ASCENT®

CENTER FOR TECHNICAL KNOWLEDGE

Autodesk® Revit® 2026 BIM Management: Template and Family Creation

Learning Guide

Imperial Units - Edition 1.0

ASCENT - Center for Technical Knowledge®
Autodesk® Revit® 2026
BIM Management: Template and Family Creation
Imperial Units - Edition 1.0

Prepared and produced by:

ASCENT Center for Technical Knowledge
11201 Dolfield Blvd, Suite 112
Owings Mills, MD 21117

866-527-2368
www.ASCENTed.com

Lead Contributor: Cherisse Biddulph

ASCENT - Center for Technical Knowledge (a division of Rand Worldwide Inc.) is a leading developer of professional learning materials and knowledge products for engineering software applications. ASCENT specializes in designing targeted content that facilitates application-based learning with hands-on software experience. For over 25 years, ASCENT has helped users become more productive through tailored custom learning solutions.

We welcome any comments you may have regarding this guide, or any of our products. To contact us please email: feedback@ASCENTed.com.

Contents

Introduction to Revit Families

Chapter 7: Creating Architectural-Specific Families   7-1

Preface

Building Information Modeling (BIM) is an approach to the entire building life cycle. Autodesk® Revit® is a powerful BIM program for architecture, MEP, and structure that supports the ability to coordinate, update, and share design data with team members throughout the design construction and management phases of a building's life. A key component in managing the BIM process is to establish a company foundation for different types of projects by creating standard templates and custom family elements. Having these in place makes the process of creating new projects flow smoothly and efficiently.

The objective of the *Autodesk® Revit® 2026 BIM Management: Template and Family Creation* guide is to enable users who have worked with the software to expand their knowledge in setting up office standards with templates that include annotation styles, preset views, sheets, and schedules, as well as creating custom system, in-place, and component families.

This guide contains practices that are specific to each discipline.

Topics Covered

- Create custom templates with annotation styles, title blocks, and custom element types.

- Create schedules, including material takeoff schedules with formulas.

- Create custom wall, roof, and floor types, as well as MEP system families.

- Set up a component family file with a parametric framework.

- Create family geometry.

- Create family types.

- Modify the visibility of components and incorporate additional family items such as controls, MEP connectors, and nested components.

- Create specific families, including in-place families, profiles, annotations, and parameters.

This guide also contains discipline-specific practices for families, including doors, windows, railings, pipe fittings, light fixtures, gusset plates, and built-up columns.

Prerequisites

- Access to the 2026.0 version of the software, to ensure compatibility with this guide. Future software updates that are released by Autodesk may include changes that are not reflected in this guide. The practices and files included with this guide are not compatible with prior versions (e.g., 2025).

- You should be comfortable with the fundamentals of the Autodesk Revit software, as found in the *Autodesk Revit 2026: Fundamentals for Architecture, Autodesk Revit 2026: Fundamentals for Structure*, or *Autodesk Revit 2026: Fundamentals for MEP* guides. Knowledge of basic techniques is assumed, such as creating standard elements, copying and moving elements, and creating and working with views. Information on Collaboration Tools, Conceptual Design, and Site Planning and Design is covered in other guides.

Note on Software Setup

This guide assumes a standard installation of the software using the default preferences during installation. This includes the Revit templates and Revit Content (Families) that can be found on the Autodesk website at *https://knowledge.autodesk.com/* by searching **How to download Revit Content**. Lectures and practices use the standard software templates and default options.

Note on Learning Guide Content

ASCENT's learning guides are intended to teach the technical aspects of using the software and do not focus on professional design principles and standards. The practices aim to demonstrate the capabilities and flexibility of the software rather than following specific design codes or standards.

Lead Contributor: Cherisse Biddulph

Cherisse is an Autodesk Certified Professional for Revit as well as an Autodesk Certified Instructor. She brings over 20 years of industry, teaching, and technical support experience to her role as a Learning Content Developer with ASCENT. With a passion for design and architecture, she received her Associates of Applied Science in Drafting and Design and has worked in the industry assisting firms with their CAD management and software implementation needs as they modernize to a Building Information Modeling (BIM) design environment. Although her main passion is the Revit design product, she is also proficient in AutoCAD, Autodesk Construction Cloud, and Autodesk Navisworks. Today, Cherisse continues to expand her knowledge in the ever-evolving AEC industry and the software used to support it.

Cherisse Biddulph has been the Lead Contributor for *Autodesk Revit BIM Management: Template and Family Creation* since 2020.

In This Guide

The following highlights the key features of this guide.

Feature	Description
Practice Files	The Practice Files page includes a link to the practice files and instructions on how to download and install them. The practice files are required to complete the practices in this guide.
Chapters	A chapter consists of the following: Learning Objectives, Instructional Content, Practices, Chapter Review Questions, and Command Summary.
	• **Learning Objectives** define the skills you can acquire by learning the content provided in the chapter.
	• **Instructional Content**, which begins right after Learning Objectives, refers to the descriptive and procedural information related to various topics. Each main topic introduces a product feature, discusses various aspects of that feature, and provides step-by-step procedures on how to use that feature. Where relevant, examples, figures, helpful hints, and notes are provided.
	• **Practice** for a topic follows the instructional content. Practices enable you to use the software to perform a hands-on review of a topic. It is required that you download the practice files (using the link found on the Practice Files page) prior to starting the first practice.
	• **Chapter Review Questions**, located close to the end of a chapter, enable you to test your knowledge of the key concepts discussed in the chapter.
	• **Command Summary** concludes a chapter. It contains a list of the software commands that are used throughout the chapter and provides information on where the command can be found in the software.
Appendices	Appendices provide additional information to the main course content. It could be in the form of instructional content, practices, tables, projects, or skills assessment.

Errata Sheets

If there are any updates or corrections to this guide, they will be published in an errata sheet.

Access it here: *https://resources.ascented.com/errata-sheets-autodesk*

or

visit **ASCENTed.com > RESOURCES > RESOURCE CENTER > Errata Sheets** and select **Autodesk** from the drop-down list.

Practice Files

To download the practice files for this guide, use the following steps:

1. Type the URL *exactly as shown below* into the address bar of your Internet browser to access the Course File Download page.

   Note: If you are using the ebook, you do not have to type the URL. Instead, you can access the page by clicking the URL below.

   https://www.ascented.com/getfile/id/longiscapusPF

   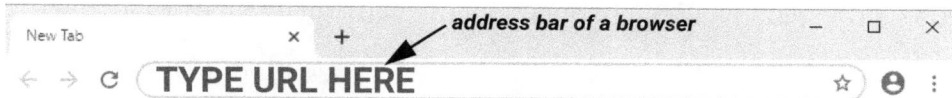

2. On the Course File Download page, click the **DOWNLOAD NOW** button, as shown below, to download the .ZIP file that contains the practice files.

3. Once the download is complete, unzip the file and extract its contents.

   The recommended practice files folder location is:
   C:\Revit 2026 BIM Management Practice Files

   Note: It is recommended that you do not change the location of the practice files folder. Doing so may cause errors when completing the practices.

   Stay Informed!
   To receive information about upcoming events, promotional offers, and complimentary webcasts, visit:
   www.ASCENTed.com/updates

Creating Custom Project Templates

Custom project templates can save you time and effort when creating similar projects by providing an efficient way to apply your organization's graphic and documentation standards. Project templates can include items such as levels, views, sheets, schedules, and annotation types for text, dimensions, and tags. A custom title block is a family that is added to project templates that ensures sheets are created with the appropriate information. You may also want to add rule-based view filters and view templates to project template files for improved workflow within the project.

Learning Objectives

- Create project templates.
- Use resource projects to store additional system families, details, schedules, and other data.
- Create standard text and dimension types for use in your projects.
- Modify callout, elevation, and section tags and specify which tags are loaded in a project template.
- Create title blocks, including detail lines, text, labels, symbols, regions, and revision schedules.
- Set up visibility/graphic override filters for various categories of elements.
- Create and apply view templates.

1.1 Preparing Project Templates

A project template is a file that contains settings and information to establish a consistent starting point for new projects. The goal is to save time by using company standards, enabling you to concentrate on the design. For example, predefined levels (as shown in Figure 1–1 for a residential project) and the associated plan views and elevations provides a starting point for a model. A project template can be created from a default project template provided by the Revit Content Library or from a blank project template that has minimal preloaded system families.

Figure 1–1

- Some items in a project template include:
    - **Project views:** Levels, schedules, legends, sheets, plan views, and view templates.
    - **Project-based settings:** Project units, object styles, fill patterns, line styles, discipline-specific settings, etc.
    - **Families:** System families, component families, custom families, and title blocks.
    - **Print settings:** Define printers and print settings.
    - **Annotation types:** Dimension style, text, arrowheads, and tags.

- You can create as many project templates as needed. If you provide constant work to a specific client (e.g., a school system or government entity), you can create a project template specific to their projects with associated title blocks and other information.

- You can also store items such as sheets, schedules, families, and drafting views (details) in a separate resource file and add them to the current project, as needed.

- As you create new project templates, families, and title blocks, it is recommended that you save them in a safe location where they will not be deleted and can be accessed by everyone, such as on a company network.

How To: Create a Project Template File

Note: Project templates are located in the C:\ProgramData\Autodesk\RVT 2026\ Templates\English (Metric) or English-Imperial folder.

1. On the Revit Home screen, click **New...** in the *Models* area, as shown in Figure 1–2.

   • Alternatively, in the *File* tab, expand ☐ (New) and click ☑ (Project).

Figure 1–2

2. In the *New Project* dialog box, in the *Template file* area, click **Browse...** to browse to a location where the project template file is stored or, from the drop-down list, either select a project template file or select **<None>** (as shown in Figure 1–3) to use a blank project file.

   Note: To save time, use an existing project or project template that includes some of the basics you need rather than starting from scratch. If using an existing project or project template, make sure to clean up and purge all existing project data that is not standard to your company.

3. In the *Create new* area, select **Project template**, as shown in Figure 1–3.

   • Project template files have the extension **.rte**.

Figure 1–3

4. Click **OK**.

- If you select **<None>** in the *Template file* list, you are prompted to specify the initial unit system for the project: **Imperial** or **Metric**, as shown in Figure 1−4. Choosing the **<None>** option requires all settings to be defined and updated versus choosing a predefined project template that is similar to your needs.

Undefined System of Measurement

Which system of measurement do you want to use in your project?

→ Imperial

→ Metric

Figure 1−4

5. In the *File* tab, select 💾 (Save As)> 📄 (Template). Alternatively, in the Quick Access Toolbar, click 💾 (Save).

6. In the *Save As* dialog box, navigate to the folder you want to save your project template to. In the *File name* field, type the desired file name and click **Save**. When using the above alternative method, make sure that the *Files of type:* is set to **Template Files (*.rte)** before clicking **Save**.

   - Add settings, families, views, etc. to the new project template file, as needed.

Managing Settings

Many of the customized settings stored in a project template file are found in the *Manage* tab> *Settings* panel, as shown in Figure 1−5. These settings include **Materials**, **Object Styles**, and **Additional Settings** (e.g., **Line Styles**, **Fill Patterns**, **Annotations**, etc.).

Figure 1−5

- Specific **Structural Settings**, **MEP Settings**, and **Panel Schedule Templates** are also included in the *Settings* panel.

For more information on managing settings, refer to the following sections in *Appendix A Additional Management Tools*:

- *A.1 General Settings*
- *A.5 Settings for Mechanical Projects*
- *A.6 Settings for Electrical Projects*
- *A.7 Settings for Structural Projects*
- *A.9 Basic User Interface Customization*

Families in Project Templates

There are two kinds of families that can be set up in project template files: *system families*, such as the duct shown in Figure 1–6, and *component families*, such as the air terminal shown in Figure 1–6.

Figure 1–6

Note: For more information on setting up system families, see **Chapter 3 Custom System Families**.

System Families are families that are predefined in Revit projects and project templates. Unlike external loadable component families, system families can be created by duplicating existing types and modifying the *Type Parameters*, as shown in Figure 1–7. This can only be done within a project and helps to establish the company standard for the families set up in a project template file. System families include walls, wall foundations, floors, structural slabs, ceilings, stairs, railings, and roofs. They also include duct, pipe, cable tray, and conduit types, along with some annotation types, such as text and dimensions, and datum families, like reference lines, grids, and levels.

Figure 1–7

*Note: For more information on creating component families, see **Chapter 4 Loadable Component Families**.*

Component Families are external loadable families that are created outside of a project in the family editor and can be loaded directly in a project template file with predefined types that are used frequently. Component families include elements such as furniture, trees, beams, columns, mechanical equipment, and electrical fixtures, as well as tags, labels, markers, and symbols.

How To: Load a Family from the Revit Library

1. In the *Insert* tab>*Load from Library* panel, click ⬇️ (Load Family).

    *   Alternatively, start a loadable family command, such as **Door** or **Electrical Fixture**, then in the *Modify* contextual tab>*Mode* panel, click ⬇️ (Load Family).

    *Note: To use the Load Family method, you must install the **Autodesk Revit 2026 Content** in your desired language from the Autodesk website. Go to the Autodesk.com website and search **Autodesk Revit 2026 Content**.*

2. In the *Load Family* dialog box, locate the folder that contains the family or families you want to load, as shown in Figure 1–8. To load more than one family at a time, hold <Ctrl> while selecting.

    *   The program remembers the last-used folder. If the *Load Family* dialog box does not default to the Revit Library folder, click on **Imperial Library** in the *Places* panel.

    *   If the *Load Family* dialog box does not default to the Revit Library folder, click on **Imperial Library** in the *Places* panel.

Figure 1–8

3. Click **Open.**

*   When inserting a family using a loadable family command, after you load the family your cursor will have the loaded element at the end of the cursor to prompt you to place the element. You will need to press <Esc> twice or click ⬚ (Modify) to end the command.

4. For some families, the *Specify Types* dialog box displays, as shown for a door in Figure 1–9. Select the types you want to include in your project and click **OK**.

- To select more than one type, hold <Shift> or <Ctrl> as you select.
- You can use the drop-down lists under the columns to filter the sizes.

Figure 1–9

5. Once the families are loaded, in Properties, expand the Type Selector, as shown in Figure 1–10, and select the type you want to use.

Figure 1–10

💡 **Hint: Using Families with This Learning Content**

For the practices in this learning content, all families that are used have been provided with the practice files. This was done to ensure that all users can easily locate and use the required files to successfully complete all practices. In general, it is recommended that you use families from the provided Autodesk Revit Content via downloaded content or the cloud, or from your own custom company library.

How To: Use Load Autodesk Family

In addition to loading families from the installed Revit Library, you can also load families from the Autodesk online library using the **Load Autodesk Family** command. A connection to the Internet is required.

1. In the *Insert* tab>*Load from Library* panel, click ⬚ (Load Autodesk Family).

2. In the *Load Autodesk Family* dialog box, filter your search by typing in what kind of family you are looking for or click on a category in the *Browse* section, as shown in Figure 1–11.

Figure 1–11

3. You can select as many families from the category as needed, and then click **Load** to load them into your project.

Review Loaded Families

You can review which families have already been loaded to determine which families still need to be loaded.

How To: Review the Loaded Families

1. In the Project Browser, expand the **Families** node.

2. Expand various nodes within the *Families* section, such as the **Cable Trays>Cable Tray with Fittings** node shown on the left in Figure 1–12, to verify which families (in this case, which cable tray families) have been loaded into the project template.

3. Select the family name, such as **Channel Cable Tray**, to review its Properties, as shown on the right in Figure 1–12.

Figure 1–12

• Alternatively, you can start a command like **Door**, **Air Terminal**, or **Plumbing Fixture** to verify from the Type Selector which families are loaded. If no families are loaded for the command, a dialog box will display (as shown in Figure 1–13). Click **Yes** to launch the *Load Family* dialog box.

Figure 1–13

Purging Unused Components

You can clean up a project template by removing unnecessary or duplicated elements from a project, including individual component types, as shown in Figure 1-14.

Remove all elements within   Remove only a few elements
a component type   from the component type

Figure 1-14

- Some elements are nested in other elements, and it might require several rounds of purging the project to remove them.

- Duplicate elements or assets that have been copied into the project template will typically have a number at the end of the name, as shown in Figure 1-15. Always verify the element before purging a potential duplicate component.

Figure 1-15

How To: Purge Unused Elements

1. In the *Manage* tab>*Settings* panel, click ⬚ (Purge Unused).

2. The *Purge Unused* dialog box opens and all elements will be selected. Click **Check None** to clear the selection.

3. Select only the elements that you want to purge.

4. Click **OK**.

Purging unused components not only helps simplify the component list, but also, more importantly, reduces the project file size.

Using Resource Projects

Although you can use a project template file to start a project, you might also want to have resource projects that include additional system and component families, pre-drawn details (as shown in Figure 1–16), schedules, and sheets. You can then copy these elements into a new project template or the current project, as needed.

Figure 1–16

*   To copy drafting views (details), sheets, schedules, or reports into the current project, use **Insert Views from File**.

*   To copy system families (e.g., wall, floor, duct, pipe, wire types, etc) or annotations (e.g., text and dimension styles, materials, etc.), use **Transfer Project Standards**. Make sure that both the template/model you want to copy from and the host template/model you are copying to are open. Also, ensure that the host template/model is the active project before you start copying.

*   To copy component families from a resource project, use **Copy to the Clipboard** and either **Paste Aligned to Selected Levels** or **Paste Aligned to Selected Views**.

- If you try to paste a family that requires a host using <Ctrl>+<V>, you may run into issues, as shown in Figure 1–17.

Click on Host Face to place Instance (Space Bar to flip the instance left/right)

Figure 1–17

How To: Insert Views from an Existing Project

1. In the *Insert* tab>*Load from Library* panel, expand ⬜ (Insert from File) and click ⬜ (Insert Views from File).

2. In the *Open* dialog box, select the RVT project file you want to copy from.

3. In the *Insert Views* dialog box, select the views you want to insert into the current project, as shown in Figure 1–18.

   - In the lower left corner, you can select **Preview selection** to preview your selection.

Figure 1–18

4. Click **OK**. The views are added to the file.

- Schedules are completed with the information in the current project. Sheets are added, but do not include any views.

How To: Transfer Project Standards

1. Open the project from which you want to transfer information.

2. Switch to the current project you are copying to.

3. In the *Manage* tab>*Settings* panel, click 🗗 (Transfer Project Standards).

4. In the *Transfer Project Standards* dialog box, expand the *Copy from* drop-down list and select the file to copy from.

   *Note: Click **Check None** or **Check All**, as needed.*

5. Select the items you want to copy into the current project, as shown in Figure 1–19, then click **OK**.

Figure 1–19

- All types of the selected category will be copied. You do not have the option to select individual types.

- If the *Duplicate Types* dialog box displays (shown in Figure 1−20), choose **Overwrite** or **New Only** to update the existing project.

Figure 1−20

- You cannot transfer any of the view types, like floor plan or reflective ceiling plan, or any visibility/graphic settings. These will need to be set up manually in your project template.

Setting Default Project Template Files

If your company uses several different project templates, you can create a list that displays in the *New Project* dialog box, as shown in Figure 1−21.

Figure 1−21

How To: Set the Default Project Template Files List

1. In the *File* tab, click **Options**.
2. In the *Options* dialog box, in the left pane, select **File Locations**, as shown in Figure 1–22.

Figure 1–22

3. Click ✚ (Add Value) to add your project templates (RTE).

   - Use ▭ (Remove Value) if you do not need a project template anymore or you want to remove the default project templates.

4. In the *Browse for Template File* dialog box, navigate to your project template. Select the project template file and click **Open**.

5. Once the project template is loaded, you can click on the name in the *Name* column to rename it or leave it with its default file name. You can also click on any of the other names in the *Name* column and change them if needed.

   - To put your project templates in order, use ⬆E (Move Rows Up) and ⬇E (Move Rows Down). Move the project templates that are used most often to the top.

- To update a project template, click on the file path in the *Path* column and select the ⬚ (Browse) button.

- In the *Browse for Template File* dialog box, navigate to and select the template file, then click **Open**.

Practice 1a
Prepare Project Templates – Architecture

Practice Objectives

- Create a new project template file.
- Load a component family.
- Review existing system and component families.
- Insert views and transfer project standards from a resource project.

In this practice, you will create a new project template file based on an existing project template. You will load and review the existing system and component families. You will then insert views and transfer project standards from a resource project, as shown for text types before and after in Figure 1–23.

Before

After

Figure 1–23

Task 1: Establish a project template file.

1. On the Home screen, click **New...** in the *Models* area, or in the *File* tab, expand ☐ (New) and click ☑ (Project).

2. In the *New Project* dialog box, click **Browse....**. Navigate to the practice files *Architectural>RTE* folder, select **Imperial-Architectural Template.rte**, and click **Open**.

3. In the *New Project* dialog box, in the *Create new* area, select **Project template**, as shown in Figure 1–24, and click **OK**.

Figure 1–24

4. In the *File* tab, select 💾 (Save As)>📄 (Template). Save the project template in the practice files *Architectural>RTE* folder as **Midrise-Template.rte**.

Task 2: Modify default levels.

1. Open an elevation view.

2. Click on the level head and rename *Level 1* to **Floor 1** and *Level 2* to **Floor 2**. Click **Yes** to rename the corresponding views.

   *Note: If you check the **Do not show me this message again** box, your choice will be applied to future levels you rename.*

3. Change the **Floor 2** height to **16'-0"**, as shown in Figure 1–25.

Figure 1–25

Task 3: Load a component family and review loaded families.

1. In the *Insert* tab>*Load from Library* panel, click ⬜ (Load Family).

   • Using the **Load Family** command, you can load any type of component. However, if you use a specific command such as **Column** or **Door**, you can only load that type of family.

2. In the *Load Family* dialog box, navigate to the practice files *Architectural>RFA* folder and select the **Doric Column.rfa** family to load, then click **Open**.

3. Save the project template.

4. In the *Architecture* tab>*Build* panel, select ▦ (Component) and review the list of families in the Type Selector. Note that the **Doric Column** does not display in the list.

5. Click ▷ (Modify).

6. In the *Architecture* tab>*Build* panel, expand **Column** and click ▯ (Column: Architectural). Note that **Doric Column** displays in the Type Selector.

7. Click ▷ (Modify).

8. In the Project Browser, expand the **Families>Columns** node and note that **Doric Column** is listed there as well, as shown in Figure 1–26.

Figure 1–26

9. At the top of the Project Browser, type **single** in the *Search* box and note the families that display with the word *single* in them. Click the **X** in the *Search* box to clear the search.

10. In the *Annotate* tab>*Text* panel, click **A** (Text).

11. Expand the Type Selector. Only a few text types are available, as shown in Figure 1–27.

Figure 1–27

12. Click ⟍ (Modify).

Task 4: Use Transfer Project Standards.

*Note: Using **Transfer Project Standards** to copy elements from a Revit model requires the model to be open when performing this task.*

1. In the *File* tab, expand ▱ (Open) and click ▨ (Project).

2. In the *Open* dialog box, navigate to the practice files *Resource Project* folder and select **Construction Resource Project.rvt**. Click **Open**.

3. Make the **Midrise-Template.rte** file the active project. You can do so by clicking on the *Floor 1* view tab.

4. In the *Manage* tab>*Settings* panel, click ▥ (Transfer Project Standards).

5. In the *Transfer Project Standards* dialog box, in the *Select items to copy* area, note that the *Copy from* drop-down list is set to **Construction Resource Project.rvt**.

6. Click **Check None** to deselect everything in the list, then select **Text Types** (as shown in Figure 1–28) and click **OK**.

Figure 1–28

7. If the *Duplicate Types* dialog box displays, select **New Only** because you do not want to overwrite existing text types in your project template.

8. Start the **Text** command, then expand the Type Selector to review the list of text types that are now available, as shown in Figure 1–29.

Figure 1–29

9. Click 🗘 (Modify).

10. Save the project template.

Task 5: Copy information from a resource project.

Note: Inserting views from another Revit model does not require the model to be open when performing this task.

1. Close any open views or projects other than the project template file.

2. In the *Insert* tab>*Load from Library* panel, expand 🗋 (Insert from File) and click 🗎 (Insert Views from File).

3. In the *Open* dialog box, navigate to the practice files *Resource Project* folder, select **Construction Resource Project.rvt,** and click **Open**.

4. In the *Insert Views* dialog box, verify that *Views:* is set to **Show all views and sheets**.

5. Click **Check None** and select a couple drafting views and schedules from the list, as shown in Figure 1–30.

Figure 1–30

6. Click **OK**.

7. If the *Duplicate Types* dialog box displays, click **OK** and close any warning messages that pop up. The last view selected opens and is the active view. Close the view.

8. In the Project Browser, review the new drafting views and schedules that are added.

9. Save the project template.

Task 6: Purge duplicate elements.

Note: This task would normally be done at the end of the project template creation. This is for practice purposes only.

1. In the *Manage* tab>*Settings* panel, click ⬛ (Purge Unused).

2. In the *Purged Unused* dialog box, click **Check None**, then expand **Doors>Single-Flush**. Select **32" x 84"1** and **34" x 84"1**, as shown in Figure 1–31.

Figure 1–31

3. Click **OK** to remove them from the project template.

4. Open the *Purge Unused* dialog box again. Expand **Doors>Single-Flush** and note that the deleted elements are no longer displayed. Click **Cancel** to close the dialog box.

5. Save and close the project template file.

End of practice

Practice 1b
Prepare Project Templates – MEP

Practice Objectives

- Create a new project template file.
- Review existing system and component families.
- Load a component family.
- Insert views and transfer project standards from a resource project.

In this practice, you will create a new project template file based on an existing project template. You will review the existing system and component families and load a component family. You will then insert views and transfer project standards from a resource project, as shown for text types before and after in Figure 1–32.

Before

After

Figure 1–32

Task 1: Establish a project template file.

1. On the Home screen, click **New...** in the *Models* area, or in the *File* tab, expand ⬜ (New) and click 🗍 (Project).

2. In the *New Project* dialog box, click **Browse....** Navigate to the practice files *MEP>RTE* folder, select **Imperial-Systems Template.rte**, and click **Open**. This project template will have electrical, mechanical, and plumbing views and families in it.

    *   There are additional project templates specifically for the mechanical, plumbing, and electrical disciplines but for the purpose of this practice, the systems project template will be used.

3. In the *New Project* dialog box, in the *Create new* area, select **Project template** (as shown in Figure 1–33) and click **OK**.

Figure 1–33

4. In the *File* tab, select 💾 (Save As)> 📄 (Template). Save the project template in the practice files *MEP>RTE* folder as **Midrise-Template.rte**.

Task 2: Load a component family and review loaded families.

1. In the *Insert* tab>*Load from Library* panel, click 🗁 (Load Family).

    *   By using the **Load Family** command, you can load any type of component. If you use a specific command, such as **Mechanical Equipment**, you can only load that type of family.

2. In the *Load Family* dialog box, navigate to the practice files *MEP>RFA* folder and select the **Indoor AHU - Horizontal - Chilled Water Coil.rfa** family to load, then click **Open**.

3. In the *Systems* tab>*Mechanical* panel, click 🛞 (Mechanical Equipment). Note that **Indoor AHU - Horizontal - Chilled Water Coil** displays in the Type Selector. Expand the Type Selector to see other mechancial equipment families.

4. Click ⬚ (Modify).

5. In the Project Browser, expand the **Families>Mechanical Equipment** node and note that **Indoor AHU - Horizontal - Chilled Water Coil** is listed there as well, as shown in Figure 1–34. Continue to expand nodes within the Project Browser to see what other families are loaded in the project.

Figure 1–34

6. At the top of the Project Browser, type **equipment** in the *Search* box and note the families that display with the word *equipment* in them. Click the **X** in the *Search* box to clear the search.

7. In the *Annotate* tab>*Text* panel, click **A** (Text).

8. Expand the Type Selector. Only a few text types are available, as shown in Figure 1–35.

Figure 1–35

9. Click ⌖ (Modify).

Task 3: Use Transfer Project Standards.

*Note: Using **Transfer Project Standards** to copy elements from a Revit model requires the model to be open when performing this task.*

1. In the *File* tab, expand 📂 (Open) and click 🖼 (Project).
2. In the *Open* dialog box, navigate to the practice files *Resource Project* folder and select **Construction Resource Project.rvt**. Click **Open**.
3. Make the **Midrise-Template.rte** file the active project. You can do so by clicking on the *1 - Mech* view tab.
4. In the *Manage* tab>*Settings* panel, click 🗔 (Transfer Project Standards).
5. In the *Transfer Project Standards* dialog box, in the *Select items to copy* area, note that the *Copy from* drop-down list is set to **Construction Resource Project.rvt**.
6. Click **Check None** to deselect everything in the list, then select **Text Types** (as shown in Figure 1–36) and click **OK**.

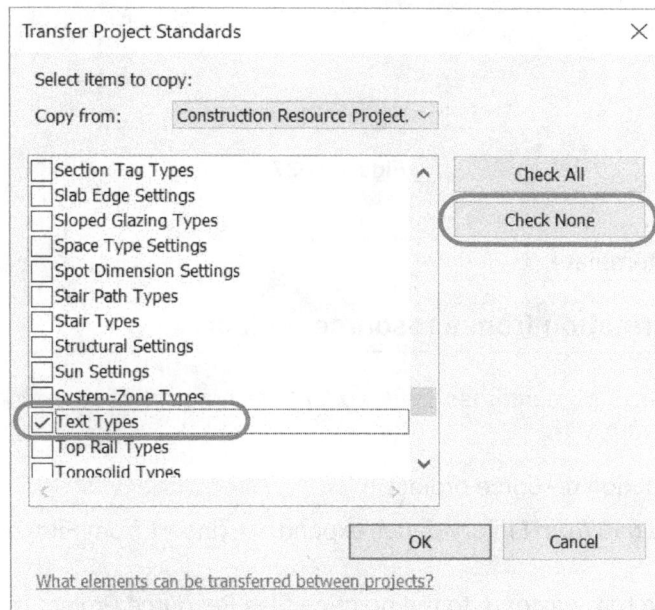

Figure 1–36

7. If the *Duplicate Types* dialog box displays, select **New Only** because you do not want to overwrite existing text types in your project template.

8. Start the **Text** command, then expand the Type Selector to review the list of text types that are now available, as shown in Figure 1–37.

Figure 1–37

9. Click ⍽ (Modify).

10. Save the project template.

Task 4: Copy information from a resource project.

Note: Inserting views from another Revit model does not require the model to be open when performing this task.

1. Close the construction resource project.

2. In the *Insert* tab>*Load from Library* panel, expand ⍽ (Insert from File) and click ⍽ (Insert Views from File).

3. In the *Open* dialog box, navigate to the practice files *Resource Project* folder, select **Construction Resource Project.rvt**, and click **Open**.

4. In the *Insert Views* dialog box, set the *Views* drop-down list to **Show all views and sheets**.

5. Click **Check None** and select a couple drafting views and schedules from the list, as shown in Figure 1–38.

Figure 1–38

6. Click **OK**.

7. If the *Duplicate Types* dialog box displays, click **OK** and close any warning messages that pop up. The last view selected opens and is the active view. Close the view.

8. In the Project Browser of your project template file, review the new drafting views and schedules that are added.

   Note: If you started with the systems or electrical template, the drafting views will be in the Coordination section in the Project Browser.

Task 5: Purge duplicate elements.

Note: This task would normally be done at the end of the project template creation. This is for practice purposes only.

1. In the *Manage* tab>*Settings* panel, click ⬚ (Purge Unused).

2. In the *Purge Unused* dialog box, click **Check None**, then expand **Air Terminals>Exhaust Grill**. Select **24 x 24 Face 12 x 12 Connection1**, as shown in Figure 1–39.

Figure 1–39

3. Click **OK** to remove it from the project template.

4. Open the *Purge Unused* dialog box again. Expand **Air Terminals>Exhaust Grill** and note that the deleted element is no longer displayed. Click **Cancel** to close the dialog box.

5. Save and close the project template file.

End of practice

Practice 1c
Prepare Project Templates – Structure

Practice Objectives

- Create a new project template file.
- Review existing system and component families.
- Load a component family.
- Insert views and transfer project standards from a resource project.

In this practice, you will create a new project template file based on an existing project template. You will review the existing system and component families and load a component family. You will then insert views and transfer project standards from a resource project, as shown for text types before and after in Figure 1–40.

Figure 1–40

Task 1: Establish a project template file.

1. On the Home screen, click **New...** in the *Models* area, or in the *File* tab, expand ⬜ (New) and click 🖼 (Project).

2. In the *New Project* dialog box, click **Browse....** Navigate to the practice files *Structural>RTE* folder, select **Imperial-Structural Template.rte**, and click **Open**.

3. In the *New Project* dialog box, in the *Create new* area, select **Project template** (as shown in Figure 1−41) and click **OK**.

Figure 1−41

4. In the *File* tab, select 💾 (Save As)>📄 (Template) and save the template in the practice files *Structural>RTE* folder as **Midrise-Template.rte**.

Task 2: Edit default levels.

1. Open an elevation view.

2. Click on the level head and rename *Level 1* to **Ground Floor** and *Level 2* to **TOS-Floor 1**. Click **Yes** to rename the corresponding views.

3. Change the **TOS-Floor 1** height to **14'-7"**, as shown in Figure 1−42.

Figure 1−42

Task 3: Load a component family and review loaded families.

1. In the *Insert* tab>*Load from Library* panel, click ⬚↓ (Load Family).

   - By using the **Load Family** command, you can load any type of component. If you use a specific command, such as **Column** or **Truss**, you can only load that type of family.

2. In the *Load Family* dialog box, navigate to the practice files *Structural>RFA* folder, select **Pipe-Column.rfa**, and click **Open**.

3. In the *Specify Types* dialog box, select **Pipe8STD** and click **OK**.

4. In the *Structure* tab>*Model* panel, select ▦ (Component) and review the list of families in the Type Selector. Note that **Pipe-Column.rfa** does not display in the list.

5. Click ⌖ (Modify).

6. In the *Structure* tab>*Structure* panel, select ⬚ (Column). Note that **Pipe8STD** is displayed in the Type Selector. Expand the Type Selector to see other columns that are loaded.

7. Click ⌖ (Modify).

8. In the Project Browser, expand the **Families>Structural Columns>Pipe-Column** node and note that **Pipe8STD** is listed there as well, as shown in Figure 1–43.

Figure 1–43

9. At the top of the Project Browser, type **truss** in the *Search* box and note the families that display with the word *truss* in them. Expand the nodes to see the different types. Click the **X** in the *Search* box to clear the search.

10. In the *Annotate* tab>*Text* panel, click **A** (Text).

11. Expand the list in the Type Selector. Only a few text types are available, as shown in Figure 1–44.

Figure 1–44

12. Click ⌖ (Modify).

Task 4: Use Transfer Project Standards.

*Note: Using **Transfer Project Standards** to copy elements from a Revit model requires the model to be open when performing this task.*

1. In the *File* tab, expand ⌂ (Open) and click ⌂ (Project).

2. In the *Open* dialog box, navigate to the practice files *Resource Project* folder and select **Construction Resource Project.rvt**. Click **Open**.

3. Make the **Midrise-Template.rte** file the active project. You can do so by clicking on the *Level 1* view tab.

4. In the *Manage* tab>*Settings* panel, click ⌂ (Transfer Project Standards).

5. In the *Transfer Project Standards* dialog box, in the *Select items to copy* area, note that the *Copy from* drop-down list is set to **Construction Resource Project.rvt**.

6. Click **Check None** to deselect everything in the list, then select **Text Types** (as shown in Figure 1–45) and click **OK**.

Figure 1–45

7. If the *Duplicate Types* dialog box displays, select **New Only** because you do not want to overwrite existing text types in your template.

8. Start the **Text** command, then expand the Type Selector to review the list of text types that are now available, as shown in Figure 1–46.

Figure 1–46

9. Click ⌖ (Modify).

Task 5: Copy information from a resource project.

1. Close any open projects other than the project template file.

2. In the *Insert* tab>*Load from Library* panel, expand ⬇ (Insert from File) and click ⬇ (Insert Views from File).

3. In the *Open* dialog box, navigate to the practice files *Resource Project* folder, select **Construction Resource Project.rvt,** and click **Open**.

4. In the *Insert Views* dialog box, verify that *Views:* is set to **Show all views and sheets**.

5. Select a couple drafting views and schedules from the list, as shown in Figure 1–47.

Figure 1–47

6. Click **OK**.

7. If the *Duplicate Types* dialog box displays, click **OK** and close any warning messages that pop up. The last view selected opens and is the active view. Close the view.

8. In the Project Browser, review the new drafting views and schedules that are added.

Task 6: Purge duplicate elements.

Note: This task would normally be done at the end of project template creation. This is for practice purposes only.

1. In the *Manage* tab>*Settings* panel, click ▧ (Purge Unused).

2. In the *Purge Unused* dialog box, click **Check None**, then expand **Floors>Floor**. Select **1 1/2" Metal Roof Deck1** and **3" LW Concrete on 2" Metal Deck 2**, as shown in Figure 1–48.

Figure 1–48

3. Click **OK** to remove them from the template.

4. Open the *Purge Unused* dialog box again. Expand **Floors>Floor** and note that the deleted elements are no longer displayed. Click **Cancel** to close the dialog box.

5. Save and close the project template file.

End of practice

1.2 Customizing Annotation Types

Establishing annotation style types is an important part of project template creation. You can customize annotation types in your project template file, including dimensions, text, arrowheads, level heads, and tags. Figure 1–49 shows the different types of annotations. Within each annotation type, you can customize font, text size, background, leaders, etc. When creating custom annotation types, it is good practice to add your company's abbreviated name or another custom identifier to indicate that it is a company-specific type.

Figure 1–49

Text, dimensions, and level arrowheads are all system families and are depicted with the label **System Family** in front of the name in their *Type Properties* (as shown in Figure 1–50) and component families. This means they have a standard set of parameters, which you can modify and save as a type.

Figure 1–50

Callout, section, and elevation tags can be modified in Revit. Most other tags, like door, window, and beam tags, are created using component families.

Creating Text Types

Text types are used to standardize text formatting (such as the font, text height, etc.), as shown in Figure 1–51. They can be created for both annotative text and model text.

ARIAL AT 1/4"

CITY BLUEPRINT AT 1/8"

ARIAL AT 3/32", BOLD

Figure 1–51

- The **Text** command places 2D text at the height you need for the final plot. The view scale controls the height of the standard text in the views.

- The *Text Size* parameter represents the height of an upper case letter. (Verify that the text in projects created in earlier versions of the software displays as expected.)

- The **Model Text** command places work plane based 3D text that is typically used on buildings, walls, doors, or signs, as shown in Figure 1–52. Text types for model text should be the actual height of the final signage element and are not affected by the view scale.

Figure 1–52

How To: Create a Text Type

1. In the *Annotate* tab>*Text* panel title, click ⌐ (Text Types). Alternatively, start the **Text** command and in Properties, click 🖼 (Edit Type).
2. In the *Type Properties* dialog box, click **Duplicate....**
3. Type a new name and click **OK**.The new type is activated.

4. Modify the parameters as needed for the new type, as shown in Figure 1–53.

Type Parameters	
Parameter	Value
Graphics	⌃
Color	◼ Black
Line Weight	1
Background	Opaque
Show Border	☐
Leader/Border Offset	5/64"
Leader Arrowhead	Arrow 30 Degree
Text	⌃
Text Font	Arial
Text Size	1/4"
Tab Size	1/2"
Bold	☐
Italic	☐
Underline	☐
Width Factor	1.000000

Figure 1–53

5. Click **OK** to finish.

How To: Create a Model Text Type

1. In the *Architecture* tab>*Model* panel, click 🅰 (Model Text). Alternatively, in the *Structure* tab>*Model* panel, click 🅰 (Model Text).

2. In the *Edit Text* dialog box, keep the default text and click **OK**, then place the text in the view.

3. Select the model text and from Properties, click **Edit Type**.

4. In the *Type Properties* dialog box, click **Duplicate...**.

5. Type a new name and click **OK**. The new type is activated.

6. Modify the parameters as needed for the new text type.

7. Click **OK** to finish.

Creating Dimension Types

Dimensions are one of the more complex system families in terms of the number of parameters you can modify. They include options for the dimension text, dimension lines, tick marks, and witness lines. You can specify information such as the units, color, and all of the gap sizes between elements, as shown in Figure 1–54.

Figure 1–54

- You can add a suffix or prefix to a dimension type by creating a type-driven dimension style. Duplicate the dimension style and specify a set prefix and suffix within the type parameters. This eliminates the need for users to manually modify the dimension every time they need to add a prefix or suffix.

How To: Create Dimension Types

1. In the *Annotate* tab>*Dimension* panel, click the *Dimension* title (as shown in Figure 1–55) to expand the panel.

Figure 1–55

2. Click one of the dimension types with the ⚲ icon next to it (as shown in Figure 1−56).

⚲ Linear Dimension Types

⚲ Angular Dimension Types

⚲ Radial Dimension Types

⚲ Diameter Dimension Types

⚲ Spot Elevation Types

⚲ Spot Coordinate Types

⚲ Spot Slope Types

Dimension

Figure 1−56

3. In the *Type Properties* dialog box, click **Duplicate...**.

   Note: You create separate types for each dimension method.

4. Type a new name and click **OK**. The new type is activated.

5. Modify the parameters as needed for the new type, as shown in Figure 1−57.

   • Values for parameters (such as text size, witness line extension, etc.) are the actual plot size for these elements. The view scale controls how large they are in the specific view.

   • Specify a prefix or suffix for *Primary Units*, as shown in Figure 1−57.

Figure 1–57

6. Click **OK** when you are finished.

- For linear dimensions, you can specify a *Leader Type*, *Shoulder Length*, and *Leader Tick Mark*, as well as the *Show Leader When Text Moves* option that is used when the text is pulled away from the dimension string. You can also specify the text inserted for *Equality Text* (the default is **EQ**).

- You can specify a *Text Background* option. If you set the value to **opaque**, it automatically masks any elements behind the text. If it is set to **transparent**, anything the text overlaps is still visible.

- If you are dimensioning doors and windows by their widths rather than their centers, you can also have the opening height displayed with the dimension. Select **Show Opening Height**.

Labeling Dimensions

If you have a distance that needs to be repeated multiple times, such as the *Wall to Window* label shown in Figure 1–58, a *clearance distance*, or one where you want to use a formula based on another dimension, you can apply a label to a dimension and associate a global parameter to it.

Figure 1–58

- To apply an existing label to a dimension, select the dimension in the view and in the *Modify | Dimensions* tab>*Label Dimension* panel, select the label in the drop-down list, as shown in Figure 1–59.

Figure 1–59

How To: Create a Label

1. In the *Manage* tab>*Settings* panel, click ▦ (Global Parameters).

2. In the *Global Parameters* dialog box, click 🗋 (New Global Parameter).

3. In the *Global Parameter Properties* dialog box, enter a *Name* and set the *Discipline*, *Data Type*, and *Group parameter under*, as shown in Figure 1–60.

   *Note: You will learn about common parameter types in **Chapter 2 Creating Schedules**.*

Figure 1–60

4. Click **OK**.

5. In the *Global Parameters* dialog box, edit the *Value* and *Formula* columns as needed.

6. Click **OK**.

How To: Create a Label from an Existing Dimension in a View

1. Select a dimension in the view.

2. In the *Modify | Dimensions* tab>*Label Dimension* panel, click ▦ (Create Parameter)

3. In the *Global Parameter Properties* dialog box, type in a *Name* and keep *Group parameter under* as **Dimensions**, as shown in Figure 1–61. Note that the *Discipline* and *Data Type* are grayed out. Click **OK**.

Global Parameter Properties	✕
Name:	☐ Reporting Parameter
Bay Length A	(Can be used to extract value from a geometric condition and report it in a formula)
Discipline:	
Common	
Data Type:	
Length	
Group parameter under:	
Dimensions	
Tooltip description:	
<No tooltip description. Edit this parameter to write a custom toolti...	
Edit Tooltip...	
How do I create global parameters?	
	OK Cancel

Figure 1–61

4. The label is applied to the dimension.

How To: Edit the Global Label Parameter

1. In the *Manage* tab>*Settings* panel, click 📓 (Global Parameters).

2. In the *Global Parameters* dialog box, modify the *Value* and *Formula*, or click 🖉 (Edit Global Parameter) to modify the *Name* and/or *Group parameter under*.

How To: Edit the Global Label Parameter from a View

1. In the view, select a labeled dimension.

2. Click 🖉 (Global Parameters), as shown in Figure 1–62.

Figure 1–62

3. In the *Global Parameters* dialog box, in the *Value* column, type the new distance, as shown in Figure 1−63.

Figure 1−63

4. Click **OK**. The selected dimension and any other dimensions using the same label are updated.

• You can also delete, modify, sort, or reposition the global parameters in this dialog box.

Loading Tags and Symbols

Tags and symbols are 2D component families that must be loaded into a project. Not all types of tags need to be in each project, so you can choose which ones you want to include in your templates. For example, if you are working in an architectural project, you can load tags such as the door, window, and wall shown in Figure 1−64.

Figure 1−64

How To: Specify Loaded Tags and Symbols

1. In the *Annotate* tab>*Tag* panel, expand the panel title and click 🗷 (Loaded Tags and Symbols).

2. In the *Loaded Tags And Symbols* dialog box, use the *Filter list* field to limit the types of tags you are looking for by discipline, as shown in Figure 1–65.

   Note: Some elements, such as Floors and Structural Fabric Reinforcement, have both tags and symbols. They can both be specified in this dialog box.

Figure 1–65

3. Click **Load Family...**.

4. In the *Load Family* dialog box, navigate to the appropriate library and folder. Note, tags are typically found in the Revit Library's *Annotations* folder and sorted within discipline sub-folders.

5. Select the required tags and click **Open**. Hold <Ctrl> or <Shift> to select multiple tags.

6. The selected tags are assigned to their appropriate categories.

7. When you have loaded all of the tags that you need for a project, click **OK**.

8. If multiple tags are loaded for a category, you can choose which one is the default tag by choosing it in the *Loaded Tags* column, as shown in Figure 1–66.

Category	Loaded Tags	Loaded Symbols ^
Bolts		
Holes		
Plates	Plate Tag : Standard	
Profiles		
Shear Studs	Shear Stud Tag : Stand	
Welds	Weld Tag : Standard	
Structural Fabric R...	Fabric Sheet Tag	Fabric Sheet Symbᵢ
Structural Foundat...	Structural Foundation	
Structural Framing	Structural Framing	
Structural Internal ...	Structural Framing Tag : Boxed	
Internal Area L...	Structural Framing Tag : Standard	

Figure 1–66

Creating Custom View Tags

Callouts, elevations, and section markers are system family view tags and can be modified or duplicated to create a custom tag to suit office standards. For example, you can create a new Elevation view type containing a tag that displays the view name by duplicating an existing one and modifying the properties, as shown in Figure 1–67. Refer to *A.9 Basic User Interface Customization* in *Appendix A Additional Management Tools* to learn how to create new view types.

Figure 1–67

How To: Create a Custom System Family Tag Type from an Existing Tag

1. In the *Manage* tab>*Settings* panel, expand ⇄ (Annotations) and select from the following to create a custom type: ⬦ (Section), ⬔ (Elevation), or ⬭ (Callout).

   - Alternatively, you can start a view command. In the *View* tab>*Create* panel, click ⬭ (Callout), ⬔ (Elevation), or ⬦ (Section), and in Properties, click ⊞ (Edit Type). In the *Type Properties* dialog box, select an existing type. Click **Duplicate** and in the *Name* dialog box (shown in Figure 1–68), name the new view type.

   Note: Each view type has different parameters.

Figure 1–68

2. Beside any of the tag parameters, click in the *Value* column and then click ⟦...⟧ (Browse), as shown in Figure 1–69.

Figure 1–69

3. In the *Type Properties* dialog box for the tag parameter, expand a *Graphics* parameter and select from an existing tag type, or duplicate a tag type and specify a new mark element from the list of families that have been loaded into the project, as shown in Figure 1–70.

Figure 1–70

4. Click **OK** to apply the tag type.

5. Modify the other parameters as needed and click **OK** to close the *Type Properties* dialog box.

• Levels (shown on the left in Figure 1–71) and grids (shown on the right) are also system families that are set up in *Type Properties* and include component families such as the *Symbol* **Level Head-Circle** and **Grid Head-Circle**.

Figure 1–71

Practice 1d
Customize Annotation Types – All Disciplines

Practice Objectives

- Set up text and dimension types.
- Load tags.
- Create a new view tag.

In this practice, you will create text types and dimension styles, adding **ASC** in front of the type name to identify it as a custom type. You will load typical tags into the project template file and then create a new elevation tag that includes the view name information.

Task 1: Create text types.

1. Open the project template **Midrise-Template.rte** that you created in the previous practice. If you did not complete the previous practice, open the template found in the practice files folder that relates to your discipline:

    - *Architectural>RTE>***Midrise-Template-A-1.rte**
    - *MEP>RTE>***Midrise-Template-MEP-1.rte**
    - *Structural>RTE>***Midrise-Template-S-1.rte**

2. In the *Annotate* tab>*Text* panel title, click ⌄ (Text Types).

3. In the *Type Properties* dialog box, click **Duplicate...**.

4. Type the *Name* **ASC_1/4" Arial** and click **OK**. The new type is the active type. Note that you can add other identifying information but for this practice, you will keep it simple.

5. In the *Graphics* section, change the *Leader Arrowhead* to **Arrow Filled 30 Degree**. In the *Text* section, set the *Text Size* to **1/4"**, as shown in Figure 1–72.

Figure 1–72

6. Click **Apply**.

7. Click **Duplicate...** again and create another new text type named **ASC_1/2" Arial**. Change the *Text Size* to **1/2"**.

8. Click **OK**.

9. Test the new text type. Start the **Text** command and verify **One Segment** is selected. In the Type Selector, select one of the new text types and place text and a leader line in the view, then repeat the process for the other new text type, as shown in Figure 1–73.

Figure 1–73

10. Click ☋ (Modify).

11. Save the project template file.

Task 2: Create dimension styles.

1. In the *Annotate* tab, expand the *Dimension* panel and select ✔ (Linear Dimension Types).

2. In the *Type Properties* dialog box, duplicate the type and name it **ASC_1/8" Arial**. Note that you can add other identifying information but for this practice, you will keep it simple.

3. In the *Text* section, change the *Text Size* to **1/8"**.

4. Click the button next to *Units Format*.

5. In the *Format* dialog box, clear the check mark for **Use project settings** and change the *Rounding* to **To the nearest 1/8"**, as shown in Figure 1−74.

Figure 1−74

6. Click **OK** twice to finish.

7. Expand the *Dimension* panel again and select **Angular Dimension Types**.

8. In the *Type Properties* dialog box, duplicate the type and name it **ASC_1/8" Arial**.

9. In the *Graphics* section, change the *Tick Mark* to **Arrow Filled 30 Degree**. In the *Text* section, change the *Text Size* to **1/8"** and change the *Units Format* to **0 decimal places**. Click **OK** twice.

10. Test the new dimension types. Model a few elements (such as walls, beams, or ducts) and add two linear and two angular dimensions, as shown in Figure 1–75. Your dimensions may differ, depending how you drew your elements.

29' - 6"

90°

Figure 1–75

11. Click ⬚ (Modify).

Task 3: Edit the new dimension type.

1. In the view, select the linear dimension. In Properties, click **Edit Type**. Move the *Type Properties* dialog box so you can see the dimension in the view.

2. In the *Type Properties* dialog box, change the *Tick Mark* to **Arrow 30 Degree** and click **Apply** to see the changes in the view.

3. Set the *Tick Mark* back to **Diagonal 1/8"**.

4. Select and delete the sample text, elements, and dimensions. Note that the types did not delete from the project.

5. Save the project template.

Task 4: Load tags.

1. In the *Annotate* tab, expand the *Tag* panel title, and click ⬚ (Loaded Tags and Symbols).

2. In the *Loaded Tags And Symbols* dialog box, set the *Filter list* to match your discipline(s). (For the MEP template, select **Mechanical**, **Electrical**, and **Piping**.)

3. Click **Load Family...** and load the following tags from the practice files *RFA* folder into the discipline-specific project template.

   • **Architecture:** Casework Tag.rfa, Furniture Tag.rfa, and Furniture System Tag.rfa

   • **MEP:** Duct Fitting Tag.rfa, Lighting Fixture Tag.rfa, Pipe Fitting Size Tag.rfa

   • **Structure:** Floor Tag.rfa and Wall Tag.rfa, Structural Column Tag-45.rfa

4. The tags are automatically assigned to the correct *Category* and display in the *Loaded Tags* column.

5. Click **OK**.

6. Save the project template file.

Task 5: Customize an existing elevation tag.

1. In the plan view, select one of the existing building elevation view markers.

2. In the Type Selector, verify that **Elevation: Building Elevation** is displayed.

3. In Properties, click **Edit Type**.

4. In the Type Parameters, select the Value beside *Elevation Tag* and then click the ⊡ (Browse) button.

5. A second *Type Properties* dialog box displays for the Elevation Tag System Family. Duplicate this type and add **-With View Name** to the end.

6. In the *Elevation Mark* drop-down list, select **Elevation Mark Body_Square: Detail Number and View Name**, as shown in Figure 1–76.

Figure 1–76

7. Click **OK** twice. All the elevation tags update in the view.

8. Click **OK** and zoom to fit the view.

9. Save and close the project template.

End of practice

1.3 Creating Title Blocks

Title blocks (as shown in Figure 1–77) are a Revit family and contain information about the company and consultants designing the project, project information (such as project name and number), and sheet-specific information (such as sheet numbers and drawn by). They are created by sketching detail lines and adding text, symbols, and regions, as well as image files for company logos. The variable information is stored in labels. Some of these parameters never change, some are project-specific, and some are sheet-specific.

Figure 1–77

- Once you have title blocks customized, you can add them to templates and set up views and sheets in the template.

How To: Create a Title Block

1. On the Home screen, in the *Families* area, click ▢ (New...). Navigate to the Revit Library's *Family Templates>English-Imperial>Titleblocks* folder.

   Note: *Title block templates are located in the C:\ProgramData\Autodesk\RVT 2026\ Family Templates\English (Metric) or English-Imperial\Titleblocks folder.*

   - Alternatively, in the *File* tab, expand ▢ (New) and click ▢ (Title Block).

2. In the *New Family - Select Template File* or *New Title Block - Select Template File* dialog box, select a template file size from the list and click **Open**.

   Note: *You can select from several preset sizes or create a custom size by selecting* **New Size.rft**.

3. A new family file opens and you will now be in Family Editor mode with a modified ribbon, as shown in part in Figure 1–78.

Figure 1–78

4. Add lines, filled regions, symbols, text, and labels (which are covered next).

    *   If you select a template with a standard size, a rectangle of that size displays in the view.
    *   If you select **New Size**, a rectangle with dimensions displays. Edit the dimensions to modify the size.
    *   You can use reference lines and dimensions to help place the elements in the title block family. They are not displayed when the title block is inserted.

5. You will save your new title block as a Revit family (.RFA) file type.

Adding Labels

Labels are not just text but elements that are assigned to specific parameters and can be added to title blocks or tags. They can change without modifying the rest of the elements. For example, you would use annotation text for the words **Drawn By:** and a label for the initials of the person who did the work (by default displaying DRW in Figure 1–79), because that varies from sheet to sheet.

Figure 1–79

*   The title block template comes with one text type and one label type already defined. You can create additional types in Properties by duplicating types. The **Text** and **Label** parameters are similar, but you must create separate types for each of them.

*   Labels use Rich Text Format so that they match text notes.

    Note: Adding text is covered in the Autodesk Revit: Fundamentals guide.

How To: Create a Sheet Label

1. To open a new title block (.RFT.), in the *File* tab, expand ⬚ (New) and click ⬚ (Title Block). To open an existing titleblock, in the *File* tab, click **Open> Family (RFA)**. If you are on the Home screen, click ⬚ (Home Screen) to view the *File* tab.

2. In the Family Editor, in the *Create* tab>*Text* panel, click $^A\boxed{\equiv}$ (Label).

3. In the *Modify | Place Label* tab>*Text* panel, specify the alignments: $\equiv$ (Align Text Top), $\equiv$ (Align Text Left), $\equiv$ (Align Text Middle), $\equiv$ (Align Text Center), $\equiv$ (Align Text Bottom), or $\equiv$ (Align Text Right).

4. Click in the view window to place the label, as shown in Figure 1–80.

Figure 1–80

5. In the *Edit Label* dialog box (shown in Figure 1–81), select a label from the *Category Parameters* list and double-click or click $\boxed{\Rightarrow}$ (Add parameter(s) to label).

    • You can select more than one by holding <Ctrl> or <Shift>.

    • Keep in mind that if you add more than one parameter, they will be added as one label.

Figure 1–81

    • To remove an added parameter, in the *Label Parameters* list, select the *Parameter Name* and click $\boxed{\Leftarrow}$ (Remove parameter from label).

    • In the *Label Parameters* area, add a prefix, sample value, or suffix, if needed.

- If you are using several parameters in one label, select **Wrap between parameters only** and **Break** (in column) options to separate them while still permitting a word wrap, as shown in Figure 1–82.

Project Name Project
Address

Two labels without break

Project Name
Project Address

Two labels with break

Figure 1–82

- Click ⬆ (Move Parameter Up) and ⬇ (Move Parameter Down) to reorder multiple parameters.

- If you select a numerical parameter such as **Assembly: Cost**, click 📐 (Edit Units Format) to change, if needed.

- Click f_x (Add calculated parameter to label) to use a formula based on other parameters.

  - When a formula is added, you can select the parameter in the list and click $f_?$ (Edit calculated parameter).

- Click 📄 (Add Parameter) to create a new parameter for the project. This option requires the use of a shared parameter. For more information, see *6.4 Working with Shared Parameters* in *Chapter 6 Additional Family Types*.

Note: For more information on creating parameters and calculated parameters, see 2.5 Working with Project Parameters in Chapter 2 Creating Schedules.

6.   Click **OK** when you have finished editing the label.

- While placing the label, you can rotate or stretch it (as shown in Figure 1–83), or select a point for an additional label.

•DRW

Figure 1–83

- You can also rotate or stretch a label once it has been placed in the title block.

Adding Revision Schedules

A table of revisions included in a project and/or sheet is typically added to a company title block, as shown in Figure 1–84. In Revit, you can create a Revision Schedule that is then linked to the Sheet Issues/Revision Table in the project.

Figure 1–84

How To: Add Revision Schedules to Title Blocks

1. To open a new title block (.RFT.), in the *File* tab, expand ⬜ (New) and click ⬛ (Title Block). To open an existing titleblock, in the *File* tab, click **Open> Family (RFA)**. If you are on the Home screen, click 🔳 (Home Screen) to view the *File* tab.

2. In the Family Editor, in the *View* tab>*Create* panel, click ☁️ (Revision Schedule).

    Note: Within the tabs, there are tools that are grayed out that you will not be able to use.

3. The *Revision Properties* dialog box displays. Click on each of the tabs along the top and modify the settings as needed.

Fields Tab

In the *Fields* tab, you can select from a list of available fields and organize them in the order in which you want them to display in the schedule. Several are already selected for you, as shown in Figure 1–85. You can also sort the available fields by Parameter Type, Discipline, or Value Type.

- In the *Available fields* area, select one or more fields that you want to add to the schedule and click ⬇ (Add parameter(s)). The field(s) are placed in the *Scheduled fields (in order)* area.

- Click ⬆ (Remove parameter(s)) to move a field from the *Scheduled fields* area back to the *Available fields* area.

  Note: You can also double-click on a field to move it from the Available fields area to the Scheduled fields area or double-click on a field to remove it from the Scheduled fields area.

- Use ⬆E (Move Parameter Up) and ⬇E (Move Parameter Down) to change the order of the scheduled fields.

Figure 1–85

Other Fields Tab Options

Select available fields from	Enables you to select additional category fields for the specified schedule. The available list of fields depends on the original category of the schedule. Typically, it includes room information.
f_x **(Add Calculated parameter)**	Enables you to create a field that uses a formula based on other fields.
(Combine Parameters)	Enables you to combine two or more parameters in one column.You can put any fields together even if they are used in another column.

Sorting/Grouping Tab

In the *Sorting/Grouping* tab, you can set how you want the information to be sorted, as shown in Figure 1–86. For example, you can sort by **Revision Sequence** and add another option in the *Then by* section(s). You can also check or uncheck the **Itemize every instance** option.

Figure 1–86

Sort by/Then by	Enables you to select the field(s) you want to sort by. You can select up to four levels of sorting.
Ascending/ Descending	Enables you to sort fields in **Ascending** or **Descending** order.
Itemize every instance	If selected, displays each instance of the element in the schedule. If not selected, displays only one instance of each type.

Formatting Tab

In the *Formatting* tab, you can control how the headers of each field display, as shown in Figure 1–87. The *Multiple values indication* options enable you to control how fields with multiple values display.

Figure 1–87

Appearance Tab

In the *Appearance* tab, you can select how you want to build the schedule: from the **Top-down** or **Bottom-up**, as shown in Figure 1–88. You can also set the *Height* to **Variable** or **User defined**.

Figure 1–88

- If the *Height* is set to **Variable**, it will add lines to the schedule as revisions are added to a project. If the *Height* is set to **User defined,** a predefined number of rows is created within the revision schedule on the title block.

- The S*tripe Rows* option allows you to highlight alternating rows within the schedule to help differentiate the rows in large schedules. You can select the option for the highlight to start on the first or second row and select the color option. This will appear on the sheet and in print.

4. Click **OK**. The schedule view displays, as shown in Figure 1–89.

Figure 1–89

5. Click on the sheet view tab (it has no name) to make it the active view, as shown in Figure 1–90.

Sheet view tab

Figure 1–90

6. In the Project Browser, expand **Views (all)>Schedules** and drag and drop the schedule onto the sheet.

- If in the revision schedule properties, on the *Appearance* tab, the height is set to **User defined**, an additional control displays at the bottom of the schedule. Use it to set the height of the schedule, as shown in Figure 1–91.

User-defined control

Figure 1–91

- In Properties, you can change the *Rotation on the Sheet* to **None, 90° Clockwise**, or **90° Counterclockwise**.

7. Save the title block.

Adding Sheets to Project Templates

In your template, you can create several sheets that are typically used in a project. For each sheet you create, you can add views to the sheet to be a placeholder for future projects. For example, a sheet can have the name of *Typical Floor Plan* and you can drag and drop *Level 1* onto the sheet, as shown in Figure 1–92. Note that the view is empty in the template, but once the template is saved as a project and you draw elements on level 1, they automatically display in the viewport that is already on the sheet.

Figure 1–92

- You can create a sheet list schedule and populate it with sheet names that can be used as placeholder sheets. See *A.8 Additional Schedule Types* in *Appendix A Additional Management Tools* for information on how to create sheet list schedules.

- You can copy sheets from a resource project.

Presetting a Starting View

When you create a project template or project, specifying a starting view can streamline opening a project model and help provide important information to the people working on the project. This can be any of the standard views, such as plan, elevation, 3D view, or one that is specifically created. This is often a drafting view (as shown in Figure 1–93), a legend view with information about the project (such as a project bulletin board), or the cover sheet for the project. You can add text as placeholders for project information you will add when the project is started.

New Project Name

Project Address
Project Address 2

Architect:
Structural Engineer:
MEP Engineer:
Civil Engineer:

Figure 1–93

How To: Set a Starting View

1. Within your company template, set up the view or sheet that you want to use as the starting view.

2. In the *Manage* tab>*Manage Project* panel, click 🔲 (Starting View).

3. In the *Starting View* dialog box, select the view or sheet that you want to use, as shown in Figure 1–94.

    Note: By default, the starting view is set to <Last Viewed>, which is the last view that was open before closing the file.

Figure 1–94

4. Click **OK** and save your template.

Practice 1e
Create Title Blocks – All Disciplines

Practice Objectives

- Draw a custom title block including detail lines, text, labels, and a revision table.
- Set up sheets in the template using the new title block.

In this practice, you will create a new title block by adding lines, text, labels, logo, and a revision schedule, similar to Figure 1–95. You will then load it into a project template file and create several standard sheets.

Figure 1–95

Task 1: Create a title block.

1. In the *File* tab, expand ▢ (New) and click ▢ (Title Block). If you are on the Home screen, click ▣ (Home Screen) to view the *File* tab.

2. In the *New Title Block - Select Template File* dialog box, navigate to the practice files *TBLK Template* folder, select **D - 36 x 24.rft**, and click **Open**.

3. In the *File* tab, select **Save as>Family** and save the title block as **Company TBLK.rfa** in the practice files *TBLK Template* folder.

4. Create the title block linework by going to the *Create* tab>*Detail* panel and clicking ⎰ (Line). Create border lines on the inside of the existing rectangle **1/4"** away from the top, bottom, and right side. Draw a line **1"** away on the left margin. Trim the lines in all four corners.

5. Draw lines for the title block in the lower-right corner, as shown in Figure 1−96.

Figure 1−96

6. In the *Create* tab>*Detail* panel, click ▦ (Symbol). When prompted to load a generic annotation family, click **Yes**.

7. In the *Load Family* dialog box, navigate to the practice files *TBLK Logo* folder, select **Company Logo.rfa**, and click **Open**. Add the symbol to the lower-left corner of the new title block, as shown in Figure 1–97. It is designed to fit within the square.

Figure 1–97

8. In the *Create* tab>*Text* panel, click A (Text). In Properties, click ⊞ (Edit Type) and create the following Text type:

Type Name	Font	Size	Bold	Background
Arial 1/16"	Arial	1/16"	No	Transparent

9. In the *Create* tab>*Text* panel, click A⊞ (Label).

10. In Properties, click ⊞ (Edit Type) and create the following Label types:

Type Name	Font	Size	Bold	Background
Arial 1/8"	Arial	1/8"	No	Transparent
Arial 1/4"	Arial	1/4"	No	Transparent

11. Using the following steps, add text and labels to the title block, as shown in Figure 1–98. You can use reference lines to place the text and labels exactly.

Figure 1–98

- **Text:**

12. Use A (Text) with the *text type* **Arial 1/16"** to add text in the lower right spacesfor the *Date*, *Project Number*, *Drawn By*, and *Sheet Number*.

- **Labels:**

13. Use A (Label) with the *label type* **Arial 1/4"** and (Align Text Center) justification to add the *Sheet Name*, *Project Name*, and *Sheet Number*. Move and stretch the labels to fit in the title block.

14. Using the *label type* **Arial 1/8"** and (Align Text Center) justification, add the *Project Address* below the *Project Name*.

15. Using the *label type* **Arial 1/8"** and (Align Text Right) justification, add the *Project Issue Date*, *Project Number*, and *Drawn By*.

Task 2: Add a revision schedule to the title block.

1. In the *View* tab>*Create* panel, click (Revision Schedule).

2. In the *Revision Properties* dialog box>*Fields* tab, verify the *Scheduled fields (in order)* list is as shown in Figure 1–99.

Figure 1–99

3. Accept the defaults for the *Sorting/Grouping* and *Formatting* tabs.

4. Select the *Appearance* tab. In the *Graphics* area, change the *Height* to **User defined**.

5. Click **OK**.

6. Return to the title block view.

7. In the Project Browser, expand **Views (all)>Schedules** to display the available schedules.

8. Drag and drop the revision schedule onto the sheet.

9. Move it above the sheet name and resize it to display several lines, as shown in Figure 1–100. Align it to the edge of the title block.

Figure 1–100

10. Save and close the title block.

Task 3: Set up sheets in a project template using the new title block.

1. Open the template found in the practice files folder that relates to your discipline:

   • *Architectural>RTE:* **Midrise-Template-A-2.rte**

   • *MEP>RTE:* **Midrise-Template-MEP-2.rte**

   • *Structural>RTE:* **Midrise-Template-S-2.rte**

2. In the *View* tab>*Sheet Composition* panel, click ⬜ (Sheet).

3. In the *New Sheet* dialog box, click **Load...**.

4. In the *Load Family* dialog box, navigate to the practice files *TBLK Template* folder, select **Company TBLK.rfa** (that you just created), and click **Open**.

   • If you did not complete the previous tasks, open **Sample TBLK.rfa** from the practice files *TBLK Template* folder. In the *New Sheet* dialog box, select the title block that you just loaded and click **OK**.

5. In the Project Browser, select the new sheet, right-click, and select **Rename**. Rename it to **CS000 – Cover Sheet**.

6. Using the **SC_1/4" Arial** text type, add text for **PROJECT DIRECTORY**, **PROJECT DATA**, and **APPLICABLE CODES**, as shown in Figure 1–101.

7. In the *Insert* tab, click **Link Image** and select **Placeholder Image.jpg** from the practice files *Placeholder Images* folder, then place it on the sheet as shown in Figure 1–101 .

Figure 1–101

8. In the *Manage* tab>*Manage Project* panel, click ⬚ (Starting View).

9. In the *Starting View* dialog box, select **Sheet: CS000 - Cover Sheet**, as shown in Figure 1–102.

Figure 1–102

10. Create another sheet with the new title block and name it according to your discipline, as follows:

   - *Architecture:* **A201 – First Floor Plan**
   - *Mechanical:* **M201 - First Floor Plan**
   - *Electrical:* **E201 - First Floor Plan**
   - *Plumbing:* **P201 - First Floor Plan**
   - *Structure:* **S201 - TOS 1 Floor Plan**

11. Open this sheet view. Drag the associated **Level 1** floor plan view onto the sheet, as shown in Figure 1–103.

Note: No elements are on the view, but it acts as a placeholder on the sheet. Elements display as they are drawn.

Figure 1–103

12. Select the view on the sheet. In the *Modify | Viewports* tab>*Positioning & View* panel, click (Save Position). In the *Save View Position* dialog box, type the sheet size and the location of the view on the sheet, for example **D_Upper Left**.

13. Click **OK** and create another sheet for another view. Place the view on the sheet.

14. With the view still selected, in the *Modify | Viewports* tab>*Positioning & View* panel, expand **Saved Position** and select the saved position that was just created.

15. Save and close the template file.

End of practice

1.4 Setting Up View Filters

Rule-based view filters used in conjunction with visibility/graphic overrides are a powerful tool that can be saved in template files. They can be used to test conditions in a project or modify the information that display in a view. For example, a fire evacuation plan might have walls with different fire ratings that display with thicker lineweights, as shown in Figure 1–104. MEP projects frequently use view filters to control which systems display in a view.

Figure 1–104

- There are two types of filters: **rule-based filters**, used in visibility/graphic overrides, and **selection-based filters**, used by selection sets.

  - Selection-based filters are not something you would set up in a template, but are used when you want to modify multiple elements at the same time in a view. You cannot add categories or apply rules to a selection-based filter like you can with a rule-based filter, but you can use selection-based filters to isolate, hide, or apply graphic settings to the set.

How To: Create a Rule-Based Filter

1. In the *View* tab>*Graphics* panel, click ⬚ (Filters). The *Filters* dialog box opens, as shown in Figure 1–105.

Figure 1–105

---

2. In the *Filters* area, select the **Rule-based Filters** node or an existing filter and click 📄 (New) or 📄 (Duplicate), as shown in Figure 1–106. Name the new filter and click **OK**.

3. In the *Categories* area, filter the list by discipline and then select the categories to include in the filter, as shown in Figure 1–106. Use **Check All** and **Check None** to help select the categories.

Create new, rename, or duplicate filter

Figure 1–106

- Although you can select multiple categories, you can only filter by the parameters the categories have in common.

4. In the *Filter Rules* area, select the *Condition* (type of filter) you want to create (**AND** or **OR**) as shown in Figure 1–107.

Condition

Figure 1–107

5. For each filter, specify the *Categories, Parameter, Operator*, and *Value*, as shown in Figure 1–108.

Figure 1–108

- Click **Add Rule** to add a rule to the existing condition.
- Click **Add Set** to add a nested condition and filters.

6. Click **Apply** to save the changes and remain in the dialog box, or click **OK** to finish.

- If you create more than one filter rule, they are applied in order.

- OR rules can reference multiple categories and all parameters from the selected categories can be used in the rule, not just those that are common to the categories.

- Building nested filters is complex. It is recommended to start with an **AND** condition and then add **OR** conditions to further identify the elements.

- Test your filters thoroughly before applying them in a template.

How To: Apply Visibility/Graphic Overrides Filters

1. Type **VG** or **VV** or in the *View* tab>*Graphics* panel, click 🖼 (Visibility/Graphics) to open the *Visibility/Graphic Overrides* dialog box for the view that you are in. Select the *Filters* tab, as shown in Figure 1–109.

Shows which view you are specifying overrides for

Visibility/Graphic Overrides for Floor Plan: 1 - Mech   ✕

Model Categories   Annotation Categories   Analytical Model Categories   Imported Categories   Filters   Revit Links

Name	Enable Filter	Visibility	Projection/Surface			Cut		Halftone
			Lines	Patterns	Transpare...	Lines	Patterns	
Mechanical - Supply	☑	☑						☐
Mechanical - Return	☑	☑						☐
Mechanical - Exhaust	☑	☑						☐

Figure 1–109

2. Click **Add** to add a filter to the list.

3. In the *Add Filters* dialog box, select the filter(s) you want to add, as shown in Figure 1–110, then click **OK**.

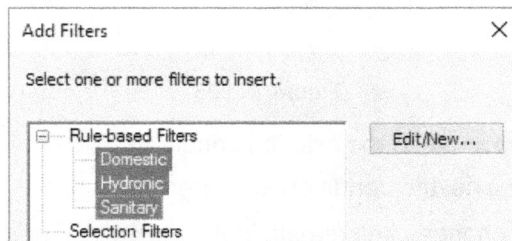

Add Filters   ✕

Select one or more filters to insert.

⊟ Rule-based Filters   Edit/New...
   Domestic
   Hydronic
   Sanitary
Selection Filters

Figure 1–110

- If the filter you want is not defined, click **Edit/New...** to open the *Filters* dialog box, where you can define a new filter or edit an existing one.
- Filters added are applied to the current view only.

4. In the *Visibility/Graphic Overrides* dialog box, assign the overrides you want for the filter, as shown in Figure 1–111.

- **Visibility:** To hide the filtered elements in the view, uncheck this box.
- **Enable Filter:** To disable the filter effects in the view, uncheck this box.

Name	Enable Filter	Visibility	Projection/Surface			Cut		Halftone
			Lines	Patterns	Transpare...	Lines	Patterns	
Domestic	☑	☑	Override...	Override...	Override...			☐
Hydronic	☑	☑						☐
Sanitary	☑	☑						☐

Figure 1–111

Practice 1f
Set Up View Filters – Architecture

Practice Objectives

- Create rule-based filters.
- Add view filters to a view and set up overrides.

In this practice, you will create rule-based filters for wall fire ratings. You will duplicate a view and add the filters with overrides set up in the *Visibility/Graphic Overrides* dialog box.

Note: This practice uses view filters in an existing project so you can add a filter and then see the impact of what it does. They should be set up originally in a template.

Task 1: Create filters.

1. In the practice files *Architectural* folder, open **Office-Fire Ratings.rvt**.
2. In the *View* tab>*Graphics* panel, click 🔲 (Filters).
3. In the *Filters* dialog box, click 🗋 (New), name the new filter **Fire Rating - 1 Hour**, and click **OK**.
4. In the *Categories* area, set the *Filter list* to **Architecture**. Select **Walls**.
5. In the *Filter Rules* area, set the **AND** condition as follows (as shown in Figure 1–112):
   - *Parameter:* **Fire Rating**
   - *Operator:* **equals**
   - *Value:* **1 Hour**

AND (All rules must be true)		Add Rule	Add Set
Walls	Fire Rating		
equals	1 Hour		

Figure 1–112

6. Click **Apply** and remain in the *Filters* dialog box.
7. Select the new **Fire Rating - 1 Hour** filter and click 🗋 (Duplicate).
8. Select the duplicated filter and click 🔠 (Rename) or right-click on the duplicated filter and click **Rename**. In the *Rename* dialog box, type **Fire Rating - 2 Hours** and click **OK**.

9. Modify the *Filter Rule* to **Fire Rating** > **equals** > **2 Hours**, as shown in Figure 1–113. Note that you will need to type in **2 Hours** because this fire rating does not yet display in the project.

Figure 1–113

10. Click **OK** to close the *Filters* dialog box.

Task 2: Test the view filters.

1. Duplicate the Floor Plans>**Level 1** view and name it **Level 1 - Fire Ratings.**

2. With only the **Level 1** and **Level 1 - Fire Ratings** views open, type **WT** to tile them side by side.

3. Zoom in on the core of the building in both views.

4. In the **Level 1 - Fire Ratings** view, open the *Visibility/Graphic Overrides* dialog box.

5. On the *Filters* tab, click **Add.**

6. In the *Add Filters* dialog box, select both Fire Rating filters, as shown in Figure 1–114, and click **OK**.

Figure 1–114

7. For the **Fire Rating - 1 Hour** filter, in the *Cut>Patterns* column, click **Override....**

8. In the *Fill Pattern Graphics* dialog box, change the *Foreground Pattern* to **Solid Fill** and *Color* to an orange, as shown in Figure 1–115. Click **OK**.

Figure 1–115

9. Repeat the process for the **Fire Rating - 2 Hours** view filter using a different color, as shown in Figure 1–116.

Figure 1–116

10. Click **OK**. The filter overrides display in the **Fire Ratings** view but not in the original view.

11. In the **Level 1 - Fire Ratings** view, select one of the exterior walls (**Basic Wall:WT-04**) and in Properties, click **Edit Type**.

Note: This is an example. Typically, exterior walls are not set up with this type of fire rating unless they are part of a fire wall.

12. Scroll down to the *Identity Data* section and beside *Fire Rating*, type in **2 Hours**, as shown in Figure 1–117. Click **OK**.

Identity Data	⌃
Type Image	
Keynote	
Model	
Manufacturer	
Type Comments	
URL	
Description	
Assembly Description	Partitions - Drywall w/ Metal Stud
Assembly Code	C1010145
Type Mark	WT-04
Fire Rating	2 Hours
Cost	

Figure 1–117

- The value of the *Fire Rating* parameter must match the name of the filter exactly. Edit the filter if the walls do not change color.

13. The filter overrides display in the **Level 1 - Fire Ratings** view, but not in the original view, as shown in Figure 1–118.

Original view   *Duplicated view with filters and overrides*

Figure 1–118

Task 3: Copy filters using Transfer Project Standards.

1. Open **Midrise-Template-A-2.rte** (that you saved) from the practice files *Architecture>RTE* folder. If you did not complete the template, open **Midrise-Template-Architecture.rte**.

2. In the *Manage* tab>*Settings* panel, click **Transfer Project Standards**.

3. In the *Transfer Project Standards* dialog box, click **Check None**, then check the checkbox next to **Filters** and click **OK**.

4. In the *View* tab>*Graphics* panel, click **Filters** and verify the two fire rating filters transferred. Click **OK**.

5. Save and close the project template and the project.

End of practice

Practice 1g
Set Up View Filters – MEP

Practice Objectives

- Create rule-based filters.
- Add view filters to a view and set up overrides.

In this practice, you will create rule-based filters. You will duplicate a view and add the filters with overrides set up in the *Visibility/Graphic Overrides* dialog box.

Note: This practice uses view filters in an existing project so you can add a filter and then see the impact of what it does. They should be set up originally in a project template.

Task 1: Create three new filters.

1. In the practice files *MEP* folder, open **Office-Velocity.rvt**.

2. In the *View* tab>*Graphics* panel, click (Filters).

3. In the *Filters* dialog box, click (New), name the new filter **Mechanical - Low Velocity**, and click **OK**.

4. In the *Categories* area, set the *Filter list* to **Mechanical**. Select **Ducts** and **Flex Ducts**.

5. In the *Filter Rules* area, set the **AND** condition as follows (as shown in Figure 1–119):

   - *Parameter:* **Velocity**
   - *Operator:* **is less than or equal to**
   - *Value:* **945.00 FPM**

Figure 1–119

6. Click **Apply** and remain in the *Filters* dialog box.

7. In the *Filters* section, select the new **Mechanical - Low Velocity** filter and click
   📄 (Duplicate).

8. Select the duplicated filter and click 🔤 (Rename) or right-click on the duplicated filter and click **Rename**. In the *Rename* dialog box, type **Mechanical - Medium Velocity** and click **OK**.

   • You will see that there is already a *Filter Rule* that was copied when duplicating the Low Velocity filter.

9. Change the existing **Velocity** rule to **is greater than or equal to**, as shown in Figure 1–120.

Figure 1–120

10. Click **Add Rule** to create a second rule and set it up as shown in Figure 1–121 using **Velocity > is less than or equal to > 1800.00 FPM**. (This filter has two rules.)

Figure 1–121

11. Click **Apply**.

12. Create an additional filter named **Mechanical - High Velocity** set up as shown in Figure 1–122. Use **is greater than** as the condition. (This filter has only one rule.)

AND (All rules must be true)		Add Rule	Add Set
All Selected...	Velocity		
is greater th...	1800.00 FPM		

Figure 1–122

13. Click **OK** to close the *Filters* dialog box.

Task 2: Test the view filters.

1. Duplicate with Detailing the Mechanical>Floor Plans>**1 - Mech** view and name it **1 - Mech - Velocity**.

2. With only the **1 - Mech** and **1 - Mech - Velocity** views open, type **WT** to tile them side by side.

3. Zoom in on the central core of the building in both views. Both views display the duct colors set up in the Duct System properties for Supply, Return, and Exhaust.

4. In the **1 - Mech - Velocity** view, open the *Visibility/Graphic Overrides* dialog box and open the *Filters* tab. Three existing filters are available for the Mechanical duct systems.

5. On the *Filters* tab, click **Add**.

6. In the *Add Filters* dialog box, select the three new filters as shown in Figure 1–123. Click **OK**.

Figure 1–123

7. Move the velocity-based filters to the top of the list using the **Up** and **Down** buttons.

8. For the **Mechanical - Low Velocity** filter, in the *Projection/Surface>Patterns* column, click **Override**.

9. In the *Fill Pattern Graphics* dialog box, change the *Pattern* to **Solid Fill** and the *Color* to an orange, as shown in Figure 1–124. Click **OK**.

Figure 1–124

10. For the other velocity filters, create a similar overrides using other colors.

11. For the Supply and Return filters, set the *Projection Lines* override *Color* to **Black**. Then, clear the *Visibility* check on the Exhaust filter, as shown in Figure 1–125.

Figure 1–125

12. Click **OK**. The filter overrides display in the **Velocity** view, but not in the original view, as shown in Figure 1–126.

Duplicated view with filters and overrides   *Original view*

Figure 1–126

Task 3: Copy filters using Transfer Project Standards.

1. Open **Midrise-Template-MEP-2.rte** (that you saved) from the practice files *MEP>RTE* folder. If you did not complete the template, open **Midrise-Template-MEP.rte**.

2. In the *Manage* tab>*Settings* panel, click **Transfer Project Standards**.

3. In the *Transfer Project Standards* dialog box, click **Check None**, then check the checkbox next to **Filters** and click **OK**.

4. In the *View* tab>*Graphics* panel, click **Filters** and verify the velocity filters transferred. Click **OK**.

5. Save and close the project template and project.

End of practice

Practice 1h
Set Up View Filters – Structure

Practice Objectives

- Create rule-based filters.
- Add view filters to a view and set up overrides.

In this practice, you will create rule-based filters for element materials. You will duplicate a view and apply the filters with overrides set up in the *Visibility/Graphic Overrides* dialog box.

Note: This practice uses view filters in an existing project so you add a filter and then see the impact of what it does. They should be set up originally in a project template.

Task 1: Create filters.

1. In the practice files *Structural* folder, open **Office-Materials.rvt**.

2. In the *View* tab>*Graphics* panel, click ⛶ (Filters).

3. In the *Filters* dialog box, click ◻ (New), name the new filter **Concrete** and click **OK**.

4. In the *Categories* area, set the *Filter list* to **Structure**. Select **Structural Columns, Structural Foundations, Structural Framing,** and **Walls**.

   Note: An alternate way to make these filters is to do one for each material.

5. In the *Filter Rules* area, set the **OR** condition and modify the existing rule as follows (as shown in Figure 1–127):
   - *Parameter:* **Structural Material**
   - *Operator:* **equals**
   - *Value:* **Concrete - Cast-in-Place Concrete**

6. Click **Add Rule** and add another rule, as follows:
   - *Parameter:* **Structural Material**
   - *Operator:* **equals**
   - *Value:* **Masonry - Concrete Masonry Units**

Figure 1–127

7. Click **Apply** and remain in the *Filters* dialog box.

8. Select the new **Concrete** filter and click 🗋 (Duplicate).

9. Select the duplicated filter and click 🔠 (Rename) or right-click on the duplicated filter and click **Rename**. In the *Rename* dialog box, type **Steel** and click **OK**.

    • The filter rules will be copied when duplicating the **Concrete Structural Material** filter.

10. Change the existing **Structural Material** filter rules to **Structural Material** > **equals** > **Metal - Steel - ASTM A500 - Grade B - Rectangular and Square** and **Metal - Steel - ASTM A992**, as shown in Figure 1–128.

Figure 1–128

11. Click **OK** to close the *Filters* dialog box.

Task 2: Test the view filters.

1. Duplicate the 3D Views>**{3D}** view and rename it to **Structural Materials - 3D**.

2. With only the **{3D}** and **Structural Materials - 3D** views open, type **WT** then **ZA** to tile them side by side and zoom all both views.

3. In the **Structural Materials - 3D view**, open the *Visibility/Graphic Overrides* dialog box.

4. On the *Filters* tab, click **Add**.

5. In the *Add Filters* dialog box, select both of the filters, as shown in Figure 1–129, and click **OK**.

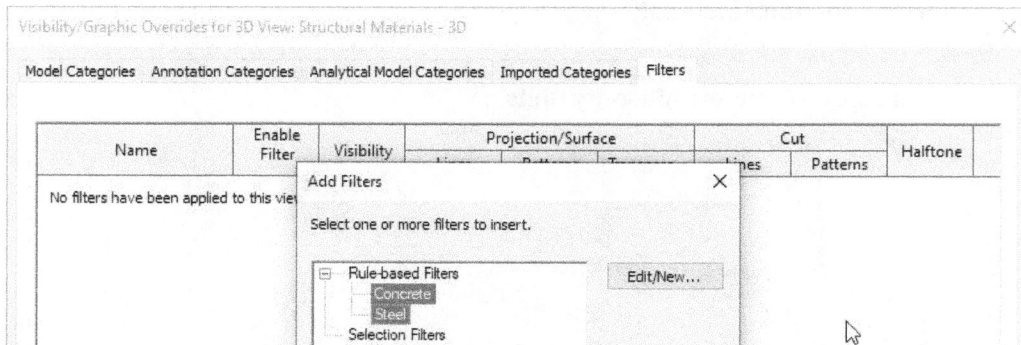

Figure 1–129

6. For the **Concrete** filter, in the *Projection/Surface>Patterns* column, select **Override**.

7. In the *Fill Pattern Graphics* dialog box, change the *Foreground Pattern* to **Solid Fill** and *Color* to an orange, as shown in Figure 1–130. Click **OK**.

Figure 1–130

8. Repeat the process for the **Steel** filter using a different color, as shown in Figure 1–131.

Figure 1–131

9. Click **OK**. The filter overrides display in the **Structural Materials** view, but not in the original view, as shown in Figure 1–132.

Figure 1–132

Task 3: Copy filters using Transfer Project Standards.

1. Open **Midrise-Template-S-2.rte** (that you saved) from the practice files *Structure>RTE* folder. If you did not complete the template, open **Midrise-Template-Structure.rte**.

2. In the *Manage* tab>*Settings* panel, click **Transfer Project Standards**.

3. In the *Transfer Project Standards* dialog box, click **Check None**, then check the checkbox next to **Filters** and click **OK**.

4. In the *View* tab>*Graphics* panel, click **Filters** and verify the two filters transferred. Click **OK**.

5. Save and close the project template and project.

End of practice

1.5 Creating and Applying View Templates

View templates applied to views, consisting of specific view properties and visibility options, ensure that company standards are applied. For example, you can create a view template that displays spaces, but hides the MEP systems in a view (as shown in Figure 1–133), while another view template displays duct systems but not plumbing fixtures (as shown in Figure 1–134).

Figure 1–133

Figure 1–134

- View templates can be applied when creating plan views or to new view types. This applies view settings and graphic properties more quickly.

- A view template can be applied to a view so that users are allowed to modify the view settings; however, you can also make the view dependent upon the view template so that changes to a single view cannot be made by users, as shown with the detail level options in Figure 1–135, which are grayed out so users cannot change them. Making a view dependent prevents users from modifying the settings and aids in establishing a company graphic standard to views.

Figure 1–135

How To: Create a View Template from an Existing View

1. Set up a view the way you want it with *Scale*, *Detail Level*, *Visibility Graphic Overrides*, and other *View Settings*. For example, you can create a view template for furniture plans that displays furniture with black lines, walls, doors, and windows as half-tone, and grid lines hidden, as shown in Figure 1–136.

Figure 1–136

2. In the Project Browser, right-click on the view and select **Create View Template from View** or, on the *View* tab>*Graphics* panel, expand ⬚ (View Template), and click 🔳 (Create Template from Current View).

3. In the *New View Template* dialog box, type a name for the view template.

4. Click **OK**.

5. In the *View Templates* dialog box, make adjustments as needed and then click **OK**.

How To: Create a View Template

1. In the *View* tab>*Graphics* panel, expand ⬚ (View Template) and then click 🔧 (Manage View Templates).

2. In the *View Templates* dialog box, under the *Names* list, select a view similar to the one you want to create and click 🗍 (Duplicate).

3. In the *New View Template* dialog box, type a new name for the view template and click **OK**.

4. Select the new view template (as shown in Figure 1–137) and modify the parameter values in the *View properties* area.

   - You can adjust the size of the *View Templates* dialog box by clicking and dragging the lower right corner.

Figure 1–137

5. Click **OK** to finish.

   Note: Note that the different view types have different view parameters. For example, 3D views have options for Rendering and plan views do not.

- To limit the number of view templates that display, filter the list by selecting an option in the *Discipline filter* and *View type filter* drop-down lists, as shown in Figure 1–138.

Figure 1–138

- If you do not want a specific view properties parameter to be controlled by the view template that is applied to views, clear the check mark in the *Include* column for the parameters you do not want to include. You can also create overrides to the view template by changing parameter values.

How To: Create a New View and Apply a View Template

1. In the *View* tab>*Create* panel, click on 🗔 (Plan Views), then click 🗔 (Floor Plan), 🗔 (Reflected Ceiling) or 🗔 (Structural Plan).

2. In the *New Floor Plan* dialog box, uncheck **Do not duplicate existing views** and select a view from the list, using the <Ctrl> or <Shift> keys to select more than one.

3. Click the **Edit Type...** button.

4. In the *Type Properties* dialog box, click on the button next to the *View Template applied to new view* parameter, as shown in Figure 1–139.

Figure 1–139

5. This opens up the *Assign View Template* dialog box, where you can select the view template you want applied. Select a view template and click **OK.**

6. In the *View Properties* dialog box, if you check the box next to **New Views are dependent on template**, the settings in the view template are used and users cannot override the settings. If it is unchecked, users can override the settings, as shown in Figure 1–140.

Identity Data	
View Template applied to new views	Structural Materials
New views are dependent on templat ☑	

| |
| Coarse |
| Medium |
| Fine |

Settings locked

Identity Data	
View Template applied to new views	Structural Materials
New views are dependent on templat ☐	

| |
| ☐ Coarse |
| ▨ Medium |
| ▨ Fine |

Settings unlocked

Figure 1–140

How To: Create a New View Type with a View Template

1. Open a view of the type you want to create. For example, if you want to create a new plan view type, select an existing Floor Plan view, or if you want to create a new elevation view type, select an existing Elevation view.

2. In Properties, click **Edit Type**.

3. Duplicate the existing type and give it a new name.

4. Specify the *Callout Tag* and *Reference Label*, set the view template for the *View Template applied to new view* option, and select **New views dependent on template**, as shown in Figure 1–141. This view is dependent on the view template settings that are applied.

Figure 1–141

5. Click **OK**.

   Note: *When you create a new view, you can select the view type from the drop-down list, as shown on the left in Figure 1–142 for a new floor plan. The view is also placed in its own section in the Project Browser, as shown on the right.*

Figure 1–142

How To: Set the Default View Template for a View

1. In the Project Browser, select one or more views.

2. In Properties, in the *Identity Data* section, click the button next to *View Template*, as shown in Figure 1–143. The name on the button varies according to the template that has already been assigned.

Figure 1–143

3. In the *Assign View Template* dialog box, select the appropriate template and click **OK**. This locks the view to be dependent on the view template settings that are applied.

- You can apply view templates to any view as many times as necessary.

- If you want to start a new view template based on an existing view, in the *Assign View Template* dialog box, select **Show Views**. The *Names* list expands to include all of the related views in the project.

💡 Hint: Temporary View Properties

As you are working, it can be helpful to temporarily override the view. You can do this by selecting a view template from the View Control Bar, as shown in Figure 1–144.

Enable Temporary View Properties

Temporarily Apply Template Properties...

Recent Templates

✓   Structural Framing Plan

Architectural Plan

Restore View Properties

Figure 1–144

1. In the *View Control* Panel, expand 🔲 (Temporary View Properties) and select **Enable Temporary View Properties**.

2. Expand 🔲 (Temporary View Properties) again and select **Temporarily Apply Template Properties**. Alternatively, if you have already used the process, you can select from a list of view templates, as shown above in Figure 1–144.

3. In the dialog box, select the view template you want to apply and click **OK**.

4. When you are finished, expand 🔲 (Temporary View Properties) and select **Restore View Properties**.

- Some companies create a "working view" template to be used as a temporary override, rather than having separate working views.

Practice 1i
Add View Templates – Architecture

Practice Objectives

- Create a view template from an existing view.
- Create a view template from within Manage View Templates.
- Duplicate views and apply the view templates.

In this practice, you will create view templates from an existing view and modify the view template using **Manage View Templates**. You will then duplicate views and apply the view templates to other views, as shown in Figure 1−145.

Figure 1−145

Note: This practice uses view templates in an existing project so you can create a view template and then see the impact of what it does. They should be set up originally in a project template.

Task 1: Create a view template from an existing view.

1. In the practice files *Architectural* folder, open **Office-Rooms.rvt**.

2. In the **Level 1 - Fire Ratings** view, hide the grids, elevations, sections, furniture, casework, lighting fixtures, specialty equipment, and plumbing fixtures. (**Hint:** Select one element of each category and type **VH**.)

3. In the Project Browser, in the *Floor Plans* section, right-click on the **Level 1 - Fire Ratings** view and select **Create View Template From View...**.

4. Name it **Fire Ratings** and click **OK**.

5. In the *View Templates* dialog box, in the *View Properties* section, next to **V/G Override Filters**, click the **Edit...** button.

6. In the *Visibility/Graphic Overrides* dialog box, *Filters* tab, review the filters and overrides and click **OK**.

7. In the *View properties* section, in the *Include* column, clear the check marks from all of the options except *Detail Level, V/G Overrides Model, V/G Overrides Annotation, V/G Overrides Filters,* and *Model Display,* as shown in Figure 1–146. Click **OK**.

Figure 1–146

Task 2: Apply view templates to views.

1. In the Project Browser, duplicate the **Level 2** view and rename it as **Level 2 - Fire Ratings.**

   • Note what the view looks like (e.g., grids, sections, elevation marks, etc.).

2. In Properties, in the *Identity Data* section, select **<None>** next to *View Template*.

3. In the *Assign View Template* dialog box, select **Fire Ratings** and click **OK**.

4. Review the View Control Bar options. Note that you cannot make any changes to the view controls of this view, as shown in Figure 1–147.

Figure 1–147

5. Switch to the **Level 1 - Fire Ratings** view. Note that you can still make changes to the View Controls of this view because a view template has not been applied to the view.

6. Return to the **Level 2 - Fire Ratings** view. Turn off the floor in this view by going to the *View* tab>*Graphics* panel, expanding (View Template) and clicking (Manage View Templates). In the *View Templates* dialog box, select **Fire Ratings**.

   *Note: You are not able to select the floor and type **VH** to hide the floor in the view because the view template that has been applied to it has the Visibility/Graphic Overrides Model categories locked.*

7. In the *View properties* section, next to *V/G Overrides Model,* click the **Edit...** button.

8. In the *Visibility/Graphic Overrides* dialog box, set the *Filter List* to **Architecture** and toggle off **Floors**.

9. Click **OK** to close each of the dialog boxes. The floor in the **Level 2 - Fire Ratings** view automatically toggles off.

10. Save the project.

Task 3: Create a view template through Manage View Templates.

1. In the *View* tab>*Graphics* panel, expand (View Template) and click (Manage View Templates).

2. In the *View Templates* dialog box, set the *View type filter* to **Floor, Structural, Area Plans**.

3. In the *Names* list, select **Architectural Plan** and click (Duplicate).

4. Name the new view **Room Plan** and click **OK**.

5. Next to *V/G Overrides Model,* click the **Edit...** button.

6. Verify the *Filter List* is set to **Architecture**.

7. Select the **All** button and click on one check mark to clear all the check marks from all of the model elements.

8. Select the **None** button to deselect everything.

9. Toggle on **Doors**, **Rooms**, **Stairs**, **Walls**, and **Windows**.

10. Expand *Rooms* and check **Interior Fill**, as shown in Figure 1–148.

Figure 1–148

11. Click **OK**.

12. In the *View Templates* dialog box, clear the check marks in the *Include* column beside *View Scale* and *View Range*. Click **OK**.

13. Use the **Duplicate with Detailing** command on the **Level 1** and **Level 2** views and rename them as **Level 1 - Rooms** and **Level 2 - Rooms**.

   • You need to include the room tags in the views so you must duplicate with detailing.

14. In the Project Browser, select both of the new room views.

15. In Properties, in the *Identity Data* section, select **<None>** next to *View Template* and apply the **Room Plan** view template to the views.

16. Review and compare the **Level 1**, **Level 1 - Fire Ratings**, and **Level 1 - Rooms** views.

17. If time permits, you can use **Transfer Project Standards** to transfer **View Templates** from this project to your project template. Remember to transfer **New Only**.

18. Save and close the project.

End of practice

Practice 1j
Add View Templates – MEP

Practice Objectives

- Create a view template from an existing view.
- Create a view template from within Manage View Templates.
- Duplicate views and apply the view templates.

In this practice, you will create view templates from an existing view and modify the view template using **Manage View Templates.** You will then duplicate views and apply the view templates to other views, as shown in Figure 1–149.

Figure 1–149

Note: This practice uses view templates in an existing project so you can create a view template and then see the impact of what it does. They should be set up originally in a project template.

Task 1: Create a view template from an existing view.

1. In the practice files *MEP* folder, open **Office-Spaces.rvt**.
2. In the Project Browser, in the *Mechanical>Floor Plans* section, right-click on the **1 - Mech - Velocity** view and select **Create View Template From View...**.
3. Name the new view template **Velocity Duct Plan** and click **OK**.
4. In the *View Templates* dialog box, in the *View Properties* section, next to **V/G Override Filters**, click the **Edit...** button.

5. The *Visibility/Graphic Overrides* dialog box opens with the *Filter* tab selected. You can see that the filters and overrides set up in the view are included in the view template.

6. Click **OK** twice to close the dialog boxes.

7. Duplicate the **2 - Mech** view and rename it as **2 - Mech - Velocity**.

8. In Properties, in the *Identity Data* section, select **<None>** next to *View Template*.

9. In the *Assign View Template* dialog box, select **Velocity Duct Plan** and click **OK**.

10. Review the View Control Bar options. Note that you cannot make any changes to the view controls of this view, as shown in Figure 1–150.

Figure 1–150

11. Switch to the **1 - Mech - Velocity** view. Note that you can still make changes to the View Controls of this view.

Task 2: Create a view template through Manage View Templates.

1. In the *View* tab>*Graphics* panel, expand 🗔 (View Template) and click 🔧 (Manage View Templates).

2. In the *View Templates* dialog box, set the *View type filter* to **Floor, Structural, Area Plans**.

3. In the *Names* list, select **Architectural Plan** and click 🗋 (Duplicate).

4. Name the new view **MEP Space Plan**.

5. Next to *V/G Overrides Model*, click **Edit....**

6. In the *Visibility/Graphic Overrides* dialog box, set the *Filter List* to **Mechanical, Electrical,** and **Piping**.

7. Select the **All** button and click on one check mark to clear all the check marks from all of the model elements.

8. Select **None** to deselect the selection.

9. Scroll down, expand *Spaces,* and select **Interior,** as shown in Figure 1–151.

Figure 1–151

10. Click **OK.**

11. In the *View Templates* dialog box, clear the check marks in the *Include* column beside *View Scale* and *View Range.*

12. Change the *Discipline* to **Coordination** and click **OK.**

13. Save the project.

Task 3: Apply the view template to views.

1. Use **Duplicate with Detailing** to duplicate the **1 - Mech** and **2 - Mech** views and rename them as **1 - Spaces** and **2 - Spaces**.

   • You need to include the space tags in the views so you must duplicate with detailing.

2. In the Project Browser, select both spaces views.

3. In Properties, in the *Identity Data* section, select **<None>** next to *View Template* and apply the **MEP Space Plan** view template to the views.

4. In the Project Browser, note that the views were automatically moved to the *Coordination* section and the spaces display in the view but none of the MEP elements display, as shown in Figure 1–152.

Figure 1–152

- If the spaces are not showing as expected, reload the linked **Office-Link.rvt** file.

5. If time permits, you can use **Transfer Project Standards** to transfer **View Templates** from this project to your project template. Remember to transfer **New Only**.

6. Save and close the project.

End of practice

Practice 1k
Add View Templates – Structure

Practice Objectives

- Create a view template from an existing view.
- Create a view template from within Manage View Templates.
- Duplicate views and apply the view templates.

In this practice, you will create a view template from an existing view and modify the view template using **Manage View Templates**. You will then duplicate views and apply the view template to other views, as shown in Figure 1–153.

Figure 1–153

Note: This practice uses view templates in an existing project so you can create a view template and then see the impact of what it does. They should be set up originally in a project template.

Task 1: Create a view template from an existing view.

1. In the practice files *Structural* folder, open **Office-View Template.rvt**.

2. In the Project Browser, in the *3D Views* section, right-click on the **Structural Materials - 3D** view and select **Create View Template From View...**.

3. Name the new view template **Structural Materials** and click **OK**.

4. Next to **V/G Override Filters**, click the **Edit...** button**.** The *Visibility/Graphic Overrides* dialog box opens with the *Filter* tab selected. You can see that the filters and overrides set up in the view are included in the view template.

5. Click **OK**.

6. In the *Include* column, clear the check marks from everything except the *Detail Level, V/G Overrides Model*, and *V/G Overrides Filters* categories, as shown in Figure 1–154, and click **OK**.

Figure 1–154

7. Save the project.

Task 2: Apply the view template to views.

1. Duplicate the Structural Plans>**Level 1** view and rename it **Level 1 - Materials**.

2. Right-click on the new view and select **Apply Template Properties**.

3. In the *Apply View Template* dialog box, set the *View type filter* to **<all>**, select **Structural Materials**, and click **OK**.

4. The plan displays with most of the design in the concrete filter color. Compare the new floor plan view with the existing **Level 1** view, as shown in Figure 1–155.

Figure 1–155

5. Duplicate the **Level 2** view and rename it as **Level 2 - Materials.**

6. In Properties, in the *Identity Data* section, select **<None>** next to *View Template*.

7. In the *Assign View Template* dialog box, set the *View type filter* to **<all>** and select **Structural Materials**. Click **OK.**

8. The material filters are applied. Review the View Control Bar options. Note that you cannot make any changes to the *Detail Levels* of this view, as shown in Figure 1–156, because they are all grayed out and controlled by the view template.

Figure 1–156

9. Switch to the **Level 1 - Materials** view. Note that you can still make changes to the *Detail Levels* of this view.

10. Save the project.

Task 3: Modify a view template through Manage View Templates.

1. Switch to the **Level 2 - Materials** view.

2. In the *View* tab>*Graphics* panel, expand (View Template) and click (Manage View Templates).

3. In the *Names* list, select **Structural Materials**.

4. Next to *V/G Overrides Model*, click **Edit....** In the **Filter list**, only turn on **Structure.**

5. In the *Visibility/Graphic Overrides* dialog box, toggle off **Floors.**

6. Click **OK** twice to close the dialog boxes. The Steel color now displays because the floor has been removed, but the masonry concrete walls do not display as expected, as shown in Figure 1–157.

Figure 1–157

7. Open **Manage View Templates** again and select **Structural Materials.**

8. Edit the *V/G Overrides Filters*.

9. In the *Visibility/Graphic Overrides* dialog box, add overrides to the *Cut Patterns* for both **Concrete** and **Steel** to match the *Projection/Surface Pattern* overrides, as shown in Figure 1–158.

Figure 1–158

10. Click **OK** to close the dialog boxes and the information is updated in the view, as shown in Figure 1–159.

Figure 1–159

11. If time permits, you can use **Transfer Project Standards** to transfer **View Templates** from this project to your project template. Remember to transfer **New Only**.

12. Save and close the project and project template.

End of practice

Chapter Review Questions

1. Which of the following items are NOT set in a template file?

   a. Units

   b. Annotation types

   c. Title blocks

   d. Keyboard shortcuts

2. What is a label?

   a. A text type used in title blocks.

   b. A dimension with text instead of numbers.

   c. A type of text with variable information.

3. When you want to create new text types, such as those shown in Figure 1–160, you need to duplicate an existing one.

   ## A FANCY FONT AT 1/4"

   A HAND LETTERING FONT AT 1/8"

   A HAND LETTERING FONT AT 3/32"

   Figure 1–160

   a. True

   b. False

4. Which of the following enables you to assign a view template consistently to a view so that no changes can be made to the view parameters?

   a. In the view's Properties, select a view template.

   b. In the Project Browser, right-click on the view and select **Apply Template Properties**.

   c. In the view's Properties, click **Edit Type** and assign a view template.

5. Which of the following parameters are included in a view template? (Select all that apply.)

   a. View Scale

   b. V/G Overrides Model

   c. Project Units

   d. Detail Level

Command Summary

Button	Command	Location
Templates		
	Callout Tags	• **Ribbon:** *Manage* tab>*Settings* panel, expand Additional Settings
	Elevation Tags	• **Ribbon:** *Manage* tab>*Settings* panel, expand Additional Settings
	Floor Plan	• **Ribbon:** *View* tab>*Create* panel, expand Plan Views
	Loaded Tags and Symbols	• **Ribbon:** *Annotate* tab>*Tag* panel, expand the panel title
	Section Tags	• **Ribbon:** *Manage* tab>*Settings* panel, expand Additional Settings
Annotation		
	Dimension Types	• **Ribbon:** *Annotate* tab>*Dimension* panel, expand the panel title
	Text	• **Family Editor** • **Ribbon:** *Create* tab>*Text* panel
Title Blocks		
	Label	• **Family Editor** • **Ribbon:** *Create* tab>*Text* panel
	New Title Block	• **Ribbon:** *File* tab>New
	Revision Schedule	• **Family Editor** • **Ribbon:** *View* tab>*Create* panel
View Templates and Filters		
	Apply Template Properties to Current View	• **Ribbon:** *View* tab>*Graphics* panel, expand View Templates • **Project Browser:** (*right-click on a view*)
	Create View Template From View	• **Ribbon:** *View* tab>*Graphics* panel, expand View Templates • **Project Browser:** (*right-click on a view*)
	Filters	• **Ribbon:** *View* tab>*Graphics* panel

Button	Command	Location
	Manage View Templates	• **Ribbon:** *View* tab>*Graphics* panel, expand View Templates
	Temporary View Properties	• View Control Bar

Creating Schedules

Schedules are a critical component of BIM projects. They gather information about the model that is used in construction documents and can also be used to test your model (for example, to verify the amount of air flow in a space). Several types of schedules can be created, including building component schedules, key schedules, and material takeoff schedules. These schedules are all created using the same basic methods. Custom parameters can be added to schedules that include additional information about elements, as well as formulas and other calculations.

Learning Objectives

- Schedule building components.
- Customize schedule tables using filters, sorting/grouping, formatting, and appearance.
- Modify the appearance and content of individual schedule cells.
- Create key style schedules by defining keys for elements with similar characteristics.
- Create material takeoff schedules.
- Apply conditional formatting to fields in a schedule.
- Embed a schedule into an existing room or space schedule.
- Create additional parameters, including calculated value fields and percentage fields.

2.1 Schedules

Schedules can be created at any point in a project or included in template files. Each schedule is a separate view and can be inserted on a sheet, as shown in Figure 2–1.

Figure 2–1

- Schedules can be created in project templates so that they can be reused in multiple projects.

    - If needed, use the **Insert Views from File** tool (*Insert* tab>*Load from Library* panel) to copy schedules into a project template, as well as **Transfer Project Standards** to copy **Panel Schedule Templates**.

- You are not required to have actual elements in the model when you are creating schedules.

- All properties that are stored in the model elements, as well as those specified by the user, can be added to schedules.

You can create the following types of schedules:

(Schedule/Quantities)	Generates schedules using parameters available at the category level. There are two types of Schedule/Quantities schedules: **Building Component** and **Key**.
(Material Takeoff)	Generates schedules from information about materials in a project and can be used to do quantity takeoffs.
(Sheet List)	Generates schedule from sheet information including who has designed and checked the sheet.
(Note Block)	Generates schedules that keep count of all of the symbols used in the project.

▣ (View List)	Generates schedules that keep count of all of the views in the project, including their scale, phase, and use on sheets.
▦ (Graphical Column Schedule)	(Structural only) Generates graphical schedules displaying heights of all columns in a project compared to levels. For more information, see the *Autodesk Revit: Fundamentals for Structure* guide.

- For more information on how to create Sheet List, Note Block, and View List schedules, see *A.8 Additional Schedule Types* in *Appendix A Additional Management Tools*.

Creating Building Component Schedules

A building component schedule is a table view of the type and instance parameters of a specific element. You can specify the parameters (fields) you want to include in the schedule. All of the parameters found in the type of element you are scheduling are available for use. For example, a door schedule (as shown in Figure 2–2) can include instance parameters that are automatically filled in (such as the **Height** and **Width**) and type parameters that may need to be filled in manually in the schedule or element type (such as the **Fire Rating** and **Frame**).

\<Door Schedule\>							
A	B	C	D	E	F	G	H
Mark	Height	Width	Fire Rating	Frame Type	Frame Material	Finish	Function
2	7' - 0"	10' - 0"	A	A	Steel	Brushed	Exterior
3	6' - 8"	3' - 0"	B	B	Wood	Paint	Interior ▼
4	6' - 8"	3' - 0"	B	B	Wood	Paint	Interior
5	6' - 8"	3' - 0"	B	B	Wood	Paint	Interior
6	6' - 8"	3' - 0"	B	B	Wood	Paint	Interior

Figure 2–2

- Schedules are automatically filled out with the information stored in the instance and type parameters of related elements that are added to the model. Fill out additional information either in the schedule or in Properties.

- When you select a schedule's row, it will highlight in blue.

- You can drag and drop the schedule onto a sheet as a placeholder.

- You can zoom in to read small text in schedule views. Hold down \<Ctrl\> and scroll in or out using the mouse wheel or press \<Ctrl\>+\<+\> to zoom in or \<Ctrl\>+\<-\> to zoom out. To reset the zoom back to the original zoom, press \<Ctrl\>+\<0\> (zero).

How To: Create a Building Component Schedule

1. In the *View* tab>*Create* panel, expand ⊞ (Schedules) and click ⊞ (Schedule/Quantities) or in the Project Browser, right-click on the *Schedule/Quantities* node and select **New Schedule/Quantities**.

2. In the *New Schedule* dialog box, select the type of schedule you want to create (e.g., **Structural Beam Systems**) from the *Category* list, as shown in Figure 2–3.

   Note: In the Filter list drop-down list, you can specify the discipline(s) to show only the categories that you want to display.

Figure 2–3

3. Revit assigns a name for the schedule. You can also type a new *Name*, if the default does not suit.

4. Select **Schedule building components.**

5. Specify the *Phase* as needed.

6. Click **OK**.

7. Fill out the information in the *Schedule Properties* dialog box. This includes the information in the *Fields*, *Filter*, *Sorting/Grouping*, *Formatting*, and *Appearance* tabs.

8. Once you have entered the schedule properties, click **OK**. A schedule view is created, displaying a report of the information configured in the schedule.

- Other elements that can be scheduled include model groups and Revit links.

Fields Tab

In the *Fields* tab, you can select from a list of available fields and organize them in the order in which you want them to display in the schedule, as shown in Figure 2–4. You can also sort the available fields by Parameter Type (such as Project Parameters), Discipline, or Data Type.

Figure 2–4

How To: Fill Out the Fields Tab

1. In the *Available fields* area, select one or more fields you want to add to the schedule and

   click 📥 (Add parameter(s)). The field(s) are placed in the *Scheduled fields (in order)* area.

   Note: You can also double-click on a field to move it from the Available fields area to the Scheduled fields area, and double-click on a field to remove it from the Scheduled fields area.

2. Continue adding fields, as required.

- Click ◀ (Remove parameter(s)) to move a field from the *Scheduled fields* area back to the *Available fields* area.

- Use ↑Ε (Move parameter up) and ↓Ε (Move parameter down) to change the order of the scheduled fields.

Other Fields Tab Options

Select available fields from	Enables you to select additional category fields for the specified schedule. The available list of fields depends on the original category of the schedule. Typically, they include room information.
Include elements in links	Includes elements that are in files linked to the current project, so that their elements can be included in the schedule.
(New parameter)	Adds a new field according to your specification. New fields can be placed by instance or by type.
fx **(Add Calculated parameter)**	Enables you to create a field that uses a formula based on other fields.
(Combine parameters)	Enables you to combine two or more parameters in one column.You can put any fields together even if they are used in another column.
(Edit parameter)	Enables you to edit custom fields. This is grayed out if you select a standard field.
(Delete parameter)	Deletes the selected custom fields. This is grayed out if you select a standard field.

Filter Tab

In the *Filter* tab, you can set up filters so that only elements meeting specific criteria are included in the schedule. For example, you might only want to show information for one level, as shown in Figure 2–5. You can create filters for up to eight values. All values must be satisfied for the elements to display.

Figure 2–5

- The parameter you want to use as a filter must be included in the schedule. You can hide the parameter once you have completed the schedule, if needed.

Filter by	
Field/Parameter	Specifies the field/parameter to filter. Not all fields/parameters are available to be used to filter.
Condition	Specifies the condition that must be met. This includes options such as **equal**, **not equal**, **greater than**, and **less than**.
Value	Specifies the value of the element to be filtered. You can select from a drop-down list of appropriate values. For example, if you set *Filter By* to **Level**, it displays the list of levels in the project.

Sorting/Grouping Tab

In the *Sorting/Grouping* tab, you can set how you want the information to be sorted, as shown in Figure 2–6. For example, you can sort by **Mark** (number) and then **Type**.

Figure 2–6

Sort by	Enables you to select the field(s) you want to sort by. You can select up to four levels of sorting.
Ascending/ Descending	Sorts fields in **Ascending** or **Descending** order based on an alphanumeric system.

Header/ Footer	Enables you to group similar information and separate it by a **Header** with a title and/or a **Footer** with quantity information.
Blank line	Adds a blank line between groups.
Grand totals	Selects which totals to display for the entire schedule. You can specify a name to display in the schedule for the Grand total.
Itemize every instance	If selected, displays each instance of the element in the schedule. If not selected, displays only one instance of each type, based on the sorting/ grouping categories.

Formatting Tab

In the *Formatting* tab, you can control how the headers of each field display, as shown in Figure 2–7. The *Multiple values indication* options enable you to control how fields with multiple values display.

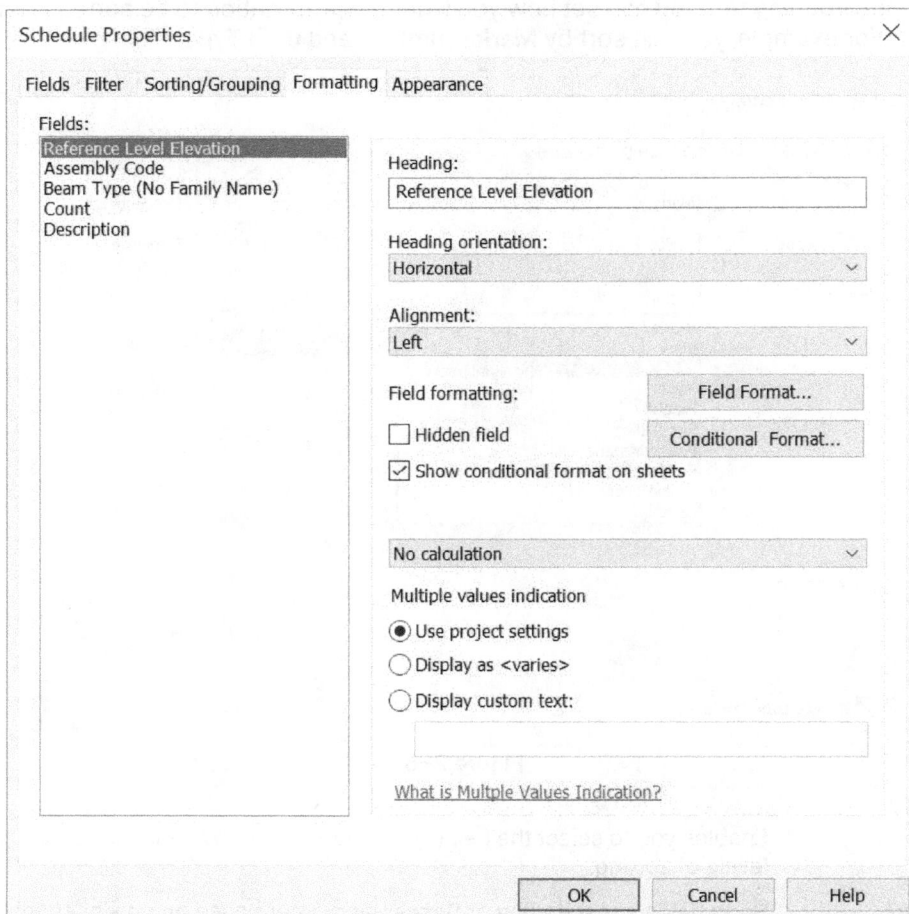

Figure 2–7

Fields	Enables you to select the field for which you want to modify the formatting.
Heading	Enables you to change the heading of the field if you want it to be different from the field name. For example, you might want to replace **Mark** (a generic name) with the more specific **Door Number** in a door schedule.
Heading orientation	Enables you to set the heading on sheets to **Horizontal** or **Vertical**. This does not impact the schedule view.
Alignment	Aligns the text in rows under the heading to be **Left**, **Right**, or **Center** justified.
Field Format...	Sets the units format for numerical fields, e.g., length, area, HVAC Air Flow, Pipe Flow, etc. By default, this is set to use the project settings.
Conditional Format...	Sets up the schedule to display visual feedback based on the conditions listed.
Hidden field	Enables you to hide a field. For example, you might want to use a field for sorting purposes, but not have it display in the schedule. You can also modify this option in the schedule view later.
Show conditional format on sheets	Select if you want the color code set up in the *Conditional Format* dialog box to display on sheets.
Calculation options	Select the type of calculation you want to use. All values in a field are: • **No Calculation:** Calculated separately. • **Calculate totals:** Added together. This enables a field to calculate and display in the Grand Totals or Footers. • **Calculate minimum:** Only the smallest amount displays. • **Calculate maximum:** Only the largest amount displays. • **Calculate minimum and maximum:** Both the smallest and largest amounts display. • Minimum and Maximum calculations only show when **Itemize every instance** is unchecked in the *Sorting/Grouping* tab.
Multiple values indication	When a schedule is not set to itemize every instance, select how the value will display.

Hint: Hiding Columns

If you want to use the field to filter or sort, but do not want it to display in the schedule, select **Hidden field**. Alternatively, once the schedule is completed, select the column header, right-click on it, and select **Hide Columns**.

Appearance Tab

In the *Appearance* tab, you can set the text style and grid options for a schedule, as shown in Figure 2–8.

Figure 2–8

Grid lines	Displays lines between each instance listed and around the outside of the schedule. Select the style of lines from the drop-down list; this controls all lines for the schedule, unless modified.
Grid in headers/footers/ spacers	Extends the vertical grid lines between the columns.
Outline	Specify a different line type for the outline of the schedule.
Blank row before data	Select this option if you want a blank row to be displayed before the data begins in the schedule.
Stripe Rows	Select this option if you want to highlight alternating rows within the schedule to help differentiate the rows in large schedules.

Show Title/Show Headers	Select these options to include the text in the schedule.
Title text/Header text/ Body text	Select the text style for the title, header, and body text.

Schedule Properties

Schedule views have properties including the *View Template, View Name, Phase, IFC Parameters*, and methods of returning to the *Schedule Properties* dialog box, as shown in Figure 2–9. In the *Other* section, select the button next to the tab that you want to open in the *Schedule Properties* dialog box. In the dialog box, you can switch from tab to tab and make any required changes to the overall schedule.

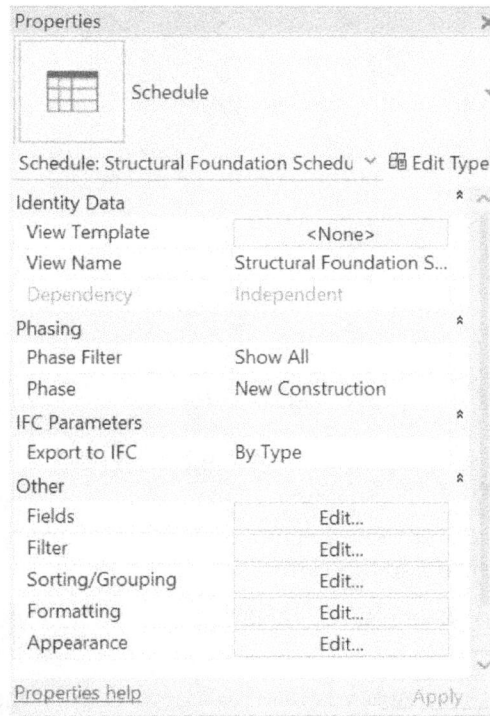

Figure 2–9

Just like other views, schedules can have *View Templates* applied. When you specify a view template directly in the view, as shown in Figure 2–10, none of the schedule properties can be modified.

Figure 2–10

- Schedule view templates are type-specific. If you apply one to a different type of element, only the *Appearance* information is applied.

- If you apply a schedule view template to a schedule of the same type, it overrides everything in the existing schedule including the fields.

- If you have a complicated schedule, you might want to create a view template for it to avoid losing that organization.

- To create schedule view templates, you need to create at least one from an existing view. Then, you can modify it and duplicate it in the *View Templates* dialog box.

Filtering Elements from Schedules

When you create schedules based on a category you might need to filter out some of the element types in that category. For example, in Revit, doors (and windows) in curtain walls are automatically added to a door schedule, as shown in the top image in Figure 2–11, but are typically estimated as part of the curtain wall rather than as a separate door. You can remove them from the schedule, as shown in the bottom image in Figure 2–11.

To remove the curtain wall doors, you can use one of two filtering methods:

- Create a filter for the door type in the schedule properties.

- Modify the elements Type Properties in the model to add a value to the elements parameter, and then use that parameter/value to filter the element out of the schedule.

	Door Size			Frame		Door Schedule- 1st
Door Type	Width	Height	Thickness	Frame Type	Frame Material	Head Detail
	8' - 3 1/2"	9' - 4 1/4"				
	3' - 0"	7' - 0"	0' - 2"	A	Aluminum	
	3' - 0"	7' - 0"	0' - 2"	B	Aluminum	
	3' - 0"	6' - 8"	0' - 2"	C	Aluminum	

Curtain wall doors displayed

	Door Size			Frame		Door Schedule- 1st
Door Type	Width	Height	Thickness	Frame Type	Frame Material	Head Detail
	3' - 0"	7' - 0"	0' - 2"	A	Aluminum	
	3' - 0"	7' - 0"	0' - 2"	B	Aluminum	
	3' - 0"	6' - 8"	0' - 2"	C	Aluminum	
	3' - 0"	6' - 8"	0' - 2"	C	Aluminum	

Curtain wall doors filtered out

Figure 2–11

- This type of filtering can be used for any schedule in any discipline.

How To: Modify an Element and Filter in a Schedule

1. Select an element (such as a door used in curtain walls) and modify the Type Parameters. Add a value to one of the parameters that you are not otherwise using in your schedule. For example, set *Construction Type* to **CW**, as shown Figure 2–12.

Type Parameters	
Parameter	Value
Construction	
Function	Exterior
Construction Type	CW

Figure 2–12

2. Create a schedule and include the field, such as *Construction Type*.

3. Modify the *Filter* of the schedule so the parameter does not equal the specified value. In the example shown in Figure 2–13, *Construction Type* **does not equal CW**. Any types that match this filter are excluded from the schedule.

Figure 2–13

4. In the final schedule, the elements display with the specified value. Right-click on the column header and select **Hide Column(s)**, as shown in Figure 2–14. It is just used as a filter and not part of the final schedule.

Figure 2–14

Note: Hiding a parameter/field in a schedule allows you to use it as a filter, but not have it visible in the schedule.

Practice 2a
Create Schedules for Architectural Projects

Practice Objectives

- Create building component schedules.
- Apply filters.
- Enter information.
- Place schedules on a sheet.

In this practice, you will create door and window schedules, filter out curtain wall doors, and add information to cells in the door schedule. You will also place the schedules on a sheet, as shown in Figure 2–15.

Figure 2–15

Task 1: Create a door schedule.

1. In the practice files *Architectural* folder, open **Clark-Hall-Schedules-Create.rvt**.

2. In the *View* tab>*Create* panel, expand ▦ (Schedules) and click ▦ (Schedule/Quantities).

3. In the *New Schedule* dialog box, set *Filter list* to **Architecture** only, to limit the number of categories, and then set *Category* to **Doors**. Name the schedule **Door Schedule-Level 1**, as shown in Figure 2–16.

Figure 2–16

4. Click **OK**.

5. In the *Schedule Properties* dialog box, in the *Fields* tab, add the following fields, as shown in Figure 2–17:

- *Level*
- *Mark*
- *Height*
- *Width*
- *Fire Rating*

- *Frame Type*
- *Frame Material*
- *Finish*
- *Comments*
- *Construction Type*

Figure 2–17

6. Click **OK** to create the schedule. Note that Level 1, Level 2, and Level 3 doors are included.

7. In Properties, in the *Other* section, next to **Filter**, click **Edit...**. The *Schedule Properties* dialog box opens with the *Filter* tab selected. Set *Filter by* to **Level** > **equals** > **Level 1**.

8. Click on the *Sorting/Grouping* tab, sort the doors by **Mark**, and click **OK** to update the schedule.

9. Save the project.

Task 2: Remove the curtain wall doors from the schedule.

1. Continue working in the new **Door Schedule-Level 1** view, The doors in the curtain walls do not display with a mark, as shown in Figure 2–18. Additionally, they are not needed in the door schedule and need to be removed.

	A	B	C	D
	Level	Mark	Height	Width
Curtain wall doors ➤	Level 1		6' - 11"	5' - 11"
	Level 1		6' - 11"	5' - 11"
	Level 1	1	7' - 0"	3' - 0"
	Level 1	2	7' - 0"	6' - 0"
	Level 1	3	7' - 0"	6' - 0"
	Level 1	4	6' - 8"	3' - 0"
	Level 1	5	6' - 8"	3' - 0"

Figure 2–18

2. In Properties, in the *Other* section, next to **Filter**, click **Edit...**.

3. In the *Schedule Properties* dialog box, in the *Filter* tab, add an additional filter for **Construction Type** > **does not equal** > **CW** (as shown in Figure 2–19), then click **OK**.

    Note: You need to type **CW** because the option does not yet exist in the project.

Schedule Properties				✕
Fields Filter Sorting/Grouping Formatting Appearance				
Filter by:	Level ▾	equals ▾	Level 1 ▾	
And:	Construction Type ▾	does not equal ▾	CW ▾	

Figure 2–19

4. In the Schedule, next to one of the curtain wall doors, in the *Construction Type* column, type **CW** and press <Enter>. An alert displays. Click **OK** and the curtain wall doors are no longer included in the schedule, as shown in Figure 2–20.

A	B	C	D
Level	Mark	Height	Width
Level 1	1	7' - 0"	3' - 0"
Level 1	2	7' - 0"	6' - 0"
Level 1	3	7' - 0"	6' - 0"
Level 1	4	6' - 8"	3' - 0"

Figure 2–20

5. Select column A (Level) to highlight the entire column. In the *Modify Schedule/Quantities* tab>*Columns* panel, select 🔲 (Hide).

6. Right-click on the *Construction Type* column header and select **Hide Columns**. This hides the columns in the schedule, as shown in Figure 2–21, but the field can still be used for sorting and filtering within the schedule.

	A	B	C	D	E	F	G	H
	Mark	Height	Width	Fire Rating	Frame Type	Frame Material	Finish	Comments
1	7' - 0"	3' - 0"						
2	7' - 0"	6' - 0"						
3	7' - 0"	6' - 0"						
4	6' - 8"	3' - 0"						
5	6' - 8"	3' - 0"						
6	6' - 8"	3' - 0"						
7	6' - 8"	3' - 0"						
8	6' - 8"	3' - 0"						

<Door Schedule - Level 1>

Figure 2–21

7. Save the project.

Task 3: Fill in additional information in the door schedule.

1. Continue working in the **Door Schedule-Level 1** view.

2. In row **1**, in the *Fire Rating* column, type the letter **B** and press <Enter>. Because the door type controls the **Fire Rating** parameter, an alert box opens, as shown in Figure 2–22. Click **OK**.

Figure 2–22

3. In row **4**, in the *Fire Rating* column, type the letter **A** and press <Enter>. Click **OK** in the alert box.

4. Open the **Floor Plans: Level 1** view and select one of the interior single doors.

5. Right-click and select **Select All Instances>In Entire Project.** In Properties, set the following parameters:

   • *Frame Type:* **22**

   • *Frame Material:* **Wood**

   • *Finish:* **Stained**

   Note: *As you enter this information, only the information for that door will be filled in. This is because these are instance parameters.*

6. Switch back to the schedule to verify that it has updated with the new information, as shown in Figure 2–23.

<Door Schedule - Level 1>							
A	B	C	D	E	F	G	H
Mark	Height	Width	Fire Rating	Frame Type	Frame Material	Finish	Comments
1	7' - 0"	3' - 0"	B				
2	7' - 0"	6' - 0"	B				
3	7' - 0"	6' - 0"	B				
4	6' - 8"	3' - 0"	A	22	Wood	Stained	
5	6' - 8"	3' - 0"	A	22	Wood	Stained	
6	6' - 8"	3' - 0"	A	22	Wood	Stained	
7	6' - 8"	3' - 0"	A	22	Wood	Stained	
8	6' - 8"	3' - 0"	A	22	Wood	Stained	
9	6' - 8"	3' - 0"	A	22	Wood	Stained	

Figure 2–23

7. In the schedule view, set the rest of the doors to the following parameters:

- *Frame Type:* **21**
- *Frame Material:* **Aluminum**
- *Finish:* **Brushed**

8. Save the project.

Task 4: Create a window schedule.

1. Create a new window schedule with the following fields: **Count**, **Type**, **Manufacturer**, and **Comments**.

2. In the *Sorting/Grouping* tab, sort the windows by **Type**. Toggle on **Grand totals** and toggle off **Itemize every instance**.

3. Click **OK** to create the schedule. It lists the total count for a single type (only one type is used in the project), as shown in Figure 2–24.

<Window Schedule>			
A	B	C	D
Count	Type	Manufacturer	Comments
39	48" x 48"		
Grand total: 39			

Figure 2–24

4. In the **Floor Plans: Level 1** view, select the three windows in the Conference Room in the office wing. In Properties change the type to **Fixed with Trim: 36" x 72"**.

5. Switch back to the schedule view. A change should display in the schedule that reflects the new window type, as shown in Figure 2–25.

<Window Schedule>			
A	B	C	D
Count	Type	Manufacturer	Comments
3	36" x 72"		
36	48" x 48"		
Grand total: 39			

Figure 2–25

6. Open the **A601- Schedules** sheet. Drag and drop the schedules to this sheet. Modify the width of each field as required.

7. Save and close the project.

End of practice

Practice 2b
Create Schedules for MEP Projects

Practice Objectives

- Create building component schedules.
- Place the schedules on a sheet.

In this practice, you will create schedules for two types of typical MEP schedules: a system schedule and a fixture schedule. In this case, they will be for duct systems and plumbing fixtures. If time permits, you will also create schedules for electrical circuits and lighting fixtures. You will then place the schedules on a sheet, as shown in Figure 2–26.

Duct Systems		
System Name	Comments	Flow
Exhaust Air		
Mechanical Exhaust Air 1		2000 CFM
Mechanical Exhaust Air 7		420 CFM
Mechanical Exhaust Air 9		200 CFM
Return Air		
Mechanical Return Air 1		0 CFM
Mechanical Return Air 2		0 CFM
Mechanical Return Air 3		205 CFM
Mechanical Return Air 4		500 CFM
Mechanical Return Air 5		500 CFM
Mechanical Return Air 6		500 CFM
Mechanical Return Air 10		0 CFM
Mechanical Return Air 14		205 CFM
Supply Air		
Mechanical Supply Air 1		4000 CFM
Mechanical Supply Air 2		2400 CFM
Mechanical Supply Air 3		2900 CFM
Mechanical Supply Air 4		3500 CFM
Mechanical Supply Air 8		0 CFM
Mechanical Supply Air 9		2900 CFM
Mechanical Supply Air 10		3900 CFM
Mechanical Supply Air 15		3090 CFM
Mechanical Supply Air 19		2400 CFM

Figure 2–26

Task 1: Create a duct system schedule.

1. In the practice files *MEP* folder, open **Freel-Office-Create.rvt**.

2. In the *View* tab>*Create* panel, expand ▦ (Schedules) and click ▦ (Schedule/Quantities).

3. In the *New Schedule* dialog box, set *Filter list* to **Mechanical** and *Category* to **Duct Systems**. Keep the name of the schedule as **Duct System Schedule**, as shown in Figure 2–27. Click **OK**.

Figure 2–27

4. In the *Schedule Properties* dialog box, in the *Fields* tab, add the following fields:

   - *System Classification*
   - *System Name*
   - *Comments*
   - *Flow*

5. In the *Sorting/Grouping* tab, sort by **System Classification**. Select **Ascending**, **Header**, and **Itemize every instance**.

6. Click **OK** to create the schedule. Stretch the columns so that you can read all of the information, as shown in Figure 2–28.

\<Duct System Schedule\>			
A	B	C	D
System Classification	System Name	Comments	Flow
Exhaust Air			
Exhaust Air	Mechanical Exhaust Air 1		2000 CFM
Exhaust Air	Mechanical Exhaust Air 7		420 CFM
Exhaust Air	Mechanical Exhaust Air 9		200 CFM
Return Air			
Return Air	Mechanical Return Air 1		0 CFM
Return Air	Mechanical Return Air 2		0 CFM
Return Air	Mechanical Return Air 3		205 CFM
Return Air	Mechanical Return Air 4		500 CFM
Return Air	Mechanical Return Air 5		500 CFM
Return Air	Mechanical Return Air 6		500 CFM
Return Air	Mechanical Return Air 10		0 CFM
Return Air	Mechanical Return Air 14		205 CFM
Supply Air			
Supply Air	Mechanical Supply Air 1		4000 CFM
Supply Air	Mechanical Supply Air 2		2400 CFM
Supply Air	Mechanical Supply Air 3		2900 CFM
Supply Air	Mechanical Supply Air 4		3500 CFM
Supply Air	Mechanical Supply Air 8		0 CFM
Supply Air	Mechanical Supply Air 9		2900 CFM
Supply Air	Mechanical Supply Air 10		3900 CFM
Supply Air	Mechanical Supply Air 15		3090 CFM
Supply Air	Mechanical Supply Air 19		2400 CFM

Figure 2–28

7. Right-click on the *System Classification* column and select **Hide Columns**, as shown in Figure 2–29. (The System Classification is specified by the header.)

Figure 2–29

8. Open the **M601- Mechanical Schedules** sheet. Drag and drop the duct system schedule to this sheet. Modify the width of each field as required.

9. Save the project.

Task 2: Create a plumbing fixture schedule.

1. In the *View* tab>*Create* panel, expand ⊞ (Schedules) and click ⊞ (Schedule/Quantities).

2. In the *New Schedule* dialog box, set *Filter list* to **Piping**, set *Category* to **Plumbing Fixtures**, and keep the name of the schedule as **Plumbing Fixture Schedule**, as shown in Figure 2–30. Click **OK**.

Figure 2–30

3. In the *Schedule Properties* dialog box, in the *Fields* tab, add the following fields:

   • *Family*
   • *Type*
   • *Manufacturer*
   • *Count*

4. In the *Sorting/Grouping* tab, sort by *Family*, and clear **Itemize every instance**.

5. Click **OK** to create the schedule. Stretch the columns so that all the words are visible, as shown in Figure 2–31.

<Plumbing Fixture Schedule>			
A	**B**	**C**	**D**
Family	Type	Manufacturer	Count
Drinking Fountain-Hi-Lo-3D	Drinking Fountain-Hi-Lo-3D		1
Shower Base-Round Corner	36" x 36"		1
Sink Kitchen-Double	42" x 21"		1
Sink Vanity-Round	19" x 19"		8
Toilet-Commercial-Wall-3D	15" Seat Height		6
Urinal-Wall-3D	Urinal-Wall-3D		2

Figure 2–31

6. Open the **P601- Plumbing Schedules** sheet. Drag and drop the schedule to this sheet. Modify the width of each field as required.

7. Save the project.

Task 3: Create electrical-related schedules.

1. In the *View* tab>*Create* panel, expand ▦ (Schedules) and click ▦ (Schedule/Quantities).

2. In the *New Schedule* dialog box, set *Filter list* to **Electrical**, set *Category* to **Electrical Circuits,** and keep the name of the schedule as **Electrical Circuit Schedule**, as shown in Figure 2–32. Click **OK**.

Figure 2–32

3. In the *Schedule Properties* dialog box, in the *Fields* tab, add the following fields:

   - *Circuit Number*
   - *Load Name*
   - *Panel*
   - *Comments*

4. Click **OK** to create the schedule. Stretch the columns so that all the words are visible, as shown in Figure 2–33.

<Electrical Circuit Schedule>			
A	**B**	**C**	**D**
Circuit Number	Load Name	Panel	Comments
1	Lighting - Dwelling Unit Office Area 1 101	400 A, 277 V/480 V, Three Phase, 4 Wires, Wye	
2	Lighting - Dwelling Unit Office Area 1 101	400 A, 277 V/480 V, Three Phase, 4 Wires, Wye	
3	Lighting - Dwelling Unit Office Area 1 101	400 A, 277 V/480 V, Three Phase, 4 Wires, Wye	
1	Lighting - Dwelling Unit Conf. Room 105	225 A, 120 V/208 V, Three Phase, 4 Wires, Wye	
2	Lighting - Dwelling Unit Room 108, 104	225 A, 120 V/208 V, Three Phase, 4 Wires, Wye	
3	Lighting - Dwelling Unit Break Room 1 112	225 A, 120 V/208 V, Three Phase, 4 Wires, Wye	

Figure 2–33

5. Open the **E601 - Electrical and Lighting Schedules** sheet. Drag and drop the schedule onto this sheet.

6. Save and close the project.

End of practice

Practice 2c
Create Schedules for Structural Projects

Practice Objectives

- Create a structural schedule that includes all types of structural elements.
- Reorganize the schedule content by sorting and grouping.
- Place the schedule on a sheet.

In this practice, you will create a schedule displaying structural elements by category. You will then place it on a sheet and modify it to fit, as shown in Figure 2-34.

Structural Schedule		
Type Mark	Family and Type	Count
Structural Columns		
P-1	Concrete-Rectangular-Column: 24 x 24	22
	W-Wide Flange-Column: W10X33	1
	W-Wide Flange-Column: W10X49	22
Structural Foundations		
F-2	Footing-Rectangular: 14'x14'x2'-0"	1
F-1	Footing-Rectangular: 36" x 36" x 12"	21
	Foundation Slab: 6" Foundation Slab	1
	Step Footing: Step Footing	4
	Wall Foundation: Bearing Footing - 24" x 12"	6
	Wall Foundation: Bearing Footing - 36" x 12"	4
	Wall Foundation: Retaining Footing - 24" x 12" x 12"	1
Structural Framing		
	HSS-Hollow Structural Section: HSS6X6X.500	9
	K-Series Bar Joist-Rod Web: 16K6	65
	W-Wide Flange: W8X10	6
	W-Wide Flange: W12X26	63
	W-Wide Flange: W14X48	62
	W-Wide Flange: W16X45	1

Figure 2-34

Task 1: Create a structural schedule.

1. In the practice files *Structural* folder, open **Axiom-Building-Create.rvt**.

2. In the *View* tab>*Create* panel, expand ⊞ (Schedules) and click ⊞ (Schedule/Quantities).

3. In the *New Schedule* dialog box, set *Filter list* to **Structure**, set *Category* to **<Multi-Category>**, and name the schedule **Structural Schedule**, as shown in Figure 2–35. Click **OK**.

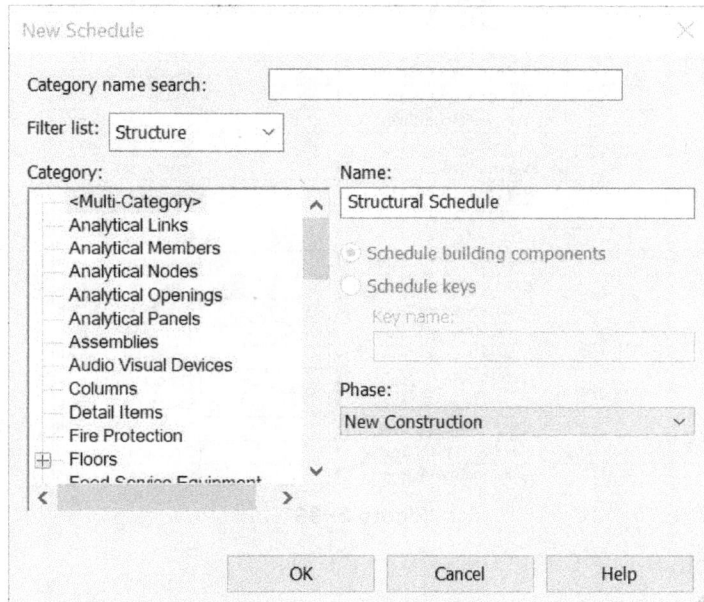

Figure 2–35

4. In the *Schedule Properties* dialog box, in the *Fields* tab, add the following fields:

    * *Type Mark*
    * *Family and Type*
    * *Count*
    * *Category*

5. Click **OK**. The new schedule displays with all of the structural elements in the project in a long list, as shown in part in Figure 2–36.

<Structural Schedule>			
A	B	C	D
Type Mark	Family and Type	Count	Category
	W-Wide Flange-Colum	1	Structural Columns
	W-Wide Flange-Colum	1	Structural Columns
	W-Wide Flange-Colum	1	Structural Columns
	W-Wide Flange-Colum	1	Structural Columns
	W-Wide Flange-Colum	1	Structural Columns
	W-Wide Flange-Colum	1	Structural Columns
	W-Wide Flange-Colum	1	Structural Columns
	W-Wide Flange-Colum	1	Structural Columns
	W-Wide Flange-Colum	1	Structural Columns
	W-Wide Flange-Colum	1	Structural Columns
	W-Wide Flange-Colum	1	Structural Columns
	W-Wide Flange-Colum	1	Structural Columns
	W-Wide Flange-Colum	1	Structural Columns
	W-Wide Flange-Colum	1	Structural Columns
	W-Wide Flange-Colum	1	Structural Columns
	W-Wide Flange-Colum	1	Structural Columns
	W-Wide Flange-Colum	1	Structural Columns
	W-Wide Flange-Colum	1	Structural Columns
	W-Wide Flange-Colum	1	Structural Columns
	Wall Foundation: Beari	1	Structural Foundati
	Wall Foundation: Beari	1	Structural Foundati
	Wall Foundation: Beari	1	Structural Foundati

Figure 2–36

6. Save the project.

Task 2: Add filtering, sorting, and grouping to the schedule.

1. In *Properties*, in the *Other* section, next to *Sorting/Grouping*, click **Edit...**. The *Schedule Properties* dialog box opens with the *Sorting/Grouping* tab selected.

2. In the *Sorting/Grouping* tab, sort by **Category**, and select **Header**. Then, sort by **Family and Type** with no header. Clear **Itemize every instance**, as shown in Figure 2–37.

Figure 2–37

3. In the *Schedule Properties* dialog box, in the *Filter* tab, add the following, as shown in Figure 2–38:

- *Filter by:* **Category** > **is greater than or equal to** > **Structural Columns**
- *And:* **Category** > **does not equal** > **Structural Rebar**
- *And:* **Category** > **does not equal** > **Structural Path Reinforcement**
- *And:* **Category** > **does not equal** > **Walls**

Figure 2–38

4. Click **OK** to update the schedule.
5. Resize the columns to see the information. Right-click on the *Category* column and select **Hide Columns**. The schedule displays as shown in Figure 2–39.

\<Structural Schedule\>		
A	B	C
Type Mark	Family and Type	Count
Structural Columns		
P-1	Concrete-Rectangular-Column: 24 x 24	22
	W-Wide Flange-Column: W10X33	1
	W-Wide Flange-Column: W10X49	22
Structural Foundations		
F-2	Footing-Rectangular: 14'x14'x2'-0"	1
F-1	Footing-Rectangular: 36" x 36" x 12"	21
	Foundation Slab: 6" Foundation Slab	1
	Step Footing: Step Footing	4
	Wall Foundation: Bearing Footing - 24" x 12"	6
	Wall Foundation: Bearing Footing - 36" x 12"	4
	Wall Foundation: Retaining Footing - 24" x 12" x 12"	1
Structural Framing		
	HSS-Hollow Structural Section: HSS6X6X.500	9
	K-Series Bar Joist-Rod Web: 16K6	65
	W-Wide Flange: W8X10	6
	W-Wide Flange: W12X26	63
	W-Wide Flange: W14X48	62
	W-Wide Flange: W16X45	1

Figure 2–39

6. Open the **S601- Schedules** sheet. Drag and drop the schedule to this sheet. Modify the width of each field as required.

7. Save the project.

Task 3: (Optional) Create additional schedules.

1. If time permits, create a structural foundation schedule and a structural foundation column schedule that incorporate the information shown in Figure 2−40 and Figure 2−41.

<Structural Foundation Schedule>				
A	B	C	D	E
Type Mark	Count	Type	Width	Length
F-1	21	36" x 36" x 12"	3' - 0"	3' - 0"
F-2	1	14'x14'x2'-0"	14' - 0"	14' - 0"
Grand total: 22				

Figure 2−40

- **Hint:** Filter by **Type Mark** > **begins with** > **F** so that only the individual footing foundations display, then on the *Sorting/Grouping* tab, set the *Sort by* to **Type Mark** with **Itemize every instance** turned off.

<Structural Foundation Column Schedule>				
A	B	C	D	E
Type Mark	Count	Type	Top Level	Base Level
P-1	22	24 x 24	Level 1	T.O. Footing

Figure 2−41

- **Hint:** Create a Structural Column Schedule, change the name, filter by **Type Mark** > **begins with** > **P** so that only the foundation columns display, and on the *Sorting/Grouping* tab, turn off **Itemize every instance**.

2. Save and close the project.

End of practice

2.2 Modifying Schedule Appearance

Modifying schedules in Revit is an essential aspect of refining data presentation and enhancing project documentation. While you assign global appearance settings in the *Schedule Properties* dialog box, you can also modify the appearance of each cell in a schedule and add other rows and columns. Title and Heading cells can include both text and parameter values and have different text formatting, as shown in Figure 2–42. You can also add images to title cells and to individual rows in a schedule.

Figure 2–42

- Most of these modifications can be accessed in the *Modify Schedule/Quantities* tab, which is available when you are in a schedule view. What is selected in the schedule will determine which tools are available in the ribbon; for example, selecting the title displays the select tools shown in Figure 2–43.

Figure 2–43

- Many of these options are also found in the right-click shortcut menu.

Setting Up Parameter Values

Parameter values and options can be set up by cells. The type of cell determines the options you can use. These options can be found in the *Modify Schedule/Quantities* tab>*Parameters* panel when the schedule view is active.

- **Title Cells:** Select the schedule's title cell and select either **Schedule** or **Project Information**, as shown on the left in Figure 2–44, then choose from the parameters available, as shown on the right.

Figure 2–44

- **Header or Data Cells:** Select a header or data cell and select options based on the type of element the schedule is made for, as shown on the left in Figure 2–45, then choose from the parameters available, as shown on the right. Changing this information also changes the field specified for the selected column.

Figure 2–45

- Parameter values in titles display in the schedule view with **< >** at either end of the value. This does not display on the sheet view.

- Additional options for modifying the parameters include (Format Unit),

  (Calculated), and (Combine Parameters). These are covered in more depth in **2.4 Advanced Schedule Options**.

Modifying Columns and Rows

The options for Columns and Rows (shown in Figure 2–46) vary according to the type of cell selected. You can **Insert**, **Delete**, and **Resize** title columns and rows. If you select a header column, you can insert, delete, resize, and hide the column.

Note: Be careful about making changes in the ribbon when you are in a data cell because any changes you make apply to the entire row or column.

Figure 2–46

How To: Hide a Column

1. Select any cell in the column that you want to hide.

2. In the *Modify Schedule/Quantities* tab>*Columns* panel, click 🔲 (Hide). Alternatively, if you have selected the header cell, right-click and select **Hide Columns**.

3. The column is hidden.

*   If you have hidden any columns and no longer want them hidden, you can click 🔲 (Unhide All) or right-click and select **Unhide All Columns** at any time.

*   Hiding columns is typically used when you want to sort or filter the field, but do not want the data to display in the final schedule.

How To: Resize a Row or Column

1. Select a cell. If the cell is a title cell you can resize both the row and column

2. In the *Modify Schedule/Quantities* tab>*Columns* panel, click ⊣⊢ (Resize (Columns)) or in the *Rows* panel, click ⊥ (Resize (Rows)).

3. In the *Resize Column* (or *Row*) dialog box (shown in Figure 2–47), type a size and click **OK**.

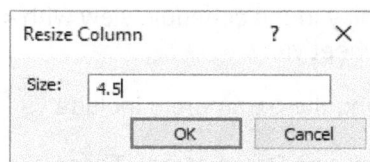

Figure 2–47

4. The column or row is resized in the schedule view and sheet.

- The row's height cannot be resized as it is controlled by the height of the text used for the body of the schedule.

Modifying Titles and Headers

The more complex and extensive a schedule, the more it can help to modify the title and header cells using the commands shown in Figure 2–48. The title cells can be merged or unmerged. You can also insert images and delete the contents of title cells. Header cells can be grouped and ungrouped. If you have a large schedule, you can turn on **Freeze Header** so the titles and headers stay at the top as you scroll through your schedule.

Figure 2–48

How To: Add and Merge Title Cells

1. Click inside a title cell.

2. In the *Modify Schedule/Quantities* tab>*Rows* panel, expand (Insert) and click (Above Selected) or (Below Selected). When inserting below the primary cell, it typically comes in matching the number of header cells, as shown in Figure 2–49.

Figure 2–49

3. Pick and drag across the cells that you want to merge.

4. Click (Merge Unmerge).

5. The cells are now merged together, as shown in Figure 2–50.

<Door Schedule>						
A	B	C	D	E	F	G
Mark	Family and Type	Height	Width	Fire Rating	Frame Material	Frame Type

Figure 2–50

6. Add a parameter, text, or image in the newly merged cell.

*   If you no longer want the cells to be merged, select the cell and click ▦ (Merge Unmerge).

*   To insert an image file (such as a .BMP, .JPG, or .PNG) in a title cell, select the title cell and

    click 🖼 (Insert Image) and select the image from the list.

*   Use 🖺 (Clear Cell) to delete the text, image, or parameter used in that cell (Titles only).

How To: Group Sub-headers

1. In the Schedule view, drag the cursor over the headers you want to group.

2. In the *Modify Schedule/Quantities* tab>*Titles & Headers* panel, click ▦ (Group).

3. A new header group is created above the selected columns. Enter a new name, as shown in Figure 2–51.

    *   Make sure all fields are added before grouping.

New header group

A	B	C	D	E
		Window Dimensions		
Window Type	Count	Height	Width	Sill Height
36 x 36	72	3' - 0"	3' - 0"	3' - 0"
36" x 48"	84	4' - 0"	3' - 0"	3' - 0"
Grand total: 156				

Figure 2–51

*   If you no longer need the grouped header cell, select the grouped cell and click

    ▦ (Ungroup).

How To: Freeze Headers

1. In a schedule view, in the *Modify Schedule/Quantities* tab>*Titles & Headers* panel, click
    ⊞ (Freeze Header).

2. Scroll down in a schedule and the header and titles stay at the top of the schedule.

3. Click ⊞ (Freeze Header) again to turn it off.

    *   In panel or graphical column schedules, you cannot use the ⊞ (Freeze Header) tool.

Setting the Appearance

The overall appearance of a schedule, including the text types used in the various cells, is set up in the Schedule Properties. You can freeze the header so you can scroll within the schedule and still see the headers, as well as modify individual title and header cells using the options in the *Appearance* panel, as shown in Figure 2–52.

Figure 2–52

⊞ **(Shading)**	Opens the *Color* dialog box in which you can select a background color for the selected cells.
⊞ **(Borders)**	Opens the *Edit Borders* dialog box in which you can specify the line style and locations of borders around the selected cells.
🖌 **(Reset)**	Returns the formatting of selected cells to the original specified in the schedule properties.
A **(Font)**	Opens the *Edit Font* dialog box in which you can specify the **Font**, **Font size**, **Font Style** (**Bold**, **Italic**, or **Underline**) and **Font Color** for the selected cells.
≡ **(Align Horizontal)**	When expanded, select how the selected cells' text will align, either ≡ (Left), ≡ (Center), or ≡ (Right) justification.
≡ **(Align Vertical)**	When expanded, select how the selected cells' text will align, either ≡ (Top), ≡ (Middle), or ≡ (Bottom) justification.

*   The changes you make using the tools in the *Appearance* panel are not included in a schedule view template.

Adding Image Fields and Images

In addition to adding images in the title cells of a schedule you can assign images to elements and have them display in the schedule on a sheet, as shown in Figure 2–53.

Lighting Fixture Types			
Type Mark	Image	Family	Count
A		Troffer Light - 2x2 Parabolic	17
B		Troffer Light - 2x4 Parabolic	48
C		Pendant Light - Hemisphere	10

Figure 2–53

- Images can be set by instance or by type parameters.

How To: Add Images to Schedules

1. In the schedule view, open the *Schedule Properties* dialog box in the *Fields* tab.

2. Add the *Image* (or *Type Image*) field to the *Scheduled fields*, as shown in Figure 2–54.

Figure 2–54

3. Complete the rest of your schedule design and click **OK**.

4. In the schedule view, the *Image* (or *Type Image*) column displays as part of the schedules, as shown in Figure 2–55.

		<Lighting Fixture Types>		
A	B	C	D	E
Type Mark	Image	Family	Manufacturer	Count
A	<None>	Troffer Light - 2x2 Parabolic		17
B	<None>	Troffer Light - 2x4 Parabolic		48
C	<None>	Pendant Light - Hemisphere		10

Figure 2–55

5. Assign the appropriate image file to the instances or types of an element, or click
   ⊡ (Browse) in the *Image* column (as shown in Figure 2–56) to open the *Manage Images* dialog box to assign an image.

Browse button

		<Lighting Fixture Types>
A	B	C
Type Mark	Image	Family
A	<None> ⊡	Troffer Light - 2x2 Parabolic
B	<None>	Troffer Light - 2x4 Parabolic
C	<None>	Pendant Light - Hemisphere

Figure 2–56

- Type images for component families (such as light fixtures) are assigned directly in the family file and are read-only in the project.

- Type images for system families (such as walls, roofs, and floors) are assigned in the *Type Properties* dialog box, as shown in Figure 2–57.

Figure 2–57

- Instance images are assigned in Properties for each individual instance of the element, as shown in Figure 2–58.

Figure 2–58

6. To display the images, place the schedule on a sheet.

How To: Assign Image Files

1. Select an element and in Properties next to the *Image* parameter (as shown in Figure 2–59), or in Type Properties next to the *Type Image* parameter, click ⊡ (Browse).

Identity Data	⌃
Image	⊡
Comments	
Mark	

Figure 2–59

- Type images for component families are assigned in the family file, not in the project.

2. In the *Manage Images* dialog box, click **Add...** (as shown in Figure 2–60) to navigate to the location of the image, or if an image is loaded, select the image that you want to use and click **OK**.

Figure 2–60

- You can also delete and reload images as you would reload linked files.
- Image file formats include .BMP, .JPG, .JPEG, .PDF, .PNG, and .TIF.

How To: Add an Image to the Title Header

1. Select the title header.
2. In the *Modify Schedule/Quantities* tab>*Titles & Headers* panel, click (Insert Image).
3. In the *Import Image* dialog box, navigate to the image file and click **Open**.
4. The image is imported into the schedule, as shown in Figure 2–61.

   • If the title header has text, the image will replaced the text.

<Window Schedule>			
A	B	C	D
Count	Type	Manufacturer	Comments

Figure 2–61

Practice 2d
Modify Schedules for Architectural Projects

Practice Objectives

- Modify the look of the schedule using parameters, and by merging and grouping cells.
- Add images to a schedule.

In this practice, you will modify the appearance of a schedule by adding parameters and text to the title and by merging group headers, as shown in Figure 2–62 (on a sheet). You will also add an image field (column) and assign images to a schedule.

<Door Schedule - Level 1>							
<Clark Hall Performing Arts Building>				Project Number: <1234.56>			
A	B	C	D	E	F	G	H
	Door Size				Frame Information		
Mark	Height	Width	Fire Rating	Frame Type	Frame Material	Finish	Comments

Figure 2–62

Task 1: Modify the appearance of the schedule.

1. In the practice files *Architectural* folder, open **Clark-Hall-Schedules-Modify.rvt**.
2. Open the **Door Schedule-Level 1** view.
3. Select the top title row of the schedule.

   Note: The name of the project displays in brackets indicating that it is a parameter rather than text.

4. In the *Modify Schedule/Quantities* tab>*Rows* panel, expand ⬚ (Insert) and click ⬚ (Below Selected).

5. Drag the cursor across the new cells above Columns A-D to highlight the cells. In the *Titles & Headers* panel, click ▦ (Merge Unmerge). The cells are merged as shown in Figure 2–63.

<Door Schedule - Level 1>							
A	B	C	D	E	F	G	H
Mark	Height	Width	Fire Rating	Frame Type	Frame Material	Finish	Comments

Figure 2–63

---

6. Select the newly merged cell. In the *Modify Schedule/Quantities* tab>*Parameters* panel, expand *Category:* and select **Project Information**. Expand *Parameter:* and select **Project Name**, as shown in Figure 2–64.

Figure 2–64

7. Merge the cells above column E and part of column G, then manually type **Project Number:**.

8. Merge the last two cells above part of column G and column H, then from the *Parameters* panel, expand *Category:* and select **Project Information**. Add the parameter **Project Number**. Your schedule will look like the one shown in Figure 2–65.

<Door Schedule - Level 1>							
<Clark Hall>				Project Number:		<1234.56>	
A	B	C	D	E	F	G	H
Mark	Height	Width	Fire Rating	Frame Type	Frame Material	Finish	Comments

Figure 2–65

9. In the *Manage* tab>*Settings* panel, click 🔲 (Project Information).

10. In the *Project Information* dialog box, update the *Project Name* to **Clark Hall Performing Arts Building**. Click **OK**. The *Project Name* updates, as shown in Figure 2–66.

<Door Schedule - Level 1>							
<Clark Hall Performing Arts Building>				Project Number:		<1234.56>	
A	B	C	D	E	F	G	H
Mark	Height	Width	Fire Rating	Frame Type	Frame Material	Finish	Comments

Figure 2–66

11. Click on the *Modify Schedule/Quantities* tab, and in the Door schedule, drag the cursor over the *Height* and *Width* header cells.

12. In the *Modify Schedule/Quantities* tab>*Titles & Headers* panel, click 🔲 (Group).

13. Select the new cell and type **Door Size**.

14. Repeat for *Frame Type, Frame Material,* and *Finish* and enter **Frame Information**, as shown in Figure 2–67.

A	B	C	D	E	F	G	H
	Door Size			Frame Information			
Mark	Height	Width	Fire Rating	Frame Type	Frame Material	Finish	Comments

Figure 2–67

15. Save the project.

Task 2: Modify the appearance of the title.

1. Select the title header cell and, in the *Modify Schedule/Quantities* tab>*Appearance* panel, click A (Font).

2. In the *Edit Font* dialog box, change the *Font size* to **1/4"** and set the *Font style* to **Bold**, then click **OK**.

3. Modify the other title and header cells to use bold text.

4. Select the *Project Number:* cell. In the *Modify Schedule/Quantities* tab>*Appearance* panel, expand **Align Horizontal** and select ≣ (Right Horizontal). Repeat this process for the project number cell and align horizontal left.

5. Select both the *Project Number:* and project number cells. In the *Modify Schedule/Quantities* tab>*Appearance* panel, select ⊞ (Borders).

6. In the *Edit Borders* dialog box, select **None** and then **Outside**, as shown in Figure 2–68, then click **OK**.

Figure 2–68

7. Modify the other title and header cells to display shading, as shown in the example in Figure 2–69.

<Door Schedule - Level 1>							
<Clark Hall Performing Arts Building>				Project Number: <1234.56>			
A	B	C	D	E	F	G	H
	Door Size				Frame Information		
Mark	Height	Width	Fire Rating	Frame Type	Frame Material	Finish	Comments

Figure 2–69

8. Open the **Sheets (all): A601-Schedules** view and adjust the column width as needed.

9. Save the project.

Task 3: Add images to a schedule.

1. Open the **Window Schedule** view.

2. Click **Edit** next to *Field*. In the *Schedule Properties* dialog box, add the **Type Mark** and **Image** parameters to the *Scheduled fields* above the **Type** parameter. Move the **Count** parameter to the bottom of the list, as shown in Figure 2–70, and click **OK**.

   *Note: In this situation, the **Type Image** is only accessible by opening and adjusting the family file. Therefore, you can use the instance **Image** parameter.*

Figure 2–70

3. In the *Window Schedule* view, select the *Image* cell for the first type and click ⬚ (Browse).

4. In the *Manage Images* dialog box, click **Add....**

5. In the *Import Image* dialog box, navigate to the practice files *Architectural>Images* folder, select the two window images, and click **Open**.

6. In the *Manage Images* dialog box, select the image that matches the window row that you are working in and click **OK**.

   - Type Mark 18 - Window Rectangle.png
   - Type Mark 19 - Window Square.png

7. Repeat the process with the other window image. The schedule should look similar to Figure 2–71.

<Window Schedule>					
A	B	C	D	E	F
Type Mark	Image	Type	Manufacturer	Comments	Count
18	Window Rectangle.png	36" x 72"			3
19	Window Square.png [...]	48" x 48"			36
Grand total: 39					

Figure 2–71

8. Open the **Sheets (all): Sheets (all): A601 - Schedules** view and adjust the column width as needed. The images should display as shown in Figure 2–72.

Window Schedule					
Type Mark	Image	Type	Manufacturer	Comments	Count
18		36" x 72"			3
19		48" x 48"			36
Grand total: 39					

Figure 2–72

9. If time permits, modify the schedule appearance to match the Door schedule by adding the Project Name and Project Number parameters below the Title row.

10. Save and close the project.

End of practice

Practice 2e
Modify Schedules for MEP Projects

Practice Objectives

- Modify the look of the schedule using parameters and by merging and grouping cells.
- Add images to a schedule.

In this practice, you will modify the appearance of a schedule by adding parameters and text to the title and by merging headers. You will also add an image field (column) and assign images to a schedule, as shown on a sheet in Figure 2–73.

Lighting Fixture Types			
Type Mark	Image	Family	Count
A		Troffer Light - 2x2 Parabolic	17
B		Troffer Light - 2x4 Parabolic	48
C		Pendant Light - Hemisphere	10

Figure 2–73

Task 1: Modify the appearance of the schedule.

1. In the practice files *MEP* folder, open **Freel-Office-Modify.rvt**.

   Note: If you do not see the linked architectural file, you will need to reload it using **Manage Links** in the Manage tab.

2. Open the **Plumbing Fixtures** schedule view.

3. Select the top title row of the schedule.

4. In the *Modify Schedule/Quantities* tab>*Row* panel, expand ⬚ (Insert) and click ⬚ (Below Selected).

5. Drag the cursor over the first two cells of the new heading columns on the left. In the *Titles & Headers* panel, click ⬚ (Merge Unmerge). The cells are merged, as shown in Figure 2–74.

<Plumbing Fixtures>			
A	B	C	D
Family	Type	Manufacturer	Count

Figure 2–74

6. Select the newly merged cell. In the *Modify Schedule/Quantities* tab>*Parameters* panel, expand *Category:* and select **Project Information**, then expand *Parameter:* and select **Project Name**, as shown in Figure 2–75. The name of the project displays in brackets, indicating that it is a parameter.

Category ⟶ Project Infor... ▾
Parameter ⟶ Project Name ▾

Parameters

Figure 2–75

7. In the middle cell, manually add the text **Project Number:**, and in the last cell, from the *Parameters* panel, expand *Category:* and select **Project Information**. Add the parameter **Project Number**. Your schedule will look like the one shown in Figure 2–76.

<Plumbing Fixtures>			
<Project Name>		Project Number:	<Project Number>
A	B	C	D
Family	Type	Manufacturer	Count

Figure 2–76

8. In the *Manage* tab>*Settings* panel, click ⬚ (Project Information).

9. In the *Project Information* dialog box, update *Project Name* to **Freel Office Building** and *Project Number* to **1234.56.** Click **OK**. The parameters update as shown in Figure 2–77.

<Plumbing Fixtures>			
<Freel Office Building>		Project Number:	<1234.56>
A	B	C	D
Family	Type	Manufacturer	Count

Figure 2–77

10. Save the project.

Task 2: Modify the appearance of the title.

1. Select the title header cell and, in the *Modify Schedule/Quantities* tab>*Appearance* panel, click ⒜ (Font).

2. In the *Edit Font* dialog box change the *Font size* to **1/4"** and set the *Font style* to **Bold**. Click **OK**.

3. Modify the other title and header cells to use bold text.

4. Select the *Project Number:* cell. In the *Modify Schedule/Quantities* tab>*Appearance* panel, expand **Align Horizontal** and select ≡ (Right Horizontal). Repeat this process for the project number cell and align horizontal left.

5. Select both the *Project Number:* and project number cells. In the *Modify Schedule/Quantities* tab>*Appearance* panel, select ⊞ (Borders).

6. In the *Edit Borders* dialog box, select **None** and then **Outside**, as shown in Figure 2–78.

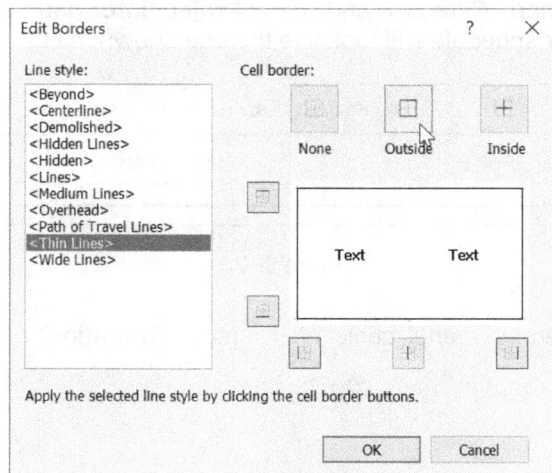

Figure 2–78

7. Click **OK**. The schedule updates as shown in the example in Figure 2–79.

\<Plumbing Fixtures\>			
\<Freel Office Building\>		Project Number: \<1234.56\>	
A	B	C	D
Family	Type	Manufacturer	Count

Figure 2–79

8. Open the **Sheets (all): P601-Plumbing Schedules** view and adjust the column widths as needed.

9. Save the project.

Task 3: Add images to a schedule.

1. Open the **Lighting Fixture Types** schedule view.

2. In the *Schedule Properties* dialog box, in the *Fields* tab, add the **Image** parameter to the Scheduled Fields after the **Type Mark** parameter, as shown in Figure 2–80, then click **OK**.

    Note: In this situation the Type Image is only accessible by opening and adjusting the family file. Therefore, you can use the instance Image parameter.

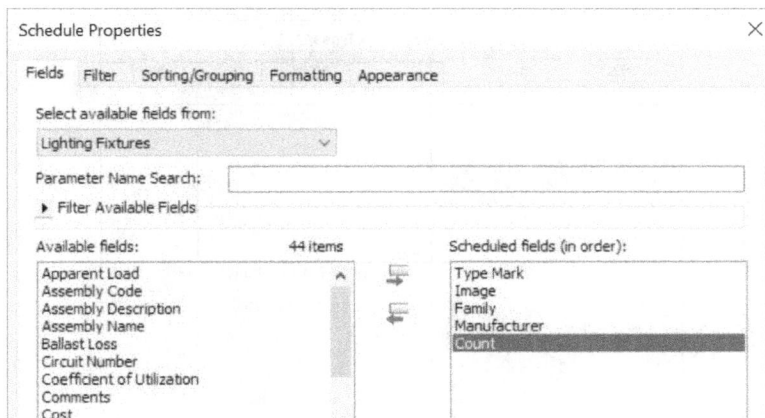

Figure 2–80

3. In the **Lighting Fixture Types** view, select the *Image* cell for the first type and click ⟨...⟩.

4. In the *Manage Images* dialog box, click **Add...**.

5. In the *Import Image* dialog box, navigate to the practice files *MEP>Images* folder, select the three light images, and click **Open**.

6. In the *Manage Images* dialog box, select the image that matches the row that you are working in (as follows) and click **OK**.

- Type Mark **A** - Troffer Light Square.jpg
- Type Mark **B** - Troffer Light Rectangle.jpg
- Type Mark **C** - Pendant Light.jpg

7. Repeat the process with the other lighting fixture images. The schedule should look similar to the one shown in Figure 2–81.

A	B	C	D
Type Mark	Image	Family	Count
A	Troffer Light Square.jpg	Troffer Light - 2x2 Parabolic	17
B	Toffer Light rectangle.jpg	Troffer Light - 2x4 Parabolic	48
C	Pendant Light.jpg	Pendant Light - Hemisphere	10

<Lighting Fixture Types>

Figure 2–81

8. Open the **Sheets (all): E601 - Electrical and Lighting Schedules** view and adjust the column widths as needed. The images should display as shown in Figure 2–82.

Figure 2–82

9. Save and close the project.

End of practice

Practice 2f
Modify Schedules for Structural Projects

Practice Objective

- Modify the look of the schedule using parameters and merging and grouping cells.

In this practice, you will modify the appearance of a schedule by adding parameters and text to the title and by merging cells, as shown in Figure 2–83.

<Structural Schedule>		
<Axiom Building>		Project Number: <1234.56>
A	B	C
Type Mark	Family and Type	Count

Figure 2–83

Task 1: Modify the appearance of the schedule.

1. In the practice files *Structural* folder, open **Axiom-Building-Modify.rvt**.

2. Open the **Structural Schedule** view.

3. Select the top title row of the schedule.

4. In the *Modify Schedule/Quantities* tab>*Row* panel, expand 🔲 (Insert) and click 🔲 (Below Selected).

5. Drag the cursor across the two new cells on the left over columns A and part of B, then, in the *Titles & Headers* panel, click 🔲 (Merge Unmerge). The cells are merged as shown in Figure 2–84.

<Structural Schedule>		
A	B	C
Type Mark	Family and Type	Count

Figure 2–84

6. Select the newly merged cell. In the *Modify Schedule/Quantities* tab>*Parameters* panel, expand *Category:* and select **Project Information**, then expand *Parameter:* and select **Project Name**, as shown in Figure 2-85. The name of the parameter displays in brackets in the schedule, indicating that it is a parameter rather than text.

Figure 2-85

7. In the middle cell, manually add the text **Project Number:**, and in the last cell, from the *Parameters* panel, expand *Category:* and select **Project Information**. Add the parameter **Project Number**. Your schedule will look like the one shown in Figure 2-86.

<Structural Schedule>		
<Project Name>	Project Number:	<Project Number>
A	B	C
Type Mark	Family and Type	Count

Figure 2-86

8. In the *Manage* tab>*Settings* panel, click 📷 (Project Information).

9. In the *Project Information* dialog box, update *Project Name* to **Axiom Building** and *Project Number* to **1234.56**. Click **OK**. The project name and number update as shown in Figure 2-87.

<Structural Schedule>		
<Axiom Building>	Project Number:	<1234.56>
A	B	C
Type Mark	Family and Type	Count

Figure 2-87

10. Open the **Sheets (all): E601 - Schedules** view and adjust the column widths as needed.

11. Save the project.

Task 2: Modify the appearance of the title.

1. Select the title header cell. In the *Modify Schedule/Quantities* tab>*Appearance* panel, click A (Font).

2. In the *Edit Font* dialog box, change the *Font size* to **1/4"** and set the *Font style* to **Bold**. Click **OK**.

3. Modify the other title and header cells to use bold text.

4. Select the *Project Number:* cell. In the *Modify Schedule/Quantities* tab>*Appearance* panel, expand **Align Horizontal** and select ≡ (Right Horizontal). Repeat this process for the project number cell and align horizontal left.

5. Select both the *Project Number:* and project number cells. In the *Modify Schedule/Quantities* tab>*Appearance* panel, select ⊞ (Borders).

6. In the *Edit Borders* dialog box, select **None** and then **Outside**, as shown in Figure 2–88.

Figure 2–88

7. Click **OK**. The schedule updates as shown in the example in Figure 2–89.

Figure 2–89

8. Open the **Sheets (all): E601 - Schedules** view and adjust the column widths as needed.

9. If time permits, modify the other two structural schedules to match the appearance by adding the project name and project number parameters as above.

10. Save and close the project.

End of practice

2.3 Additional Schedule Types

Two important types of schedules are used in construction documents to help clarify information that is not included in a standard building component schedule.

- *Key schedules* lists provide information that is not automatically included in an element, such as the finish or frame type of a door. By grouping this information into keys, you can enter it more quickly.

- *Material takeoff schedules* gather information about the materials in a project (such as the area and volume) so you can calculate the amount and price of the material, as shown in Figure 2-90.

<CMU - Material Takeoff>				
A	B	C	D	E
Material: Description	Material: Area	Material: Cost	Total Cost	Total Units of Block
CMU	604 SF	8.00	$4830	4226
CMU: 14	604 SF		$4830	4226

Figure 2-90

Creating Key Schedules

Schedule key styles are useful when you have a large number of elements that need to have the same finish information, as shown in Figure 2-91. Fields in key styles are typically controlled by instance rather than by type. Grouping styles together makes it easier to apply this information to large numbers of instances.

<Room Style Schedule>					
A	B	C	D	E	F
Key Name	Wall Finish	Floor Finish	Base Finish	Ceiling Finish	Comments
Corridor	Painted	Carpet	Vinyl	Painted	
Executive Office	Wall Paper	Wood	Wood	ACT	
Standard Office	Painted	Carpet	Vinyl	ACT	
Utility	Painted	Vinyl	Vinyl	ACT	

Figure 2-91

How To: Create a Schedule Key Style

1. Start a new schedule.

2. In the *New Schedule* dialog box, select a category.

3. Select the **Schedule keys** option and type a *Key name*, as shown in Figure 2–92. This adds a *Room Style* instance parameter in Properties for the selected category (as shown on the right in Figure 2–92) and adds a *Key Name* field to the schedule (as shown on the left in Figure 2–92).

    *   Use the *Filter list* to limit the number of categories that you can select from.

Figure 2–92

4. Click **OK**.

5. In the *Schedule Properties* dialog box, the *Fields* tab displays the new **Key Name** that has already been added to the *Scheduled fields*, as shown in Figure 2–93.

6. Add other fields from the list of *Available fields*, as shown in Figure 2–93.

   • If needed, expand **Filter Available Fields** and you can search by parameter name or filter the available fields by Parameter Type, Value Type, and Discipline.

Figure 2–93

7. Fill out the rest of the tabs as needed and click **OK**. The new schedule opens with only the fields displayed, as shown in Figure 2–94.

Figure 2–94

8. With nothing in the schedule selected, in the *Modify Schedule/Quantities* tab>*Rows* panel,

   click [icon] (Insert Data Row), or right-click on the schedule and select **Insert Data Row**. A new row with the default label **1** displays, as shown in Figure 2–95.

Figure 2–95

9. Continue adding rows, then fill in the values for the rows as shown in Figure 2-96.

<Room Style Schedule>					
A	B	C	D	E	F
Key Name	Wall Finish	Floor Finish	Base Finish	Ceiling Finish	Comments
Corridor	Painted	Carpet	Vinyl	Painted	
Executive Office	Wall Paper	Wood	Wood	ACT	
Standard Office	Painted	Carpet	Vinyl	ACT	
Utility	Painted	Vinyl	Vinyl	ACT	

Figure 2-96

10. After all of the Room Style Schedule's values have been filled in, switch to a floor plan view and select a room within the view. Set the parameter within the *Identity Data* section in Properties for the key styles, as shown in Figure 2-97. This will auto-fill the values you entered in the schedule.

Figure 2-97

11. Create a new room schedule and verify that **Schedule Building Components** is selected. Add fields to the schedule (such as *Room Style*, *Wall Finish*, and *Base Finish*), similar to the room schedule shown in Figure 2–98.

<Room Schedule>					
A	B	C	D	E	F
Room Style	Wall Finish	Floor Finish	Base Finish	Ceiling Finish	Comments
Corridor	Painted	Carpet	Vinyl	Painted	
Executive Office	Wall Paper	Wood	Wood	ACT	
Standard Office	Painted	Carpet	Vinyl	ACT	
Standard Office	Painted	Carpet	Vinyl	ACT	
(none)					
(none)					
Corridor					
Executive Office					
Standard Office					
Utility					

Figure 2–98

12. Because you have already created a key schedule for all the rooms in your project, they will auto-populate in a building components room schedule.

Creating Material Takeoff Schedules

Creating material takeoff schedules follows the same procedure as when creating building component schedules, except that it uses a different command in order to create one. This type of schedule gives more detail about the assembly or material that is in a component, like quantity, cost, and finish type.

How To: Create a Material Takeoff Schedule

1. In the *View* tab>*Create* panel, expand ▦ (Schedules) and click 🚚 (Material Takeoff), or in the Project Browser, right-click on the **Schedule/Quantities** node and select **New Material Takeoff**.

2. In the *New Material Takeoff* dialog box, select a category, as shown in Figure 2–99. Modify the name and select a phase, if needed, and click **OK**.

Figure 2–99

- After a category to report on has been specified, the options for fields in the *Material Takeoff Properties* dialog box include all of the material parameters, as shown in Figure 2–100.
  - If needed, expand **Filter Available Fields** and you can search by parameter name or filter the available fields by Parameter Type, Value Type, and Discipline.

Figure 2–100

- When creating a Material Takeoff Schedule, it can help to modify the unit settings for the various fields. In the *Formatting* tab, select a field and click **Field Format...**. In the *Format* dialog box, clear the **Use project settings** option and modify the options, as shown in Figure 2–101. This is only available for numerical fields.

Note: A numerical value can be assigned a currency. Zeros can be suppressed. Spaces can be suppressed and large numbers can include commas as separators.

Figure 2–101

- Most material properties used in material takeoff schedules can be set by material. In the *Manage* tab>*Settings* panel, click 🔘 (Materials). In the *Material Browser*, select the material that you want to modify. In the *Identity* tab, you can add information, such as *Manufacturer* and *Cost*, as shown in Figure 2–102.

Figure 2–102

2.4 Advanced Schedule Options

An important use of schedules, in addition to showing quantities and other information for construction documents, is to analyze and modify the information stored in the elements in the project. You can use conditional formatting that adds a background color to schedule cells that meet the condition. For schedules based on rooms or spaces, you can also create nested schedules to show information such as the number of casework elements in a room or if the supply airflow to a space meets the expected setting.

Conditional Formatting

Conditional formatting can be applied to any field where you need to display specific information that can easily be seen at a glance. For example, in Figure 2–103, the *Area* field is highlighted according to a conditional test for any size over **10000 SF**.

Note: Conditional formatting is generally used for testing specific criteria and not something that is typically included in a schedule when placed on a sheet

Area Schedule Over 10000 SF			
A	B	C	D
Number	Name	Area Type	Area
1	Office	Building Common Area	2657 SF
2	Auditorium	Building Common Area	9694 SF
3	Classrooms	Building Common Area	13533 SF
4	Area	Building Common Area	3682 SF

Figure 2–103

How To: Add Conditional Formatting in a Schedule

1. Open the schedule you want to work in, and then in Properties, select the **Edit...** button beside the *Formatting* parameter.

2. On the *Formatting* tab, select the field that you want to apply the conditional formatting to.

3. Click the **Conditional Format...** button.

4. In the *Conditional Formatting* dialog box, set the *Field* and *Test*, and specify a *Value* to meet the condition you need, as shown in Figure 2–104.

Figure 2–104

5. Click the **Background Color** button and select a color to display in the schedule when the conditions are met.

6. You can select additional fields and values to further refine the conditional statements.

7. When you are finished, click **OK** to close the dialog box and continue working on the Schedule Properties.

Embedded Schedules

When working with schedules that refer to spaces, rooms, duct systems, piping systems, or electrical circuits, you can use embedded schedules. For example, in Figure 2–105, a space schedule that is displaying the **Space Number** and **Name**, also has an embedded schedule displaying information about the air terminals in each space.

*   This is most frequently used with MEP schedules but also works with any elements that you may want to group by room or space.

Figure 2–105

How To: Add an Embedded Schedule

1. Create or select a Space or Room schedule.

2. In Properties, click the **Edit** button next to *Embedded Schedule*. In the *Schedule Properties* dialog box, select the **Embedded Schedule** checkbox and then select a category type from the *Category* list, as shown in Figure 2–106.

Figure 2–106

3. Click the **Embedded Schedule Properties** button.

4. In the *Schedule Properties* dialog box, *Field* tab, add the required fields, then add any filters, sorting, and formatting as needed.

5. Click **OK** until the schedule displays. The fields display in order directly under the base schedule columns, as shown in Figure 2–107.

Figure 2–107

2.5 Working with Project Parameters

Project parameters apply only to the project in which they are created, and they can be assigned to multiple categories, including loadable component families, sheets, schedules, and views. Because they exist solely within a single project file, the information they contain cannot be shared directly with other projects. These parameters are especially useful for organizing and reporting data as they support more precise scheduling, sorting, and filtering of the families and elements placed in the model. When you are working with a variety of schedules, you may want to add additional parameters, create fields that use formulas (such as the rounded area example shown in Figure 2–108), or even combine parameters to generate the information you need.

<Room Schedule>			
A	B	C	D
Number	Name	Area	Floor Area
101	Office	280.49 SF	280 SF
102	Conference	337.38 SF	340 SF
103	Office	199.63 SF	200 SF
104	Office	199.63 SF	200 SF
105	Office	193.17 SF	190 SF
106	Office	243.22 SF	240 SF
107	Work Room	154.77 SF	150 SF
108	Reception	327.48 SF	330 SF
109	Library	404.78 SF	400 SF

Figure 2–108

Autodesk Revit includes many parameters used in families and schedules:

- **Family parameters** are specific to a family, and they constrain or flex geometry and assign attributes, such as material. You will learn more about this parameter type in *Chapter 4 Loadable Component Families*.

- **Project parameters** can be assigned to schedules and are available only in the current project.

- **Shared parameters** can be referenced in multiple locations, such as projects, families, tags, and schedules, and shared between projects. You will learn more about this parameter type in *Chapter 6 Additional Family Types*.

- Project parameters can be used in schedules and families, but not in tags. You must instead create shared parameters. Shared parameters can also be used in other projects and exported to a database. For more information, see *6.4 Working with Shared Parameters* in *Chapter 6 Additional Family Types*.

How To: Create a Project Parameter in a Schedule

1. In the *Schedule Properties* dialog box, in the *Fields* tab, click 🗋 (New parameter).

2. In the *Parameter Properties* dialog box, select **Project parameter**, as shown in Figure 2–109.

Figure 2–109

3. In the *Parameter Data* area (shown in Figure 2–110), set the value as **Instance** or **Type**. Specify a new *Name* for the parameter and select the *Discipline*, *Data Type*, and *Group parameter under* category from the drop-down lists. You can also add a custom tooltip.

Figure 2–110

- **Type:** Modify all instances of a specific type. For example, if you create a **Material** parameter for a furniture component, changing the material for one component changes all furniture components of that family's type.

- **Instance:** Set for each instance of the associated element. For example, if you create a **Material** parameter when you are creating a furniture schedule, you can assign a different material to each individual instance of the component.

- **Values are aligned per group type:** (Instance Parameters only.) If an element that includes this parameter is part of multiple groups, the value remains the same for all of the groups. Changing the value in one group changes the value in all of the groups.

- **Values can vary by group instance:** (Instance Parameters only.) If an element that includes this parameter is part of multiple groups, the value can vary according to the group. Changing the value in one group changes the value for all other instances of that group, but does not change the value for instances of other groups that also include the element.

- The *Discipline* can be set to **Common**, **Structural**, **HVAC**, **Electrical**, **Piping**, **Infrastructure**, or **Energy**.

- The *Data Type* specifies how the parameter value is stored, The options available for Discipline impact the types of parameters in the list, as shown in Figure 2–111.

Figure 2–111

Common Parameter Types

Text	A text parameter can host any type of information that consists of both numbers and letters. Examples could be the fabric color or part number of the element.
Integer	Any value that is always represented by a whole number. Examples could be the number of chairs that fit around a conference table or the number of shelves in a bookcase.
Number	Any numeric value: whole, decimal, or fraction. You can use formulas with **Number** parameters.
Length	When you label dimensions, you create **Length** parameters. You can use formulas with **Length** parameters.
Area	Establishes the area of an element. It is numeric and can have formulas applied to it.

Volume	Establishes the volume of an element. It is numeric and can have formulas applied to it.
Angle	Establishes the angle of an element. It is numeric and can have formulas applied to it.
Slope	Displays a slope, as set up in the Field Format.
Currency	Displays the amount in dollars or other currencies, as set up in the Field Format.
Mass Density	Displays the mass per unit volume of material.
URL	Specifies a link to a website.
Material	Provides a place to assign a material from the list of materials that are set up in the project.
Image	Creates a parameter in which you can add a raster image connected to the family.
Yes/No	Used with instance parameters where you need a **Yes** or **No** answer to a question listed in the name. The default is **Yes**.
<Family Type>	Opens a dialog box where you can select from the list of family types, such as doors, furniture, or tags.

The *Group parameter under* drop-down list, as shown in Figure 2–112, lists groups that categorize parameters in the *Properties* and *Family Types* dialog boxes, as shown in Figure 2–113.

Figure 2–112

Figure 2–113

How To: Create Project Parameters (Outside of Schedules)

1. In the *Manage* tab>*Settings* panel, click ⬛ (Project Parameters).

2. In the *Project Parameters* dialog box, click 🗋 (New Parameter).

3. In the *Parameter Properties* dialog box, select **Project parameter** and set up the *Parameter Data* (i.e., the same information that is in the *Parameter Properties* dialog box for the schedule).

4. In the *Categories* area, select one or more related categories, as shown in Figure 2–114. Use the *Filter list* drop-down box to specify the discipline to limit the number of items that display.

Figure 2–114

5. Click **OK**. The parameter is now available in the properties of the selected categories.

> **Hint: Creating a Tooltip for New Parameter**
>
> When creating a new parameter, you can add a tooltip description that can be viewed when you hover the cursor over the parameter in Properties (as shown in Figure 2–115).

Figure 2–115

- To create this tooltip, click the **Edit Tooltip...** button at the bottom of the *Parameter Properties* dialog box.

Creating Fields from Formulas

In a variety of schedules, you need to gather numerical information and apply formulas to it to create a new calculated parameter. For example, you can include cost and quantity information in a Material Takeoff, as shown in the schedule in Figure 2–116. Formulas can only reference fields that are already included in the schedule.

<Brick - Material Takeoff>					
A	B	C	D	E	F
Material: Name	Material: Area	Material: Manufacturer	Material: Cost	Total Cost	Total Units of Brick
Masonry - Brick	22160 SF	XYZ Masonry	3.00	$66480	155123
Masonry - Brick: 14	22160 SF			$66480	155123

Figure 2–116

- You can create calculated value fields to add formulas to a schedule, or create a percentage field using values in the schedule.

- Gather the information you need to use to create formulas, including the exact name of any fields, before you start the process of creating the calculated value.

- Formula outcomes can be rounded off.

How To: Create a Calculated Value Field

1. In the *Schedule Properties* dialog box, in the *Fields* tab, click f_x (Add calculated parameter). The *Calculated Value* dialog box opens, as shown in Figure 2–117.

Figure 2–117

2. Type a *Name* for the new field.
3. Specify **Formula** as the type of field.
4. Select the *Discipline* and *Type*.
5. Type the formula you want to use in the *Formula* field.

   - If a warning displays about inconsistent units, clarify the units by adding ***1** or **/1** to a formula. After doing this, the software should then apply the correct units.

   - To ensure you get the exact field name, click ⬚ (Browse) to select from a list of fields, as shown in Figure 2–118.

   Note: Formulas can only reference fields that are already included in the schedule.

Figure 2–118

6. Click **OK**.

Percentage Fields

Percentage fields can be used with area schedules, as shown in Figure 2–119.

<Area Schedule (Rentable)>		
A	B	C
Name	Area	Percent of Total Area
Office	2657 SF	9%
Auditorium	9694 SF	33%
Classrooms	13533 SF	46%
Area	3682 SF	12%

Figure 2–119

How To: Create a Percentage Field

1. In the *Schedule Properties* dialog box, in the *Fields* tab, click f_x (Add calculate parameter). The *Calculated Value* dialog box opens, as shown in Figure 2–120.

Figure 2–120

2. Type a *Name* for the new field.

3. Specify **Percentage** as the type of field.

4. Select the field you want to take a percentage *Of*.

5. Select the field you want to take a percentage *By*.

   • The default option is **<Grand total>**, which calculates the percentage based on the total of the entire schedule.

   • If you have created groups in the *Sorting/Grouping* tab, they are also available. For example, if *Fields* are sorted by **Level**.

6. Click **OK**.

Combining Parameters

Parameters can be combined to create a new parameter. For example, you might want to include the height, width and depth of casework in one **Size** parameter, as shown in Figure 2–121.

<Casework Schedule>				
A	B	C	D	E
Family	Size	Cost	Count	Comments
Base Cabinet-2 Bin	2' - 10 1/2" x 1' - 6" x 2' - 0"		1	
Base Cabinet-4 Drawers	2' - 10 1/2" x 2' - 0"		2	
Base Cabinet-Double Door Sink Unit	2' - 10 1/2" x 3' - 0" x 2' - 0"		1	
Base Cabinet-Single Door & Drawer	2' - 10 1/2" x 2' - 0" x 2' - 0"		1	

Figure 2–121

- Combined parameters are schedule-specific and need to be created for each schedule.

How To: Create Combined Parameters

1. In the *Schedule Properties* dialog box, in the *Fields* tab, click (Combine Parameters).

2. In the *Combine Parameters* dialog box, in the *Combined Parameter Name* text box, type a new name for the parameter.

3. Select two or more *Schedule Parameters* from the list on the left and click (Add parameter(s)) to add it to the *Combined Parameter* list on the right.

4. Modify the *Separator* between each parameter, as shown in Figure 2–122.

Figure 2–122

- You can also add a *Prefix* or *Suffix* and modify the *Sample Value* name.
- A preview of the combined parameter value will display at the bottom of the dialog box.
- Parameters in the combined parameter do not need to already be in the schedule's Scheduled field.

5. Click **OK**.

Practice 2g
Create Complex Schedules for Architectural Projects

Practice Objectives

- Create material takeoff schedules.
- (Optional) Create a percentage-based calculated value field for use in a schedule.

In this practice, you will create a material takeoff schedule that includes several calculated value formulas. You will then add it to a sheet, as shown in Figure 2–123, and test it and other material takeoff schedules by modifying the wall type and material properties. As an optional task, you will create a percentage-based field for an area schedule.

Brick - Material Takeoff					
Material: Name	Material: Area	Material: Manufacturer	Material: Cost	Total Cost per SF	Total Units of Brick
Masonry - Brick	2749 SF	XYZ Masonry	3.00	$8250	19242
Masonry - Brick: 11	2749 SF			$8250	19242

Figure 2–123

Task 1: Create a material takeoff schedule.

1. In the practice files *Architectural* folder, open **Mall-Addition.rvt**.
2. In the *View* tab>*Create* panel, expand ▦ (Schedules) and click 🗔 (Material Takeoff).
3. In the *New Material Takeoff* dialog box, in the *Filter* list, select **Architecture**, and in the *Category* list, select **Walls**. Name the schedule **Brick – Material Takeoff** and select **New Construction** from the *Phase* list.
4. Click **OK**.

5. In the *Fields* tab of the *Material Takeoff Properties* dialog box, add the fields **Material: Name**, **Material: Area**, **Material: Manufacturer**, and **Material: Cost**, as shown in Figure 2–124.

Figure 2–124

6. Click f_x (Add calculated parameter) and set the following parameters, as shown in Figure 2–125. (Ensure that you account for the spaces in the field names when typing the formulas. There should be a space after the colon for the software to recognize **Material: Area** as a field.)

    *   *Name:* **Total Cost per SF**
    *   Select **Formula**
    *   *Discipline:* **Common**
    *   *Type:* **Currency**
    *   *Formula:* **(Material: Area/1SF)*Material: Cost**

    Note: *Area and Cost are two different types of parameters. Therefore, in this practice, you need to divide the **Material: Area** parameter by 1 to cancel out the SF units of the Area.*

Figure 2–125

Note: You can click ⌐⋯⌐ (Browse) to select from a list of fields as you are creating the formula to prevent you from misspelling parameter names.

7. Click **OK**.

8. Create another calculated parameter field using the following parameters. (There are seven standard bricks in a square foot. The type and size of bricks being used might vary and that can affect the number of bricks.)

   - *Name:* **Total Units of Brick**
   - Select **Formula**
   - *Discipline:* **Common**
   - *Type:* **Number**
   - *Formula:* **(Material: Area/1)*7**

9. Click **OK**.

10. In the *Filter* tab, filter the schedule using **Material: Name > equals > Masonry - Brick**, as shown in Figure 2–126.

Figure 2–126

11. In the *Sorting/Grouping* tab, sort by **Material: Name** and select **Footer**, as shown in Figure 2–127.

Figure 2–127

12. In the *Formatting* tab, in the *Fields* list, select **Material: Area**, **Total Cost per SF**, and **Total Units of Brick**. Expand the *No calculation* drop-down list and select **Calculate totals**, as shown in Figure 2–128.

Figure 2–128

13. Click **OK**.

Task 2: Modify the material takeoff schedule.

1. The units for the *Total Cost per SF* and *Total Units of Brick* fields have six decimal places, as shown in Figure 2–129. This is more than required.

<Brick - Material Takeoff>					
A	B	C	D	E	F
Material: Name	Material: Area	Material: Manufact	Material: Cost	Total Cost per SF	Total Units of Brick
Masonry - Brick	192 SF		4.00	769.675167	1346.931543
Masonry - Brick	756 SF		4.00	3023.630924	5291.354117
Masonry Brick	474 SF		4.00	4889.292022	2204.020205

Figure 2–129

2. In Properties, next to *Formatting*, click **Edit...**. The *Material Takeoff Properties* dialog box opens with the *Formatting* tab selected.

3. Select the *Total Cost per SF* field and click **Field Format...**.

4. In the *Format* dialog box, clear the **Use project settings** option. Verify *Units* is set to **Currency**, and set *Rounding* to **To the nearest 10** and *Unit symbol* to **$**, as shown in Figure 2–130. Click **OK**.

Figure 2–130

5. Select the *Total Units of Brick* field and click **Field Format...**.

6. In the *Format* dialog box, clear the **Use default settings** option. Set the *Units* to **Fixed** and *Rounding* to **0 decimal places**. Click **OK**.

7. Click **OK** to close the dialog box.

8. In the schedule view, enter a manufacturer's name and set the *Material: Cost* of the brick to **3.00**. The *Total Cost* updates, but the *Total Units of Brick* remains the same.

Task 3: Test the material takeoff schedule.

1. Open the **A102 – Plan and Schedules** sheet.

2. Zoom in on the existing schedules to one side of the sheet.

3. Add the new **Brick – Material Takeoff** schedule to the sheet. Use grips to modify the size of the schedule as needed.

4. This schedule is different from other schedules because it includes all the instances of brick. In the Project Browser, select the **Brick - Material Takeoff** schedule (you do not have to open it to change the properties).

5. In Properties, in the *Other* section, next to *Sorting/Grouping*, click **Edit...**.

6. In the *Material Takeoff Properties* dialog box, in the *Sorting/Grouping* tab, clear the **Itemize every instance** option and click **OK**. The schedule updates on the sheet.

7. Open the **3D Views: Front View**. Tile and adjust the views so that you can see the **Front View** and, in the **A102 - Plan and Schedules** sheet, the top two schedules on the sheet, as shown in Figure 2–131.

Figure 2–131

8. In the 3D view, select one of the walls on the tower to the left and change its wall type to **Basic Wall: FCE – Exterior – EIFS on Mtl.Stud**, as shown in Figure 2–132.

Figure 2–132

9. The schedules change to display a smaller amount of the stone used and adds to the EIFS schedule that was blank before, as shown in Figure 2-133.

Stone - Material Takeoff			
Material: Description	Material: Area	Material: Cost	Total Cost
Facestone	865 SF	0.00	0
Facestone: 6	865 SF		0

EIFS - Material Takeoff			
Material: Description	Material: Area	Material: Cost	Total Cost
EIFS	298 SF	12.00	3574
EIFS: 1	298 SF		3574

Figure 2-133

10. Double-click on the **Stone - Material Takeoff** schedule in the sheet to open the related schedule view.

11. Change the *Material: Cost* to **10** and click in the next cell.

12. The *Material: Cost* and *Total Cost* fields update on the sheet as well.

13. In Properties, click **Edit...** next to *Formatting*.

14. In the *Material Takeoff Properties* dialog box, select **Material: Cost** and click **Field Format**. In the *Format* dialog box, verify that *Units* is set to **Currency**, then change the *Unit symbol* to **$** and click **OK**. Repeat for **Total Cost**.

*Note: If needed, uncheck **Use project settings** to edit the information in the Format dialog box.*

Task 4: (Optional) Create a percentage-based Calculated Value field.

1. Using ⊞ (Schedule/Quantities), create a new area schedule by selecting the **Area (Rentable)** category. Leave the name as the default **Area Schedule (Rentable)**.

2. Add the fields *Name* and *Area*.

3. Click f_x (Add calculated parameter) and add the new *Calculated Value* field, as shown in Figure 2–134.

Figure 2–134

4. Click **OK** twice to create the schedule.

5. Open the **A103 – Area Plans** sheet and add the new area schedule to the sheet next to the colored legend, as shown in Figure 2–135.

Figure 2–135

6. Save and close the project.

End of practice

Practice 2h
Create Complex Schedules for MEP Projects

Practice Objectives

- Create a base schedule and add an embedded schedule into it.
- Test the scheduled information using conditional formatting.

In this practice, you will create a base schedule including a Calculated Value and Conditional Formatting. You will then add an embedded schedule to create a Space Air Flow Check schedule, as shown in Figure 2–136.

A	B	C	D	E	F
\<Space Air Flow Check \>					
Space Number	Name	Condition Type	Actual Supply Airflo	Calculated Supply A	Airflow Check
Diffuser ID	Family and Type	Flow			
101	Office Area 1	Heated and cooled	0 CFM	2833 CFM	-2833 CFM
102	Office Area 2	Heated and cooled	0 CFM	2546 CFM	-2546 CFM
103	Vestibule 1	Heated and cooled	0 CFM	351 CFM	-351 CFM
104	Foyer 1	Heated and cooled	0 CFM	718 CFM	-718 CFM
105	Conf. Room	Heated and cooled	800 CFM	519 CFM	281 CFM
1	Supply Diffuser1: D-	400 CFM			
2	Supply Diffuser1: D-	400 CFM			
106	Women's 1	Heated and cooled	500 CFM	203 CFM	297 CFM
13	Supply Diffuser1: D-	500 CFM			
107	Mens 1	Heated and cooled	500 CFM	201 CFM	299 CFM
14	Supply Diffuser1: D-	500 CFM			
108	Hall 1	Heated and cooled	500 CFM	864 CFM	-364 CFM
8	Supply Diffuser1: D-	500 CFM			
109	Mech. Room	Heated and cooled	100 CFM	90 CFM	10 CFM
50	Supply Diffuser1: D-	100 CFM			
110	Elec. Room	Heated and cooled	100 CFM	168 CFM	-68 CFM
49	Supply Diffuser1: D-	100 CFM			
111	Utility	Heated and cooled	0 CFM	54 CFM	-54 CFM
112	Break Room 1	Heated and cooled	500 CFM	527 CFM	-27 CFM
9	Supply Diffuser1: D-	500 CFM			
113	Vestibule 2	Heated and cooled	0 CFM	150 CFM	-150 CFM
114	Stair	Heated and cooled	0 CFM	53 CFM	-53 CFM
115	Elev.	Heated and cooled	0 CFM	25 CFM	-25 CFM
201	Office Space 3	Heated and cooled	0 CFM	7327 CFM	-7327 CFM
202	Office Space 4	Heated and cooled	0 CFM	6196 CFM	-6196 CFM
203	Foyer 2	Heated and cooled	0 CFM	867 CFM	-867 CFM
204	Womens 2	Heated and cooled	0 CFM	203 CFM	-203 CFM
205	Mens 2	Heated and cooled	140 CFM	201 CFM	-61 CFM
37	Supply Diffuser1: D-	140 CFM			
206	Hall 2	Heated and cooled	500 CFM	1003 CFM	-503 CFM
25	Supply Diffuser1: D-	500 CFM			
207	Stair	Heated and cooled	0 CFM	238 CFM	-238 CFM
208	Break Room 2	Heated and cooled	410 CFM	497 CFM	-87 CFM
24	Supply Diffuser1: D-	205 CFM			
34	Supply Diffuser1: D-	205 CFM			
209	Mechanical Room 2	Heated and cooled	0 CFM	268 CFM	-268 CFM

Figure 2–136

Task 1: Create a base schedule.

1. In the practice files *MEP* folder, open **Office-Airflow.rvt**.

    *   If you do not see the linked architectural file, you will need to reload it.

2. In the *View* tab>*Create* panel, expand ⊞ (Schedules) and click ⊞ (Schedule/Quantities).

3. In the *New Schedule* dialog box, filter the list by *Mechanical* and select **Spaces**. Name the schedule **Space Air Flow Check** and click **OK**.

4. Add the following fields: **Number**, **Name**, **Condition Type**, **Actual Supply Airflow**, and **Calculated Supply Airflow**, as shown in Figure 2-137.

    Note: You can use the Parameter Name Search to find available fields.

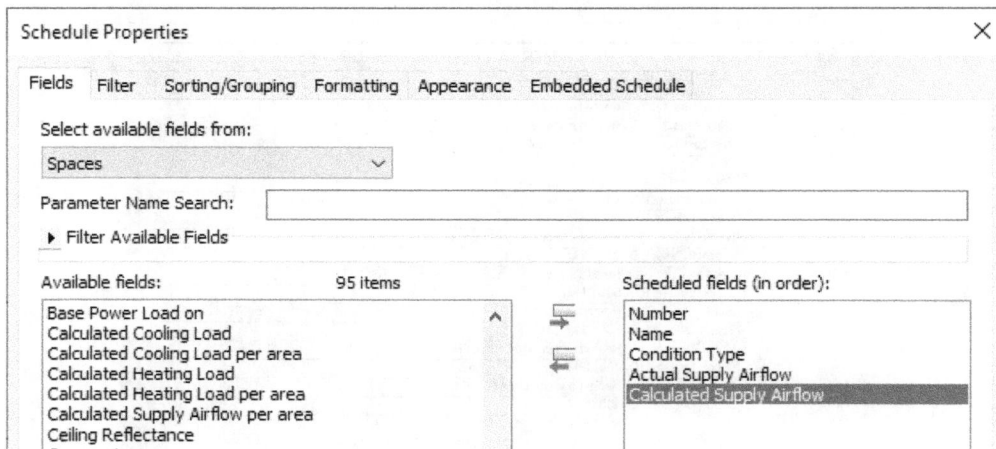

Figure 2-137

5. While still in the *Fields* tab, click f_x (Add calculated parameter) and set the following parameters, as shown in Figure 2–138. (Ensure that you account for the spaces in the field names when typing the formulas.)

    *   *Name:* **Airflow Check**
    *   Select **Formula**
    *   *Discipline:* **HVAC**
    *   *Type:* **Air Flow**
    *   *Formula:* **Actual Supply Airflow-Calculated Supply Airflow**

    Note: You can click [...] *(Browse) to select from a list of fields as you are creating the formula to prevent you from misspelling parameter names.*

Figure 2–138

6. Click **OK**.
7. In the *Sorting/Grouping* tab, sort by **Number**.
8. In the *Formatting* tab, select **Airflow Check** and click **Conditional Format...**.

9. In the *Conditional Formatting* dialog box, specify the different fields (as shown in Figure 2–139), and click **OK**. You can select any color you want.

Figure 2–139

10. Click **OK** again to display the schedule. Expand the columns, as shown in Figure 2–140.

<Space Air Flow Check>					
A	B	C	D	E	F
Number	Name	Condition Type	Actual Supply Airfl	Calculated Supply	Airflow Check
101	Office Area 1	Heated and cooled	0 CFM	2833 CFM	-2833 CFM
102	Office Area 2	Heated and cooled	0 CFM	2546 CFM	-2546 CFM
103	Vestuble 1	Heated and cooled	0 CFM	351 CFM	-351 CFM
104	Foyer 1	Heated and cooled	0 CFM	718 CFM	-718 CFM
105	Conf. Room	Heated and cooled	800 CFM	519 CFM	281 CFM
106	Women's 1	Heated and cooled	500 CFM	203 CFM	297 CFM
107	Mens 1	Heated and cooled	500 CFM	201 CFM	299 CFM
108	Hall 1	Heated and cooled	500 CFM	864 CFM	-364 CFM

Figure 2–140

11. Click inside the **Number** heading and change it to **Space Number**.

12. Save the project.

Task 2: Add an embedded schedule.

1. While still in the Space Air Flow Check schedule view, in Properties, beside *Embedded Schedule*, click **Edit...**.

2. In the *Schedule Properties* dialog box, in the *Embedded Schedule* tab, check the checkbox next to **Embedded Schedule**.

3. In the *Category* list, select **Air Terminals**.

4. Click **Embedded Schedule Properties**.

5. In the *Schedule Properties* dialog box, in the *Fields* tab, add the following fields:

    * *System Classification*

    * *Mark*

    * *Family and Type*

    * *Flow*

6. In the *Filter* tab, filter by: **System Classification > equals > Supply Air**.

7. In the *Sorting/Grouping* tab, set *Sort by* as **Mark** and *Then by* as **Family and Type**, as shown in Figure 2–141.

Figure 2–141

8. In the *Formatting* tab, select the *Field* **System Classification** and check the checkbox next to **Hidden field**.

9. Select **Mark** and change the *Heading* name to **Diffuser ID**. Set *Heading orientation* as **Horizontal** and *Alignment* as **Right**.

10. Select **Family and Type** and change the *Heading* name to **Diffuser Type**. Set *Heading orientation* as **Horizontal** and *Alignment* as **Left**.

11. Select **Flow** and change the *Heading* name to **Diffuser Airflow**. Set *Heading orientation* as **Horizontal** and *Alignment* as **Left**.

12. Click **OK** until the schedule displays, as shown in part in Figure 2–142.

<Space Air Flow Check >					
A	B	C	D	E	F
Space Number	Name	Condition Type	Actual Supply Airflo	Calculated Supply A	Airflow Check
Diffuser ID	Family and Type	Flow			
101	Office Area 1	Heated and cooled	0 CFM	2833 CFM	-2833 CFM
102	Office Area 2	Heated and cooled	0 CFM	2546 CFM	-2546 CFM
103	Vestibule 1	Heated and cooled	0 CFM	351 CFM	-351 CFM
104	Foyer 1	Heated and cooled	0 CFM	718 CFM	-718 CFM
105	Conf. Room	Heated and cooled	800 CFM	519 CFM	281 CFM
1	Supply Diffuser1: D-	400 CFM			
2	Supply Diffuser1: D-	400 CFM			
106	Women's 1	Heated and cooled	500 CFM	203 CFM	297 CFM

Figure 2–142

13. If time permits, work with the project to establish the correct air flow for the various spaces.

14. Save and close the project.

End of practice

Practice 2i
Create Complex Schedules for Structural Projects

Practice Objectives

- Create project parameters and modify an existing schedule using them.
- Modify and group headers in a schedule to graphically link the parameter types.

In this practice, you will create project parameters for structural footing types. You will then add the new parameters to a schedule, add an additional parameter, add headers to the schedule, and fill in the schedule, as shown in Figure 2–143.

A	B	C	D	E	F	G	H	I	J
		Dimensions			Reinforcement				
					Cover		Bars		
Type	Length	Width	Thickness	Top Cover	Bottom Cover	Major Bars	Minor Bars	Count	Volume
FC3.0		3' - 0"	1' - 0"	0' - 3"	0' - 1 1/2"	#4 @ 1'-0"	#4 @ 1'-0"	4	715.22 CF
FC5.0	139' - 10"	5' - 0"	1' - 0"	0' - 3"	0' - 2"	#4 @ 0'-9"	#4 @ 0'-9"	1	553.47 CF
FS6.0	6' - 0"	6' - 0"	1' - 0"	0' - 3"	0' - 1 1/2"	#4 @ 1'-0"	#4 @ 1'-0"	27	972.00 CF
FS8.0	8' - 0"	8' - 0"	1' - 0"	0' - 3"	0' - 2"	#4 @ 0'-9"	#4 @ 1'-0"	3	192.00 CF
Grand total: 35								35	2432.69 CF

Above the table: `<Structural Foundation Schedule>`

Figure 2–143

Task 1: Add project parameters.

1. In the practice files *Structural* folder, open **Century-Building.rvt**.

2. In the Project Browser, in the *Schedules/Quantities* section, open the **Structural Foundation Schedule,** as shown in Figure 2–144. This schedule is limited to existing parameters and does not include any rebar information. Also, the **Foundation Thickness** parameter is recorded for continuous footing (FC) types but not for spot footings (FS) types.

A	B	C	D	E	F
		Dimensions			
Type	Length	Width	Foundation Thickness	Count	Volume
FC3.0	<varies>	3' - 0"	1' - 0"	4	715.22 CF
FC5.0	139' - 10"	5' - 0"	1' - 0"	1	553.47 CF
FS6.0	6' - 0"	6' - 0"		27	972.00 CF
FS8.0	8' - 0"	8' - 0"		3	192.00 CF
Grand total: 35				35	2432.69 CF

Above the table: `<Structural Foundation Schedule>`

Figure 2–144

3. Open the **Structural Plans: T.O.F.** view.

---

4. Select one of the spot footings.

5. In Properties, click ⊞ (Edit Type).

6. In the *Type Properties* dialog box, there are parameter sections for *Dimensions* and *Identity Data*, as shown in Figure 2–145, but no information about the rebar that typically needs to be included in a foundation schedule.

   *Note: You can see a **Thickness** parameter, but this does not link into schedules.*

Figure 2–145

7. Click **Cancel** to close the dialog box and click in the view to clear the footing selection.

8. In the *Manage* tab>*Settings* panel, click ▥ (Project Parameters).

9. In the *Project Parameters* dialog box, click ▢ (New Parameter).

10. In the *Parameter Properties* dialog box, create a *Project parameter* named **Bottom Cover**. Make it a **Type** parameter and set *Discipline* to **Common**, *Data Type* to **Length**, and *Group parameter under* to **Rebar Set**. In *Categories*, set the *Filter list* to **Structure**, and select **Structural Foundations**, as shown in Figure 2–146.

Figure 2–146

11. Click **OK**.

12. Add additional **Type** parameters. Set *Discipline* as **Common** and *Group parameter under* as **Rebar Set** with the following additional information:

Name	Data Type	Categories
Top Cover	Length	Structural Foundations
Major Bars	Text	Structural Foundations Walls
Minor Bars	Text	Structural Foundations Walls

13. When you are finished, the four parameters display as shown in Figure 2–147. Click **OK**.

Figure 2–147

14. Select a footing again and open the *Type Properties* dialog box. This time the *Rebar Set* section of parameters displays above *Dimensions*, as shown in Figure 2–148. Click **OK**.

Figure 2–148

15. Save the project.

Task 2: Modify a foundation schedule.

1. Switch back to the **Structural Foundation Schedule**.

2. In *Properties*, next to *Fields*, click **Edit...**.

3. In the *Schedule Properties* dialog box, in the *Fields* tab, add the following fields: **Top Cover**, **Bottom Cover**, **Major Bars**, and **Minor Bars**. Place them in the order shown in Figure 2–149.

   * Note you can use the *Parameter Name Search* to find available fields.

Figure 2–149

4. In the *Scheduled fields (in order)* area, remove the existing **Foundation Thickness** parameter.

5. In the *Fields* tab, click ⬜ (New parameter).

6. In the *Parameter Properties* dialog box, select **Project parameter**, and enter the *Name* **FS and FC Foundation Thickness**. Set it as a **Type** parameter with *Discipline* set to **Common**, *Data Type* set to **Length**, and *Group parameter under* to **Dimensions**, as shown in Figure 2–150.

Figure 2–150

7. Click **OK**.

8. Click ⬆E (Move parameter up) to place it below the existing **Width** parameter.

9. Select the new parameter and click ✏ (Edit parameter).

10. The full *Parameter Properties* dialog box opens. The **Structural Foundations** category is already selected because you are working in that type of schedule. Additionally, select the **Walls** category.

11. Click **OK** twice to close the dialog boxes. The schedule displays as shown in Figure 2–151.

<Structural Foundation Schedule>									
A	B	C	D	E	F	G	H	I	J
	Dimensions		FS and FC Foundation Thickness						
Type	Length	Width		Bottom Cover	Major Bars	Minor Bars	Top Cover	Count	Volume
FC3.0	<varies>	3' - 0"						4	715.22 CF
FC5.0	139' - 10"	5' - 0"						1	553.47 CF
FS6.0	6' - 0"	6' - 0"						27	972.00 CF
FS8.0	8' - 0"	8' - 0"						3	192.00 CF
Grand total: 35								35	2432.69 CF

Figure 2–151

12. Save the project.

Task 3: Modify and apply headers.

1. Click inside the header for FS and FC Foundation Thickness. Delete **FS and FC Foundation** so it displays as only *Thickness*.

2. To fix the *Dimensions* header, select it in the schedule view, then from the *Modify Schedule/ Quantities* tab>*Titles & Headers* panel, click 🔲 (Ungroup).

3. Press and drag the cursor over the columns from *Length* to *Thickness*.

4. In the *Titles & Headers* panel, click 🔲 (Group).

5. Type a header name of **Dimensions**.

6. Repeat the group process to create a header from *Top Cover* to *Minor Bars* with the name **Reinforcement**.

7. Group *Top Cover* and *Bottom Cover* and name the header **Cover**.

8. Group *Major Bars* and *Minor Bars* and name the header **Bars**. The schedule displays as shown Figure 2–152.

\<Structural Foundation Schedule>									
A	B	C	D	E	F	G	H	I	J
	Dimensions			Reinforcement					
				Cover		Bars			
Type	Length	Width	Thickness	Top Cover	Bottom Cover	Major Bars	Minor Bars	Count	Volume
FC3.0	\<varies>	3' - 0"						4	715.22 CF
FC5.0	139' - 10"	5' - 0"						1	553.47 CF
FS6.0	6' - 0"	6' - 0"						27	972.00 CF
FS8.0	8' - 0"	8' - 0"						3	192.00 CF
Grand total: 35								35	2432.69 CF

Figure 2–152

9. Set the *Thickness* to **1'-0"** for each of the types, clicking **OK** in the *Apply Changes* dialog box.

10. Open the **Structural Plans: T.O.F.** view and select one of the larger **FS8.0** spot footings close to the center of the building.

11. In Properties, click ⊞ (Edit Type). The **FS and FC Foundation Thickness** parameter has been added and set to **1'-0"**. Fill out the rest of the information for the *Cover* and *Bars*, as shown in Figure 2–153, and close the *Type Properties* dialog box.

Type Properties			✕
Family:	Footing-Rectangular ⌄		Load...
Type:	FS8.0 ⌄		Duplicate...
			Rename...

Type Parameters

Parameter	Value	=	^
Rebar Set			≋
Bottom Cover	0' 2"		
Major Bars	#4 @ 0'-9"		
Minor Bars	#4 @ 1'-0"		
Top Cover	0' 3"		
Dimensions			≋
Width	8' 0"		
Length	8' 0"		
Thickness	1' 0"		
FS and FC Foundation Thickness	1' 0"		

Figure 2–153

12. In the Type Properties of each foundation type or in the schedule view, fill out the rest of the information as shown in the table below.

Type	Bottom Cover	Major Bar	Minor Bar	Top Cover
FC3.0	0' - 1 1/2"	#4 @ 1'-0"	#4 @ 1'-0"	0' - 3"
FC5.0	0' - 2"	#4 @ 0'-9"	#4 @ 0'-9"	0' - 3"
FS6.0	0' - 1 1/2"	#4 @ 1'-0"	#4 @ 1'-0"	0' - 3"

13. Switch to the Structural Foundation schedule as shown in Figure 2–154. Adjust the columns as needed.

Structural Foundation Schedule									
A	B	C	D	E	F	G	H	I	J
		Dimensions			Reinforcement				
				Cover		Bars			
Type	Length	Width	Thickness	Top Cover	Bottom Cover	Major Bars	Minor Bars	Count	Volume
FC3.0	<varies>	3' - 0"	1' - 0"	0' - 3"	0' - 1 1/2"	#4 @ 1'-0"	#4 @ 1'-0"	4	715.22 CF
FC5.0	139' - 10"	5' - 0"	1' - 0"	0' - 3"	0' - 2"	#4 @ 0'-9"	#4 @ 0'-9"	1	553.47 CF
FS6.0	6' - 0"	6' - 0"	1' - 0"	0' - 3"	0' - 1 1/2"	#4 @ 1'-0"	#4 @ 1'-0"	27	972.00 CF
FS8.0	8' - 0"	8' - 0"	1' - 0"	0' - 3"	0' - 2"	#4 @ 0'-9"	#4 @ 1'-0"	3	192.00 CF
Grand total: 35								35	2432.69 CF

Figure 2–154

14. Save and close the project.

End of practice

2.6 Importing and Exporting Schedules

Schedules are views and can be copied into your project from other projects. Only the formatting information is copied; the information about individually scheduled items is not included. That information is automatically gathered from the elements in the current project. You can also export the schedule information to be used in spreadsheets.

How To: Import Schedules

1. In the *Insert* tab>*Load from Library* panel, expand ⬜ (Insert From File) and click ⬛ (Insert Views From File).

2. In the *Open* dialog box, locate the project file containing the schedule that you want to use.

3. Select the schedules that you want to import. If the referenced project contains many types of views, change *Views:* to **Show schedules and reports only**, as shown in Figure 2–155.

Figure 2–155

4. Click **OK**.

How To: Export Schedule Information

1. Switch to the schedule view that you want to export.

2. In the *File* tab, expand ⬜→ (Export)> ⬜ (Reports) and click ⊞ (Schedule), as shown in Figure 2–156.

Figure 2–156

3. In the *Export Schedule* dialog box, select a folder location, type a name for the text file, and set the *Files of types* to either **CSV (delimited) (*.csv)** or **Text (delimited)(*.txt)**, as shown in Figure 2–157.

Figure 2–157

4. Click **Save**.

5. In the *Export Schedule* dialog box, set the options in the *Schedule appearance* and *Output options* areas that best suit your spreadsheet software, as shown in Figure 2–158.

Figure 2–158

6. Click **OK**. A new file is created that you can open in a spreadsheet, as shown in Figure 2–159.

Figure 2–159

Chapter Review Questions

1. You are required to have actual elements in the model when you are creating schedules.

   a. True

   b. False

2. Which type of schedule allows you to list style information, such as the finish or frame type of a door, that is not automatically included in the element's properties?

   a. Material Takeoff

   b. Quantities

   c. Key

   d. Building Component

3. When creating *Calculated Value* fields (such as shown in Figure 2–160), the parameters you use must first be added to the list of fields in the schedule.

Figure 2–160

   a. True

   b. False

4. When creating a material takeoff schedule, where do you modify information about the material, such as the cost or manufacturer, as shown in Figure 2–161? (Select all that apply.)

Stone - Material Takeoff			
Material: Description	Material: Area	Material: Cost	Total Cost
Stone	865 SF	0.00	0
Stone: 6	865 SF		0

EIFS - Material Takeoff			
Material: Description	Material: Area	Material: Cost	Total Cost
EIFS	298 SF	12.00	3574
EIFS: 1	298 SF		3574

Figure 2–161

a. In the *Type Properties* dialog box.

b. In the schedule, fill out the columns related to the type information.

c. In the Material Editor.

d. In the Material Browser.

5. In an MEP or architectural schedule, which of the following should be created before you can create an embedded schedule, as shown in Figure 2–162?

A	B
SPACE NO.	NAME
DIFFUSER ID	DIFFUSER TYPE
1501	CLASSROOM
29	Supply Diffuser - Perforated - Round Neck - Ceiling Mounted:
30	Supply Diffuser - Perforated - Round Neck - Ceiling Mounted:
31	Supply Diffuser - Perforated - Round Neck - Ceiling Mounted:
32	Supply Diffuser - Perforated - Round Neck - Ceiling Mounted:
1502	CLASSROOM
45	Supply Diffuser - Perforated - Round Neck - Ceiling Mounted:
46	Supply Diffuser - Perforated - Round Neck - Ceiling Mounted:
47	Supply Diffuser - Perforated - Round Neck - Ceiling Mounted:
48	Supply Diffuser - Perforated - Round Neck - Ceiling Mounted:

Figure 2–162

a. Rooms, spaces, systems, or circuits

b. Elements covered in the schedule

c. The schedule that you want to embed into

d. A key schedule

Command Summary

Button	Command	Location
Schedule Types		
	Graphical Column Schedule	• **Ribbon:** *View* tab>*Create* panel, expand Schedules (*Structural Columns only*)
	Material Takeoff Schedule	• **Ribbon:** *View* tab>*Create* panel, expand Schedules
	Note Block	• **Ribbon:** *View* tab>*Create* panel, expand Schedules
	Schedule/ Quantities	• **Ribbon:** *View* tab>*Create* panel, expand Schedules
	Sheet List	• **Ribbon:** *View* tab>*Create* panel, expand Schedules
	View List	• **Ribbon:** *View* tab>*Create* panel, expand Schedules
Schedule Appearance		
	Align Horizontal	• **Ribbon:** *Modify Schedule/Quantities* tab>*Appearance* panel
	Align Vertical	• **Ribbon:** *Modify Schedule/Quantities* tab>*Appearance* panel
	Borders	• **Ribbon:** *Modify Schedule/Quantities* tab>*Appearance* panel
fx	**Calculated**	• **Ribbon:** *Modify Schedule/Quantities* tab>*Parameters* panel
	Clear Cell	• **Ribbon:** *Modify Schedule/Quantities* tab>*Titles & Headers* panel
	Combine Parameters	• **Ribbon:** *Modify Schedule/Quantities* tab>*Parameters* panel
	Delete (Columns)	• **Ribbon:** *Modify Schedule/Quantities* tab>*Columns* panel
	Delete (Rows)	• **Ribbon:** *Modify Schedule/Quantities* tab>*Rows* panel
A:	**Font**	• **Ribbon:** *Modify Schedule/Quantities* tab>*Appearance* panel

Button	Command	Location
	Format Unit	• **Ribbon:** *Modify Schedule/Quantities* tab>*Parameters* panel
	Freeze Header	• **Ribbon:** *Modify Schedule/Quantities* tab>*Titles & Headers* panel
	Group	• **Ribbon:** *Modify Schedule/Quantities* tab>*Titles & Headers* panel
	Hide (Columns)	• **Ribbon:** *Modify Schedule/Quantities* tab>*Columns* panel
	Insert Data Row	• **Ribbon:** *Modify Schedule/Quantities* tab>*Rows* panel
	Insert (Columns)	• **Ribbon:** *Modify Schedule/Quantities* tab>*Columns* panel
	Insert Image	• **Ribbon:** *Modify Schedule/Quantities* tab>*Titles & Headers* panel
	Insert (Rows)	• **Ribbon:** *Modify Schedule/Quantities* tab>*Rows* panel
	Merge Unmerge	• **Ribbon:** *Modify Schedule/Quantities* tab>*Titles & Headers* panel
	Reset	• **Ribbon:** *Modify Schedule/Quantities* tab>*Appearance* panel
	Resize (Columns)	• **Ribbon:** *Modify Schedule/Quantities* tab>*Columns* panel
	Resize (Rows)	• **Ribbon:** *Modify Schedule/Quantities* tab>*Rows* panel
	Shading	• **Ribbon:** *Modify Schedule/Quantities* tab>*Appearance* panel
	Ungroup	• **Ribbon:** *Modify Schedule/Quantities* tab>*Titles & Headers* panel
	Unhide All (Columns)	• **Ribbon:** *Modify Schedule/Quantities* tab>*Columns* panel

Introduction to Revit Families

Families are the backbone of Autodesk Revit. They are the elements you add as you model a building and its services, as well as the tools you use when annotating views. There are three kinds of families, all of which are customizable.

- *System families* are preset in the templates used to create projects (e.g., walls, roofs, slabs, ducts, pipes, and conduit, as well as text and dimensions). You create new types by duplicating an existing type and modifying the type parameters. System families are covered in *Chapter 3 Custom System Families*.

- *Component families* (e.g., doors, air handling units, columns, as well as tags and symbols, etc.) are defined in the Family Editor and loaded into a project. One family can have many types. Component families can be standalone or hosted by other elements such as walls, floors, or ceilings. Component families are the most complicated elements to create. Component families are covered in *Chapter 4 Loadable Component Families*, *Chapter 5 Advanced Family Techniques*, and *Chapter 6 Additional Family Types*.

- *In-place families* are component families created directly in a project and are dependent on the model geometry (e.g., custom gutters, special trim, or built-in columns). Use these only for unique situations where a component family does not work.

   Note: *In-place families are covered in **6.3 Creating In-Place Families** in **Chapter 6 Additional Family Types**.*

There are also three additional chapters of discipline-specific family creation practices:

- *Chapter 7 Creating Architectural-Specific Families*

- *Chapter 8 Creating MEP-Specific Families*

- *Chapter 9 Creating Structural-Specific Families*

Custom System Families

System families are embedded in a Revit® project or template file, and their parameters can be changed by editing the type properties of the family. Walls, roofs, floors, and compound ceiling types each have an assembly of layers that can be modified. MEP system families include duct, pipe, conduit, cable tray, and wire type families. Structural system families include wall foundations, floors, slabs, and walls.

Learning Objectives

- Create system family types for walls, roofs, floors, and ceilings.
- Modify wall types vertically to include split materials, profiles, and reveals.
- Create a vertically stacked wall from two or more wall types.
- Create duct and pipe types using routing preferences.
- Create cable tray, conduit, and wire types using type properties.

3.1 Creating Wall, Roof, Floor, and Ceiling Types

System families are modified in a project or template file by duplicating an existing element type. Some of these system families (such as walls, roofs, floors, and some ceilings) are compound or layer-based. For example, to modify a compound wall, you edit the type and select the **Structure** parameter. This opens the *Edit Assembly* dialog box (shown in Figure 3–1), which enables you to specify each layer of the assembly.

Figure 3–1

- Walls are used as the primary example, but floors, roofs, and compound ceilings follow the same pattern.

- Structural floors often use profiles for metal decking. Creating this type of floor is covered in the profile families topic.

- System families, such as wall, roof, floor, and ceiling types, can be copied between projects using the **Transfer Project Standards** command.

How To: Create a Compound Wall, Floor, Roof, or Ceiling

1. Start the wall, floor, roof or ceiling command.
2. In Properties, select a type similar to the one you want to create and click ⊞ (Edit Type).
3. In the *Type Properties* dialog box, click **Duplicate...**.

4. In the *Name* dialog box, enter a name for the new type and click **OK**.

5. Next to the **Structure** parameter, click **Edit...**.

6. In the *Edit Assembly* dialog box, modify the layers of the assembly and click **OK**.

7. Modify any Type Parameters in the *Type Properties* dialog box.

8. Click **OK** to close the dialog box.

💡 Hint: Basic Ceilings

The basic ceiling system family does not include a structure parameter and is intended to be used for open framed/exposed ceiling spaces where a ceiling truly would not exist. Instead, modify the Type by specifying a *Material* for the entire thickness of the ceiling.

Editing Wall, Roof, and Floor Assemblies

In the *Edit Assembly* dialog box, you can define the layers that make up the compound structure, as shown in Figure 3–2.

Figure 3–2

- To better visualize the wall, click **<< Preview** to open the preview pane and see the layers in the structure. You can preview the structure in a plan or section view, and zoom or pan in the preview pane.

- To change the way the element displays in the preview pane, expand ▦ (Visual Style) in the lower-left corner, as shown in Figure 3–3. By default, it is set to **Shaded**.

Figure 3–3

Assembly Information

The top of the dialog box lists the *Family* (such as **Basic Wall** or **Floor**), the *Type* name that you assigned to the new type, and the *Total thickness* (which is the sum of the layers defined in the wall), as shown in Figure 3–4. It also includes *Resistance (R)* and *Thermal Mass* which are automatically calculated from the materials assigned to the layers. You can also set a *Sample Height* for your wall design.

Family:	Basic Wall		
Type:	Exterior - Brick on CMU		
Total thickness:	1' 7 1/2"	Sample Height:	20' 0"
Resistance (R):	31.6278 (h·ft²·°F)/BTU		
Thermal Mass:	28.6462 BTU/°F		

Figure 3–4

Layers

When you specify the layers for the compound element, you assign them a *Function, Priority, Material, Thickness*, etc., as shown in Figure 3–5.

Layers

EXTERIOR SIDE

	Function	Priority	Material	Thickness	Wraps	Structural Material	Variable
1	Finish 1	4	Brick, Common	0' 3 5/8"	☑	☐	☐
2	Thermal/Air Layer	3	Air	0' 3"	☑	☐	☐
3	Membrane Layer		Air	0' 0"	☑	☐	☐
4	Substrate	2	Plywood, Sheat	0' 0 3/4"	☑	☐	☐
5	**Core Boundary**		**Layers Above W**	0' 0"			
6	Structure	1	Metal Stud Lay	0' 6"	☐	☑	☐
7	**Core Boundary**		**Layers Below Wr**	0' 0"			
8	Membrane Layer		Vapor Retarder	0' 0"	☑	☐	☐
9	Finish 2	5	Gypsum Wall B	0' 0 1/2"	☑	☐	☐

INTERIOR SIDE

Insert	Duplicate	Delete	Up	Down

Figure 3–5

- Use the buttons to insert additional layers and to rearrange them in the layer list. You can also delete layers from the list.

- The *Core Boundary* function separates the core or structural portion of the wall, floor, roof, or ceiling from the layers above and below the wrapping; a heavier line displays when in a plan or section in the *Edit Assembly* Preview.

- Editing a wall assembly works from the exterior side at the top of the list to the interior side at the bottom. For floors and roofs, you work around the layers above and below the wrap of the *Core Boundary*.

Options

Function and Priority		Select from a set list of functions in the drop-down list with a priority of highest (1) to lowest (5). Higher priority layers connect with another element's layer of the same priority before lower priority layers. For example, a wall with a layer of **Structure** with a priority of **1** will connect first with another wall that has a layer with a priority of **1** regardless of the function.
	Structure	The structural support for the wall, floor, or roof.
	Substrate	A material that acts as a foundation for another material, such as plywood sheathing or gypsum board.
	Thermal/Air Layer	An open layer for rigid insulation or air space.
	Finish 1	The exterior finish layer, such as brick for an exterior wall type, or one side of finish on an interior wall type. For floors, roofs, and ceilings, this represents the top finish layer of the assembly
	Finish 2	The interior finish layer, such as drywall on the inside of an exterior wall type, or the opposite side of finish on an interior wall type. For floors, roofs, and ceilings, this represents the bottom finish layer of the assembly.
	Membrane Layer	A vapor barrier. Typically, this layer represents vapor or moisture barrier/retarder within a wall, floor, roof, or ceiling assembly. Due to the barrier actually being so thin, it is set to a 0'-0" thickness and, therefore, it does not have a priority code.
	Structural Deck	(Floors only) A structural support based on a Deck Profile. You can also specify the Deck Usage with a **Bound Layer Above** or a **Standalone Deck**. Structural Deck Properties Deck Profile: Form Deck_Non-Composite : 2" x 6 ∨ Deck Usage: Bound Layer Above ∨
Material		Select from a list of available materials. Layers clean up if they share the same material and function. If they do not, a line displays at the join.
Thickness		Set the thickness of the particular layer.

Wraps	Set up individual layers to wrap when the Default Wrapping area has been specified - select the Wraps option at the end of each layer.
Structural Material	When selected, the physical asset of the layers material is used in the structural analytical model.

Wall Only Options

Sample Height	Displays the height of a wall in section when you are creating it. It does not impact the height of the wall in the project but is used when editing the vertical material changes and additions of sweeps or reveals.
Default Wrapping	Controls how the layers within the assembly wrap at the end of a wall (At Ends) or an opening (At Inserts) within the wall.
Variable	Controls which layer within the assembly will have a variable width. This must be set before creating a tapered wall type.

- Wall wrapping can be set in the assembly or in the *Type Properties*, as shown in Figure 3−6.

Wrapping at Inserts	Do not wrap
Wrapping at Ends	None

Figure 3−6

Slanted Wall

You can draw a slanted wall type and specify the **Angle From Vertical** degree value in Properties. The slant degree needs to be within -90° to 90°. You can also change a vertically drawn wall to a slanted wall type. If there are any doors, door openings or window added to the wall, you will need to select those objects and, in Properties, specify their *Orientation*. The direction to which the wall has been drawn (right to left or left to right) will determine the direction the angle will go. Figure 3−7 shows that when drawing from left to right the wall slant will go in the negative direction, and drawing from right to left the slant wall goes in the positive direction.

Figure 3−7

- Slanted walls can be modified in a plan, 3D, section, and perspective views.

- You can create a slanted wall with curved, circle, arc, polygon, or elliptical paths.

- If the angle is not going in the correct direction, + or -, you can add a (negative) - symbol in front of the degree value in Properties.

Tapered Wall

You can create a tapered wall from any wall type except walls with sweeps and reveals, stacked walls, and curtain walls. You must first edit the structure of the wall to set the variable thickness for the available wall layers. If not, you are prompted to set this before drawing the wall, as shown in Figure 3–8.

Figure 3–8

- To set the default angles of the tapered wall, in *Type Properties*, you can set the *Default Exterior Angle* and *Default Interior Angle*.

- If you have multiple instances of the same tapered wall type, you can select a tapered wall and, in Properties, override the angles by selecting the **Override Type Properties** option and setting the *Exterior Angle* and *Interior Angle*, as shown in Figure 3–9.

Cross-Section	Tapered
Override Type Properties	☑
Exterior Angle	5.00°
Interior Angle	0.00°

Figure 3–9

How To: Create a Tapered Wall

1. In the *Architecture* tab>*Build* panel, click ⬜ (Wall) or type the shortcut **WA**.

2. In Properties, click **Edit Type...**.

3. In the *Type Properties* dialog box, in the *Type* drop-down list, select the wall type you want to duplicate to create a tapered wall type.

4. Click **Duplicate...**.

5. In the *Name* dialog box, type a name and click **OK**.

6. In the *Type Properties* dialog box, in the *Construction* section, click **Edit...** next to *Structure*.

7. In the *Edit Assembly* dialog box, in the *Variable* column, check the checkbox next to the layer you want to have the variable width, as shown in Figure 3–10.

Figure 3–10

8. Click **OK**.

9. In the *Type Properties* dialog box, you will now have the ability to set the *Cross Section Properties,* as shown in Figure 3–11.

Figure 3–11

10. When finished, click **OK**.

11. To verify that the wall was created correctly, in Properties verify that your new wall type is showing in the Type Selector.

12. In the *Cross-Section Definition* section, set the *Cross-Section* to **Tapered**, as shown in Figure 3–12. Note that every time you need to draw a **Tapered** or **Slanted** wall type, you need to specify the *Cross-Section* in Properties accordingly as the last-selected *Cross-Section* will be the default the next time the **Wall** command is started.

*Note: If you select **Slanted**, the entire wall will slant at the angle specified in the Type Properties.*

13. In the view, draw the wall and view it in the default 3D view to test the new parameters, as shown on the right in Figure 3–12.

Figure 3–12

14. If the parameters are not correct, click **Edit Type...** to edit them. Once correct, delete the wall from the view to keep your template clean.

Additional Parameters

Roofs, floors, and structural slabs have an additional parameter that relates to sloping for drains. When *Variable* is not selected, the slab is set to a constant thickness and the entire element slopes, as shown on the top in Figure 3–13. When *Variable* is selected, only the variable layer gets thicker or thinner, as shown on the bottom in Figure 3–13.

Variable not checked

Variable checked

Figure 3–13

Practice 3a
Create an Architectural Wall Type

Practice Objective

- Create an exterior wall type with multiple of layers on the interior and the exterior of a core structural layer.

In this practice, you will create a custom exterior wall type, as shown in Figure 3–14.

Edit Assembly

Family:	Basic Wall
Type:	Exterior - Custom
Total thickness:	1' 1 7/8" (Default)
Resistance (R):	18.7300 (h·ft²·°F)/BTU
Thermal Mass:	7.5454 BTU/(ft²·°F)

Sample Height: 20' 0"

Layers

EXTERIOR SIDE

	Function	Priority	Material	Thickness	Wraps	Structural Material	Variable
1	Finish 1	4	Concrete Masonry Units	0' 3 5/8"	☑		☐
2	Thermal/Air Layer	3	Air	0' 3"	☑		☐
3	Membrane Layer		Air Infiltration Barrier	0' 0"	☑		☐
4	Substrate	2	Plywood, Sheathing	0' 0 3/4"	☑		☐
5	Core Boundary		Layers Above Wrap	0' 0"			
6	Structure	1	Metal - Stud Layer	0' 6"	☐	☑	☐
7	Core Boundary		Layers Below Wrap	0' 0"			
8	Membrane Layer		Vapor Retarder	0' 0"	☑		☐
9	Finish 2	5	Gypsum Wall Board	0' 0 1/2"	☑		☐

INTERIOR SIDE

Figure 3–14

Task 1: Create a custom wall type.

1. Start a new project based on the **Imperial-Architectural Template.rte** file found in the practice files *Architectural>RTE* folder, and save it as **Custom Wall Types.rvt** in the practice files *Architectural* folder.

2. In the *Architecture* tab>*Build* panel, click ⬚ (Wall).

3. In Properties, click ⬚ (Edit Type).

4. In the *Type Properties* dialog box, select **Generic - 8"**, click **Duplicate...**.

5. In the *Name* dialog box, type **Exterior - Custom** and click **OK**.

6. In the *Type Properties* dialog box, click **Edit...** next to the *Structure* parameter.

7. In the *Edit Assembly* dialog box, the simple wall type and layers display, as shown in Figure 3–15.

Figure 3–15

8. Click **<<Preview** and set the *View:* to **Floor Plan: Modify type attributes**.

9. In the *Layers* area, click **Insert** and then **Up** so a new layer is placed above the top **Core Boundary** layer, as shown in Figure 3–16. Editing a wall assembly works from the exterior side at the top of the list to the interior side at the bottom, so this location is considered the exterior side.

Figure 3–16

10. Click **Insert** three more times for a total of four layers above the top *Core Boundary* layer, then add two layers below the bottom *Core Boundary* layer. At the moment, they all have a *Function* of **Structure**, a *Priority* of **1**, and no materials or thicknesses.

11. On layer 1, in the *Function* column, click and expand the first **Structure** and set it to **Finish 1**, then expand the *Priority* column and select **4**. In the *Thickness* column, type **3 5/8"** as shown in Figure 3–17.

12. Set the rest of the *Function* and *Thickness* columns as shown in Figure 3–17.

Layers

EXTERIOR SIDE

	Function	Priority	Material	Thickness	Wraps	Structural Material	Variable
1	Finish 1	4	<By Category>	0' 3 5/8"	☑		☐
2	Thermal/Air Layer	3	<By Category>	0' 3"	☑		☐
3	Membrane Layer		<By Category>	0' 0"	☑		☐
4	Substrate	2	<By Category>	0' 0 3/4"	☑		☐
5	**Core Boundary**		**Layers Above Wrap**	**0' 0"**			
6	Structure	1	<By Category>	0' 6"	☐	☑	☐
7	**Core Boundary**		**Layers Below Wrap**	**0' 0"**			
8	Membrane Layer		<By Category>	0' 0"	☑		☐
9	Finish 2	5	<By Category>	0' 0 1/2"	☑		☐

INTERIOR SIDE

Figure 3–17

13. On layer 6, select **<By Category>** in the *Material* column and click ⬚ (Browse).

14. In the *Material Browser*, select **Metal Stud Layer**. (You can limit the number of materials you see by typing **stud** in the search box, as shown in Figure 3–18.) Click **OK**.

Material Browser - Metal Stud Layer

stud ✕   Identity

Project Materials: All ▼ ▾   ☰ ▾

Search results for "stud"   Descriptiv‹

Name

Metal Stud Layer

Figure 3–18

15. In the *Edit Assembly* dialog box, in the *Thickness* column, type **6"**, as shown in Figure 3–19.

16. Add the materials shown in Figure 3–19 to the other layers.

Figure 3–19

17. Click **OK** twice to close the dialog boxes.

18. Add a couple of walls to the project to see how the new wall functions.

19. Change the *Detail Level* to **Medium** or **Fine** to see the different layers of the wall.

20. Save the project.

Task 2: Create a tapered wall type.

1. Start the **Wall** Command again.

2. In the Type Selector, select the **Basic Wall: Exterior - CMU on Mtl. Stud** wall type.

3. In Properties, select **Edit Type...**.

4. In the *Type Properties* dialog box, click **Duplicate...**.

5. In the *Name* dialog box, type **Exterior - Custom Variable** and click **OK**.

6. In the *Type Properties*, in the *Construction* section, click **Edit...** next to *Structure*.

7. For **Finish 1** (layer 1), in the *Variable* column, check the checkbox to set this layer to allow a variable width, as shown in Figure 3–20.

Layers

EXTERIOR SIDE

	Function	Priority	Material	Thickness	Wraps	Structural Material	Variable
1	Finish 1	4	Concrete Masonry Units	0' 7 5/8"	✓		✓
2	Thermal/Air Layer	3	Air	0' 3"	✓		
3	Membrane Layer		Air Infiltration Barrier	0' 0"	✓		
4	Substrate	2	Plywood, Sheathing	0' 0 3/4"	✓		
5	**Core Boundary**		**Layers Above Wrap**	**0' 0"**			
6	Structure	1	Metal Stud Layer	0' 6"		✓	
7	**Core Boundary**		**Layers Below Wrap**	**0' 0"**			
8	Membrane Layer		Vapor Retarder	0' 0"	✓		
9	Finish 2	5	Gypsum Wall Board	0' 0 1/2"	✓		

Figure 3–20

8. Click **OK**.

9. In the *Type Properties* dialog box, in the *Cross-Section Definition* section, set the *Default Interior Angle* to **5** (degrees), as shown in Figure 3–21.

Cross-Section Definition		☆
Default Exterior Angle	0.00°	
Default Interior Angle	5.00°	
Width Measured At	Top	

Figure 3–21

10. Click **OK**.

11. In Properties, verify the new wall type is showing in the Type Selector.

12. In the *Cross-Section Definition* section, set the *Cross-Section* to **Tapered**.

13. To verify the wall is correct, draw the new wall in a plan view and then open the default 3D view to view the new wall, as shown in Figure 3–22.

Figure 3–22

14. Save and close the project.

End of practice

Practice 3b
Create a Structural Floor Type

Practice Objectives

- Load a custom profile into a project.
- Create a new structural floor type using the profile.

In this practice, you will load a metal deck profile into a project, use it to create a new metal deck floor type, as shown in Figure 3–23, and test the new floor type.

Figure 3–23

Task 1: Load the profile and create a structural floor.

1. Start a new project based on the **Imperial-Structural Template.rte** file found in the practice files *Structural>RTE* folder, and save it as **Custom Floor Types.rvt** in the practice files *Structural* folder.

2. Open the **Structural Plans: Level 2** view.

3. In the *Insert* tab>*Load from Library* panel, click ⬇ (Load Family).

4. Navigate to the practice files *Structural>RFA* folder, select **Custom-Metal-Deck-Profile.rfa**, and click **Open**.

5. In the *Structure* tab>*Structure* panel, click ⌢ (Floor: Structural).

6. In the Type Selector, verify that **Floor: 3"LW Concrete on 2" Metal Deck** is selected.

7. In the *Modify | Create Floor Boundary* tab>*Draw* panel, use the **Line** or **Rectangle** tool to draw a slab of any shape or size, as shown in Figure 3–24.

Figure 3–24

*   If the span direction is not horizontal, click ⬚ (Span Direction) in the *Draw* panel and select a boundary sketch line.

8. Click ✔ (Finish Edit Mode).

9. In the Quick Access Toolbar, click ◊ (Section) and place a section vertically through the slab from north to south.

10. Open the new section view and change the *Scale* to **3/4"=1'-0"** and the *Detail Level* to **Fine**. You might need to adjust the crop region and/or zoom in on the slab section. It should look similar to the one shown in Figure 3–25.

Figure 3–25

11. Save the project.

Task 2: Create a new floor type.

1. Select the floor.

2. In Properties, click ⊞ (Edit Type).

3. In the *Type Properties* dialog box, click **Duplicate...**.

4. In the *Name* dialog box, type **6" Concrete on 3" Comp Metal Deck** and click **OK**.

5. In the *Type Properties* dialog box, click **Edit...** next to the *Structure* parameter.

6. Expand **Preview>>** so that you can see the changes in the preview pane.

7. For the **Structure** layer (layer 2), change the *Thickness* to **6"**, as shown in Figure 3–26.

Layers

	Function	Priority	Material	Thickness
1	**Core Boundary**		**Layers Above Wrap**	**0' 0"**
2	Structure	1	Concrete, Lightweight - 4 ksi	0' 6"
3	Structural Deck	1	Metal Deck	0' 0"
4	**Core Boundary**		**Layers Below Wrap**	**0' 0"**

Figure 3–26

8. Select the **Structural Deck** layer (layer 3).

9. In the *Structural Deck Properties* area, in the *Deck Profile* drop-down list, select **Custom-Metal-Deck-Profile : 3"**, as shown in Figure 3–27.

Layers

	Function	Priority	Material	Thickness
1	**Core Boundary**		**Layers Above Wrap**	**0' 0"**
2	Structure	1	Concrete, Lightweight - 4 ksi	0' 6"
3	Structural Deck	1	Metal Deck	0' 0"
4	**Core Boundary**		**Layers Below Wrap**	**0' 0"**

Insert	Duplicate	Delete	Up

Structural Deck Properties

Deck Profile	Deck Usage
Custom-Metal-Deck-Profile : 3"	Bound Layer Above

Custom-Metal-Deck-Profile : 3"
Form Deck_Composite : 1 1/2" x
Form Deck_Composite : 2" x 6"
Form Deck_Composite : 3" x 8"

Figure 3–27

10. Click **OK** to close all of the dialog boxes. The section should display the new metal deck profile, as shown in Figure 3–28.

Figure 3–28

11. Save and close the project.

End of practice

3.2 Modify Compound Walls

Compound walls are made of regions of different materials, as well as optional permanent sweeps or reveals, as shown in Figure 3–29. Several options help you create these walls: **Modify**, **Split Region**, **Merge Regions**, **Assign Layers**, **Wall Sweeps**, and **Reveals**.

Figure 3–29

In the *Edit Assembly* dialog box, you must have the preview's *View:* set to **Section: Modify type attributes** to work with the *Modify Vertical Structure* tools, as shown in Figure 3–30.

Figure 3–30

How To: Duplicate a Wall Type

1. In the *Architecture* tab>*Build* panel, click ⬜ (Wall), or in the *Structure* tab>*Structure* panel, click ⬜ (Wall).
2. In Properties, click ▦ (Edit Type).
3. In the *Type Properties* dialog box, click **Duplicate...**. Give the type a new name and click **OK**.
4. In the *Type Properties* dialog box, click **Edit...** next to the *Structure* parameter. In the *Edit Assembly* dialog box, create any additional layers that might be required.
5. Open the preview pane and set the *View:* to **Section: Modify Type Attributes**. This activates the *Modify Vertical Structure (Section Preview only)* tools, as shown in Figure 3–31.

Figure 3–31

6. Zoom in to see the various layers.
7. In the *Layers* list, select the row you want to work with. The selected layer highlights in the preview pane.
8. Use the various tools that are outlined below.
9. Click **OK** until all of the dialog boxes are closed to save the wall type.

*   When making changes to the vertical structure of a wall type it helps to have the *Sample Height* set to the shortest expected height for the wall type so the changes display more clearly.

How To: Split Regions on a Wall Layer

1. Duplicate an existing wall type and click **Edit...** next to *Structure* in the *Construction* section.
2. In the *Edit Assembly* dialog box, click **Split Region**.

3. In the section preview pane, move the cursor to the edge of the wall or layer and a dimension will display. Move the cursor up the wall layer's edge, as shown in Figure 3–32, and click to split the wall's layer.

Wall layer edge

3' - 10"

Figure 3–32

- When splitting regions, it is helpful to move the cursor along the outer edge of the region being split. Look for the horizontal line across the region before picking the point to split, as shown in Figure 3–33.

Horizontal split region line

Figure 3–33

4. Click (Modify).

- You can create as many split regions as required on one layer, but it is important to understand that you should not create more than you need. There is no undo option in this dialog box. To save your work as you go, click **OK** in the *Edit Assembly* dialog box, then click **Edit...** next to *Structure* to go back in to edit the assembly.

5. To change the height (dimension) of the split region, select the border (split region line) between the two regions. An arrow displays when the border is selected, as shown in Figure 3-34.

Figure 3-34

- You can either drag the border (split region line) to the new location or select the dimension text, type a new distance (as shown in Figure 3-35), and press <Enter>.

Figure 3-35

6. To modify the width of the layer in the preview pane, click **Modify** and select the outer boundary (left edge of the region) to display a temporary dimension (as shown in Figure 3–36), then click on the dimension text, change the width, and press <Enter>. Note that this will change the width for the entire layer regardless of how many split regions there are.

Figure 3–36

How To: Create New Layers

1. In the *Layers* area, click **Insert**. Click **Up** or **Down** as needed to move the new layer into place. Assign a *Function*, *Priority,* and *Material,* as required. Do not modify the *Thickness* (keep it at 0).

   • In the example shown in Figure 3–37, two layers have the function **Finish 1** with a *Priority* of **4,** and each layer has a different material. When a region is split, the thickness of the original layer is set to **Variable** and cannot be modified in the *Layers* area of the *Edit Assembly* dialog box.

	Function	Priority	Material	Thickness	Wraps	Structural Material	Variable
1	Finish 1	4	Brick, Common	Variable	☑	☐	☐
2	Finish 1	4	Stone, Natural So	0' 0"	☑	☐	☐
3	Thermal/Air Layer	3	Air	0' 3"	☑	☐	

Figure 3–37

How To: Assign Split Regions to Layers

1. In the *Edit Assembly* dialog box, in the preview pane, zoom in so you can see the areas that have been split, as shown in Figure 3–38.

2. In the *Layers* area, select the row that has the layer you want to assign.

3. In the *Modify Vertical Structure* area, click **Assign Layers**.

4. In the preview pane, select the exterior edge of the split region where you want the selected layer applied. The section should highlight, as shown in Figure 3–38.

Figure 3–38

5. Repeat the steps to assign the other split regions.

Merging Regions

The **Merge Regions** tool allows you to combine adjacent layers or regions that have previously been split within a wall assembly. As you move your cursor across the boundary, a tooltip and merge icon will appear, indicating which layer will remain after the merge and displaying the names of the layers involved. Figure 3–39 shows the difference between the cursor's hover and how the merge will result in different outcomes. It is important to note that only layers directly next to each other can be merged using this tool.

Figure 3–39

- After merging layers, the layer that was merged will remain in the the *Layers* list with the thickness set to **0** and the layer that remains displays the total thickness of the two merged layers.

Wall Sweeps and Reveals

When editing a wall assembly, you can add a sweep, which adds material to a wall using a profile shape, as well as a reveal, which voids material from a wall using a profile shape, as shown in Figure 3–40. You can also specify the material (sweeps only), orientation, offset, distance from top or base, if the wall profile will be on the exterior or interior side, and the option to flip the wall profile.

Edit wall assembly   *View of placed wall in section view*

Figure 3–40

How To: Add a Sweep

1. In the *Edit Assembly* dialog box, click **Sweeps** to open the *Wall Sweeps* dialog box.

2. In the *Wall Sweeps* dialog box, click **Add**. A default row is added.

3. In the *Profile* column, select from the drop-down list of the existing profiles in the project. If needed, click **Load Profile** to add a profile.

4. Continue setting up the profile by selecting a *Material* and setting the *Distance* from the top or bottom, interior or exterior *Side*, and the *Offset* from that side, as shown in Figure 3–41. If needed, place a check mark in the *Flip* column to flip the profile.

	Profile	Material	Distance	From	Side	Offset	Flip	Setback	Cuts Wall	Cuttable	^
1	Parapet Cap-	Concrete,	0' 0"	Top	Exterior	0' 0"	☐	0' 0"	☑	☐	
2	Wall Sweep-	Brick, Soldi	-1' 4"	Top	Exterior	-0' 3 5/	☐	0' 0"	☑	☐	
3	Sill-Precast :	Concrete,	3' 4"	Base	Exterior	0' 0"	☐	0' 0"	☑	☐	

Figure 3–41

5. Click **Apply** to see the sweep in the preview before you click **OK** to finish.

- Reveals work the same way, except that you do not assign a material to a reveal. The whole shape of the reveal profile is visible in the section view, but you only see the cut in the project.

Practice 3c
Create a Vertically Compound Wall

Practice Objectives

- Add material.
- Add wall sweeps and reveals.
- Split wall to create a vertically compound wall.

In this practice, you will modify the vertical structure of a wall type using **Split Region** and **Assign Layers**. You will then add wall sweeps and reveals, as shown in Figure 3–42.

Figure 3–42

Task 1: Add materials to the project.

1. In the practice files *Architectural* folder, open **Custom Wall Types-Vertical.rvt.**

2. In the *Manage* tab>*Settings* panel, click 🌑 (Materials).

3. Verify you can see the *Material Libraries* section (as shown in Figure 3–43) in the lower-left side of the *Material Browser* dialog box.

Figure 3–43

- If you do not see the material libraries at the bottom of the *Material Browser* dialog box, expand the *Material Libraries* section, as shown in Figure 3–44.

Figure 3–44

- If you do not see the *AEC Materials* library at the bottom of the dialog box, click **Shows/ Hides library tree**, as shown in Figure 3–45.

Figure 3–45

- If needed, change the view to display a *View Type* of **List View** and a *Thumbnail Size* of **64 x 64**, as shown in Figure 3–46.

Figure 3–46

4. Expand the *AEC Materials* folder and select **Masonry**. In the *Name* list, scroll down and select **Brick, Common, Grey** and click [↑] (Adds material to document.), as shown in Figure 3–47.

Figure 3–47

5. Repeat the process and add the **CMU, Split Face** material to the project.

6. Click **OK** to close the *Material Browser* dialog box.

7. Save the project.

Task 2: Split regions in the wall's *Edit Assembly* dialog box.

1. In the **{3D}** view, select the existing wall. In Properties, verify that the Type Selector is set to **Exterior - Custom** and click [⊞] (Edit Type).

2. In the *Type Properties* dialog box, click **Edit...** next to the *Structure* parameter.

3. In the upper-right corner of the *Edit Assembly* dialog box, verify the *Sample Height* is set to **30'-0"**.

4. Click **<< Preview**.

5. Set the *View:* to **Section: Modify type attributes**.

6. In the *Layers* area, select row 1 and click **Insert** twice so two new layers are placed at the top of the list. Set the *Function* for both to **Finish 1** with a *Priority* of **4**, as shown in Figure 3–48. Editing a wall assembly works from the exterior side at the top of the list to the interior side at the bottom, so this location is considered the exterior side.

7. Set the materials as shown in Figure 3–48. Do not specify a thickness. Once you apply a layer to part of the split region, it will take on the appropriate thickness.

Layers

	Function	Priority	Material	Thickness
			EXTERIOR SIDE	
1	Finish 1	4	CMU, Split Face	0' 0"
2	Finish 1	4	Brick, Common, Grey ···	0' 0"
3	Finish 1	4	Concrete Masonry Units	0' 3 5/8"
4	Thermal/Air Layer	3	Air	0' 3"
5	Membrane Layer		Air Infiltration Barrier	0' 0"
6	Substrate	2	Plywood, Sheathing	0' 0 3/4"
7	**Core Boundary**		**Layers Above Wrap**	**0' 0"**
8	Structure	1	Metal Stud Layer	0' 6"
9	**Core Boundary**		**Layers Below Wrap**	**0' 0"**
10	Membrane Layer		Vapor Retarder	0' 0"
11	Finish 2	5	Gypsum Wall Board	0' 0 1/2"

Figure 3–48

8. In the *Modify Vertical Structure (Section Preview only)* area, click **Split Region**.

9. In the preview pane, move the cursor along the left edge of the exterior finish region (the leftmost region) to a point **3'-6"** above the base, as shown in Figure 3–49. Zoom in to ensure that you split the finish layer and not the central structural layer.

3' - 6"

Figure 3–49

10. Add three additional splits to the same layer, as shown in Figure 3–50.

Figure 3–50

- If you make a mistake with the split sizes, click **Modify** and zoom in to the split that needs to be fixed so that you can see both the split region line and the dimension that you need to edit. Select the split region line, as shown on the left in Figure 3–51, then select the dimension and change it, as shown on the right. Press <Enter> to update the dimension.

Figure 3–51

Task 3: Assign layers in a wall type.

1. Zoom in or out and use the slide bars along the right and bottom sides of the preview pane so you can see just the areas that have been split, as shown in Figure 3–52.

2. In the *Layers* area, select the **Brick, Common, Gray** layer.

3. In the *Modify Vertical Structure* area, click **Assign Layers**.

4. In the preview pane, select the **2'-0"** portion of the wall where you want the finish applied. The section should highlight, as shown in Figure 3–52.

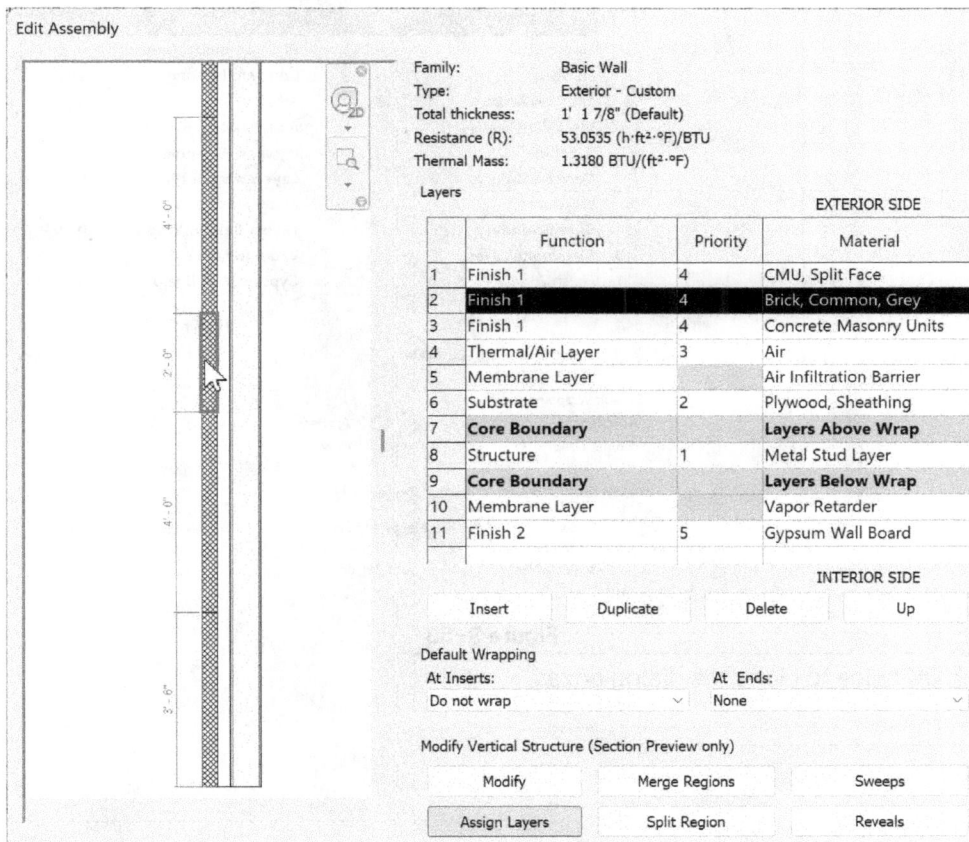

Edit Assembly

Family: Basic Wall
Type: Exterior - Custom
Total thickness: 1' 1 7/8" (Default)
Resistance (R): 53.0535 (h·ft²·°F)/BTU
Thermal Mass: 1.3180 BTU/(ft²·°F)

Layers

EXTERIOR SIDE

	Function	Priority	Material
1	Finish 1	4	CMU, Split Face
2	Finish 1	4	Brick, Common, Grey
3	Finish 1	4	Concrete Masonry Units
4	Thermal/Air Layer	3	Air
5	Membrane Layer		Air Infiltration Barrier
6	Substrate	2	Plywood, Sheathing
7	**Core Boundary**		**Layers Above Wrap**
8	Structure	1	Metal Stud Layer
9	**Core Boundary**		**Layers Below Wrap**
10	Membrane Layer		Vapor Retarder
11	Finish 2	5	Gypsum Wall Board

INTERIOR SIDE

Insert	Duplicate	Delete	Up

Default Wrapping
At Inserts: Do not wrap
At Ends: None

Modify Vertical Structure (Section Preview only)

Modify	Merge Regions	Sweeps
Assign Layers	Split Region	Reveals

Figure 3–52

5. Repeat with the **CMU, Split face** material in each of the **4'-0"** sections. The top and bottom of the wall remain using the **Concrete Masonry Units** material.

6. Click **Modify** to finish the process. The list of layer thicknesses displays as shown in Figure 3-53.

Edit Assembly

Family: Basic Wall
Type: Exterior - Custom
Total thickness: 1' 1 7/8" (Default)
Resistance (R): 54.0217 (h·ft²·°F)/BTU
Thermal Mass: 7.1826 BTU/(ft²·°F)

Layers

EXTERIOR SIDE

	Function	Priority	Material	Thickness
1	Finish 1	4	CMU, Split Face	Variable
2	Finish 1	4	Brick, Common, Grey	0' 3 5/8"
3	Finish 1	4	Concrete Masonry Units	Variable
4	Thermal/Air Layer	3	Air	0' 3"
5	Membrane Layer		Air Infiltration Barrier	0' 0"
6	Substrate	2	Plywood, Sheathing	0' 0 3/4"
7	**Core Boundary**		**Layers Above Wrap**	**0' 0"**
8	Structure	1	Metal Stud Layer	0' 6"
9	**Core Boundary**		**Layers Below Wrap**	**0' 0"**
10	Membrane Layer		Vapor Retarder	0' 0"
11	Finish 2	5	Gypsum Wall Board	0' 0 1/2"

INTERIOR SIDE

Insert | Duplicate | Delete | Up | Down

Default Wrapping
At Inserts: | At Ends:
Do not wrap | None

Modify Vertical Structure (Section Preview only)
Modify | Merge Regions | Sweeps
Assign Layers | Split Region | Reveals

Figure 3-53

7. Click **OK** twice to close the dialog boxes.

8. Set the *Visual Style* of the 3D view to **Texture** to see the layout of the materials, as shown in Figure 3–54.

Figure 3–54

9. Save the project.

Task 4: Add sweeps and reveals to the wall type.

1. Edit the structure of the same wall type.

2. In the *Edit Assembly* dialog box, in the *Modify Vertical Structure (Section Preview only)* area, click **Sweeps**.

3. In the *Wall Sweeps* dialog box, click **Add** twice and set up two wall sweeps using the information shown in Figure 3–55. Leave other options at their default settings.

Wall Sweeps

Wall Sweeps

	Profile	Material	Distance	From	Orientation	Side
1	Parapet Cap-Precast : 16"	Concrete, Cast-in-Place gray	0' 0"	Top	Perpendicular to Face	Exterior
2	Sill-Precast : 5" Wide	Concrete, Cast-in-Place gray	3' 4"	Base	Perpendicular to Face	Exterior

Figure 3–55

4. Click **OK** to exit the *Wall Sweeps* dialog box.

5. In the preview of the *Edit Assembly* dialog box, you should see the two sweeps when you zoom in, as shown for both the sill and the cap in Figure 3–56.

Figure 3–56

6. In the *Edit Assembly* dialog box, in the *Modify Vertical Structure (Section Preview only)* area, click **Reveals**.

7. In the *Reveals* dialog box, click **Add** three times and set up the reveals as shown in Figure 3–57. Click **OK**. Note that in the preview pane, the reveals look like a solid, similar to the sweeps, but a reveal will remove material away from the wall.

	Profile	Distance	From	Orientation	Side	Offset	Flip	Setback	
1	Reveal-Brick Course : 1 Brick	13' 5"	Base	Perpendicular	Exterior	0' 0"	☐	0' 0"	
2	Reveal-Brick Course : 1 Brick	9' 5"	Base	Perpendicular	Exterior	0' 0"	☐	0' 0"	
3	Reveal-Brick Course : 1 Brick	7' 5"	Base	Perpendicular	Exterior	0' 0"	☐	0' 0"	

Figure 3–57

8. Click **OK** twice to close the dialog boxes. The wall displays complete with sweeps and reveals. Rotate the wall around to see the protruding sweeps and the reveals that have removed material from the wall.

9. Save and close the project.

End of practice

3.3 Stacked Walls

A vertically stacked wall is a specific system family that takes two or more existing basic walls and stacks them on top of each other at specific heights, as shown in Figure 3–58. One wall must be variable in height. The basic wall types have to be in place before you create the stacked wall. These walls are created by copying and editing an existing Vertically Stacked Wall type.

Figure 3–58

How To: Create a Vertically Stacked Wall

1. Start the **Wall** command.

2. In Properties Type Selector, select an existing stacked wall type and click ⊞ (Edit Type).

3. Duplicate the wall type and give it a new name.

4. In the *Type Properties* dialog box, click **Edit...** next to the *Structure* parameter.

5. In the *Edit Assembly* dialog box, set the *Offset* for how the walls should align when they are stacked and a *Sample Height* for the preview, as shown in Figure 3–59.

Figure 3–59

6. In the *Name* column, select the wall types you want to add to the stacked wall, as shown in Figure 3–60.

Figure 3–60

7. For each wall type, set the appropriate height and location (Up or Down) in the list. One height must be variable. Set the *Offset* of the wall as required.

8. Click **<< Preview** to see the wall, as shown in Figure 3–61.

Figure 3–61

9. Click **OK** until all of the dialog boxes are closed.

💡 Hint: Embedding a Wall Inside Another Wall

Another way of creating a compound wall is to embed one wall inside another wall, as shown in Figure 3–62. When you have drawn a host wall, draw another wall on top of, or parallel to it near the host. A warning box opens and recommends that you use **Cut Geometry** to embed the wall in the host wall.

Figure 3–62

1. Add the embedded wall to the host wall.

2. Close the warning box.

3. In the *Modify* tab>*Geometry* panel, click ⌀ (Cut).

4. Select the host wall.

5. Select the wall that cuts the host wall.

- The only way to have an embedded wall in a project template is to copy and paste the host and the embedded wall into the project template.

- Embedded walls work similar to windows. You can modify the embedded wall with controls.

- Some curtain wall types are created to be automatically embedded in another wall. The type **Curtain Wall: Storefront** is an example. The Type Parameter *Automatically Embed* is available for all curtain wall types.

- You can separate embedded walls. In the *Modify* tab>*Geometry* panel, expand

  ⌀ (Cut) and click ⌀ (Uncut Geometry).

Practice 3d
Create Stacked and Embedded Walls

Practice Objectives

- Create a vertically stacked wall type.
- Embed a wall into a stacked wall.

In this practice, you will create a vertically stacked wall and use it in a project. You will also embed a curtain wall and another wall type into a host wall, as shown in Figure 3–63.

Figure 3–63

Task 1: Create a stacked wall.

1. Start a new project based on the **Imperial-Architectural Template.rte** file found in the practice files *Architectural>RTE* folder, and save it as **Warehouse.rvt** in the practice files *Architectural* folder.

2. Start the **Wall** command. In the Type Selector, select **Basic Wall: Exterior - Brick on Mtl. Stud**.

3. Edit and duplicate the type. Rename the duplicated type to **Exterior - Render on Mtl. Stud** and click **OK**.

4. Edit the structure of the new wall.

5. In the *Edit Assembly* dialog box, set the *Thickness* for the **Finish 1** layer to **1"**. In the *Materials* column, click on the material and click the **Browse** button.

6. In the *Material Browser* dialog box, search for **render**, as shown in Figure 3–64. Note that there are no materials called *render* in the *Project Materials* list, but there are in the *Material Libraries*. Click **Adds material to document** next to **Render, Tan, Textured** (as shown in Figure 3–64) to add it to the *Project Materials* list.

Figure 3–64

7. In the Project Materials list, select **Render, Tan Textured**, then click **OK** three times to close all the dialog boxes.

8. You should still be in the **Wall** command. In the Type Selector, select the **Stacked Wall: Exterior – Brick Over CMU w Metal Stud** type.

9. Edit the type and duplicate it to create a new wall type named **Exterior – Render over Brick/ CMU**.

10. Edit the structure of the new wall.

11. For the top wall (layer 1), expand the name and select **Exterior – Render on Mtl. Stud** from the drop-down list. Leave the *Height* as **Variable** and set the *Offset* to **4"**.

12. For the bottom wall, select **Exterior – Brick on CMU** and set the *Height* to **6'-0"**.

13. Click **OK** to close all of the open dialog boxes.

14. Draw a rectangular building **50'-0" x 30'-0"** using the new wall style. The wall height is an *Unconnected Height* of **20'-0"**.

15. Click ⌖ (Modify).

16. Set the *Detail Level* to **Fine**.

17. Display the walls in 3D to verify that the Brick/EIFS displays on the exterior.

18. Set the *Visual Style* to **Realistic**.

19. Save and close the project.

End of practice

3.4 Creating MEP System Family Types

Revit project templates for mechanical, electrical, and plumbing are preloaded with system families for ducts (shown in Figure 3–65), pipes, cable trays, conduits, wire types, and basic conductor and cable types. You can modify the existing types or create custom ones to suit your company and project needs.

Figure 3–65

How To: Create System Duct Types

1. Start the **Duct** command, select one of the existing types, and click ⊞ (Edit Type).

2. In the *Type Properties* dialog box, click **Duplicate...**, type a new name in the *Name* dialog box, and click **OK**.

3. Next to the *Routing Preferences* parameter, click **Edit...**.

4. The *Routing Preferences* dialog box displays, as shown in Figure 3–66. This is where you will set up the fittings that will be used when routing ducts of this type.

Figure 3–66

5. To modify the duct sizes being used in the project (not just for the duct type being created), click **Duct Size...** to open the *Mechanical Settings* dialog box. In the *Duct Settings* area, you can add or remove the typical sizes used in the project.

6. Click **Load Family...** to add more duct fittings or accessory families that you want to use in the type that are not already loaded in the project.

7. For each of the fittings, expand the drop-down list and select the size that you want to use, as shown in Figure 3–67.

Figure 3–67

8. If you need to include more than one option for a fitting, click ✛ (Add row) and select the secondary option for the fitting. You can also use ↑E (Move row up) or ↓E (Move row down) to specify the order in which the fittings are applied by default or click ▬ (Remove Row) to delete the ones you do not need to use.

9. When you have finished assigning fittings, click **OK** to close the *Routing Preferences* dialog box.

10. Fill in the other parameters for the *Type Properties* as required and click **OK** to finish the new duct type.

• Flex ducts do not have routing preferences; the fitting selection takes place directly in the *Type Properties*, as shown in Figure 3–68.

Figure 3–68

How To: Create Pipe Types

1. Start the **Pipe** command, select one of the existing types, and click ⊞ (Edit Type).

2. In the *Type Properties* dialog box, click **Duplicate...**, type a new name in the *Name* dialog box, and click **OK**.

3. Next to the **Routing Preferences** parameter, click **Edit...**.

4. The *Routing Preferences* dialog box opens, as shown in Figure 3–69.

Content	Min. Size	Max. Size
Pipe Segment		
Copper - K	1/4"	12"
Elbow		
Elbow - Generic: Standard	All	
Preferred Junction Type		
Tee	All	
Junction		
Tee - Generic: Standard	All	
Cross		
Cross - Generic: Standard	All	
Transition		
Transition - Generic: Standard	All	
Union		
Coupling - Generic: Standard	All	
Flange		
None	None	
Cap		
Cap - Generic: Standard	All	

Routing Preferences

Pipe Type: Custom Pipe Type

Segments and Sizes...   Load Family...

OK   Cancel

Figure 3–69

5. To modify the segments and sizes being used in the project (not just for the pipe type being created), click **Segments and Sizes...** to open the *Mechanical Settings* dialog box. In this dialog box, specify the segment types and sizes for the various types of pipe as shown in Figure 3–70. Click **OK** when finished.

Note: Segment types can be added or removed here.

Figure 3–70

6. Click **Load Family...** to add any pipe fittings that you want to use in the type that have not already been loaded in the project.

7. For the *Pipe Segment* type and each of the fittings, expand the drop-down list and select the size that you want to use as shown in Figure 3–71.

Figure 3–71

8. If you want to include more than one option for a fitting, click ✛ (Add row) and select the secondary option for the fitting.

9. You can also use ⬆E (Move row up) or ⬇E (Move row down) to specify the order in which the fittings are applied by default or ▭ (Remove Row) to delete the ones you do not need to use.

10. When you have finished assigning fittings, click **OK** to close the *Routing Preferences* dialog box.

11. Fill in the other parameters for the type properties as required and click **OK** to finish the new pipe type.

   * Flex pipes do not have routing preferences; the fittings selection takes place directly in the *Type Properties* dialog box, as shown in Figure 3–72.

Figure 3–72

How To: Create Cable Tray and Conduit Types

1. Start the **Cable Tray** or **Conduit** command, select one of the existing types, and click 🔲 (Edit Type).

2. In the *Type Properties* dialog box, click **Duplicate**, type a new name in the *Name* dialog box, and click **OK**.

3. Select the fittings that you want to use as shown in Figure 3–73. For example, you may want to specify a more specific type of coupler for the *Union* parameter.

   Note: Most of the cable tray types you need are preloaded in the default electrical and systems templates. You can only change some of the options, such as the radius size.

Figure 3–73

- For conduit, you first need to specify the *Electrical Standard* that you are using, as shown in Figure 3–74.

Figure 3–74

4. Fill in the values for any of the *Identity Data* information you might have and click **OK** to finish.

How To: Create a Wire Type

1. Start the **Wire** command, select one of the existing types, and click ⊞ (Edit Type).

2. In the *Type Properties* dialog box, click **Duplicate**, type a new name in the *Name* dialog box, and click **OK**.

3. Select the information that you want to use, as shown in Figure 3-75.

Figure 3-75

- Wire types for THWN and XHHW are preset in the default electrical and systems templates.

- Another use of wire types is to show wire differently based on certain conditions. For example, create a type called **THWN - Above Ceiling** that is an exact duplicate of the basic **THWN** type, then create a view filter using this type name and change the line style to hidden or dashed.

3.5 Electrical Conductor and Cable Settings

In a project template, you need to establish conductor (wire) size, cable (collection of conductors) size, and cable types. These settings are defined in the *Electrical Conductor and Cable Settings* dialog box, as shown in Figure 3–76. They include the type of wires available, based on material, temperature, and insulation ratings, and specify which wire types can be used in a project.

Figure 3–76

- These settings should be set up in your project template. If needed, these settings can be transferred from another project template or project using the **Transfer Project Standards** tool.

Conductor Details	Specify *Conductor Materials*, *Temperature Ratings*, and *Insulation Materials*. These can all be used when creating cable types.
Conductor Sizes	Define the project's wire sizes by adding, deleting, or modifying the existing list of wires and sizes.
Cable Sizes	Create various cable sizes with different configurations or groups of conductors. A cable size can include a variation of number and size of hot, neutral, and ground conductors or other sizes of conductors.
Cable Types	Create cable types that will be used in the project. The settings use the previous settings on the other tabs, such as cable name, conductor material, temperature rating, insulation material, and core type, as well as specify which cable sizes will be used for the different cable types.

How To: Define Electrical Conductor and Cable Settings

1. In the *Manage* tab>*Settings* panel, expand (MEP Settings) and click (Electrical Conductor and Cable Settings).

2. In the *Electrical Conductor and Cable Settings* dialog box, click on the tabs to review the default types, modify types, or create new ones.

Conductor Details and Conductor Sizes Tabs

1. On the *Conductor Details* tab, review the default types for the *Conductor Materials* (shown in Figure 3–77), *Temperature Ratings*, and *Insulation Materials*.

   - To add a new type, click **+ Add** and modify the name.

   - If there is a type that is not needed, select it and click 🗑 **Delete**.

Figure 3–77

2. Select the *Conductor Sizes* tab to review the sizes. By default, there are some standard American wire gauge (AWG) sizes. Click **Add** or **Delete** to add or delete sizes as needed.

Cable Sizes Tab

1. Select the *Cable Sizes* tab. Note that there are no cable sizes added in the default templates. Above the *Name* column, click **Add**. A new cable size line appears in the list.

2. In the *Name* column, click **New Cable Size** and type a name, as shown in Figure 3–78.

3. Set the parameters for the new cable size by typing in a value in the *# Of Hot Conductor* column, then in the *Hot Conductor Size* column, expand the drop-down list and select one of the available options.

4. Continue entering in the rest of the values for the neutral conductor/size and ground conductor/size, as shown in Figure 3–78.

Figure 3–78

- To duplicate a cable size, click **Duplicate** at the top of the list of cable sizes. A copy of the cable size appears in the list. Click on the name to change it, then edit the necessary column values.
- If needed, click **Delete** to remove a cable size.

Cable Types Tab

1. By default, THWN and XHHW cable types are available. You can add, duplicate, or delete the cable types.

2. To assign cable sizes, in the *Name* column, select a cable type, then in the flyout panel, select the applicable cable sizes, as shown in Figure 3–79, and click **OK**.

   Note: *If needed, you can click* ▮➜ *(Expand side panel) in the upper-right corner to open the flyout panel.*

Electrical Conductor and Cable Settings						×
Conductor Details Conductor Sizes Cable Sizes **Cable Types**						

THWN

Cable Size	Usable
1-#10, 1-#10, 1-#10	☑
1-#12, 1-#12, 1-#12	☑
3-#8, 1-#8, 1-#8	☐
3-#10, 1-#10, 1-#10	☐

Name	Comments	Conductor Material	Temperature Rating (°C)	Insulation Material	Core Type
THWN		Copper	60	THWN	Single-core
XHHW		Copper	60	XHHW	Single-core

How do I configure conductors and cables?   OK   Cancel

Figure 3–79

Practice 3e
Create a Duct System Type

Practice Objective

- Create a new duct system type.

In this practice, you will sketch ducts that show the various fittings that come with the default information. You will then duplicate and modify a duct system family, by loading additional fittings and assigning them to the system family, as shown in Figure 3–80.

Rectangular Duct: Radius Elbow / Tees

Rectangular Duct: Radius Elbow / Taps - DTL

Figure 3–80

1. In the practice files *MEP>RTE* folder, open **Midrise-Template-MEP-Systems.rte.**
2. Open the Mechanical>HVAC>Floor Plans>**1 - Mech** view.

3. Start the **Duct** command and using the **Rectangular Duct: Radius Elbows / Tees** type, add some ducts in an arrangement similar to Figure 3–81. The exact size and length does not matter.

Figure 3–81

4. Right-click on the end of the far right open pipe and select **Cap Open End**. Repeat on the other three open ends.

5. Make a copy of the entire duct system below the original making sure they don't touch.

6. Select one of the new ducts and in Properties, click ⊞ (Edit Type).

7. In the *Type Properties* dialog box, click **Duplicate...**.

8. In the *Name* dialog box, type **Radius Elbows / Taps - DTL** and click **OK**.

9. Next to the **Routing Preferences** parameter, click **Edit...**.

10. In the *Routing Preferences* dialog box, click **Load Family...**.

11. In the *Load Family* dialog box, navigate to the practice files *MEP>RFA* folder. Select the families listed below and click **Open**.

- **Rectangular Endcap - DTL.rfa**
- **Rectangular Elbow Eccentric Radius - DTL.rfa**
- **Rectangular Radius Tap - DTL.rfa**
- **Rectangular Length Eccentric Transition - DTL.rfa**

12. In the *Routing Preferences* dialog box, assign the families to the appropriate section, as shown in Figure 3-82.

Content
Elbow
Rectangular Elbow Eccentric Radius - DTL: Standard
Preferred Junction Type
Tap
Junction
Rectangular Tee: Standard
Rectangular Radius Tap - DTL: Standard
Cross
Rectangular Cross: Standard
Transition
Rectangular Length Eccentric Transition - DTL: Standard
Multi-shape Transition Rectangular to Round
Rectangular to Round Transition - Angle: 45 Degree
Multi-shape Transition Rectangular to Oval
Rectangular to Oval Transition - Length: Standard
Multi-shape Transition Oval to Round
None
Union
Rectangular Union: Standard
Cap
Rectangular Endcap - DTL: Standard

Figure 3-82

13. Click **OK** twice to close the dialog boxes.

14. Highlight the new system and, in the *Modify | Multi-Select* tab>*Edit* panel, click ⊞ (Change Type).

Note: Sometimes, the first selection does not update as expected, so select a different one before trying to apply the new type.

15. In Properties, select one of the other types to see the change and then select **Rectangular Duct: Radius Elbow /Taps - DTL**. The duct updates as shown in Figure 3–83.

Figure 3–83

16. Select all the ducts and duct fittings and press <Delete>.

17. Save and close the template.

End of practice

Practice 3f
Create a Pipe System Type

Practice Objective

- Create a new pipe system type.

In this practice, you will sketch pipes that show the various fittings that come with the default information as shown on the top in Figure 3−84. You will then duplicate and modify a pipe system family, by loading additional fittings and assigning them to the new system family, as shown on the bottom in Figure 3−84.

Pipe Types: Standard

Pipe Types: Ductile Iron - Flanged - 250lb

Figure 3−84

1. In the practice files *MEP>RTE* folder, open **Midrise-Template-MEP-Systems.rte.**

2. Open the Plumbing>Plumbing>Floor Plans>**1 - Plumbing** view.

3. Start the **Pipe** command and verify **Pipe Types: Standard** is showing in the Properties Type Selector.

4. In Properties, under the *Mechanical* section, set the *System Type* parameter to **Domestic Cold Water**.

   *Note: If the pipe no longer displays when you switch the System Type, open the Visibility/ Graphic Overrides dialog box. On the Filter tab, check the checkbox in the Visibility column for **Domestic**.*

5. Set the *Detail Level* to **Fine**.

6. Add some pipes in an arrangement similar to Figure 3–85. The exact size and length does not matter.

Figure 3–85

7. Click **Modify**.

8. Right-click on the end of the far right open pipe and select **Cap Open End**. Repeat on the other open ends.

9. Make a copy of the entire system below the original ensuring that they do not touch.

10. Select one of the pipes in the new system.

11. In Properties, click (Edit Type).

12. In the *Type Properties* dialog box, click **Duplicate...**.

13. In the *Name* dialog box, type **Ductile Iron - Flanged - 250lb** and click **OK**.

14. Next to the **Routing Preferences** parameter, click **Edit...**.

15. In the *Routing Preferences* dialog box, click **Load Family...**.

16. In the *Load Family* dialog box, navigate to the practice files *MEP>RFA* folder. Select the families listed below and click **Open**.

   • **Flange - Blind - GI - Class 250.rfa**

   • **Flange - Threaded - GI - Class 250.rfa**

   • **Cross - Flanged - GI - Class 250.rfa**

   • **Elbow - Flanged - GI - Class 250.rfa**

   • **Reducer - Flanged - GI - Class 250.rfa**

   • **Tee Reducing - Flanged - GI - Class 250.rfa**

17. Assign the families to the appropriate section, as shown in Figure 3–86. In the *Min. Size* column, verify it is set correctly for all the options.

Figure 3–86

18. Click **OK** twice to close the dialog boxes.

19. Highlight the new system and in the *Modify | Multi-Select* tab>*Edit* panel, click 🔲 (Change Type).

20. In Properties, select **Pipe Types: Ductile Iron - Flanged - 250lb**. The pipe updates as shown in Figure 3–87.

Figure 3–87

21. Select all the pipes and pipe fittings and press <Delete>.

22. Save and close the template.

End of practice

Practice 3g
Define Electrical Conductor and Cable Settings

Practice Objective

- Create a new insulation material, conductor size, cable size and cable type.

In this practice, you will open the *Electrical Conductor and Cable Settings* dialog box and create a new insulation material, conductor size, and cable size. You will then assign these new settings to a cable type.

1. In the practice files *MEP>RTE* folder, open **Midrise-Template-MEP-Systems.rte**.

2. In the *Manage* tab>*Settings* panel, expand (MEP Settings) and click (Electrical Conductor and Cable Settings).

3. In the *Electrical Conductor and Cable Settings* dialog box, on the *Conductor Details* tab, select **Insulation Materials** on the left and click **Add**. In the *Name* column, a new row displays with the name **New Insulation**, as shown in Figure 3–88. Click **New Insulation** and rename it to **TFN**, then press <Enter>.

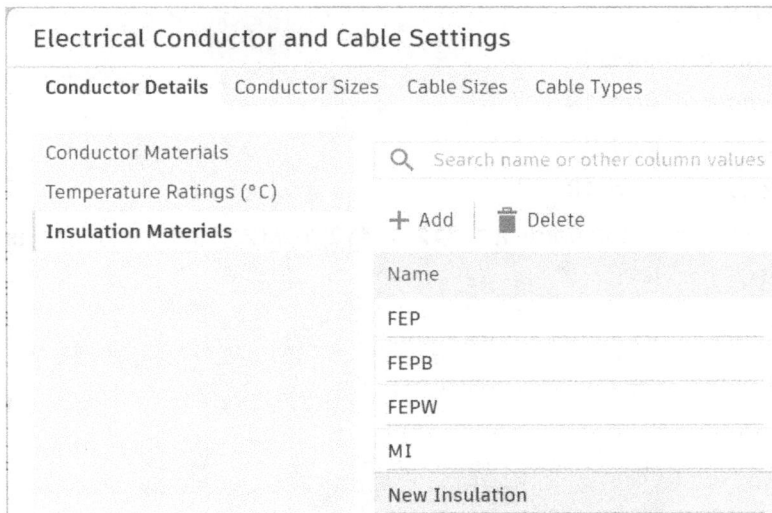

Figure 3–88

4. At the top of the dialog box, select the *Conductor Sizes* tab, then click **Add**. In the *Name* column, click **New Conductor Size** and rename it to **18**. In the *Diameter* column, type **0.0403** and press <Enter>. The row should appear as shown in Figure 3−89.

Electrical Conductor and Cable Settings

Conductor Details   **Conductor Sizes**   Cable Sizes   Cable Types

Q   Search name or other column values

+ Add | 🗑 Delete

Name	Diameter
18	0.040300"

Figure 3−89

5. Select the *Cable Sizes* tab, then click **Add**. A new cable size line appears. Click **New Cable Size** and rename it to **1-#18, 1-#18, 1-#18**. Set the values in the columns as follows (as shown in Figure 3−90):

- *# Of Hot Conductor*: **1**
- *Hot Conductor Size*: **18**
- *# Of Neutral Conductor*: **1**
- *Neutral Conductor Size*: **18**
- *# Of Ground Conductor*: **1**
- *Ground Conductor Size*: **18**

6. Add another cable size and name it **1-#12, 1-#12, 1-#12**. Enter the values as shown in Figure 3−90.

Electrical Conductor and Cable Settings

Conductor Details   Conductor Sizes   **Cable Sizes**   Cable Types

Q   Search name or other column values

+ Add | 📄 Duplicate | 🗑 Delete

Name	Comments	# Of Hot Conductor	Hot Conductor Size	# Of Neutral Conductor	Neutral Conductor Size	# Of Ground Conductor	Ground Conductor Size	# Of Other Conductor
1-#12, 1-#12, 1-#12		1	12	1	12	1	12	0
1-#18, 1-#18, 1-#18		1	18	1	18	1	18	0

Figure 3−90

7. At the top of the list of cable sizes, click **Duplicate**. A copy of the cable size appears in the list.

8. Click on the copied size's name and change it to **2-#12, 1-#12, 1-#12**. In the *# Of Hot Conductor* column, change the value to **2**.

9. At the top of the dialog box, select the *Cable Types* tab.

10. Click **Add**, then click on **New Cable Type** and rename it to **TFN**. For the *Conductor Material*, expand the drop-down list and select **Copper**. For *Temperature Rating*, select **90** and for *Insulation Material* select **TFN**.

11. In the upper-right corner, click ▐→ (Expand side panel) if the panel flyout is not already open.

12. Check the checkbox next to **1-#18, 1-#18, 1-#18**, as shown in Figure 3–91.

Electrical Conductor and Cable Settings						TFN ▐→	
Conductor Details Conductor Sizes Cable Sizes **Cable Types**						🔍	
🔍 Search name or other column values						Cable Size	Usable
+ Add 📄 Duplicate 🗑 Delete						1-#12, 1-#12, 1-#12	☐
Name	Comments	Conductor Material	Temperature Rating (°C)	Insulation Material	Core Type	1-#18, 1-#18, 1-#18	☑
TFN		Copper	90	TFN	Single-core	2-#12, 1-#12, 1-#12	☐
THWN		Copper	60	THWN	Single-core		
XHHW		Copper	60	XHHW	Single-core		

Figure 3–91

13. In the *Name* column, select **THWN**. In the flyout panel, select all the cable sizes except for **1-#18, 1-#18, 1-#18** and click **OK**.

14. Save and close the project template.

End of practice

Chapter Review Questions

1. When creating a compound wall, you assign a function for each layer. The *Priority* numbers indicate the priority of the layers when they are joined together with other walls, as shown in Figure 3–92. Which of the following priorities connects first?

Figure 3–92

   a. Membrane Layer

   b. Substrate with a *Priority* of 2

   c. Structure with a *Priority* of 1

   d. Thermal/Air Layer with a *Priority* of 3

   e. Finish 2 with a *Priority* of 5

2. How do you create a wall type that has more than one finish material on the vertical plane, like the stucco and brick wall shown in Figure 3–93, and has the remaining layers stay the same?

Figure 3–93

   a. Create separate wall types for the stone and stucco. Duplicate an existing Stacked Wall type and set the wall types to stone and stucco.

   b. Draw two walls on top of each other and use ⬦ (Join Geometry) to link them.

   c. Duplicate an existing Basic Wall type and use **Split Region** and **Assign Layers** to apply the stone and stucco materials to separate parts of the wall.

   d. Draw the first wall, draw the other wall on top of the first, and use ⬦ (Cut Geometry) to cut the second wall out of the first wall.

3. Which command do you need to use to embed a wall inside another wall?

   a. Wall Joins

   b. Cut Geometry

   c. Cope

   d. Split Face

4. (MEP only) When setting up a new duct or pipe type, which of the following items can be set by type?

   a. System Type

   b. Width and Height

   c. Preferred Junction Type

   d. Justification

5. (MEP only) When creating a new conduit or cable tray type, you need to assign Routing Preferences.

   a. True

   b. False

Command Summary

Button	Command	Location
	Cable Tray	• **Ribbon:** *Systems* tab>*Electrical* panel • **Shortcut:** CT
	Conduit	• **Ribbon:** *Systems* tab>*Electrical* panel • **Shortcut:** CN
	Cut Geometry	• **Ribbon:** *Modify* tab>*Geometry* panel
	Duct	• **Ribbon:** *Systems* tab>*HVAC* panel • **Shortcut:** DT
	Edit Type	• **Ribbon:** *Modify* tab>*Properties* panel • **Properties Palette**
	Pipe	• **Ribbon:** *Systems* tab>*Plumbing & Piping* panel • **Shortcut:** PI
	Uncut Geometry	• **Ribbon:** *Modify* tab>*Geometry* panel, expand Cut
	Wall: Architectural	• **Ribbon:** *Architecture* tab>*Build* panel or *Structure* tab>*Structure* panel, expand Wall • **Shortcut:** WA
	Wall: Structural	• **Ribbon:** *Architecture* tab>*Build* panel or *Structure* tab>*Structure* panel, expand Wall • **Shortcut:** WA
	Wire	• **Ribbon:** *Systems* tab>*Electrical* panel • **Shortcut:** EW

Chapter

4

Loadable Component Families

Loadable component families are the heart of the Autodesk® Revit® software. They include furniture; doors and windows; mechanical, electrical, and plumbing equipment; and structural framing. While some families are included with the software, it is important to know how to create custom families yourself. The basics include creating a parametric framework, adding solid geometry, and creating family types.

Learning Objectives

- Understand the different types of families that can be created in the software.
- Set up a parametric framework using reference planes, dimensions, and labels.
- Flex the framework to test all of the parameters.
- Create solid/void forms including extrusions, blends, revolves, sweeps, and swept blends.
- Create family types.
- Load and test families in a project.

4.1 Creating Loadable Component Families

Loadable component families are elements or annotation elements that have been grouped together and set up with dimensions and other parameters based on a family template. Families are parametric, meaning that they can be changed without having to recreate the geometry. For example, when you change the *Width* and *Depth* of the base cabinet shown in Figure 4–1, other parts move as well.

Figure 4–1

Families are created in the Family Editor, which has a slightly different set of ribbon tabs from the standard interface, as shown in Figure 4–2.

(Ribbon continued)

Figure 4–2

- Component families (e.g., doors, air handling units, columns, etc.) are defined in the Family Editor and loaded into a project. One family can have many types.

- Many families are complex and time-consuming to create, but creating them all follows the same basic process and principles.

- Sometimes, it is easier to modify an existing component family than to create a family from scratch.

Preparing to Create Families

Before you create a custom loadable component family, you should plan ahead by asking a variety of questions, including the following:

- Is this family going to be used in one project (in-place) or in many projects (component)?

- What family template should be used? Is this going to be a host-based or free-instance family? If a generic family is being created, the **Generic Model.rft** family template file is often used.

- Where should the origin point (insertion point) be located? The origin point should be located where users would logically expect to begin placement. For example, for casework that is placed along a wall, it would be best to have the origin point at the back of the family instead of at the center of the family.

- How much detail is needed in the family? More details added to a family increases the file size and can possibly over-constrain the family.

- Do you need 2D and 3D representations in different views? What about 3D geometry?

- Will the family need to be used in a room calculation?

- Does the family need a room calculation point to be room aware to associate the family to a room or space for accurate reporting and scheduling?

> ### 💡 Hint: Host-Based vs. Free-Instance Families
>
> *Host-based* families are dependent on a host. Examples include downlights (which require a ceiling) and sconces (which require a wall), as shown in Figure 4–3.
>
> *Free-instance* families do not need a host. Examples include the desk and table lamp shown in Figure 4–3.

Figure 4–3

Selecting a Family Template

When creating a Revit family, choosing the right family template (.RFT) is important because it defines the category and behavior of the family within a project. The type of family you need, such as duct, data device, or mechanical equipment, will guide your choice. Most templates are named to reflect their category (e.g., Duct.rft) and may also include descriptors like *wall-based*, *ceiling-based*, or *line-based* to indicate how the family will be placed in a model. Selecting the appropriate template ensures the family functions correctly in its intended purpose.

- Family templates may contain several different views, geometry, and notes to help with the family creation.

- If you select a family template that does not match the needed category, you can change the category without having to start over. However, it may be difficult to change a hosted family without needing to recreate it.

- Some of the basic family template types are listed in the following table:

Standalone (Free-instance)	Standalone family templates are used when a host is not needed. For example, furniture, ducts, air handling units, or columns. These family templates are named according to the type of family that needs to be created (e.g., **Casework.rft**, **Electrical Fixture.rft**, and **Mechanical Equipment.rft**).
Host-based	Host-based family templates include any family template that includes a descriptor of *wall based*, *ceiling based*, *floor based*, or *roof based* in the template name. Family template type examples would be **Casework wall based.rft**, **Electrical Fixture ceiling based.rft**, and **Mechanical Equipment wall based.rft**. There are some families that are host-based that do not include the descriptor in the template name, like the **Door.rft** or **Window.rft** family templates.
Line-based	Lined-based family templates are used when you want the element to repeat in a line between two pick points in a model. For example, architectural wall quoining.
Profile	Profile family templates are for creating 2D profiles. When opened, they do not have an option to draw a family in a 3D view. Profiles can be applied to geometry to shape their profile, like for stair railings.
Adaptive	Adaptive family templates are for families that need multiple selection points for placement in a model.

How To: Create a Component Family (Overview)

1. On the Home screen, under *Families*, click **New...**, or (if a project file is already open) in the *File* tab, expand ▭ (New) and click ▣ (Family).

2. In the *New Family - Select Template File* dialog box, navigate to and select the family template you want to use and click **Open**.

   * Set up the origin point of the family with two intersecting reference planes in a view. Most family templates have predefined origin points that can be modified if needed.

   * Set the parametric framework by adding reference planes/lines in plan and elevation views. This is a very important step when working with parametric families.

   * Dimension and label the reference planes/lines to control the movement of the geometry and to create parameters.

   * Flex the family throughout the creation process to ensure the parameters change as expected.

   *Note: To **flex a family** means changing the dimension values to test its parametric relationship.*

- Use the *Forms* tools (shown in Figure 4–4) to draw the geometry.

Extrusion Blend Revolve Sweep Swept Void
                            Blend Forms

Forms

Figure 4–4

- Lock the geometry to the reference planes/lines.
- Flex the geometry or reference planes/lines again by changing the parameters to ensure that they are working.
- Create family types with different parameters, as required.

3. Save the family.

4. Click ⊞ (Load into Project) to test the family in a project.

Saving Custom Family Files

When you create custom family files, you should save them to a location shared by the entire company, so others can access them. You will want to label the family name with your company name or abbreviation. For easy access, set the custom library as the primary or secondary library available when you load a family.

How To: Specify the File Location for Custom Libraries

1. In the *File* tab, click **Options**.

2. In the *Options* dialog box, select the *File Locations* tab.

3. Click **Places...**.

4. In the *Places* dialog box, click ✛ (Add Value). A new *Library Name* is added to the list. Specify the name and path for the library, as shown in Figure 4–5. You can also modify the existing library names and locations if needed.

5. Click ↑E (Move Rows Up) and ↓E (Move Rows Down) to reorder the list of library names.

6. Click ▬ (Remove Value) to delete the values you do not need to use.

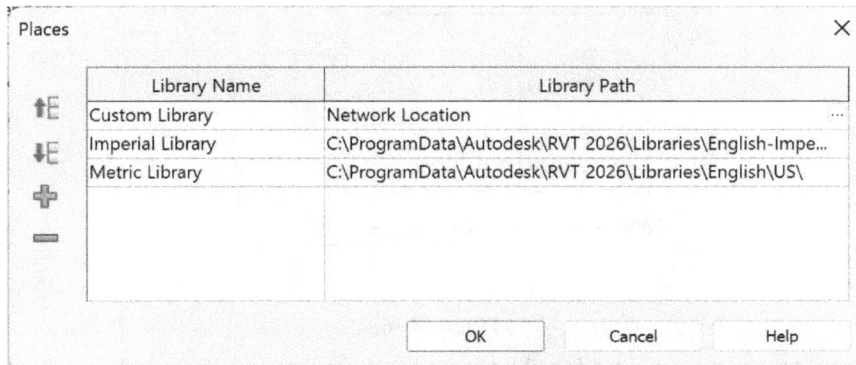

	Library Name	Library Path
	Custom Library	Network Location
	Imperial Library	C:\ProgramData\Autodesk\RVT 2026\Libraries\English-Impe...
	Metric Library	C:\ProgramData\Autodesk\RVT 2026\Libraries\English\US\

Places ✕

↑E ↓E ✛ ▬

OK   Cancel   Help

Figure 4–5

7. Click **OK** to close the dialog boxes. The library at the top of the list will be the default location when loading families.

4.2 Creating the Parametric Framework

Autodesk Revit families can be parametric (i.e., controlled by family parameters). These parameters are the framework for creating family geometry. They are based on reference planes/lines that are dimensioned and labeled, as shown in Figure 4–6.

Figure 4–6

Before you draw any geometry in a family, set up the parametric framework:

1. Place reference planes/lines at critical locations and set the origin point.

2. Dimension the reference planes/lines and label some of them so they can be manipulated.

3. Lock any dimension that must remain constant in the family by selecting the dimension and clicking the lock icon.

4. Flex the dimensioned and labeled references to ensure that they function as expected.

    *   Flexing the geometry of the family is a way to test your family's stability. After you add a label to a dimension, you can go into the *Family Types* dialog box and change the measurements to see if you get any errors or if it moves in the correct direction. Flex as often as possible to avoid errors like over-constraining.

Reference Planes

You can sketch *reference planes* (displayed as dashed green lines) and snap to them whenever you need to line up elements. Reference planes display in associated views because they are infinite planes and not just lines.

*   Intersecting reference planes have the ability to define the family's origin or insertion point. By default, the origin point of a family is the center of the space where you create the family. In most templates, this is located at the intersection of the existing reference planes. You can also specify your own origin point by selecting the intersecting reference planes and then selecting the **Defines Origin** option in Properties, as shown in Figure 4–7.

Other		⌃
Is Reference	Front	
Defines Origin	☑	

Figure 4–7

- Subcategories can be created to control reference plane object styles, making it easier to differentiate between reference planes during family creation.

- Reference planes do not display in the project when you insert the family type, but might impact snap and alignment behavior.

- After placing a reference plane, you can name it by clicking on **<Click to name>** and typing in the text box, as shown in Figure 4–8, or in Properties. Naming a reference plane enables you to use it to set the work plane when you are ready to add geometry to the family.

Figure 4–8

Reference Lines

Reference lines are similar to reference planes, but they have start and end points that can be controlled and four faces that you can sketch geometry on, as shown on the right in Figure 4–9. They appear as solid lines, as shown in Figure 4–9, and can be customized by assigning a subcategory. Unlike reference planes, a reference line's length can be adjusted by selecting it and modifying the temporary dimension value. They can be drawn using various shapes, such as rectangles, circles, or arcs. Reference lines are useful when needing to control a geometry rotation, setting lengths, or defining angled dimensions in a family.

Figure 4–9

- In Properties, you can set the *Subcategory*. You can create a subcategory using the same process as reference planes.

How To: Draw a Reference Plane or Line

1. In the Family Editor, in the *Create* tab>*Datum* panel, click ⬚ (Reference Plane) or
    ⬚ (Reference Line).

2. In the *Modify | Place Reference Plane* or *Lines* tab>*Draw* panel, select one of the draw tools.

3. Draw or select the lines that define the location. The number of reference planes/lines you need depends on what you are drawing.

*   Reference planes display in plan and elevation views, but not in 3D views, and reference lines display in all views.

*   Reference planes can be named while reference lines cannot be named.

*   In Revit family creation, the *Is Reference* (for reference planes) or *Reference* (for reference lines) property determines how a reference plane/line interacts with dimensions and alignments in a project, as follows:

    *   **Not a Reference:** The plane/line is invisible to the project environment. It cannot be used for snapping, dimensioning, or alignment once the family is loaded.

    *   **Weak Reference:** The lowest priority for snapping to or selection. While weak references can be dimensioned, they are secondary to strong references. You often need to use <Tab> to cycle through and highlight a weak reference for selection.

    *   **Strong Reference:** The highest priority for snapping to or selection. Strong references take precedence over wall centerlines and are the first targets highlighted when placing permanent dimensions. For reference planes, strong references can include names (e.g., Left, Center, or Front).

How To: Create a Reference Plane Subcategory

1. Start the **Reference Plane** or **Reference Line** command.

2. In the *Modify | Place Reference Plane* or *Lines* tab>*Subcategory* panel, expand the *Subcategory* drop-down list and select **<Create New Subcategory>**, as shown Figure 4–10.

Figure 4–10

3. In the *New Subcategory* dialog box, enter a name and specify if it is for **Reference Planes** or **Reference Lines**. Click **OK**.

4. In the *Object Styles* dialog box, modify the *Line Weight*, *Line Color*, and *Line Pattern* and click **OK**.

Adding Dimensions and Labels

Add dimensions and labels to reference planes or lines to start the constraining process, as shown in Figure 4–11. For example, you might want to run a string of dimensions and then set the distances to be equal by clicking on the associated **EQ** symbol. This moves the reference planes into place. Labeling a dimension creates a parameter that can be modified in the *Family Types* dialog box. Another way to constrain the framework is to click the lock icon to lock the dimension's distance. Any time a family is flexed, the locked dimension remains the same.

Figure 4–11

- Before creating new labels (family parameters), you need to verify if the dimension that is controlling the family's framework needs to be controlled in a project as a instance or type property. These can easily be changed during the family creation or after.

    - There are two types of parameters that can be created: **family parameters** and **shared parameters**. A family parameter helps control the family's framework and cannot be used in schedules or tags, while a shared parameter can.

How To: Label a Dimension

1. Dimension the family's framework, then select the dimension you want to label. In the *Modify | Dimensions* tab>*Label Dimension* panel, select an existing label from the drop-down list, as shown on the left in Figure 4–12. You can also right-click on the dimension text, select **Label**, and choose a label from the drop-down list, as shown on the right in Figure 4–12.

    *   If there are no parameters to choose from, click 🖹 (Create Parameter) to create a new parameter.

Figure 4–12

How To: Create a New Label (Family Parameter)

1. Select the dimension you want to label.

2. In the *Modify | Dimensions* tab>*Label Dimension* panel, click 🖹 (Create Parameter).

3. In the *Parameter Properties* dialog box, in the *Parameter Type* area, select **Family parameter**, as shown in Figure 4–13.

    *Note: Shared parameters are covered in **6.4 Working with Shared Parameters** in **Chapter 6 Additional Family Types**.*

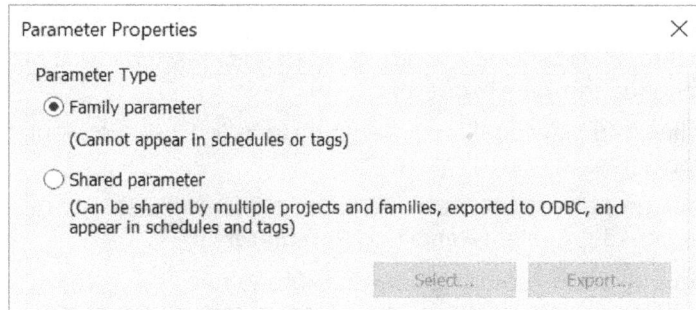

Figure 4–13

4. In the *Parameter Data* area, specify the *Name*, as shown in Figure 4–14. The *Discipline* and *Data Type* are automatically set and grayed out. The *Group parameter under* is set to **Dimensions**; this field determines which section the parameter will display under in Properties.

    *   When creating a new label (parameter) for a dimension, the **Common** discipline is automatically used because it includes basic data types like *Length*, *Text*, and *Number*. The *Discipline* option is grayed out since this is the only discipline compatible with dimensions. Similarly, the *Data Type* field is also grayed out because it is determined by the type of dimension you are using. For example, if you select an angular dimension and create a new label, the *Data Type* will automatically be set to **Angle** and cannot be changed.

    *   When naming a parameter, it is good practice to use title casing and a short name without abbreviations. Parameters are case sensitive. Do not use any symbols that are considered a math function, like -, /, +, and *, as this will cause problems when adding formulas later.

Figure 4–14

5. Select **Type** or **Instance**.

- **Type** applies it to all instances of a family when it is inserted into a project. To modify it, you need to change the Type Properties.

- **Instance** applies it to individual instance when inserted into a project. It can be modified directly in Properties.

- For an instance property, if you want the dimension information to be used in a formula or placed in a schedule, select **Reporting Parameter**.

6. Click **Edit Tooltip...** to add a tooltip description, if required.

7. Click **OK**. The dimension is labeled and ready to be flexed.

Note: If you add too many labeled dimensions to the same geometry, the software warns that you have over-constrained the sketch. You cannot ignore this warning. The label is not created in this case.

- You can change the label to be a type or instance parameter. Select the related dimension in the view and in the *Modify Dimensions* tab>*Label Dimension* panel, select either

  ⬚ (Instance) or ⬚ (Type). This can also be modified in the *Family Types* dialog box by selecting the parameter and clicking **Edit**. The *Family Types* dialog box is discussed further in the next sections.

Flexing Geometry

Once you have established dimensions and labeled them, you need to verify that the parameters work correctly with each other. To do this, flex the geometry by changing the value of a dimension (as shown in Figure 4–15), or using the *Family Types* dialog box.

Figure 4–15

- You may find that you need to lock a dimension to keep it from moving when a family gets flexed or if you need to keep a specific dimension fixed.

- Select the labeled dimension and then the dimension value to change it.

- To see all of the values you can flex at one time and to add formulas and non-dimension parameters, you need to work in the *Family Types* dialog box.

How To: Flex the Geometry in the Family Types Dialog Box

1. In the *Create* or *Modify* tab>*Properties* panel, click ▣ (Family Types). The *Family Types* dialog box displays, as shown in Figure 4–16.

   Note: You might have to move the dialog box to view what you are adjusting.

Family Types			✕
Type name:			
Search parameters			
Parameter	Value	Formula	Lock
Constraints			
Default Elevation	0' 0"	=	☐
Dimensions			
TrimWidth (default)	3' 2"	=	☐
Wall Edge to Door Opening	3' 2"	=	☐
Wall To Window	3' 2"	=	☐
IFC Parameters			
Type IFC Predefined Type		=	
Export Type to IFC As		=	
Identity Data			

Figure 4–16

2. Change the parameters and click **Apply**.

3. Does the geometry or reference planes/lines move correctly? Try several modifications.

4. Set the parameters and click **OK** to finish the command.

- If there is a check mark in the *Lock* column, this means that you are locking the constraint of that parameter.

- When you open a family file, Revit automatically checks the constraints in the family. If there are any issues, a dialog box offers information.

Creating and Modifying Parameters

In addition to creating labels (parameters specifically for dimensions), you can add dimension parameters that can be used when adding labels or parameters that store other information, such as the material of the element (as shown in Figure 4–17), the wattage of a light fixture, or the reinforcement cover setting in concrete. You can also add formulas to parameters so that they change when a related parameter changes.

Figure 4–17

- Instance parameters include (default) after the name, as shown in Figure 4–17. The assigned value is then used when the component is inserted into a project. It can be changed in Properties when the component is selected.

- The *Family Types* dialog box contains options for editing, creating, and organizing parameters, as shown in Figure 4–18.

Figure 4–18

	Edit Parameter	Displays the *Parameter Properties* dialog box, where you can change the name, group, or tooltip, or switch between **Type** and **Instance**. You can also change the parameter to reference a shared parameter. If a family template has built-in parameters, you cannot edit them and the information will be grayed out.
	New Parameter	Opens the *Parameter Properties* dialog box, where you can set up a new parameter.
	Add Parameter From Service	Use this feature to manage shared parameters. Parameters can be stored and imported from anywhere using Autodesk Construction Cloud.

	Duplicate Parameter	Creates a duplicate of the selected parameter. This is not applicable for shared parameters.
	Delete parameter	Removes the selected parameter. If a family template has built-in parameters, you cannot delete them.
↑E , ↓E	Move parameter up/down	Enables you to organize the parameters in each group.
↓Z , ↑Z	Sort parameters in ascending/descending order	Sets the order of the parameters to alphabetical order and removes any changes you might have made.

How To: Create Parameters

1. In the Family Editor, in the *Create* or *Modify* tab>*Properties* panel, click ▦ (Family Types).

2. In the *Family Types* dialog box, click ▭ (New Parameter).

   *Note: Shared parameters are covered in **6.4 Working with Shared Parameters** in **Chapter 6 Additional Family Types**.*

3. In the *Parameter Properties* dialog box, set up the *Parameter Data* (as shown in Figure 4–19) and click **OK**.

   *Note: The Discipline can be set to **Common**, **Structural**, **HVAC**, **Electrical**, **Piping**, **Energy**, or **Infrastructure**. The Data Type list changes according to the discipline.*

Figure 4–19

Common Parameter Types

Area	Establishes the area of an element. It is numeric and can have formulas applied to it.
Angle	Establishes the angle of an element. It is numeric and can have formulas applied to it.
Cost per Area	Defines cost per area for any element or subcomponent.
Currency	Displays the amount in dollars or other currencies, as set up in the Field Format.
Distance	Used to create a numerical distant parameter.
<Family Type>	Opens a dialog box where you can select from the list of family types, such as doors, furniture, or tags.
Image	Creates a parameter at which you can add a raster image connected to the family.
Integer	Any value that is always represented by a whole number. Examples could be the number of chairs that fit around a conference table or the number of shelves in a bookcase.
Length	When you label dimensions, you create **Length** parameters. You can use formulas with **Length** parameters.
Mass Density	Displays the mass per unit volume of material.
Material	Provides a place to assign a material from the list of materials that are set up in the project.
Multiline Text	Used when the use of longer multiline text strings is needed.
Number	Any numeric value: whole, decimal, or fraction. You can use formulas with **Number** parameters.
Rotation Angle	Establishes an element or subcomponents rotation angle.
Slope	Displays a slope, as set in the Field Format.
Speed	Used to define a speed related parameter.
Text	A text parameter can host any type of information that consists of both numbers and letters. Examples could be the fabric color or part number of the element.
Time	Used to define a time related parameter.
URL	Specifies a link to a web site.
Volume	Establishes the volume of an element. It is numeric and can have formulas applied to it.
Yes/No	Used with instance parameters where you need a **Yes** or **No** answer to a question listed in the name. The default is **Yes**.

How To: Add Formulas to Parameters

1. In the *Create* or *Modify* tab>*Properties* panel, click ▣ (Family Types).

2. In the *Family Types* dialog box, in the *Formula* column, add formulas to the parameters. In the example shown in Figure 4–20, the *Shelf Height* is defined as the **Height** divided by **4**. When you change the *Shelf Height* or *Height*, the other value updates according to the formula.

Dimensions			⌃
Depth	2' 0"	=	☑
Height	6' 0"	=	☑
ShelfHeight	1' 6"	= Height / 4	☑
TrimWidth	0' 2"	=	☐
Width	4' 0"	=	☑

Figure 4–20

You can use several types of formulas with families:

Arithmetic	Basic arithmetic operations in formulas include addition (+), subtraction (-), multiplication (*), division (/), exponentiation, logarithms, and square roots.
Trigonometric	Trigonometric functions include sine, cosine, tangent, arcsine, arccosine, and arctangent.
Conditional	Conditional functions include comparisons in a condition (e.g., <, >, =, etc.) and Boolean operators with a conditional statement (e.g., AND, OR, NOT, etc.). See the Autodesk Revit Help files for more information about creating conditional statements.

- You can enter numbers as integers, decimals, or fractions. Conditional statements can include numeric values, numeric parameter names, or **Yes/No** parameters.

- Formulas are case-sensitive. Therefore, if you have created a dimension label named **Height**, ensure that the formula that uses this label also has the H capitalized (e.g., **Height * 2**).

> 💡 **Hint: Formulas in Projects**
>
> You can use a formula to specify the length of a wall by typing it in the temporary dimension. Start with an equal sign (e.g., =12 / 3 + 4). The example shown in Figure 4–21 returns the number 8 (interpreted as 8'-0") in the dimension. Formulas also work with numerical values in Properties.

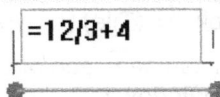

=12/3+4

Figure 4–21

Practice 4a
Set Up a Bookcase Family

Practice Objectives

- Add reference planes.
- Dimension and label reference planes.
- Add a formula to a parameter.
- Flex the framework.

In this practice, you will create a family file based on a template and view the existing reference planes. You will also create reference planes, dimension them, and label the dimensions, as shown in Figure 4–22. You will add a formula to control a parameter and then test the framework by changing parameter values.

Figure 4–22

Task 1: Open a family template.

1. Close all open projects.
2. On the Home page, under the *Families* area, click **New…**.
3. In the *New Family - Select Template File* dialog box, select the template **Furniture.rft** from the practice files *Architectural>RFT* folder and click **Open**.
4. In the *View* tab>*Windows* panel, click ▢▢ (Tile) (or type **WT**).
5. The four open views display so you can see each of them. Type **ZA** (the shortcut for **Zoom All to Fit**) to fit the view in all of the windows.
6. Two existing reference planes are included in the file, as well as **Ref.Level**.
7. Save the family in the practice files *Architectural> RFA* folder as **Barrister Bookcase.rfa**.

Task 2: Create plan view reference planes.

1. Click inside the **Ref. Level** view and type **TW** to maximize the view.
2. Create four new reference planes, one on each side of the existing planes, as shown in Figure 4–23. Do not worry about the exact location yet.

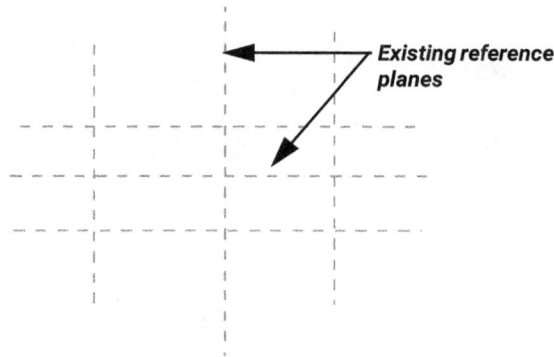

Figure 4–23

3. Add dimensions between each reference plane across the top and side, and then an overall dimension, as shown in Figure 4–24. Set the interior dimensions to **Equal**.

    Note: Your dimensions might vary depending on where you originally placed the reference planes.

Figure 4–24

4. Select the overall horizontal dimension. In the *Modify | Dimensions* tab>*Label Dimension* panel, click ⬚ (Create Parameter).
5. In the *Parameter Properties* dialog box, leave the **Parameter Type** to Family parameter. In the *Parameter Data* area, ensure that **Type** is selected and then type the name **Width**. Verify the *Group parameter under:* is set to **Dimensions**. Click **OK**.
6. Repeat the process for the overall vertical dimension and name the parameter **Depth**.

7. Select the *Width* dimension and click on the text. Change it to **3'-0"**. Repeat the process and set the *Depth* to **1'-4"**, as shown in Figure 4–25.

Figure 4–25

8. Create one more horizontal reference plane **1"** inside the front reference plane.

9. Select the reference plane, then select **<Click to name>** and name the reference plane **Door Face**, as shown in Figure 4–26.

Figure 4–26

10. Click in an empty area in the view to deselect the reference plane.

11. Dimension and lock the dimension in place, as shown in Figure 4–27.

Figure 4–27

12. Zoom out to see all the reference planes.

13. Flex the framework using the Family Editor. In the *Create* or *Modify* tab>*Properties* panel, click ⬛ (Family Types). Change the *Width* dimension to **3'-6"** and the *Depth* dimension to **1'-1"**. Click **OK**.

14. Verify that the other reference planes have remained in place.

15. Save the family file.

Task 3: Create front view reference planes.

1. Open the **Elevations: Front** view.

2. Create the reference planes and dimensions and label them, as shown in Figure 4–28.

Figure 4–28

- Each of the shelf height dimensions must be separate. Once you have created one shelf height parameter, you can apply the same label to the other dimensions.

3. In the *Modify* (or *Create*) tab>*Properties* panel, click ⬛ (Family Types).

4. In the *Family Types* dialog box, in the *Formula* column, set the formula for the *Shelf Height* to **(Height - Base) / 4**, as shown in Figure 4–29.

5. In the *Lock* column, check the checkbox for the ***Height*** parameter and note that the related *Base* and *Shelf Height* parameters also lock.

    Note: *The parameters automatically display in alphabetical order. You can reorganize them as required.*

Parameter	Value	Formula	Lock
Dimensions			^
Base	0' 4"	=	☑
Depth	1' 1"	=	☐
Height	6' 0"	=	☑
Shelf Height	1' 5"	= (Height - Base) / 4	☑
Width	4' 0"	=	☐

Family Types

Type name:

Search parameters

Figure 4–29

6. Move the dialog box to one side and try several different values for the parameters. Click **Apply** to apply the changes to the family. Verify that all of the reference planes move together. Click **OK**.

7. Save and close the family file.

End of practice

Practice 4b
Set Up a Heat Pump Family

Practice Objectives

- Add reference planes.
- Dimension and label reference planes.
- Add a formula to a parameter.
- Flex the framework.

In this practice, you will create a family file based on a template and view the existing reference planes. You will also create reference planes, dimension them, label the dimensions, as shown on the left in Figure 4–30, and use a formula in parameters, as shown on the right.

Width = 38 7/8"	CenterY = 17 3/8"
	Depth = 34 3/4"
CenterX = 17 3/8"	

Family Types ✕

Type name:

Search parameters

Parameter	Value	Formula	Lock
Constraints			
Default Elevation	0"	=	☐
Dimensions			
CenterX	17 3/8"	=CenterY	☐
CenterY	17 3/8"	=Depth / 2	☐
Depth	34 3/4"	=	☐
Height	45"	=	☐
Width	38 7/8"	=	☐

Figure 4–30

Task 1: Open a family template.

1. Close all open projects.

2. On the Home screen, under the *FAMILIES* area, click **New...**.

3. In the *New Family - Select Template File* dialog box, select the template **Mechanical Equipment.rft** from the practice files *MEP>RFT* folder and click **Open**.

4. In the *View* tab>*Windows* panel, click ☐ (Tile), or type **WT.**

5. The four open views display. Type **ZA** to fit the view in all of the windows. Two existing reference planes are included in the file, as well as **Ref. Level**.

6. Type **UN** to open the *Project Units* dialog box. In the *Format* column, click the value next to *Length*.

7. In the *Format* dialog box, change the *Units* to **Fractional inches**, then set the *Rounding* to **To the nearest 1/8"** and the *Unit symbol* to ".

---

8. Click **OK** until all of the dialog boxes are closed.

9. Save the family in the practice files *MEP>RFA* folder as **Heat Pump.rfa**.

Task 2: Create plan view reference planes.

1. Click inside the **Ref. Level** view and type **TW** to maximize the view.

2. Create two new reference planes, one above and one to the right of the existing planes, as shown in Figure 4–31. Do not worry about the exact location yet.

Existing reference planes

Figure 4–31

3. Add the dimensions shown in Figure 4–32.

Note: Your dimensions might vary depending on where you originally placed the reference planes. The scale in the graphics have been changed to display the dimensions more clearly.

Figure 4–32

4. Select the horizontal dimension. In the *Modify | Dimensions* tab>*Label Dimension* panel, click ▤ (Create Parameter).

5. In the *Parameter Properties* dialog box, in the *Parameter Data* area, ensure that **Type** is selected and then type the name **Width**. Click **OK**.

6. Repeat the process for the overall vertical dimension and name the parameter **Depth**.

7. Add two more reference planes inside the other reference planes. Dimension and label them as shown in Figure 4–33.

Note: These new dimensions are not at the center of the unit but a specific distance from the right side and the top reference planes. The exact distance is not required at this time.

Figure 4–33

8. Open the Elevations: **Front** view.

9. Create the reference planes and dimensions shown in Figure 4–34. Name the top and bottom reference planes **Top of Unit** and **Top of Base**. Label the *Height* dimension and lock the **1"** and **EQ** dimensions into place. Do not lock the top **1"** dimensions.

   • Note that you might need to zoom in to do this.

Figure 4–34

10. Save the family.

Task 3: Flex the parameters.

1. Remain in elevation view.

2. Select the ***Height*** parameter dimension and change it to a different height. Verify that the top dimensions moves with the height and the bottom one stays in place.

3. Try a different height to fully check it.

4. Return to the **Floor Plans: Ref. Level** view.

5. In the *Modify* (or *Create*) tab>*Properties* panel, click ▦ (Family Types).

6. In the *Family Types* dialog box, set up a formula for *CenterY* and *CenterX*, as shown in Figure 4–35. Lock one of the center parameters and the related parameters also lock.

Figure 4–35

7. Move the dialog box to one side and try several different values. Click **Apply** to apply the changes to the family. Verify that all of the reference planes move together. Click **OK**.

8. Save and close the family file.

End of practice

Practice 4c
Set Up a Structural Column Family

Practice Objectives

- Add reference planes and reference lines.
- Add dimensions and labels.
- Add a formula to a parameter.

In this practice, you will create a family file based on a template and view the existing reference planes. You will also create reference lines and reference planes, dimension them, label the dimensions, as shown in Figure 4–36, and use a formula in parameters.

Figure 4–36

Task 1: Open a family template.

1. Close all open projects.
2. On the Home screen, under the *FAMILIES* area, click **New...**.
3. In the *New Family - Select Template File* dialog box, select the template **Structural Column.rft** from the practice files *Structural>RFT* folder and click **Open**.
4. Open a 3D view and the **Elevations: Front** views.
5. In the *View* tab>*Windows* panel, click ▦ (Tile) or type **WT.** The three open views display so you can see each of them. Type **ZA** (the shortcut for **Zoom All to Fit**) to fit the view in all of the windows.

6. Several existing reference planes and some dimensions are included in the file, as well as **Lower Ref.Level** and **Upper Ref. Level**, which set the height of the column once it is used in a project.

7. Save the family in the practice files *Structural>RFA* folder as **Y-Column.rfa**.

Task 2: Create reference planes.

1. Click inside the **Lower Ref. Level** view and type **TW** to maximize the view.

2. Add an overall dimension across the top and side, as shown in Figure 4–37.

Figure 4–37

3. Click ⬚ (Modify).

4. Select the overall horizontal dimension. In the *Modify | Dimensions* tab>*Label Dimension* panel, click ⬚ (Create Parameter).

5. In the *Parameter Properties* dialog box, in the *Parameter Data* area, ensure that **Type** is selected and then type the name **Base Width**. Click **OK**.

6. Repeat the process for the overall vertical dimension and name the parameter **Base Depth**. The labels display as shown in Figure 4–38.

Figure 4–38

7. Add the additional reference planes along with the EQ and overall dimensions and label for *Top Depth* horizontally, and *Top Width* vertically, shown in Figure 4–39.

Figure 4–39

8. Add two more reference planes vertically along with the EQ and overall dimensions and label for *Column Depth,* as shown in Figure 4–40.

Figure 4–40

9. Save the family file.

Task 3: Set up formulas and flex the parametric framework.

1. In the *Create* or *Modify* tab>*Properties* panel, click ⬚ (Family Types).

2. In the *Family Types* dialog box, set the *Value* column and formulas as shown in Figure 4–41 and click **Apply**.

Parameter	Value	Formula	Lock
Materials and Finishes			⌃
Structural Material (default)		=	
Dimensions			⌃
Base Depth	2' 0"	=	☑
Base Width	2' 0"	=Base Depth	☑
Column Depth	1' 0"	=	☐
Top Depth	1' 4"	=Base Depth / 1.5	☑
Top Width	1' 4"	=Top Depth	☑

Figure 4–41

3. Change the *Base Depth* to **3'-0"** and click **Apply**. Verify that all of the reference planes update as expected.

4. Test other sizes.

5. Change the *Base Depth* back to **2'-0"** and click **OK**.

6. Save the family.

Task 4: Add a parametric framework to the elevation view.

1. Switch to the **Elevations: Front** view.

2. Change the *Upper Ref. Level* to **12'-0"**.

3. Extend the reference planes past the upper level marker.

   - If required, to modify the **Center (Left/Right)** reference plane, select the reference plane and click the ⊙ (Prevent or allow change of element position) icon. Once you have moved it, click the ⤴ (Prevent or allow change of element position) icon to repin it.

4. Add a reference plane and name it **Top of Base.**

5. Dimension and label the dimension as shown in Figure 4–42. Set the dimension to **1'-6"**.

Figure 4–42

6. In the *Create* tab>*Datum* panel, click ⺁ (Reference Line).

7. To draw a reference line from the intersection shown in Figure 4–43, hover your cursor over the intersection, right-click, and select **Snaps Overrides>Intersections**. When you see the intersections snap, click to place the reference line's start point. Draw the reference line at an angle past the **Upper Ref. Level**. The exact angle does not matter at this point.

8. Use the **Align** tool to align the end point of the reference line to the reference plane. If the point does not highlight, press <Tab> to cycle through the selection options.

Upper Ref. Level
12' - 0"

12' - 0"

Reference line

Lock the reference line to the vertical reference plane

Make sure you select the intersection of the reference planes

Base Height = 1'- 6"

0' - 4"
19.00°

Lower Ref. Level
0' - 0"

Figure 4–43

9. Repeat the process on the other side of the center line and add angular dimensions and labels, as shown in Figure 4–44.

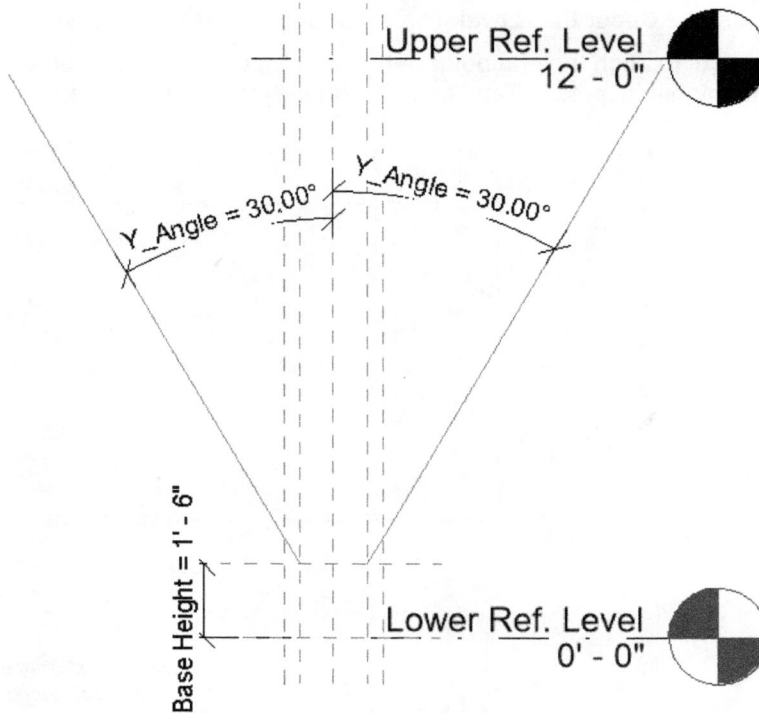

Figure 4–44

10. Flex the *Y_Angle* parameter and end on **30.00°**, and the *Base Height* parameter and end on **1'-6"**.

11. Save and close the family file.

End of practice

4.3 Creating Family Geometry

Once the parametric framework has been created and flexing has been done, and it is verified that it works as expected, it is recommended to add actual geometry to the family file, as shown in Figure 4–45. The components in a family can include 3D solids and voids, as well as 2D symbolic lines. You can also include model lines, model text, and annotation text.

Figure 4–45

Creating 3D Geometry

There are five methods of creating solid forms, as shown in Figure 4–46. Each method uses a sketched 2D profile as the basis of the 3D shape.

Figure 4–46

- **Extrusion** pushes the profile out in one direction.
- **Blend** links two profiles together.
- **Revolve** rotates the profile around an axis.
- **Sweep** extends a profile along a path.
- **Swept Blend** connects two different profiles along a path.

Note: Void forms use the same creation methods.

> **Hint: Selecting Void Forms**
>
> Solids and voids are considered separate categories. You can use the **Filter** command to select them separately, as shown in Figure 4–47.

Figure 4–47

Extrusions

Extrusions are the simplest geometry to create. All you need to do is draw a closed profile using Revit sketch tools and assign a depth for the extrusion, as shown in Figure 4–48.

Profile   *Extruded Solid*

Figure 4–48

How To: Create Solid Extrusions

1. In the *Create* tab>*Forms* panel, click ▣ (Extrusion).

2. In Properties, you can set the following:

    *   *Extrusion Start* and *Extrusion End:* By default, *Start* is at the work plane and *End* is at the depth, as shown in Figure 4–49.

    *   *Visible:* To control the visibility of the selected extrusion in a project, you can use the *Visible* checkbox, as shown in Figure 4–49. Checking it will show the extrusion, while unchecking it will hide the extrusion.

        *   For more flexibility, you can create and assign a **Yes/No** parameter to the *Visible* parameter. This creates a checkbox that allows users to easily turn the extrusion on or off when the family is loaded into a project. You will learn more about this feature in *Chapter 5 Advanced Family Techniques*.

Figure 4–49

- *Visibility/Graphics Overrides:* Click **Edit...** to specify what views the family will display and what it will look like once loaded into a project. You will learn more about this in *5.2 Visibility Display Settings* in *Chapter 5 Advanced Family Techniques*.

- *Subcategory:* If needed, you can specify a subcategory.

- *Solid/Void:* If needed, you can change the extrusion from a **Solid** to a **Void** or vice versa.

3. In the *Modify | Create Extrusion* tab>*Extrusion* panel, enter a value for the *Depth* of the extrusion.

   - A positive value for the depth extrudes up or toward you depending on the work plane. A negative value extrudes down or away from you.

4. In the *Modify | Create Extrusion* tab>*Draw* panel, use the sketch tools to create the profile for the extrusion. The extrusion profile must form a closed loop. You can add dimensions and reference planes as needed to create the profile. They will not display when the extrusion is finished.

5. If you need to create an extrusion on top of another or change the direction of the extrusion based on other geometry, you can set the work plane. In the *Modify | Create Extrusion* tab> *Work Plane* panel, click ▦ (Set Work Plane) to select the plane on which you want to draw.

6. In the *Mode* panel, click ✔ (Finish Edit Mode) to create the extrusion.

    *   To modify the extrusion, select the extrusion and in the *Modify | Extrusion* tab (shown in Figure 4–50), click **Edit Extrusion** (in the *Mode* panel) to go back into edit mode. You can also access the visibility/graphic overrides settings, change the depth of the extrusion, and edit the work plane.

Figure 4–50

Blends

Blends are defined by two 2D profile sketches: one for the base (bottom) and one for the top. The two sketches are blended together to create a solid 3D shape. The blend can be modified by either the top profile sketch or the bottom profile sketch, or by adjusting the vertex connection, as shown in Figure 4–51.

> **Note:** *If the entire blended element is not displayed in plan view, select the view name in the Project Browser, then modify the View Range Cut Plane in Properties.*

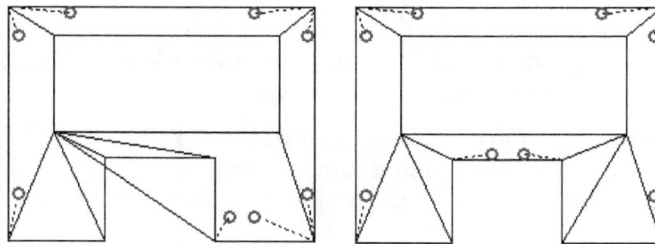

Figure 4–51

How To: Create Solid Blends

1. In the *Create* tab>*Forms* panel, click ⏢ (Blend).
2. In the *Modify | Create Blend Base Boundary* tab>*Draw* panel, use the sketch tools to draw the base profile.
3. In the *Mode* panel, click ⏢ (Edit Top).
4. In the *Blend* panel, set the *Depth* for the top.

5. In Properties, you can set the *Second End* and *First End, Visible* setting, *Subcategory, and Solid/Void* setting.

6. Draw the top profile using the sketch tools.

7. If the intersections are complex, click ⬡ (Edit Vertices) and ensure that all of the connections work correctly.

• When you click ⬡ (Edit Vertices), open blue dots display on the lines. These lines are suggested connections. Select the dot to toggle the connection on or off (as shown in Figure 4–52), and repeat with other corners to obtain the required connections. If needed, select one of the options to modify the vertices by ⟲ (Twist Right), ⟳ (Twist Left), ⬡ (Reset), ⬡ (Controls on Base), or ⬡ (Controls on Top).

Figure 4–52

8. In the *Modify | Create Blend* contextual tab>*Mode* panel, click ✔ (Finish Edit Mode) to create the blend.

9. The *Modify | Blend* tab displays with tools you can use to edit the base or the top. You also have access to the properties of the blend.

Revolves

A revolved solid form requires a 2D profile sketch and an axis around which it is revolved, as shown in Figure 4–53. The profile often needs to be sketched in a work plane perpendicular to the *ground*. Before sketching the profile, create a reference plane that you can use for the work plane. For example, if you are creating a dome, create two intersecting reference planes at the center of the dome and name them. Then, when you start the revolution, you can select one reference plane for your work plane and the other for your axis.

Note: You can name a reference plane in Properties.

Profile with axis   **Revolved solid**

Figure 4–53

How To: Create a Solid Revolve

1. In a view, draw a reference plane and give it a name so that you can use it when specifying a new work plane.

2. In the *Create* tab>*Forms* panel, click (Revolve).

3. In the *Modify | Create Revolve* tab>*Work Plane* panel, click (Set). In the *Work Plane* dialog box, select the plane on which you want to draw the profile. A prompt warns you if you need to change views to draw in that work plane.

4. In the *Draw* panel, click (Boundary Line) and draw the profile.

5. In the *Draw* panel, click (Axis Line) and draw or select the axis about which the profile will rotate.

    Note: The axis can be an edge of the profile or some distance away if there is an opening.

6. In Properties, edit the *End Angle* and *Start Angle* degree and any other properties, like *Visible*, *Visibility/Graphics Overrides*, *Material*, and *Subcategory*.

7. Click (Finish Edit Mode) to create the solid.

8. To edit the revolve, in the *Modify | Revolve* tab>*Mode* panel, select (Edit Revolve) to modify the boundary lines or axis line. You can also change the properties (such as the *End Angle* and *Start Angle*).

Sweeps

A sweep is a 3D shape that follows a defined path and can have multiple segments. Sweeps are created by sketching a 2D profile or using a loaded profile family, as shown in Figure 4–54. You define the path first and then create the profile on the path. If the path is moved or modified, the sweep will follow.

Profile

Path

Figure 4–54

How To: Create a Solid Sweep

1. In the *Create* tab>*Forms* panel, click (Sweep).
2. In the *Modify | Sweep* tab>*Sweep* panel, click (Sketch Path) or (Pick Path). Draw a path or select an edge or line you want the sweep to follow.
3. In Properties, modify the available options, if needed.
4. Click (Finish Edit Mode).
5. To select a profile, in the *Sweep* panel, expand the *Profile:* drop-down list and select a profile or click (Load Profile) to load additional profiles. The profile is added at the work planes' intersection.

   - For selected profiles only: To edit the profile's *Horizontal Profile Offset*, *Vertical Profile Offset*, *Angle*, or *Project is Flipped* parameters, click (Select Profile) in the *Sweep* panel. In Properties, modify the available parameters. Dimensions also display in the view at the intersection of the path and profile, as shown in Figure 4–55. You can manually enter a distance for the *Horizontal* and *Vertical Profile Offset* by clicking on the temporary dimension value and typing in a measurement.

Figure 4–55

6. To sketch a profile, set the *Profile:* drop-down list to **<By Sketch>**, then click (Edit Profile). In the Project Browser, open any view needed to sketch the profile, then in Properties, modify the available parameters as needed. Draw the profile for the sweep on the profile work plane, as shown in Figure 4-56.

- When you are ready to add a profile (shown in a 3D view in Figure 4-56), there will be a red dot and green dashed lines to act as visual indicators for your profile. The red dot represents the origin point where the profile and path intersect, while the green lines represent the work plane where you will sketch the profile.

Figure 4-56

7. Click (Finish Edit Mode) twice to complete the process.

8. The *Modify | Sweep* tab displays, where you can edit the sweep. In Properties, you can change several options of the profile along with the other standard options.

Swept Blends

A swept blend combines the Sweep and Blend tools. It consists of a path and, instead of one profile, you have the option to specify two profiles, as shown in Figure 4–57. The path must be one segment, which can be a line, an arc, or a spline. The profiles can be sketched or a loaded profile family can be selected. Both profiles can be different shapes.

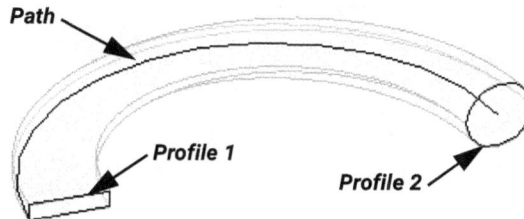

Figure 4–57

How To: Create Solid Swept Blends

1. In the *Create* tab>*Forms* panel, click (Swept Blend).
2. In the *Modify | Swept Blend* tab>*Swept Blend* panel, click (Sketch Path) or (Pick Path). Draw or select the path you want the swept blend to follow. You can only have one segment in the path.
3. Click (Finish Edit Mode).
4. In the *Swept Blend* panel, click (Select Profile 1).
5. Select a profile from the list or create a new profile using (Edit Profile).
6. In Properties, modify the parameters as needed.
7. Click (Finish Edit Mode).
8. Click (Select Profile 2) and repeat the process. It does not need to be the same size or shape as the first profile.
9. Click (Finish Edit Mode).
10. In the *Swept Blend* panel, click (Edit Vertices). The tools are the same as when creating a blend.
11. In the *Modify | Swept Blend* tab>*Mode* panel, click (Finish Edit Mode).

Aligning and Locking Geometry

It is important to lock and align sketches to reference planes (rather than other family elements) so that they can be flexed parametrically. The padlock symbol displays when you snap to reference planes while drawing. Select the padlock to lock the element to the reference plane, as shown in Figure 4–58.

Figure 4–58

- When using the (Pick Line) option, in the Options Bar, you can select **Lock** to automatically lock the sketch line to the selected reference plane.

- You can also use the **Align** command to align and lock elements to reference planes.

- You can temporarily hide other elements before sketching to ensure that you only work with the reference planes.

- Tangency Locks display when you add arcs that are tangent to other lines, as shown in Figure 4–59. Close the padlock to keep the tangency as the element is flexed.

Figure 4–59

Practice 4d
Create Family Geometry for the Bookcase

Practice Objectives

- Create solid extrusion elements.
- Align and lock the elements to reference planes.
- Join the geometry of elements.

In this practice, you will create extruded solids for the base, frame, shelves, and back of a bookcase, and lock them in place with dimensions. You will also join the solid elements together to form one unit, as shown in Figure 4–60.

Figure 4–60

Task 1: Create a base for the bookcase.

1. In the practice files *Architectural>RFA* folder, open **Barrister-Bookcase-Geometry.rfa**.
2. Open the **Floor Plans: Ref. Level** view.
3. In the *Create* tab>*Forms* panel, click ▢ (Extrusion).
4. In the *Modify | Create Extrusion* tab>*Extrusion* panel, set the *Depth* to **4"**.

5. In the *Modify | Create Extrusion* tab>*Draw* panel, use the sketch tools to draw a rectangle across the outside intersections of the reference planes, as shown in Figure 4–61.

    • **Hint:** Type **SI** to force the snap to the intersection of the reference planes.

6. In the *Modify* tab>*Modify* panel, click ▦ (Align). In the *Align* panel, check the checkbox next to **Lock**. Align the four sketch lines to their respective reference planes, as shown in Figure 4–61.

    *Note: If you use the **Pick Lines** tool, you can set it to automatically lock on the Options Bar.*

Figure 4–61

7. In the *Modify | Create Extrusion* tab>*Mode* panel, click ✔ (Finish Edit Mode).

8. Open the **Elevations: Front** view.

9. Align the top of the extrusion to the *Base* reference plane and lock it, as shown in Figure 4–62.

Figure 4–62

10. Open the *Family Types* dialog box and flex the *Base* parameter to verify the extrusion follows the changes in size correctly.

11. Save the family.

Task 2: Create the frame and shelves for the bookcase.

1. Continue working in the **Front** view.

2. In the *Create* tab>*Work Plane* panel, click ⊞ (Set).

3. In the *Work Plane* dialog box, set the *Name* to **Reference Plane : Door Face** and click **OK**.

4. Start the **Extrusion** command.

5. In the *Create* tab>*Datum* panel, draw four reference planes **2"** inside the existing reference planes for the outer frames. Dimension and label them as shown in Figure 4–63.

    *   Ensure that you dimension to the reference planes and not any existing geometry.

    Note: Drawing the reference planes inside the extrusion creation helps to keep the primary views from getting cluttered.

Figure 4–63

6. Before drawing the extrusion, in the *Family Types* dialog box, flex the *Height* and *Width* of the overall bookcase to verify that the new *Frame Width* parameters move as expected.

7. Return to the *Modify | Create Extrusion* tab>*Draw* panel and select **Rectangle**.

8. In the *Modify | Create Extrusion* tab>*Extrusion* panel, set the *Depth* to **1'-0"**.

9. Draw and lock two rectangular sketches to the reference planes, as shown in Figure 4–64.

Figure 4–64

10. Click ✔ (Finish Edit Mode).

11. Start the **Extrusion** command again.

12. Draw two reference planes **1/2"** on either side of the three shelf height reference planes.

13. To make the labels more readable, change the scale to **1"=1'-0"**.

14. Create an equal and an overall dimension, then create and add a label as shown in Figure 4–65. Repeat with the other two shelf height locations.

Figure 4–65

*Note: You can edit the existing dimension type by duplicating it and in the Type Properties dialog box, in the Text section, setting the Read Convention to **Horizontal**. Use the new type for the **Shelf** Thickness parameter so it reads horizontally, as shown above in Figure 4–65.*

15. In the *Modify | Create Extrusion* tab>*Draw* panel, select **Rectangle**.

16. In the *Modify | Create Extrusion* tab>*Extrusion* panel, ensure that the *Depth* is set to **1'-0"**.

17. Draw the sketch around each shelf (as shown in Figure 4–66) using the **Rectangle** draw tool. Ensure that you lock the sketches to the reference planes.

Figure 4–66

18. Click ✔ (Finish Edit Mode).

19. Open the *Family Types* dialog box and move the *Height*, *Width*, and *Depth* to the top of the parameters list by selecting each parameter and clicking ⬆E (Move parameter up).

20. Flex the *Height* and *Width* of the overall bookcase to verify the new **Shelf Thickness** parameters move as expected. Finish the flexing with the *Height* set to **5'-0"** and the *Width* to **3'-0"**.

21. Save the family.

Task 3: Create the back of the bookcase.

1. Open the **Elevations: Left** view.

2. Align and lock the back of the frame and shelf extrusions to the back reference plane (on the left).

3. Open the **Floor Plans: Ref. Level** view.

4. Start the **Extrusion** command again.

5. Add a reference plane **1/4"** from the back of the bookcase. Dimension it and lock the dimension in place, as shown in Figure 4−67.

    Note: Create a label if you want to change the size of the back.

Figure 4−67

6. Return to the *Modify | Create Extrusion* tab and select **Rectangle**.

7. In the *Modify | Create Extrusion* tab>*Extrusion* panel, set the *Depth* to **2'-6"**. (This is less than the bookcase height. You will adjust it later.)

8. Draw a rectangular sketch across the back and lock the four sides of the extrusion to the reference planes, as shown in Figure 4−68.

Figure 4−68

9. Click ✔ (Finish Edit Mode).

10. Open the **Elevations: Left** view. If needed, switch the *Visual Style* to ⬡ (Hidden Line). The back extrusion is shown in Figure 4–69.

Figure 4–69

11. Align and lock the top of the back panel with the top reference plane, as shown in Figure 4-70.

Figure 4-70

12. Switch to a 3D view. If needed, set the *Visual Style* to **Hidden Lines** and rotate it. The base, frame, shelves, and back are all separate elements, as shown in Figure 4-71.

Figure 4–71

13. In the *Modify* tab>*Geometry* panel, click (Join) and join the four elements. The bookcase should display as shown in Figure 4–72.

Figure 4–72

14. Save and close the family.

End of practice

Practice 4e
Create Family Geometry for the Heat Pump

Practice Objective

* Create extrusions and blends.

In this practice, you will create extruded and blended solids for the base, cabinet, top, and fan unit of a heat pump, as shown in Figure 4−73.

Figure 4−73

Task 1: Create the main cabinet of a heat pump.

1. In the practice files *MEP>RFA* folder, open **Heat Pump-Geometry.rfa**.

2. Ensure that the **Floor Plans: Ref. Level** view is open.

3. Add four reference planes **3"** to the inside of each exterior reference plane. Dimension and lock the dimensions into place, as shown in Figure 4−74.

4. In the *Create* tab>*Datum* panel, click ⌐ (Reference Line).

5. In the Options Bar, toggle off **Chain**.

6. Draw an angled reference line at each of the four corners, as shown in Figure 4–74. Ensure that you lock any open padlocks that display as you draw each line. There should be two locks for each reference line you draw.

    *   **Hint:** Type **SI** to force the snap to the intersection of the reference planes.

Figure 4–74

7. Open the *Family Types* dialog box and flex the framework by changing the *Width* and *Depth*.

8. In the *Create* tab>*Work Plane* panel, click ▦ (Set).

9. In the *Work Plane* dialog box, set *Name* as **Reference Plane : Top of Base** and click **OK**.

10. In the *Create* tab>*Forms* panel, click ⬚ (Extrusion). In the *Modify | Create Extrusion* tab> *Extrusion* panel, set the *Depth* to **30"**.

11. Sketch and lock the shape to the reference lines shown in Figure 4–75.

   - **Hint:** Use **Pick Lines** with the **Lock** option set, or in the *Modify* tab>*Modify* panel, click

     (Align). In the *Align* panel, check the checkbox next to **Lock** and then trim the excess, as required.

Figure 4–75

12. Click ✓ (Finish Edit Mode).

13. Open the **Elevations: Front** view. Align and lock the top of the unit extrusion to the **Top of Unit** reference plane, as shown in Figure 4–76. Note that the bottom of the three reference planes is the Top of Unit reference plane.

Figure 4–76

14. Save the family.

Task 2: Create the top and base of the heat pump.

1. Return to the **Floor Plans: Ref. Level** view.

2. Use **Temporary Hide/Isolate** to hide the existing extrusion.

3. Set the Work Plane to the **Top of Unit** reference plane.

4. In the *Create* tab>*Forms* panel, click 🔲 (Blend).

5. In the *Modify | Create Blend Base Boundary* tab>*Draw* panel, click ⟍ (Pick Lines).

6. In the *Modify | Create Blend Base Boundary* tab>*Blend* panel, set the *Depth* to **1/2"** and the *Offset* to **1"**. Verify **Lock** is unchecked.

7. Position the offset inside the reference planes and click on the outer-most reference planes and reference lines. Use **Trim/Extend to Corner** to clean up the sketch for the base, as shown in Figure 4–77.

8. Click 🔲 (Edit Top). Select ⟍ (Pick Lines), and then set the *Depth* to **1/2"** and the *Offset* to **1 1/2"**.

9. Use and trim the same reference planes and reference lines to create a sketch for the top, as shown in Figure 4–77.

   Note: Using reference planes to establish the sketch of the blend, rather than other elements, ensures the accuracy of the elements.

Figure 4–77

10. Click ✔ (Finish Edit Mode).

11. Flex the framework to ensure that the blend is working.

12. Return to the **Floor Plans: Ref. Level** view, if you switched to a 3D view.

13. Use **Temporary Hide/Isolate** to hide the existing blend.

14. Set the *Work Plane* to **Level: Ref. Level**.

15. In the *Create* tab>*Forms* panel, click 🗇 (Extrusion). In the *Modify | Create Extrusion* tab> *Extrusion* panel, set the *Depth* to **1"**.

16. In the *Modify | Create Extrusion* tab>*Draw* panel, use the ⬍ (Pick Lines) tool to draw a boundary at **1/2"** inside the unit reference planes, as shown in Figure 4–78 (the figure has been enhanced for clarity).

Unit reference planes

Figure 4–78

17. Click ✔ (Finish Edit Mode).

18. Reset Temporary Hide/Isolate.

19. Open the **Elevations: Front** view.

20. Temporarily hide the main cabinet extrusion.

21. In the *Modify* tab>*Modify* panel, click 🗔 (Align) and align the top of the base extrusion to the second plane from the top and lock it, as shown in Figure 4–79.

Figure 4–79

22. Reset Temporary Hide/Isolate.

23. Open a 3D view.

24. Open the *Family Types* dialog box and reorder the parameters so that *Width, Height,* and *Depth* are at the top by selecting each parameter and clicking ↑E (Move parameter up).

25. Flex the dimensions to check that everything is working as expected. If one of the solid elements is not working as expected, check all of the alignments to ensure that they are locked in place.

26. Save the family.

Task 3: Add the fan.

1. Return to the **Floor Plans: Ref. Level** view.

2. Set the Work Plane to the **Top of Unit** reference plane.

3. Start the **Extrusion** command and in the *Modify | Create Extrusion* tab>*Extrusion* panel, set the *Depth* to **1"**.

4. Draw a circle from the intersection of the CenterX and CenterY reference planes with a radius close to the outside, as shown in Figure 4–80. The exact dimension does not matter for this step.

- **Hint:** To turn off snaps, type **SO**; to turn it back on, type **SO** again.

Figure 4–80

5. Dimension the radius of the circle and create a new label based on the dimension named **Radius of Fan**.

6. Open the *Family Types* dialog box and move the **Radius of Fan** parameter below all of the others.

7. Next to **Radius of Fan**, in the *Formula* area, type **Depth / 2 - 1"**.

8. Click **Apply**.

9. Flex the element by changing the *Depth*. When it works as expected, click **OK**.

10. Click ✔ (Finish Edit Mode).

11. Open the **Elevations: Front** view. Hide the blend at the top of the unit, then make sure to reset when finished.

12. Align and lock the top of the fan to the top reference plane (as shown in Figure 4–81), and the bottom of the fan to the **Top of Unit** reference plane.

Figure 4–81

13. In the *Modify* tab>*Geometry* panel, click (Join).

14. Join the unit and the beveled blend together, then join the fan to the unit and the base to the unit.

15. View the unit in 3D, as shown in Figure 4–82.

Figure 4–82

16. Save and close the family file.

End of practice

Practice 4f
Create Family Geometry for the Structural Column

Practice Objectives

- Create a blend and an extrusion.
- Add dimensions and labels.

In this practice, you will create a blended extruded solid for the base and an extruded Y-framework of the column. You will lock the geometry to the reference planes and lines and flex the parameters of the column. The final version is shown in Figure 4–83.

Figure 4–83

Task 1: Create a base for the column.

1. In the practice files *Structural>RFA* folder, open **Y-Column-Geometry.rfa**.

2. Ensure you are in the **Floor Plans: Lower Ref. Level** view.

3. In the *Create* tab>*Work Plane* panel, click ▦ (Set).

4. In the *Work Plane* dialog box, set *Name* as **Level : Lower Ref. Level** and click **OK**.

5. In the *Create* tab>*Forms* panel, click ⬢ (Blend). In the *Modify | Create Blend Base Boundary* tab>*Blend* panel, set the *Depth* as **1'-0"**.

6. Use the **Rectangle** option to add and lock the sketch based on the *Base Width* and *Base Depth*, as shown in Figure 4–84.

    *   **Hint:** Type **SI** to force the snap to the intersection of the reference planes.

Figure 4–84

7. In the *Modify | Create Blend Base Boundary* tab>*Mode* panel, click ◇ (Edit Top).

8. Sketch and lock a rectangle based on the *Top Depth* and *Top Width*, as shown in Figure 4–85.

9. If needed, in the *Modify* tab>*Modify* panel, click ⬒ (Align). In the *Align* panel, check the checkbox next to **Lock**. Align the four sketch lines to their respective reference planes.

Figure 4–85

10. Click ✓ (Finish Edit Mode).

11. Open the **Elevations: Front** view.

12. Set the *Visual Style* to **Shaded**.

13. In the *Modify* tab>*Modify* panel, click 🔲 (Align) and verify **Lock** is checked. Align the top of the blend to the **Top of Base** reference plane (as shown in Figure 4–86).

14. Open the *Family Types* dialog box and flex the *Base Height* parameter to verify the extrusion follows the changes in size correctly.

Figure 4–86

15. Save the family.

Task 2: Create the Y-frame for the column.

1. Continue working in the **Elevations: Front** view.

2. Temporarily hide the base blend element.

3. Add two reference lines to the inside of the existing angled lines, as shown in Figure 4–87.

   To create the reference lines, select the ⬉ (Pick Lines) tool, and in the Options Bar, select **Lock** and set the *Offset* to **1'-0"**, then click on the existing angled reference lines.

4. Align and lock the two new reference lines' end points to the **Top of Base** reference line, as shown in Figure 4–87.

Top of Base reference

Reference Lines : Reference Lines : Reference

Figure 4–87

5. Add a dimension between both angle reference lines and lock the dimension to maintain the **1'-0"** between the lines, as shown in Figure 4–88.

1'-0"

1'-0"

Base Height = 1' - 6"

Figure 4–88

6. Add the angled dimensions above the previous angled dimension, then apply labels as shown in Figure 4–89. Assign the labels one at a time. If you try to do both of them at the same time, the reference planes will move unexpectedly. Undo and try again.

Figure 4–89

7. Flex the *Y_Angle* parameter and finish by setting the angle to **30.00°**.

8. Start the **Extrusion** command.

9. Verify the work plane is set to **Center (Front/Back)** and in the *Modify | Create Extrusion* tab> *Extrusion* panel, set the *Depth* to **1'-0"**.

10. Draw the sketch shown in Figure 4–90 using the following instructions:

- Use ⛏ (Pick Lines) and in the Options Bar, select **Lock**.

- Use ◁▷ (Split Element) and ⌐ (Trim Element) to create the lines, as required.

- Ensure that the sketch is completely closed.

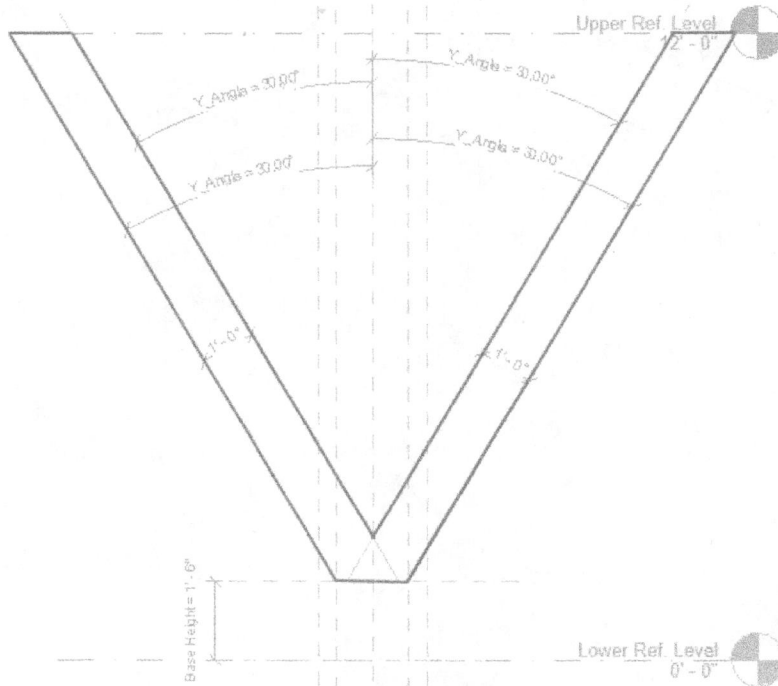

Figure 4–90

11. Click ✔ (Finish Edit Mode).

12. Flex the Y_Angle again to verify that the extrusion is moving with the angles.

13. Open the **Floor Plans: Lower Ref. Level** view.

14. Set the *Visual Style* to **Shaded**.

15. Align and lock the extrusion to the reference planes defined by the *Column Depth,* as shown in Figure 4-91. Flex the geometry for Column Depth to make sure it is working correctly.

Figure 4-91

16. Open the **3D Views: View 1** view.

17. Set the *Visual Style* to **Shaded**.

18. Rotate the view so you can see the Y framework and flex the parameters.

19. Save and close the family.

End of practice

4.4 Creating Family Types

An important aspect of family types is that it helps if you *flex* or test the parametric dimensions as you set them up. They also help you create formulas for parameters. A further use for family types is the ability to create preset sizes for a project. When you select the related command, the different types display in the Type Selector, as shown in Figure 4–92 for a dining table.

Figure 4–92

How To: Create Family Types

1. In the *Family Editor*, in the *Create* or *Modify* tab>*Properties* panel, click ⬒ (Family Types).

2. At the top of the *Family Types* dialog box, click 📄 (New Type), as shown Figure 4–93.

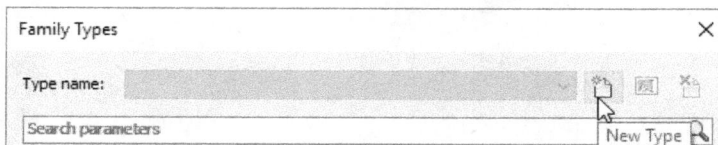

Figure 4–93

3. In the *Name* dialog box, type a name for the family type (as shown in Figure 4–94) and click **OK**.

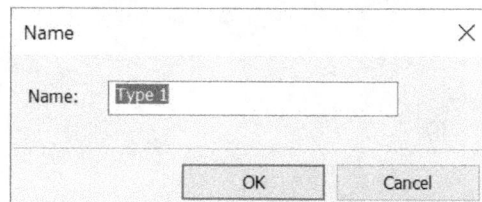

Figure 4–94

- Select a name that is useful for the entire set of types, typically a size.
  - The name of the family always precedes the name of the type. Therefore, you do not need to re-enter that information.

4. In the *Family Types* dialog box, set the *Value(s)* for that size (as shown in Figure 4–95) and click **Apply**.
   - You can type a part or all of a parameter's name to limit the number of parameters that display. This enables you to modify the values more quickly.

Figure 4–95

5. Repeat the process. You can create as many different types as you need.
6. Verify that all of the types are functioning correctly.
7. Click **OK** to finish the command.
8. Save the family.
9. Load the family into a test project and test the new types you have created.

- In the *Family Types* area, click [AI] (Rename Type) and (Delete Type), as required, to modify the list.

- To edit a type, select the type name, change the value(s), and click **Apply**.

> ### 💡 Hint: Exporting and Importing Family Types
>
> Family types can be exported to a text file and then imported into a related family. This can save you time when creating different versions of the same basic category.
>
> - In the *File* tab, expand ➡ (Export), scroll down and click ⬛ (Family Types). In the *Export As* dialog box, select a location and name. Click **Save**.
>
> - In the *Insert* tab>*Import* panel, click ⬛ (Import Family Types). In the *Import Family Types* dialog box, select the required text file and click **Open**.

Working with Families in Projects

To continue testing your family, it helps to see how it works in a project. You can load a family into one or more projects while in the Family Editor. You must have a project open before doing this.

How To: Load a Family into a Project

1. In the *Family Editor* panel, click 🔲 (Load into Project). The panel displays in all of the *Family Editor* tabs.

2. If only one project is open, the family is automatically loaded into it. If you have more than one project open, the *Load into Projects* dialog box opens. Select the project(s) to load into, as shown in Figure 4–96.

Figure 4–96

3. The project opens with the family loaded. Often, the related command is started with the new family selected in the Type Selector.

- If you have finished working on the family, you can click ⬛ (Load into Project and Close) when loading it into a project.

Practice 4g
Create Family Types for the Bookcase

Practice Objectives

- Create family types of different sizes.
- Test the family in a project.

In this practice, you will create family types for different sizes of the bookcase. You will then test the bookcase family in a project by placing each of the different types, as shown in Figure 4–97.

Figure 4–97

Task 1: Create family types.

1. In the practice files *Architectural*>RFA folder, open **Barrister-Bookcase-Types.rfa**.
2. In the *Create* or *Modify* tab>*Properties* panel, click ▣ (Family Types).
3. In the *Family Types* dialog box, click 🗋 (New Type).
4. In the *Name* dialog box, type **3'-0" x 5'-0"** and click **OK**.

5. In the *Dimensions* area, verify or set the following values for the parameters, as shown in Figure 4–98:

   - *Width:* **3'-0"**
   - *Height:* **5'-0"**
   - *Depth:* **1'-1"**
   - *Base:* **4"**

Family Types				
Type name: 3'-0" x 5'-0"				
Search parameters				
Parameter	Value	Formula		Lock
Constraints				⌃
Default Elevation	0' 0"	=		☐
Dimensions				⌃
Width	3' 0"	=		☐
Height	5' 0"	=		☑
Depth	1' 1"	=		☐
Base	0' 4"	=		☑
Frame Width	0' 2"	=		☐
Shelf Thickness	0' 1"	=		☐
Shelf Height	1' 2"	= (Height - Base) / 4		☑

Figure 4–98

6. Click **Apply**.

7. Repeat the steps to create another new type for the following sizes. (Note: Do not change the *Depth* and *Base* values.)

   - **3'-0" x 6'-0"**
   - **3'-6" x 5'-0"**
   - **3'-6" x 6'-0"**

8. In the *Family Types* dialog box, test the family types by selecting the *Name* and clicking **Apply** after each selection.

9. Click **OK**.

10. Save the family.

Task 2: Use the family in a project.

1. In the practice files *Architectural* folder, open **Barrister-Bookcase-Project.rvt**.

2. Switch to one of the Bookcase family views.

3. In the *Family Editor* panel, click ⬆ (Load into Project).

    * If there is only one project open, the family file is automatically loaded into that project.

    * If more than one project is open, the *Load into Projects* dialog box opens. Select the project you want to load and click **OK**.

4. The **Component** command is automatically started with the Barrister Bookcase family selected.

5. Place one of each type in the project.

6. Create a 3D view to see the differences.

7. Save and close the project and family files.

End of practice

Practice 4h
Create Family Types for the Heat Pump

Practice Objectives

- Create family types of different sizes.
- Test the family in a project.

In this practice, you will create and apply family types of different sizes to a heat pump and test the family in a project, as shown in Figure 4–99.

Figure 4–99

Task 1: Create family types.

1. In the practice files *MEP>RFA* folder, open **Heat Pump-Types.rfa**.
2. In the *Create* tab>*Properties* panel, click ⬚ (Family Types).
3. In the *Family Types* dialog box, click ⬚ (New Type).
4. In the *Name* dialog box, type **HP060C** as the name.
5. In the *Dimensions* area, verify or set the following values for the parameters, as shown in Figure 4–100:
   - *Width:* **38 7/8"**
   - *Height:* **44 3/4"**
   - *Depth:* **34 3/4"**

Figure 4–100

6. Click **Apply**. The family resizes to match the new information.

7. Create the other models as follows:

Model	Width	Height	Depth
HP048C	38 7/8"	37"	34 3/4"
HP030C	32 7/8"	32 3/4"	28 3/4"
HP024C	32 7/8"	28 5/8"	28 3/4"

8. In the *Family Types* dialog box, test the family types by selecting the *Name* and clicking **Apply** after each selection.

9. Click **OK**.

10. Save the family.

Task 2: Use the family in a project.

1. In the practice files *MEP* folder, open **Heat-Pump-Project.rvt**.

2. Switch to one of the Heat Pump family views.

3. In the *Family Editor* panel, click 📤 (Load into Project).

   • If there is only one project open, the family file is automatically loaded into that project.

   • If more than one project is open, the *Load into Projects* dialog box opens. Select the project you want to load and click **OK**.

4. The **Component** command is automatically started with the new family selected.

5. Place one of each type in the project.

6. Create a 3D view to see the differences.

7. Save and close the project and the family files.

End of practice

Practice 4i
Create Family Types for the Structural Column

Practice Objectives

* Create family types.
* Use the family in a project.

In this practice, you will create and apply family types for the column. You will add the column family to a project and test the columns by modifying levels, as shown in Figure 4–101.

Figure 4–101

Task 1: Create family types.

1. In the practice files *Structural*>RFA folder, open **Y-Column-Types.rfa**.
2. In the *Create* or *Modify* tab>*Properties* panel, click ⬚ (Family Types).
3. In the *Family Types* dialog box, click 🗋 (New Type).
4. In the *Name* dialog box, set the name as **Over 12'-0"** and click **OK**.

5. In the *Dimensions* section, set the *Base Depth* to **3'-0"**, as shown in Figure 4–102.

Figure 4–102

6. Click **Apply**.

7. Create another new family type with the name **Under 12'-0"**.

8. In the *Dimensions* area, set the *Base Depth* to **2'-0"**.

9. Click **OK**.

10. Save the family.

Task 2: Use the family in a project.

1. In the practice files *Structural* folder, open **Y-Column-Project.rvt**.

2. Open the **Structural Plans: Level 2** view.

3. Switch to the Y-column family view.

4. In the *Family Editor* panel, click (Load into Project).

   - If there is only one project open, the family file is automatically loaded into that project.

   - If more than one project is open, the *Load into Projects* dialog box opens. Select the project you want to load and click **OK**.

5. The **Structural Column** command is automatically started with the Y-Column family selected. Verify that (Vertical Column) is selected.

6. Place one of each type in the project using the default information.

7. Open the **Elevations: South** view.

   Note: Change the Top Level first, so that the column does not go in the wrong direction.

---

8. Select the **Under 12'-0"** column. In Properties, set the *Top Level* to **Level 2,** the *Top Offset* to (negative) **-6"**, and the *Base Level* to **Level 1** with no *Base Offset*.

9. Select the **Over 12'-0"** column. In Properties, set the *Top Level* to **Level 3**, the *Top Offset* to (negative) **-6"**, and the *Base Level* to **Level 1** with no *Base Offset*, as shown in Figure 4–103.

Figure 4–103

10. Change the height of the levels to see how the look of the column changes.

11. Save and close the project and the family files.

End of practice

Chapter Review Questions

1. In which of the following views do the reference planes, as shown in Figure 4–104, display? (Select all that apply.)

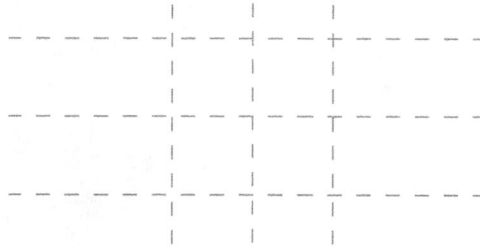

Figure 4–104

    a. Plan

    b. Elevation

    c. 3D

    d. Section

2. Which of the following is created when you label a dimension?

    a. Family

    b. Type

    c. Parameter

    d. Value

3. For which of the commands shown in Figure 4–105 can you use a profile instead of sketches? (Select all that apply.)

Extrusion Blend Revolve Sweep Swept Blend Void Forms

Forms

Figure 4–105

    a. Extrusion

    b. Blend

    c. Revolve

    d. Sweep

    e. Swept Blend

4. Which of the following commands creates the element shown in Figure 4–106?

Figure 4–106

a. Extrusion

b. Blend

c. Revolve

d. Sweep

e. Swept Blend

5. In which dialog box do you create sizes for component types?

a. Family Editor

b. Family Types

c. Family Categories

d. Family Properties

Command Summary

Button	Command	Location
Forms		
	Blend	• **Ribbon:** *Create* tab>*Forms* panel
	Extrusion	• **Ribbon:** *Create* tab>*Forms* panel
	Revolve	• **Ribbon:** *Create* tab>*Forms* panel
	Sweep	• **Ribbon:** *Create* tab>*Forms* panel
	Swept Blend	• **Ribbon:** *Create* tab>*Forms* panel
	Void Forms	• **Ribbon:** *Create* tab>*Forms* panel
Other Tools		
	Align	• **Ribbon:** *Modify* tab>*Modify* panel
	Family Types	• **Ribbon:** *Create* or *Modify* tab>*Properties* panel
	Load Family	• **Ribbon:** *Insert* tab>*Load from Library* panel
	Load into Project	• **Ribbon:** *all tabs*>*Family Editor* panel
Reference and Work Plane		
	Reference Line	• **Ribbon:** *Create* tab>*Datum* panel
	Reference Plane	• **Ribbon:** *Create* tab>*Datum* panel
	Set	• **Ribbon:** *Create* tab>*Work Plane* panel

Advanced Family Techniques

Once you have created basic families with parametric framework, geometry, and family types, you can enhance the families with additional parameters, elements, and settings. Possible enhancements include controls for flipping the family or connectors for MEP system elements. You can also nest families into other families, and then coordinate the parameters between the two. Visibility display settings enable you to specify the elements you want to display at various detail levels.

Learning Objectives

- Add controls, room calculation points, connectors, and openings.
- Insert components and associate the parameters.
- Control the display of elements in views at various detail levels using visibility settings.
- Create masking regions to block elements that would otherwise display through a family.
- Add model and symbolic lines.

5.1 Additional Tools for Families

Once you have created the basic framework of your family, added solid elements, established family types, and tested it in a project, you can start to add items that will make the family even more powerful. Some family-specific functions include the following:

- Controls that flip and mirror the family.

- A room calculation point that makes a family room-aware.

- Connectors (MEP elements only) that contain information, such as pipe or duct size, electrical data, power, cable tray size, and conduit size.

- Openings in a host, such as a wall or ceiling.

- The ability to nest or insert additional families to create a combined family, as shown in the kitchenette in Figure 5–1.

Figure 5–1

Adding Controls

You can place control arrows to flip or mirror geometry in the family, as shown in Figure 5–2. The controls also display on doors and other elements. Some family templates already include controls, but you can add as many as needed.

Figure 5–2

How To: Add Controls

1. In the *Create* tab>*Control* panel, click ⊹ (Control).

2. In the *Modify | Place Control* tab>*Control Type* panel, click one of the following controls:

   - ⟨ (Single Vertical)

   - ⌃ (Single Horizontal)

   - ⊹ (Double Vertical)

   - ⊹ (Double Horizontal)

3. Click in the view to place the control. If needed, you can move the controls once you have placed them by first clicking **Modify**, then selecting the control in the view and moving it.

Setting Room Calculation Points

Some families (e.g., lighting fixtures, specialty equipment, casework, furniture, etc.) can be placed so that the default center of the element is not in the room where it needs to be counted, as shown in Figure 5–3. You can adjust this by modifying the room calculation point, making the family a room-aware family.

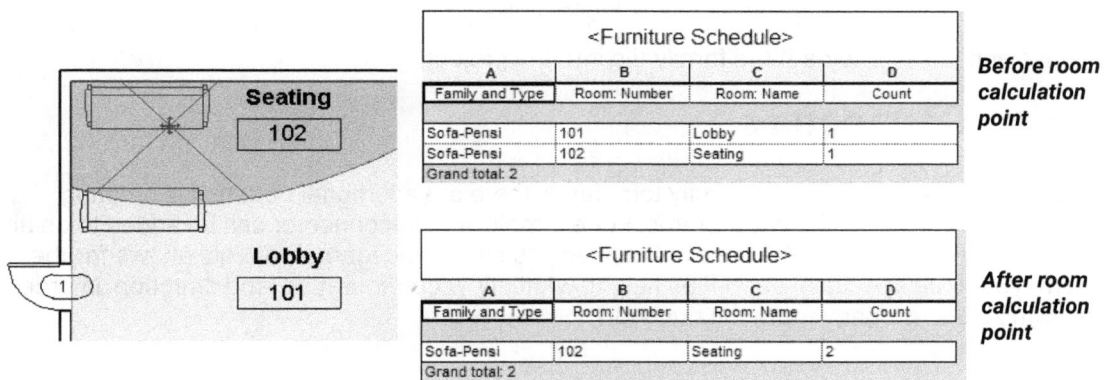

Figure 5–3

- Room calculation points can only be set in the family.

- The room calculation point defaults to the family's insertion point and can be adjusted in the X-, Y-, and Z-axis.

How To: Set a Room Calculation Point

1. Open the family file.

2. In *Properties*, check the checkbox for *Room Calculation Point*, as shown on the left in Figure 5–4.

3. To ensure the room calculation point does not interfere with model geometry and is properly recognized by an intended room or space, move it to the appropriate location within the family, as shown on the right in Figure 5–4.

Figure 5–4

4. Save and load (or reload) the family file into the project.

Adding Connectors

In the MEP-specific and generic family templates, there are additional options for creating connectors specific to different systems. For example, a duct connector can be added to an air terminal at the point where the duct will connect, as shown in Figure 5–5. This allows for the system type to be specified, as well as height, width, flow configuration, and direction, in order to recognize and properly route the ductwork.

Figure 5–5

- If you are using imported 3D shapes in a family, you can place connectors on the geometry. These tools are found on the *Create* tab>*Connectors* panel, as shown in Figure 5–6.

Electrical Connector | Duct Connector | Pipe Connector | Cable Tray Connector | Conduit Connector

Connectors

Figure 5–6

How To: Add a Connector

1. In the *Create* tab>*Connectors* panel, select the type of connector you want to use.
2. In the Options Bar, specify the type of connector (if applicable), as shown for an electrical connector in Figure 5–7. This will determine the system type that is created in a project.

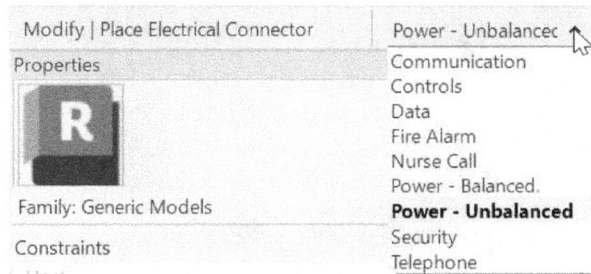

Figure 5–7

3. In the *Modify | Place Connector* tab>*Placement* panel, click 🖐 (Face) or ◈ (Work Plane).
4. Select a face or work plane that matches the location and direction of the connector.

   - The connector will host to the middle of the face that it is hosted and cannot be moved from that center.

5. Select the connector and make any necessary adjustments in Properties.

Adding Openings

You can create a custom opening using a host-based family template, like wall, floor, ceiling, or roof, and you can control the parameters for the dimensions of that opening. This is useful when needing to create a custom archway (as shown in Figure 5–8) or windows, doors, or skylights that need to cut through the entire host. This differs from a void form, which also cuts through a host but has the ability to control the cut's depth.

Figure 5–8

How To: Add an Opening to a Host Element

1. In the *Create* tab>*Model* panel, click ▢ (Opening).

    Note: This tool will be grayed out if you are not in a host-based family template.

2. In the *Modify | Create Opening Boundary* tab>*Draw* panel, use the sketch tools to create the opening. Use reference planes and dimensions as needed; they will not display when loading the opening into a project.

3. Click ✔ (Finish Edit Mode).

4. With the opening still selected, in the Options Bar, for the *Transparent in* option, select **3D** and/or **Elevation**.

- If you set the opening to be transparent (in 3D, elevation, or both), you will be able to see objects beyond the opening when it is loaded into a project, as shown in a project's 3D view in Figure 5–9.

3D is checked   **3D is unchecked**

Figure 5–9

5. You can make changes to the opening by clicking ✎ (Edit Sketch) in the *Modify | Opening Cut* tab>*Opening* panel.

Nesting Families

Adding a family to another family produces a nested family. In most cases, you want to do this with elements that are used multiple times in other families, such as the hardware shown in Figure 5–10.

Figure 5–10

- Nesting families will increase the file size.

- There are two types of components:

    - ⊞ **(Component):** In the *Create* tab>*Model* panel, places model components that display in all views.

    - ⊞ **(Detail Component):** In the *Annotate* tab>*Detail* panel, places detail components that display only in the current view.

Associating Family Parameters

To control a family's instance or type parameters, you can associate a family parameter. When loaded into a project, users can see these associated parameters and make adjustments depending on the associated parameter. When you are working with nested families, you might need to associate parameters in the host family with the nested family in order to control the nested family's parameters.

How To: Associate Family Parameters

Note: While not required, it is easier to have the parameters that are going to be associated inside of a host family be instance parameters instead of type parameters.

1. Select the element(s) whose parameters need to be associated.

2. In *Properties*, in the row where you want to connect the parameters, click ⬛ (Associate Family Parameter), as shown in Figure 5–11.

Figure 5–11

3. In the *Associate Family Parameter* dialog box, select the related parameter, as shown in Figure 5–12. Click **OK**.

Note: Type part of the parameter name in the search box to speed up selection.

Figure 5–12

- The parameter is now grayed out and the button displays the = sign, as shown in Figure 5–13.

Figure 5–13

Practice 5a
Add a Component to the Bookcase

Practice Objectives

- Add a component to a family.
- Associate parameters between the component and the family.
- Copy and align the component.

In this practice, you will insert a glass door component into the bookcase family. You will fit the component to the correct location on one shelf by aligning it and associating door width and height parameters with the related parameters in the family. You will then copy and align that door to other shelves, as shown in Figure 5–14. Optionally, you will add a Material parameter and test the options in a project.

Figure 5–14

Task 1: Add door components.

1. In the practice files *Architectural*>RFA folder, open **Barrister-Bookcase-Component.rfa**.
2. Open the **Floor Plans: Ref. Level** view.
3. In the *Insert* tab>*Load from Library* panel, click ⬇ (Load Family).
4. In the *Load Family* dialog box, in the practice files *Architectural*>RFA folder, select **Shelf-Door-Glass.rfa** and click **Open**.
5. In the *Create* tab>*Model* panel, click ⬛ (Component).

6. Place a copy of the door in the view aligned to the **Center L/R** reference plane, as shown in Figure 5-15. The width might not match the bookcase width.

Figure 5-15

7. Use ⬚ (Align) to lock the center of the bookcase with the center reference plane, as shown in Figure 5-16.

Figure 5-16

8. Use ⬚ (Align) to line up the back of the door with the **Door Face** reference plane and lock it, as shown in Figure 5-17.

- Make sure to select the Door Face reference plane first when you are aligning.

Figure 5-17

9. Save the family.

Task 2: Associate parameters.

Note: The Door Width and Door Height parameters are instance parameters, meaning you do not have to click Edit Type to associate the parameters. This keeps you from having to have multiple types of door panels for the nested family.

1. Click ⌨ (Modify) and select the door.

2. In Properties, scroll down to the *Other* area. Beside **Door Width**, at the end of the row, click ⬚ (Associate Family Parameter).

3. In the *Associate Family Parameter* dialog box, select **Width**, as shown in Figure 5–18, then click **OK**.

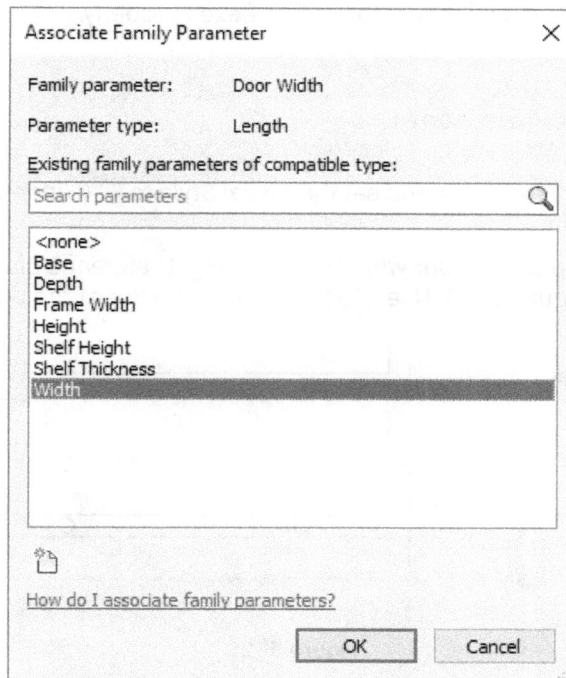

Figure 5–18

4. Repeat the process to associate **Door Height** with **Shelf Height**. The parameters in Properties gray out and an equal sign displays in the button, as shown on the left in Figure 5–19. The door should now fit in the shelf, as shown on the right.

Other		☆
Door Width	3' 0"	
Door Height	1' 3"	
Label	<None>	

Figure 5–19

5. Open the *Family Types* dialog box, expand *Type Name*, and change it to a different size. Click **Apply** each time you change it to verify it flexes properly.

6. Save the family.

Task 3: Align and copy the doors.

1. Open the **Elevations: Front** view and set the *Visual Style* to ▱ (Hidden Line). The door needs to be aligned vertically.

2. Align and lock the top of the door with the shelf height reference planes for the bottom shelf, as shown in Figure 5–20. Use <Tab> to select the top of the door.

Shelf Height reference plane

Base = 4"

Shelf Height = 1' - 3"

Figure 5–20

3. Copy the door to the other shelves and align and lock the top of each copied door with the associated reference plane, as shown in Figure 5–21. Ensure that the **Multiple Alignment** option is not selected in the *Align* panel.

Figure 5–21

4. Open the *Family Types* dialog box and change the *Type Name* to different sizes. Click **Apply** each time to verify it flexes properly.

5. Open the **Elevations: Left** view and find the **Door Face** reference plane. Align the back of the top three door faces with the **Door Face** reference plane. Figure 5–22 shows the alignment names.

Alignment first pick

Reference Planes : Reference Plane : Door Face

Alignment second pick

Furniture : Shelf-Door-Glass : Shelf-Door-Glass : Center (Front/Back) : Center F/B

Figure 5–22

6. Switch to a 3D view, as shown in Figure 5–23. Use family types to flex the model again to ensure that everything is working together.

Figure 5–23

7. Save the family.

Task 4: (Optional) Add and test a material parameter.

1. In the *Create* tab>*Properties* panel, click (Family Types).
2. In the bottom left corner of the *Family Types* dialog box, click (New Parameter).

3. Create a family parameter with the *Parameter Data* set, as shown in Figure 5–24. Click **OK**.

   Note: *Setting the type as an* **Instance** *makes modifying this parameter in the project file easier.*

Figure 5–24

4. In the *Family Types* dialog box, leave the **Material** parameter set to **<By category>**, as shown in Figure 5–25. Click **OK** to close the dialog box.

Figure 5–25

5. In the 3D view, select all of the bookcase components, but not the doors. **Hint:** Select everything and use <Shift> to remove the doors from the selection.

6. In Properties, a new instance parameter labeled **Material** displays under *Materials and Finishes*.

7. In the *Material* row, click ▢ (Associate Family Parameter), as shown in Figure 5–26.

Figure 5–26

8. In the *Associate Family Parameter* dialog box, select the **Material** parameter, as shown in Figure 5–27. Click **OK**.

Figure 5–27

- The *Material* is now marked with the **=** sign, as shown in Figure 5–28.

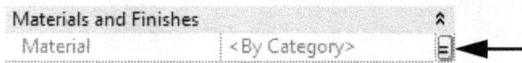

Figure 5–28

9. Select one of the bookcase doors.

10. In Properties, click ▦ (Edit Type).

11. In the *Type Properties* dialog box, associate the **Door Material** parameter with the **Material** parameter.

12. Click **OK**.

13. Save the family.

14. Open the **Barrister-Bookcase-Project.rvt** file and delete any existing bookcase elements.

15. Switch to the bookcase family and load it into the project.

16. Place one of each type of the **Barrister-Bookcase-Component** family types in the project. An older version of the family might also be in the project.

17. Create a 3D view to see the differences.

18. In the View Control Bar, set the *Visual Style* to 🔲 (Consistent Colors).

19. Select a bookcase. In Properties, in the *Materials and Finishes* area, next to the **Material** parameter, click ⬜ (Browse).

20. In the *Material Browser*, in the search, narrow your search down to *Bookcase*. Select a material and click **OK** to apply it to the bookcase. (Several materials starting with the word **Bookcase** are available for you to use.) Because you changed the bookcase's material instance parameter, you changed just that one bookcase's material.

21. Repeat with the other bookcases using different materials, such as those shown in Figure 5–29.

Figure 5–29

22. Save and close the project and family files.

End of practice

Practice 5b
Add a Component and Connectors to the Heat Pump

Practice Objectives

- Add a void element.
- Add a component to a family.
- Add electrical and piping connectors.
- Associate parameters.

In this practice, you will add a void element to cut out part of the main unit of the heat pump. You will then insert a panel component into that void. You will create additional extrusions and add connectors to these and other extrusions in the panel component. Finally, you will create and associate parameters to set pipe sizes. The completed family is shown in Figure 5–30.

Figure 5–30

Task 1: Add a void.

1. In the practice files *MEP>RFA* folder, open **Heat Pump-Connectors.rfa**.
2. Open the **{3D}**, **Ref. Level**, and **Front** views. Tile the views so that all three are visible on the screen.

3. In the **Front** elevation view, add two references planes to the lower left corner of the unit and dimension them as shown in Figure 5−31.

4. Select the lower reference plane and name it **Bottom of Void**, as shown in Figure 5−31.

Figure 5−31

5. Activate the **Ref. Level** view and zoom in on the lower-left corner of the equipment.

6. Change the *Scale* to **1 1/2"=1'-0"** to make the annotation smaller.

7. Draw and dimension the reference planes shown in Figure 5−32 and lock the dimensions.

   Note: Existing 3" dimensions shown for clarity.

Figure 5−32

8. In the *Create* tab>*Forms* panel, expand (Void Forms) and click (Void Extrusion).

9. In the *Modify | Create Void Extrusion* tab>*Work Plan* panel, click (Set).

10. In the *Work Plane* dialog box, select the *Name* **Reference Plane : Bottom of Void** and click **OK**.

11. Draw and lock the sketch, as shown in Figure 5-33.

Figure 5-33

12. In *Properties*, set the *Extrusion End* to **9"**.

13. Click ✔ (Finish Edit Mode) and click in an empty area in the view to release the selection.

14. In the **Elevation: Front** view, align and lock the top of the extrusion to the reference plane, as shown in Figure 5-34.

Figure 5-34

15. Rotate the 3D view so you can see the new void, as shown in Figure 5–35.

Figure 5–35

16. Save the project.

Task 2: Insert a component.

1. Activate the **Floor Plan: Ref. Level** view.

2. In the *Create* tab>*Model* panel, click (Component).

3. When prompted to load a family, click **Yes**.

4. Navigate to the practice files *MEP>RFA* folder and open **Connector Panel.rfa**.

5. Insert the component, as shown in Figure 5–36.

Insertion point

1/2"

1/2"

1/2"   1/2"

Figure 5–36

6. Align and lock the back and side of the component to the reference planes. Press <Tab> to rotate through edges to select the connector's edge and not the void's face, as shown in Figure 5–37.

Generic Models : Connector Panel : Connector Panel :
Reference

Figure 5–37

7. In the **Elevations: Front** view, align and lock the top of the component to the top of the void reference plane, as shown in Figure 5–38.

Figure 5–38

8. Save the family.

Task 3: Add extrusions for piping connections.

1. Activate the **Floor Plan: Ref. Level** view.

2. Draw a section in front of the angled reference line at 45 degrees and open it. (This section is not cutting anything, but acts similar to an elevation.) Adjust the length of the section by dragging the arrows, as needed.

3. Start the **Extrusion** command.

4. In the *Work Plane* dialog box, select **Pick a plane** and click **OK**. Select the edge of the plane shown in Figure 5–39.

5. Add the reference planes, dimensions, and the extrusion shown in Figure 5–39. Set the extrusion *Depth* to **1/4"**.

    Note: You might need to zoom in closer to place the smaller circle.

Figure 5–39

6. Click ✔ (Finish Edit Mode).

7. Join the extrusion to the rest of the unit.

8. Save the family.

Task 4: Add connectors.

1. Open the 3D view and modify the view to display the corner of the unit where the connectors need to be applied.

2. In the *Create* tab>*Connectors* panel, click ⚡ (Electrical Connector).

3. In the Options Bar, select **Power-Balanced**.

4. Select the face of the top circular extrusion, as shown in Figure 5–40.

5. Click ⌖ (Modify) and select the new connector.

6. In *Properties*, in the *Identity Data* area, in the *Connector Description*, type **Electric Power Supply**.

7. Continue adding the other connectors as shown in Figure 5–40. For the Pipe Connectors, before selecting the location, in *Properties*, set the *Round Connector Dimension* to **Use Radius**.

Pipe Connector:
Other
Connector Description:
Gas Line

Pipe Connector:
Other
Connector Description:
Liquid Line

Electrical Connector:
Power-Balanced
Connector Description:
Electric Power Supply

Electrical Connector:
Power-Balanced
Connector Description:
Low Voltage

Figure 5–40

8. Save the family.

Task 5: Create and assign new parameters for piping connectors.

1. In the *Properties* panel, click 🖳 (Family Types).

2. In the lower left corner, click 📄 (New Parameter) and add the following type parameters:

Name	Discipline	Data Type	Group
Gas Line Service Valve	Piping	Pipe Size	Mechanical
Liquid Line Service Valve	Piping	Pipe Size	Mechanical
Gas Line Radius	Piping	Pipe Size	Dimensions
Liquid Line Radius	Piping	Pipe Size	Dimensions

- The **Radius** parameters are going to be linked to **Radius** parameters in the connectors. Revit reads this and sets the correct diameter for the connector in the family when it is inserted into a project.

3. Assign the following values:

   - *Gas Line Service Valve:* **7/8"**

   - *Liquid Line Service Valve*: **3/8"**

4. Type in the following formulas:

   - *Gas Line Radius*: **Gas Line Service Valve / 2**

   - *Liquid Line Radius:* **Liquid Line Service Valve / 2**

5. Move the two radius parameters to the end of the *Dimensions* section. The final set of parameters is shown in Figure 5–41.

Parameter	Value	Formula	Lock
Dimensions			☒
Width	38 7/8"	=	☐
Height	44 3/4"	=	☐
Depth	34 3/4"	=	☐
CenterX	17 3/8"	= CenterY	☐
CenterY	17 3/8"	= Depth / 2	☐
Radius of Fan	16 3/8"	= Depth / 2 - 1"	☐
Gas Line Radius	7/16"	= Gas Line Service Valve /	☐
Liquid Line Radius	3/16"	= Liquid Line Service Valve	☐
Mechanical			☒
Gas Line Service Valve	7/8"	=	☐
Liquid Line Service Valve	3/8"	=	☐

Figure 5–41

6. Click **OK**.

7. In *Properties*, under the *Dimensions* heading, verify that the *Round Connector Dimension* is set to **Use Radius**.

8. Select the Gas Line connector.

9. In *Properties*, in the *Dimensions* area, in the **Radius** parameter, click ⬛ (Associate Family Parameter).

10. In the *Associate Family Parameter* dialog box, select **Gas Line Radius**, as shown in Figure 5–42, then click **OK**.

Figure 5–42

11. Repeat the process for the Liquid Line connector and associate the **Liquid Line Radius** to it.

12. When it is finished the connectors should be sized accordingly in the family, as shown in Figure 5–43.

Note: Select the connector and click the Flip control if the Z-axis is pointing into the heat pump.

Figure 5–43

13. Save and close the family.

End of practice

Practice 5c
Modify the Structural Column

Practice Objectives

- Add and test material parameters.
- Associate parameters.
- Add parameters to an existing extrusion.

In this practice, you will add a sweep element around the base of the column. You will then add a material parameter and test it in a project, as shown in Figure 5–44.

Figure 5–44

Task 1: Add a sweep around the base of the column.

1. In the practice files *Structural>RFA* folder, open **Y-Column-Advanced.rfa.**
2. Open the **Floor Plans: Lower ref. Level** view.
3. Select the existing column and base elements and temporarily hide them.
4. In the *Create* tab>*Forms* panel, click (Sweep).
5. In the *Modify | Sweep* tab>*Sweep* panel, click (Sketch Path).
6. Set the Work Plane to **Level: Lower Ref. Level.**

7. Add and lock the sketch as shown in Figure 5–45.

Figure 5–45

8. Click ✔ (Finish Edit Mode).

9. In the *Sweep* panel, click ⬚ (Edit Profile).

10. In the *Go To View* dialog box, select **Elevation: Left** and click **Open View**.

11. Zoom in on the area near the red dot.

12. Use the sketch tools to add a profile similar to Figure 5–46. The exact size and design does not matter but ensure that you are locking the edges to the angled reference line and level reference plane.

Figure 5–46

13. Click ✔ (Finish Edit Mode) twice to apply the sweep.

14. Open the 3D view to see the sweep, as shown in Figure 5−47.

Figure 5−47

15. Save the family.

Task 2: Add a material parameter.

1. In the *Create* tab>*Properties* panel, click ⬚ (Family Types).

2. Select the *Structural Material (default)* parameter and click ✎ (Edit Parameter).

3. In the *Parameter Properties* dialog box, you can see that this is a *Built-in parameter* and most of the information cannot be changed. Select **Type**, as shown in Figure 5–48. Click **OK**.

Figure 5–48

4. For the *Structural Material*, click the **Browse** button in the *Value* column, as shown in Figure 5–49.

Parameter	Value	Formula	Lock
Materials and Finishes			
Structural Material	<By Category>		

Figure 5–49

5. Select one of the **Concrete, Cast-in-Place** materials. You will need to load it into the project from the AEC Materials library, as shown in Figure 5–50.

Figure 5–50

6. In the *Family Types* dialog box, click 🗋 (New Parameter).

7. Create a **Family parameter** and set the *Parameter Data,* as shown in Figure 5–51. Click **OK**. Ensure that you select **Instance** so you can modify the parameter of each column individually.

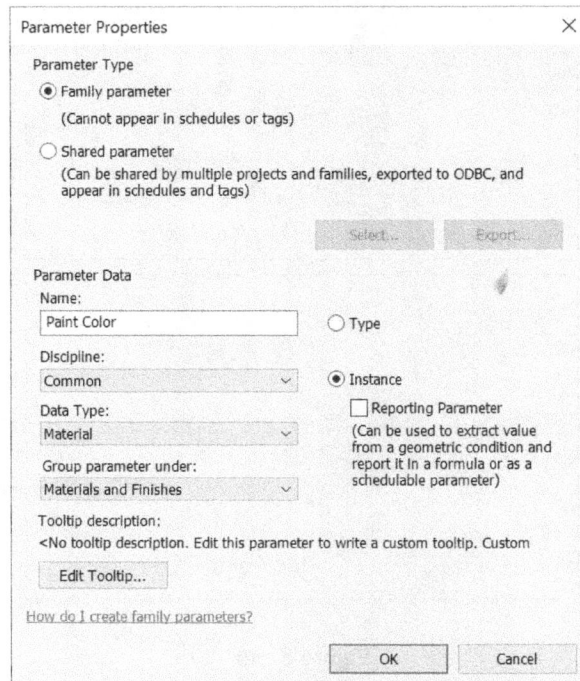

Figure 5–51

8. In the *Family Types* dialog box, ensure that the **Paint Color** parameter is set to **<By category>**, as shown in Figure 5–52.

Parameter	Value	Formula	Lock
Materials and Finishes			⌃
Paint Color (default)	<By Category>	=	
Structural Material	Concrete, Cast-in-Place	=	

Figure 5–52

9. Click **OK** to close the dialog box.

10. In *Properties*, in the *Structural* area, set the *Material for Model Behavior* to **Concrete**, as shown in Figure 5–53.

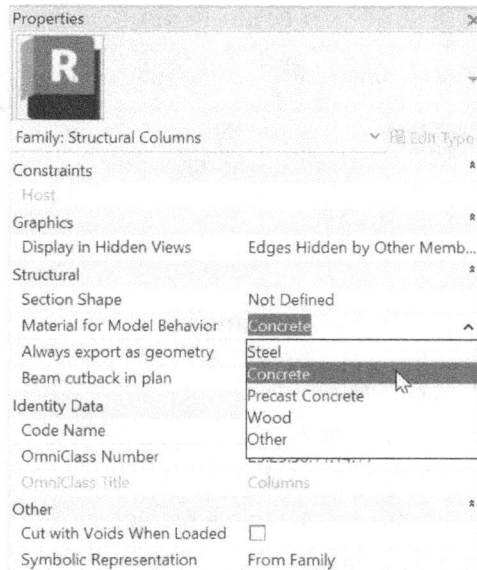

Figure 5-53

11. In the 3D view, select the three parts of the column.

12. In *Properties*, in the *Materials and Finishes* area, a parameter labeled **Material** displays.

13. In the *Material* row, click ⬚ (Associate Family Parameter), as shown in Figure 5-54.

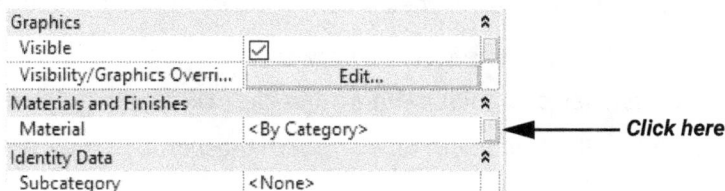

Figure 5-54

14. In the *Associate Family Parameter* dialog box, select **Paint Color,** as shown in Figure 5-55. Click **OK**.

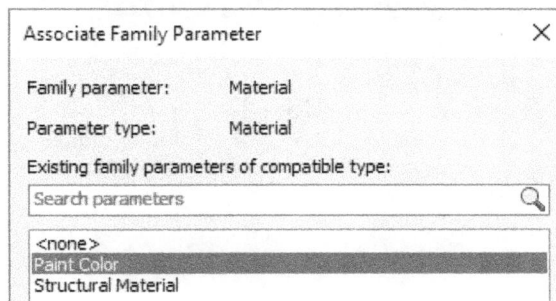

Figure 5-55

- The *Material* is now marked with the = sign, as shown in Figure 5-56.

Figure 5-56

15. Close all of the views except the 3D view.

16. Save the family.

Task 3: Modify the material of the columns.

1. Open the **Y-Column-Project.rvt** file.

2. Open the **Structural Plans: Level 2** view.

3. Delete any existing columns from previous practices.

4. Switch to the column family and load it into the project.

5. Add several columns at different heights. Set the base and top of each column in properties.

6. Open the **Elevations: South** view.

7. In the View Control Bar, set the *Visual Style* to 🔲 (Consistent Colors).

8. Select one of the columns.

9. In *Properties*, in the *Materials and Finishes* area, beside *Paint Color,* in the <By Category> box, click ⬚ (Browse) to open the *Material Browser.*

10. In the *Material Browser*, select a paint material and click **OK** to apply it to the column.

    - Several materials of different colors (starting with the words **Metal - Paint Finish**) are available for you to use.

11. Repeat with the other columns using different materials.

12. Save and close the project and family files.

End of practice

5.2 Visibility Display Settings

You can make families more versatile by controlling what displays in various views and at different detail levels. For example, you can set the **Coarse** view to display only 2D symbolic lines while the **Fine** detail view displays the full 3D model, as shown in Figure 5–57. To do this, change the visibility of the elements. You can also add masking regions to elements in a family to obscure other elements.

Fine detail level   *Coarse detail level*

Figure 5–57

How To: Control the Display of Elements

1. In the family, select the elements that you want to modify.

2. In the *Modify* contextual tab>*Visibility* panel, click (Visibility Settings).

3. In the *Family Element Visibility Settings* dialog box, specify the views and detail level in which you want the elements to display, as shown in Figure 5–58.

   - Alternatively, you can select the element and in Properties, click **Edit...** next to *Visibility/ Graphics Overrides*.

Figure 5–58

4. Click **OK**.

- All model elements (not detail elements) typically display in 3D views. You can select how they display in plan and elevation views.

- How a family displays in a project's plan view is determined by the cut plane specified by the *View Range*. Some elements, such as furniture and mechanical equipment, cannot be cut in plan view, while structural columns can.

- The *Detail Levels* area controls whether or not the element displays at various levels of detail in a view (**Coarse**, **Medium**, and **Fine**). If you clear the check mark from a level and the view in the Family Editor is set to that detail level, the lines defining the element turn gray in the family file. They do not display at that detail level when inserted into the project.

- To aid in assigning elements to various detail levels, you can preview the visibility. In the View Control Bar, expand 🖥 (Preview Visibility Off) and select 🖥 (Preview Visibility On). When the preview is on, you can change the *Detail Level* and only the elements assigned to that level display, as shown in Figure 5–59.

Detail Level: Medium   Detail Level: Fine

Figure 5–59

- When the category permits, you can also set **Preview Visibility On (Not Cut)**, as shown in Figure 5–60.

Figure 5–60

Adding Lines

Lines are often used to enhance a family without adding additional model geometry, which helps keep a family lighter in file size. This is often used to display the model elements in plan and elevation views at the **Coarse** (and sometimes **Medium**) detail level. There are two types of lines:

- ⬡ (Model Line) in the *Create* tab>*Model* panel is shown in all views.

- ⬡ (Symbolic Line) in the *Annotate* tab>*Detail* panel is visible in views parallel to the view in which it was drawn.

Lines can also be used in other situations. For example, you could use model lines to draw door hardware that is not three-dimensional, or use symbolic lines to draw the door swing (as shown in Figure 5–61) so that it does not display in 3D views.

Figure 5–61

- Use the standard sketch tools in the *Draw* panel to draw model and symbolic lines. You can also specify a subcategory with an associated line type (as shown in Figure 5–62 for a door family).

Figure 5–62

- You can create entire families of model and symbolic lines if they are only going to be used in a 2D view. For example, create a 2D family for a hospital bed, as shown in Figure 5-63, and use it in a large hospital layout where most of the instances do not need to be full 3D.

  Note: 2D families can still be robust in the number and types of parameters they hold for use in schedules and quantity takeoffs.

Figure 5-63

Creating Masking Regions

When you do not want to see all or part of the geometry while creating a family, you can create a mask region around the area. This will obscure the objects when loaded into a project. For example, in the desk family shown in Figure 5-64, a chair placed under the desk is masked but the lamp on top of the desk is not.

Figure 5-64

How To: Create Masking Regions

1. Open a plan or elevation view.

2. In the *Annotate* tab>*Detail* panel, click ⬚ (Masking Region).

3. In the *Modify | Create Masking Region Boundary* tab>*Subcategory* panel, select the subcategory you want to use for the boundary of the region. Select **<Invisible Lines>** if you do not want the boundary to display.

4. In the *Draw* panel, select the tools to sketch the region.

5. In Properties, you can set the *Visibility/Graphics Overrides* of the masked region to only display in certain detail levels or to only show if the instance is cut (based on a project's *View Range*).

6. Click ✔ (Finish Edit Mode) and click in an empty space to finish the command.

Practice 5d
Modify the Visibility of Elements in the Bookcase

Practice Objectives

- Modify visibility settings.
- Create symbolic lines.

In this practice, you will modify the visibility settings of the main 3D elements so that they display at the **Medium** and **Fine** detail levels. You will also create a simple extrusion for 3D views and sketch symbolic lines for 2D views to display at the **Coarse** detail level. The elevation views of the three detail levels are shown in Figure 5–65.

Coarse   Medium   Fine

Figure 5–65

Task 1: Modify the visibility settings of the 3D elements.

1. In the practice files *Architectural>RFA* folder, open **Barrister-Bookcase-Visibility.rfa**.
2. Open the **Floor Plans: Ref. Level** and **Elevation: Front** views. Tile the views so you see the 3D view along with the two opened views.
3. Activate the 3D view and set the *Visual Style* to ⬛ (Hidden Line).
4. In the View Control Bar, expand 🖼 (Preview Visibility Off) and select 🖼 (Preview Visibility On).
5. By default, the *Display Level* is set to **Medium** so all elements should be visible.

6. Hover the cursor over part of the bookcase element (but not the doors) and press <Tab> until the **Joined Solid Geometry** highlights, as shown in Figure 5–66. Click to select it.

Figure 5–66

7. In the *Modify | Joined Solid Geometry* tab>*Visibility* panel, click (Visibility Settings).

8. In the *Family Element Visibility Settings* dialog box, in the *Detail Levels* area, clear the **Coarse** option and select **Medium** and **Fine**, as shown in Figure 5–67. Then, click **OK**.

Note: This has to be done in two steps because the doors are a different element (a nested family) from the rest of the elements.

Figure 5–67

9. Select the door elements and in the *Modify | Lines* tab>*Visibility* panel, click (Visibility Settings).

10. In the *Family Element Visibility Settings* dialog box, in the *Detail Levels* area, clear the **Coarse** and **Medium** options and select **Fine**. Click **OK**. The doors no longer display, as shown in Figure 5–68.

Figure 5–68

11. Change the *Detail Level* to **Fine**. The doors should display as shown in Figure 5–69.

Figure 5–69

12. Change the *Detail Level* to **Coarse**. Nothing should display in the 3D view.

13. Save the family.

Task 2: (Optional) Create an extrusion for coarse detail in 3D views.

In this task, you will create an extrusion of the bookcase to help you visualize what it looks like in 3D.

1. In the **Elevation: Front** and **Floor Plans: Ref. Level** views, select ▦ (Preview Visibility On).

2. The *Detail Level* is set to **Coarse** so none of the 3D elements display.

3. In the **Ref. Level** view, create a new extrusion with the footprint shown in Figure 5–70. Set

    the *Depth* to **2'-6"** and click ✔ (Finish Edit Mode).

    Note: *Lock all sketch lines.*

Figure 5–70

4. In the **Elevations: Front** view, align and lock the top of the new extrusion to the top reference plane, as shown on the left in Figure 5–71. The simple extrusion also displays in the 3D view as shown on the right.

Figure 5–71

5. Select the new extrusion.

6. In the *Modify | Extrusion* tab>*Mode* panel, click (Visibility Settings).

7. In the *Family Element Visibility Settings* dialog box, clear all of the options for the *View Specific Display* and all the *Detail Levels* except **Coarse**, as shown in Figure 5–72.

    Note: You do not want this element displaying in the 2D views at any detail level.

Family Element Visibility Settings ✕

View Specific Display
  Display in 3D views and:
  ☐ Plan/RCP
  ☐ Front/Back
  ☐ Left/Right
  ☐ When cut in Plan/RCP (if category permits)

Detail Levels
  ☑ Coarse   ☐ Medium   ☐ Fine

  [OK]   [Cancel]   [Default]   [Help]

Figure 5–72

8. The simple extrusion should only display in the 3D view.

9. Save the family.

Task 3: Add symbolic lines to elevation and plan views.

1. In the **Elevations: Front** view, verify that the *Detail Level* is set to **Coarse**.

2. In the *Annotate* tab>*Detail* panel, click (Symbolic Line).

3. Draw a rectangle around the outside of the bookcase and lock it to the reference planes, as shown in Figure 5–73.

Figure 5–73

4. Select all of the lines.

5. In the *Modify | Lines* tab>*Visibility* panel, click (Visibility Settings).

6. In the *Family Element Visibility Settings* dialog box, in the *Detail Levels* area, select **Coarse** and clear the **Medium** and **Fine** options, as shown in Figure 5–74. Click **OK**.

    *Note: Symbolic lines display in views parallel to the view where they were drawn. Therefore, the lines in the **Front** view will automatically display in the **Back** view.*

Figure 5–74

7. Repeat the process in the **Floor Plans: Ref. Level** view, as shown in Figure 5–75.

Figure 5–75

8. Select all of the lines and set the *Visibility Settings* to **Coarse**.

9. Open the **Elevations: Left** view and repeat the process. (Toggle on **Preview Visibility** to hide the 3D elements at the **Coarse** detail level.)

10. Check the detail levels in each of the views.

11. Save the family.

Task 4: Load and test the family in a project.

1. Open the **Barrister-Bookcase-Project.rvt** file.

2. Delete any existing bookcases.

3. Switch to the bookcase family file and load it into the project.

4. Add at least one copy of the new bookcase.

5. In the View Control Bar, set the *Visual Style* to **Shaded**.

6. Change the detail levels to see the differences, as shown in Figure 5–76.

Detail Level: Coarse *Detail Level: Medium* *Detail Level: Fine*

Figure 5–76

7. Test in other views to ensure that the detail levels display the way you want them to.

8. Save and close the project and family files.

End of practice

Practice 5e
Modify the Visibility of Elements in the Heat Pump

Practice Objectives

- Modify visibility settings.
- Create symbolic lines.

In this practice, you will modify the visibility settings of the 3D elements so that they display differently at various levels of detail, as shown in Figure 5–77. You will also create elements that display at a **Coarse** detail level, including a simple extrusion for 3D views and symbolic lines for plan and elevation views.

Coarse *Medium* *Fine*

Figure 5–77

- The electrical and piping connectors are hidden in these views for clarity.

Task 1: Modify the visibility settings of the 3D elements.

1. In the practice files *MEP>RFA* folder, open **Heat Pump-Visibility.rfa**.
2. Open the **Floor Plans: Ref. Level** and **Elevation: Front** views. Tile the views so you see the 3D view along with the two opened views.
3. In each of the views, in the View Control Bar, expand ⬚ (Preview Visibility Off) and select ⬚ (Preview Visibility On).
4. Activate the 3D view and set the *Visual Style* to ⬚ (Hidden Line).

5. By default, the *Detail Level* is set to **Medium** so all elements should be visible, as shown in Figure 5–78.

Figure 5–78

6. Rotate the view and select the panel component.

7. In the *Modify | Joined Solid Geometry* tab>*Visibility* panel, click (Visibility Settings).

8. In the *Family Element Visibility Settings* dialog box in the *Detail Levels* area, clear the **Coarse** and **Medium** options and select **Fine**. Click **OK**.

9. Repeat the process with the connector extrusions. Neither of these elements should display in the **Medium** detail level, as shown in Figure 5–79, although the pipe connector elements still display.

Figure 5–79

10. Hover the cursor over part of the heat pump element and press <Tab> until the **Joined Solid Geometry** highlights, as shown in Figure 5–80. Click to select it.

Figure 5–80

11. In the *Family Element Visibility Settings* dialog box, in the *Detail Levels* area, clear the **Coarse** option and select **Medium** and **Fine**, as shown in Figure 5–81. Click **OK**.

Figure 5–81

12. Change the *Detail Level* to **Fine**. The panel and connector extrusions should display.

13. Change the *Detail Level* to **Coarse**. No 3D elements should display in any of the views that are set to **Coarse**.

14. Save the family.

Task 2: (Optional) Add elements for the Coarse detail view.

In this task, you will create an extrusion of the heat pump to help you visualize what it looks like in 3D.

1. Activate the **Floor Plans: Ref. Level** view.

2. Set the work plane to **Ref. Level**.

3. Create a new extrusion with the footprint shown in Figure 5–82. Set the *Depth* to **40"** and click ✔ (Finish Edit Mode).

Figure 5–82

4. Switch to the **Elevations: Front** view.

5. Set the *Visual Style* to **Shaded** to display the extrusion.

6. Align and lock the top and bottom of the new extrusion to the reference planes, as shown in Figure 5–83.

Figure 5–83

7. Select the extrusion.

8. In the *Modify | Extrusion* tab>*Mode* panel, click ⬚ (Visibility Settings).

9. In the *Family Element Visibility Settings* dialog box, clear all of the options except **Coarse**, as shown in Figure 5–84.

Note: You do not want this element displaying in the 2D views at any detail level.

Figure 5–84

10. While still in the **Elevation: Front** view, in the *Annotate* tab>*Detail* panel, click ⬚ (Symbolic Line).

11. Draw a rectangle using the outermost reference planes of the heat pump and lock it to the reference planes.

12. Select all of the lines.

13. In the *Modify | Lines* tab>*Visibility* panel, click ⬚ (Visibility Settings).

14. In the *Family Element Visibility Settings* dialog box, in the *Detail Levels* area, select **Coarse** and clear the **Medium** and **Fine** options, as shown in Figure 5–85. Click **OK**.

*Note: Symbolic lines display in views parallel to the view where they were drawn. Therefore, the lines in the **Front** view will automatically display in the **Back** view.*

Figure 5–85

15. Return to the **Ref. Level** view and draw and lock symbolic lines to the outer reference planes using the same footprint as the extrusion. Set the visibility settings, as shown in Figure 5–85.

16. Open the **Elevations: Left** view and repeat the process. (Toggle on **Preview Visibility** to hide the 3D elements at the **Coarse** detail level.)

17. Check the detail levels in each of the views.

18. Close all but one view of the family.

19. Save the family.

Task 3: Load and test the family in a project.

1. Open the **Heat-Pump-Project.rvt** file.

2. Delete any existing Heat Pump components.

3. Open the Mechanical>HVAC>**Floor Plans: 1 - Mech** view.

4. Switch to the heat pump family file and load it into the project.

5. Add at least one copy of the new heat pump.

6. In the View Control Bar, set the *Visual Style* to **Shaded**.

7. Change the detail levels to display the differences, as shown in Figure 5–86.

Detail Level: Coarse   **Detail Level: Medium**   **Detail Level: Fine**

Figure 5–86

8. Open a 3D view, rotate it so that the connector locations display and test the detail levels.

9. Save and close the project and family files.

End of practice

Practice 5f
Modify the Visibility of Elements in the Structural Column

Practice Objectives

- Modify visibility settings.
- Create a simple extrusion.
- Add symbolic lines.

In this practice, you will modify the visibility settings of the 3D elements so that they display differently at various levels of detail. You will also create elements that display at a **Coarse** detail level, including a simple extrusion for 3D views and symbolic lines for plan and elevation views, as shown in Figure 5–87.

View: Plan
Detail Level: Coarse

View: Front Elevation
Detail Level: Medium

View: 3D
Detail Level: Fine

Figure 5–87

Task 1: Modify the visibility settings of the 3D elements.

1. In the practice files *Structural>RFA* folder, open **Y-Column-Visibility.rfa**.
2. Close any other open files.
3. Open the **Floor Plans: Lower Ref. Level**, **Elevation: Front**, and **Elevation: Left** views. Tile the views so you see the 3D view along with the other opened views.
4. In each of the views, in the View Control Bar, expand ⬚ (Preview Visibility Off) and select ⬚ (Preview Visibility On).

5. Activate the 3D view. By default, the *Detail Level* is set to **Medium** and all elements should be visible, as shown in Figure 5–88.

Figure 5–88

6. Select the curved part of the base element and in the *Family Element Visibility Settings* dialog box, in the *Detail Levels* area, clear the **Coarse** and **Medium** options and select **Fine**, as shown in Figure 5–89. Click **OK**. The curved base should be removed from the view.

Figure 5–89

7. Switch the 3D views detail level from **Medium** to **Fine**, and the curved base should display. Return the view back to medium detail.

8. Save the family.

Task 2: Add symbolic lines.

1. Activate the **Floor Plans: Lower Ref. Level** view.
2. In the View Control Bar, change the *Visibility Preview* to ▨ (Preview Visibility On (Not Cut)).
3. In the *Annotate* tab>*Detail* panel, click ▢ (Symbolic Lines).
4. In the *Modify | Place Symbolic Lines* tab>*Subcategory* panel, expand the *Subcategory* list and select **Structural Columns [projection]**, if not already selected. Add symbolic lines around the edge of the base and lock them in place, as shown by the solid lines in Figure 5–90.
5. Set the *Subcategory* to **Hidden Line (projection)** and add the lines on either side of the base to show the area of the Y-Column above. The exact length of the lines is not important at this time.

Figure 5–90

6. If you isolate just the symbolic lines, it will display as shown in Figure 5–91.

Figure 5–91

7. Select all the symbolic lines and set the visibility settings to display only at the **Coarse** detail level, as shown in Figure 5–92.

Figure 5–92

8. Open the **Elevations: Front** and **Elevations: Left** views.

9. Hide the Y-column temporarily.

10. Start the **Symbolic Lines** command.

11. In *Properties*, set the lines to display only at the **Coarse** *Detail Level* (set the *Subcategory* to **Structural Columns [projection]**).

12. In the *Draw* panel, select **Pick Lines** and click the checkbox next to **Lock** on the Options Bar.

13. Add symbolic lines around the edge of the base.

14. Reset Temporary Hide/Isolate.

15. Add symbolic lines around the Y-column, as shown in Figure 5–93. Verify the lines are locking to the Y-column. Trim as needed.

Figure 5–93

16. Select the Y-column and base. In the *Family Elements Visibility Settings* dialog box, select the **Front/Back** and **Left/Right** options and uncheck **Course**, as shown in Figure 5–94.

Figure 5–94

17. Check the detail levels in each of the views.

18. Close all but one open view.

19. Save the family.

Task 3: Load and test the family in a project.

1. Open **Y-Column-Project.rvt**.
2. Switch to the Y-Column family file and load it into the project.
3. Select one of the existing columns and replace it with the new **Y-Column-Visibility** type of the same size.

   - The paint color is not retained because it is an instance parameter, not a type parameter.

4. Delete the other columns.
5. Open the **Structural Plans: Level 1** and **Elevations: South** views and tile the views.
6. Test the visibility settings in the different views including the **Elevations: Front** view shown in Figure 5–95.

Detail Level: Coarse   *Detail Level: Medium*   *Detail Level: Fine*

Figure 5–95

7. Save and close the project and family files.

End of practice

Chapter Review Questions

1. If your family's direction can be flipped (such as a door swing), what needs to be added?
    a. Mirror
    b. Connector
    c. Control
    d. Calculation

2. (MEP only) When adding a connector, where do you specify the system type (e.g., Power-Balanced, Exhaust Air, or Domestic Hot Water)?
    a. In the shortcut menu
    b. In the Options Bar
    c. In the expanded *Connectors* panel
    d. In the *Type Properties* dialog box

3. In which of the following situations would you use a nested family?
    a. When the family is used multiple times in other families.
    b. When the family is used multiple times in one project.
    c. When the family is used multiple times in several projects.

4. Why would you want to associate a family parameter? (Select all that apply.)
    a. The parameter will be visible in the project.
    b. The parameter will be used in a schedule.
    c. You want a user-created parameter to control another parameter.
    d. You want the parameter to reference a project parameter.

5. For the elements in a family to display differently at Coarse and Fine detail levels (as shown in Figure 5-96), you must draw everything in 2D.

Figure 5-96

a. True

b. False

Command Summary

Button	Command	Location
Connectors		
	Cable Tray Connector	• **Ribbon**: *Create* tab>*Connectors* panel, expand Connector
	Conduit Connector	• **Ribbon**: *Create* tab>*Connectors* panel, expand Connector
	Duct Connector	• **Ribbon**: *Create* tab>*Connectors* panel, expand Connector
	Electrical Connector	• **Ribbon**: *Create* tab>*Connectors* panel, expand Connector
	Pipe Connector	• **Ribbon**: *Create* tab>*Connectors* panel, expand Connector
Other Tools		
	Component	• **Ribbon:** *Create* tab>*Model* panel
	Control	• **Ribbon:** *Create* tab>*Control* panel
	Detail Component	• **Ribbon**: *Annotate* tab>*Detail* panel
	Masking Region	• **Ribbon:** *Annotate* tab>*Detail* panel
	Model Line	• **Ribbon:** *Create* tab>*Model* panel
	Opening	• **Ribbon:** *Create* tab>*Model* panel
	Symbolic Line	• **Ribbon:** *Annotate* tab>*Detail* panel
	Visibility Settings	• **Ribbon:** Various contextual tabs>*Mode* panel

Additional Family Types

Beyond the basics of family creation, there are several special cases. These include a variety of 2D detail and annotation families, 2D profiles used as the basis of other family geometry creation, line-based families that work with 2D and 3D elements, and in-place families that are only available in the current project. Shared parameters are frequently required when you create tags with information you want to include in schedules.

Learning Objectives

- Create 2D detail families.
- Create 2D profiles that are used to create sweeps, reveals, railings, nosings, and other elements.
- Create 2D symbol families using drawing tools, filled regions, text, and labels.
- Create 2D and 3D line-based families with and without arrays.
- Create in-place families directly in a project.
- Create shared parameters that can be used in both tags and schedules in multiple projects.

6.1 Creating 2D Families

2D elements can be inserted into views and families to give additional information and level of detail about a design, as shown in Figure 6–1. These families include detail items, profiles, tags, and symbols.

Ceiling Tile

Recessed Fluorescent Light Fixture

Detail Items : Suspended Acoustic Ceiling-Square Edge- Section

Figure 6–1

Creating Detail Items

Detail components can be added into drafting views and nested into families. There are many sample files found in the Revit Library's *Detail Items* folder, organized by CSI specification divisions, as shown for a concrete joist section in Figure 6–2.

Figure 6–2

Detail families are created using the **Detail Item.rft** template, which only includes two reference planes used to define the insertion point. Then, you use the tools found on the *Create* tab>*Detail* panel to add elements such as lines and filled regions, as shown in Figure 6–3 for the front of a dock bumper, to create the detail.

Figure 6–3

- Standard family tools such as reference planes, dimensions, labels, controls, and family types also apply to detail families.

Creating Profiles

Profiles are 2D elements that are used in a variety of commands to create 3D elements. For example, you need a profile to create wall sweeps (as shown in the Base profile in Figure 6–4) and reveals, gutters, fascias, and floor slab edges. They are also used in families for curtain wall mullions, railings, stair nosings, and solid sweeps.

Profile   **Profile used in a wall sweep**

Figure 6–4

Several profile templates are supplied with the Autodesk® Revit® software: **Profile**, **Profile-Hosted**, **Profile-Mullion**, **Profile-Rail**, **Profile-Reveal**, and **Profile-Stair Nosing**. These are created with existing reference planes to help you place the elements correctly on the host element.

- All profiles must be closed shapes.

- Profile families can include detail components.

Creating Tags and Symbols

Tags and symbols are created using specific templates related to the type of element you want to tag, as shown in the Revit Library's *Annotations* folder in Figure 6–5. You can also create Generic and Multi-Category tags, as well as generic annotations such as a north arrow. Click **Imperial Library** in the *Places* panel if you do not default to the Revit Library folder.

Note: You can modify tags and symbols that are supplied with Revit to fit your company standards.

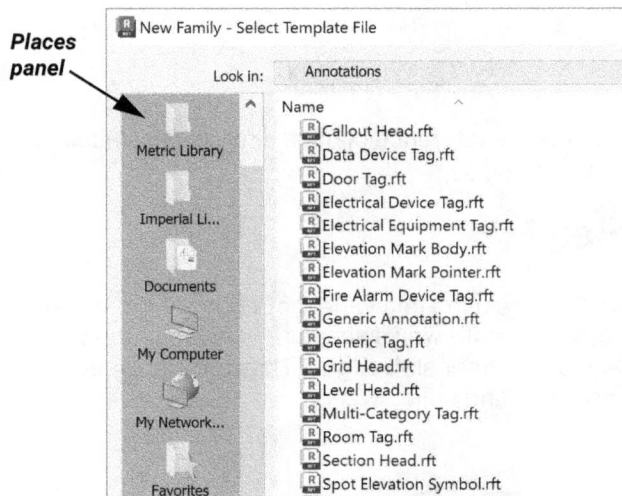

Annotation templates in Revit

Figure 6–5

The drawing tools for annotation families include the standard line sketching tools, filled region, text, and label. You can also add existing symbols to the family.

- Most annotation symbols do not have family types. They are designed to change size according to the view scale.

  Note: Practices for creating tags are included with shared parameters practices.

- Some annotation family templates include notes to help you create the symbol. Delete them before using the family.

- Tags are frequently created using shared parameters that are both associated with elements and can be scheduled.

Adding Labels

Many tags (as well as title blocks) use labels. Labels are not just text, but elements that are assigned to specific parameters. They can change without modifying the rest of the elements. For example, in a tag, you add a label (such as **Extension** shown in Figure 6–6) that can later be adjusted either by the type or instance parameter in the project.

Figure 6–6

How To: Create a Label

1. Starting in an annotation or title block family template, in the *Create* tab>*Text* panel, click $A_\boxdot$ (Label).

2. In the *Modify | Place Label* tab>*Text* panel, specify the alignments: **Align Text Left**, **Align Text Center**, **Align Text Right**, **Align Text Top**, **Align Text Middle**, or **Align Text Bottom**.

3. Click in the view window to place the label.

4. In the *Edit Label* dialog box (shown in Figure 6–7), select a label in the *Category Parameters* list and double-click, or click $\overline{\overline{\underline{\overline{}}}}$ (Add parameter(s) to label). You can select more than one by holding <Ctrl> or <Shift>.

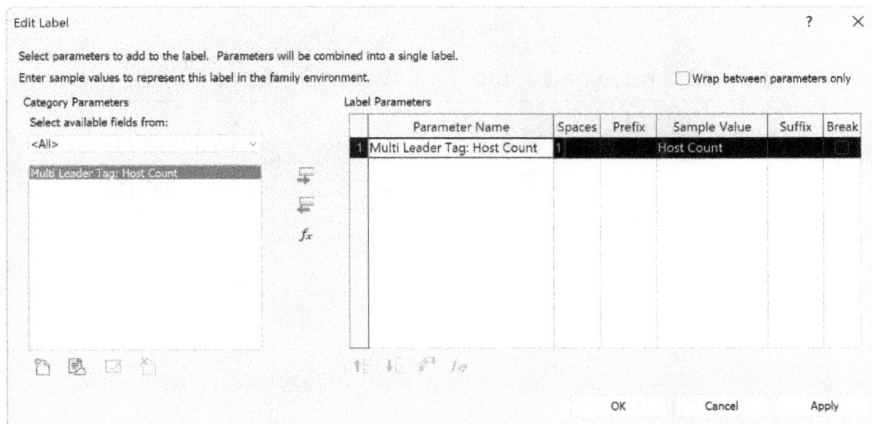

Figure 6–7

5. Enter the *Sample Value* and specify any other options, as needed.

6. Click **OK** when you have finished editing the label.

- While placing the label, you can rotate or stretch it (as shown in Figure 6–8), or select a point for an additional label.

•DRW

Figure 6–8

- You can also rotate or stretch a label once it has been placed in the family. However, you cannot extend the length of a label once loaded into a project.

💡 Hint: Modifying Labels

When you add labels, the length of the boundary box impacts the way the text word-wraps. For example, the Viewport: Title w Line tag that comes with the default metric template does not have enough room for a long title, as shown in Figure 6–9.

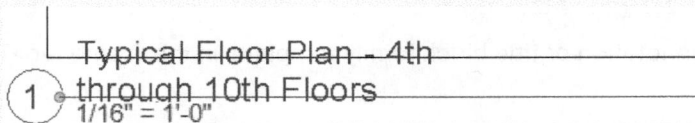

Typical Floor Plan - 4th
1 | through 10th Floors
1/16" = 1'-0"

Figure 6–9

To modify it, open the related family file (in this case **View Title.rfa**) and stretch the length of the label boundary, as shown in Figure 6–10.

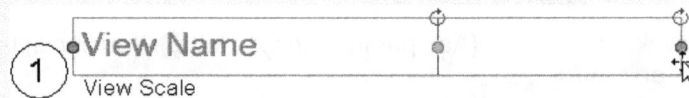

1 | View Name
View Scale

Figure 6–10

Save the annotation family and reload it into the project. The length of the title expands to fit the longer title, as shown in Figure 6–11.

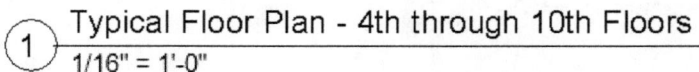

1 | Typical Floor Plan - 4th through 10th Floors
1/16" = 1'-0"

Figure 6–11

Practice 6a
Create 2D Families – Arrow Symbol

Practice Objectives

- Create an annotation symbol.
- Add a filled region.
- Test the symbol in a project.

In this practice, you will create an annotation symbol and apply it to a project, as shown in Figure 6–12.

View Scale 1/2"=1'-0"   *View Scale 1/4"=1'-0"*

Figure 6–12

Task 1: Create an annotation symbol.

1. Create a new annotation symbol family based on the **Generic Annotation.rft** template found in the practice files *Architectural>RFT* folder.

   - Note the red notes providing some guidance on family category and insertion points. Make sure to delete the red text before saving and inserting it into the project.

2. Save the family to your practice files *Architectural>RFA* folder as **Arrow.rfa**.

3. In the *Create* tab>*Detail* panel, click ⌐ (Line) and sketch the arrow as shown in Figure 6–13. The dimensions are for reference only; do not add them to the sketch.

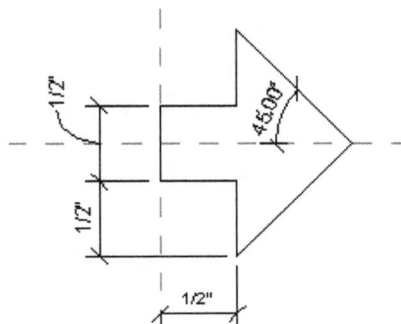

Figure 6–13

4. In the *Create* tab>*Detail* panel, click ⬚ (Filled Region). Add a filled region by using the draw tools to sketch the outline of the arrow. You can add the default solid pattern, or if time permits, create a new pattern similar to the pattern shown in Figure 6–14.

Figure 6–14

5. Save the family.

Task 2: Add the symbol to a project.

1. Open a new project file.
2. Switch back to the arrow family and click ⬚ (Load into Project and Close).
3. In the project, place the arrow symbol. (If required, in the *Annotate* tab>*Symbol* panel, click

    ⬚ (Symbol) to start the command if it is not automatically started and select the **Arrow** type.)
4. Add some other full-scale elements near the arrow.
5. Change the *View Scale*, as shown previously in Figure 6–12. The arrow should resize according to the new view scale.
6. Close the project. You do not need to save it.

End of practice

Practice 6b
Create 2D Families – Curtain Wall Mullion Profile

Practice Objectives

- Create a profile family including reference planes, dimensions, and a label.
- Insert a detail family.
- Modify the visibility of the detail family.

In this practice, you will create a mullion profile by creating a parametric framework of reference planes, dimensions, and a label, and then add lines, as shown in Figure 6–15. You will then insert an existing detail designed to work with the profile and modify it so it fits the new profile. Finally, you will set the visibility settings of the detail family so it only shows when the *Detail Level* is set to **Fine**, as shown on the right in Figure 6–15.

Figure 6–15

Task 1: Create a profile.

1. Close all open files.
2. On the Home screen, in the *Families* area, click **New....**

3. In the *New Family - Select Template File* dialog box, navigate to the practice files *Architectural>RFT* folder and select **Profile-Mullion.rft** and click **Open**. The template includes some text and reference planes as shown in Figure 6–16.

Center Of Mullion

Interior

Curtain Panels are trimmed to where the profile sketch intersects the Center (Front/Back) Ref Plane.

Center Front/Back Reference Plane

Exterior

Figure 6–16

4. Change the *Scale* to **3"=1'-0"**.

5. Type **UN** to open the *Project Units* dialog box. In the *Format* column, click the value next to *Length*.

6. In the *Format* dialog box, set the *Units* to **Fractional inches**, leave the *Rounding* as is, and set the *Unit symbol* to ". Click **OK**.

7. Click **OK**.

8. Save the family as **Mullion Profile.rfa** to the practice files *Architectural>RFA* folder.

9. Add the reference planes, dimensions, and lines shown in Figure 6–17.

10. To create a depth label for the dimensions, as shown in Figure 6–17, select the dimension and in the *Modify | Dimensions* tab>*Label Dimension* panel, click 🔲 (Create Parameter).

Figure 6–17

11. Lock all profile lines to their aligned reference planes.

Task 2: Add a detail component to the profile.

1. In the practice files *Architectural>RFA* folder, open **Mullion Detail Center.rfa**. This is a detail family that is based on the same shape as the mullion profile you just created, as shown in Figure 6–18.

Figure 6–18

2. In the *Modify* tab>*Family Editor* panel, click ⬚ (Load into Project). Load the detail into the **Mullion Profile.rfa** project.

3. Start the **Detail Component** command. Place the detail at the intersection of the original reference planes and click ▷ (Modify). The detail does not fit with the profile yet, as shown in Figure 6–19.

Figure 6–19

4. Select the detail element and edit the type.

5. In the *Type Properties* dialog box, beside the **Depth** parameter, click the **Associate Family Parameter button,** as shown in Figure 6–20.

6. In the *Associate Family Parameter* dialog box, select **Depth** and click **OK**, as shown in Figure 6–20.

Figure 6–20

7. The mullion detail now matches the profile, as shown in Figure 6–21.

Figure 6–21

8. Align and lock the detail centers (Horizontal and Vertical) to the original reference planes to keep them from moving.

9. With the mullion detail still selected, in the *Modify | Detail Items* tab>*Visibility* panel, click ⬚ (Visibility Settings).

10. In the *Family element visibility settings* dialog box, clear the check marks from each of the *Detail Levels* except **Fine**, as shown in Figure 6–22. Click **OK**.

Figure 6–22

11. Toggle on the **Preview Visibility** and test the different detail levels.

12. Toggle off the **Preview Visibility**.

13. Save and close the family files.

• If time permits, you can add the mullion profile to a mullion type in a project (as shown in Figure 6–23) and test it in a curtain wall. Mullion types are system families.

Figure 6–23

End of practice

Practice 6c
Create 2D Families – Electrical Trunking Line Profile

Practice Objectives

- Create a profile family including reference planes, dimensions, and a label.
- Add a formula to parameters.

In this practice, you will create a profile by creating a parametric framework of reference planes, dimensions, and labels, and then add lines, as shown in Figure 6–24. You will also add a formula in the *Family Types* dialog box.

Figure 6–24

1. Close all open files.
2. On the Home screen, in the *Families* area, click **New....**
3. In the *New Family - Select Template File* dialog box, navigate to the practice files *MEP>RFT* folder, select **Profile.rft,** and click **Open**. The template includes two reference planes that define the insertion point of the profile.
4. Save the family as **Trunking Profile.rfa** in the practice files *MEP>RFA* folder.
5. To make the information easier to read as you proceed, change the *Scale* to **3"=1'-0"**.
6. Type **UN** to open the *Project Units* dialog box. In the *Format* column, click the value next to *Length*.

7. In the *Format* dialog box, set the *Units* to **Fractional Inches**, leave the *Rounding* as is, and set the *Unit symbol* to ". Click **OK**.

8. Add the reference planes, dimensions, and lines, as shown in Figure 6–25. Lock all profile lines to their aligned reference planes.

9. Create labels for the dimensions as shown in Figure 6–25 by selecting a dimension and in the *Modify | Dimensions* tab>*Label Dimension* panel, click ▤ (Create Parameter).

Figure 6–25

10. In the *Create* tab>*Properties* panel, click ⊞ (Family Types). Set the *Formula* for *Nominal Height* to **Nominal Width**, as shown in Figure 6–26. Click **OK**.

Parameter	Value	Formula	Lock
Dimensions			⌃
Land	1"	=	☐
Nominal Height	4"	= Nominal Width	☐
Nominal Width	4"	=	☐

Figure 6–26

11. Zoom in on the top of the angled line and add a **1/32"** notch **3/8"** off each end of angled line, as shown in Figure 6–27.

Figure 6–27

12. Mirror the notch to the other end of the angled line. Split and trim, as required.

13. Save and close the profile family.

End of practice

Practice 6d
Create 2D Families – Structural Floor Profile

Practice Objectives

- Create a profile to use in defining a composite metal deck.
- Load the profile into a project and create a new structural floor type using the profile.
- Test the new floor and change the span direction.

In this practice, you will create a profile for a composite metal deck and save it to a library. You will then load the profile into a project, use it to create a new Metal Deck Floor type, as shown in Figure 6–28, and test the new floor type.

Figure 6–28

Task 1: Create a composite metal deck profile.

1. Close all open files.

2. On the Home screen, in the *Families* area, click **New....**

3. In the *New Family - Select Template File* dialog box, navigate to the practice files *Structural>RFT* folder, select **Profile.rft,** and click **Open.**

4. Save the family to your practice files *Structural>RFA* folder as **Composite-Metal-Deck.rfa.**

5. To make the information easier to read as you proceed, change the *Scale* to **3"=1'-0".**

6. Type **UN** to open the *Project Units* dialog box. In the *Format* column, click the value next to *Length.*

7. In the *Format* dialog box, set the *Units* to **Fractional Inches**, leave the *Rounding* as is, and set the *Unit symbol* to ".

8. Add reference planes as shown in Figure 6-29 (the dimensions are shown for reference only).

Figure 6-29

9. Sketch the profile and lock all profile lines to their aligned reference planes, as shown in Figure 6-30.

Figure 6-30

10. In the *Create* tab>*Properties* panel, click ⊞ (Family Types).

11. At the top of *Family Types* dialog box, click 🗋 (New Type).

---

12. In the *Name* dialog box, set the name to **3"**, and click **OK**.

13. Click **OK** again to close the dialog box.

14. Save the family without closing the file.

Task 2: Load the composite metal deck profile.

1. Start a new project based on the **Imperial-Structural Template** file found in the practice files *Structural>RTE* folder. Open the **Structural Plans: Level 2** view.

2. Switch back to the **Composite-Metal-Deck.rfa** or press <Ctrl>+<Tab> to toggle back to the family file and load it into the project.

3. In the *Structure* tab>*Structure* panel, click ⌒ (Floor: Structural).

4. In the Type Selector, verify that **Floor: 3"LW Concrete on 2" Metal Deck** is selected.

5. In the *Modify | Create Floor Boundary* tab>*Draw* panel, use the **Line** or **Rectangle** tool to draw a slab of any type or size. Set the *Span Direction* to **Horizontal**.

6. Click ✔ (Finish Edit Mode).

7. In the Quick Access Toolbar or *View* tab>*Create* panel, click ◇ (Section) and place a section vertically through the slab from north to south.

8. Open the new section view and change the *Scale* to **3/4"=1'-0"** and the *Detail Level* to **Fine**. It should look similar to the one shown in Figure 6–31.

Figure 6–31

9. Select the slab.

10. In Properties, click ⬚ (Edit Type).

11. Duplicate the existing type. Name the duplicated type **6" Concrete on 3" Comp Metal Deck**.

12. Edit the **Structure** parameter.

13. Modify the **Structure, 1, Concrete, Lightweight - 4 ksi** layer to a *Thickness* of **6"**, as shown in Figure 6–32.

Layers			EXTERIOR SIDE				
	Function	Priority	Material	Thickness	Wraps	Structural Material	Variable
1	**Core Boundary**		**Layers Above Wrap**	0' 0"			
2	Structure	1	Concrete, Lightweight, 4 ksi	0' 6"		☑	☐
3	Structural Deck	1	Metal - Deck	0' 0"		☐	☐
4	**Core Boundary**		**Layers Below Wrap**	0' 0"			

Figure 6–32

14. Select the **Structural Deck** layer. In the *Structural Deck Properties* area, in the *Deck Profile* drop-down list, select **Composite-Metal-Deck: 3"**, as shown in Figure 6–33.

Figure 6–33

15. Click **OK** to close all of the dialog boxes. The section should display the metal deck profile that was previously created, as shown in Figure 6–34.

Figure 6–34

Task 3: Change the flute direction of a composite metal deck.

1. Return to the **Structural Plans: Level 2** view.

2. Select the **Span Direction Symbol**. Note that the **Direction Symbol** extends to the edges of the slab. The closed arrowheads represent the flute direction and the open arrowheads represent the extents of the slab in the perpendicular direction.

3. Start the **Rotate** command and rotate the span direction 90 degrees.

4. Return to the section view. The orientation of the composite metal deck has changed, as shown in Figure 6–35.

Figure 6–35

5. Save the project as **New Floor.rvt** and close the project.

6. Save and close the file **Composite-Metal-Deck.rfa**.

End of practice

6.2 Creating Line-Based Families

Line-based families enable you to draw repeating elements in a line by selecting two points. These families can be made up of 2D detail elements (such as the filled region in Figure 6–36 that is used to show GWB in a wall section) or an array of 3D elements, such as the solar panels shown in Figure 6–37. These families are created using a line-based family template that has a default **Length** parameter that controls the start and end points of the family and a reference line built in.

Length = 4' - 0"

Detail Items : Filled region : Detail Filled Region

Figure 6–36

Length = 9' - 0"

Panel Distance = 4' - 0"

Model Groups : Model Group : Array Group 1

Figure 6–37

- When using a line-based model component in a project, place the components on a face or on a work plane, as shown in Figure 6-38.

Figure 6-38

How To: Create a Simple Line-Based Family

1. Start a new family based on a family template with **line based** as the descriptor.

2. The template includes reference planes, a labeled dimension, and a reference line, as shown in Figure 6-39.

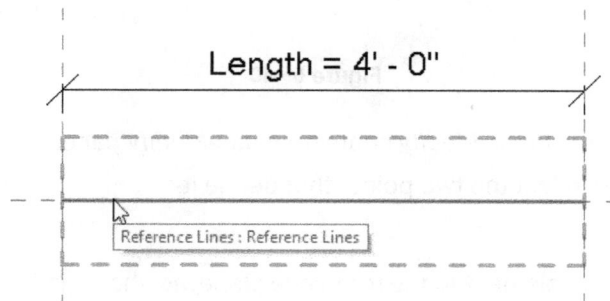

Figure 6-39

3. Add any other framework information, as needed.

4. Add elements that make up the family.

   - Detail elements include lines, detail components, symbols, masking regions, filled regions, text, and controls.
   - Model elements include all of the form tools along with components, model lines and text, connectors, and controls.

5. Flex the **Length** parameter to verify that what you have added works as expected.

6. Add parameters and family types, if needed.

7. Load the family in a project to test it.

How To: Create Line-Based Family with an Array

1. Start a new family based on a family template with **line based** as the descriptor.

2. Add any other framework information, as needed.

3. Insert a component or symbol or create model elements that you want to array.

4. Locate the element at the first point of the array. In the example shown in Figure 6–40, a square extrusion is aligned and locked to the reference planes.

Figure 6–40

5. Select the element and in the *Modify* contextual tab>*Modify* panel, click ▦ (Array).

6. Set up the array and select the two points that define it.

7. Click ⏳ (Modify).

8. Align and lock the last element to the reference plane, as shown in Figure 6–41.

Figure 6–41

9. Flex the **Length** parameter to verify that the elements stay within the reference planes, as shown in Figure 6–42.

Length = 8' - 0"

Figure 6–42

- To control the array, you can select the array edge and create a label (family parameter) by going to the *Modify | Array* tab>*Labeling* panel and clicking 🔲 (Create Parameter).

Family Category and Parameters

The *Family Category and Parameters* dialog box (shown in Figure 6–43) lets you assign your family to a category, like **Electrical Equipment**, **Furniture**, or **Specialty Equipment**, based on the needed behavior in a project. You can click in the *Category name search* field and type the category you are looking for or use the *Filter list* drop-down list to limit your selection by discipline, as shown in Figure 6–43. In the *Family Parameters* area, you can then specify the parameters that will control the behavior of the family, like *Cut with Voids When Loaded*. The available options differ based on the selected category. Some options will be grayed out, such as *Classification Title*, which indicates that it is a fixed parameter that cannot be modified.

Figure 6–43

- Specifying a category also helps when creating schedules.

How To: Set the Family Category and Parameters of a Family

1. Within the family editor, select ⬚ (Family Category and Parameters).

2. In the *Family Category and Parameters* dialog box, in the *Family Category* area, select the category you want to assign your family to.

3. In the *Family Parameters* area, scroll through the choices and select all parameters that apply.

Practice 6e
Create Line-Based Families – GWB Detail

Practice Objectives

- Create a line-based detail family.
- Add family types.
- Test the family in a project.

In this practice, you will create a line-based detail family using a filled region to represent Gypsum Wall Board (GWB) in details. You will add reference planes, a label, and a flip control to help you create this family, as shown in Figure 6–44. You will create family types and test the family in a project.

Figure 6–44

Task 1: Create a line-based detail family.

1. On the Home screen, in the *Families* area, click **New...**.

---

2. In the *New Family* dialog box, navigate to the practice files *Architectural>RFT* folder, select **Detail Item line based.rft**, and click **Open**. The family template includes three reference planes, a reference line, and a labeled dimension, as shown in Figure 6−45.

Figure 6−45

3. Save the family as **Detail Component-GWB.rfa** in the practice files *Architectural>RFA* folder.

4. Add a horizontal reference plane above the existing and dimension it as shown in Figure 6−46.

Figure 6−46

5. In the *Create* tab>*Detail* panel, click ▨ (Filled Region).

6. In the *Draw* panel, use the **Rectangle** tool to create the outline of the fill, snapping and locking the lines in place, as shown in Figure 6–47.

Figure 6–47

7. In the Type Selector, select **Filled region: Gypsum**.

8. Click ✔ (Finish Edit mode).

9. Flex the **Length** dimension to verify that the filled region moves as expected, as shown in Figure 6–48.

Figure 6–48

10. Finish with a length of **4'-0"**.

11. Select the **2"** dimension and in the *Modify | Dimensions* tab>*Label Dimension* panel, click 🗒 (Create Parameter).

12. Create a **Thickness** label (Type Parameter), then change the **2"** dimension to **5/8"**, as shown in Figure 6–49.

13. In the *Create* tab>*Control* panel, click ↟ (Control).

14. In the *Modify | Place Control* tab>*Control Type* panel, click ↟ (Double Vertical).

15. Place the control as shown in Figure 6–49.

Figure 6–49

16. Save the family.

Task 2: Create family types and test the family in a project.

1. In the *Create* or *Modify* tab>*Properties* panel, click ▦ (Family Types).

2. In the *Family Types* dialog box, click 🗅 (New Type).

3. Type in the *Name* **GWB 5/8"** and click **Apply**.

4. Create two additional types named **GWB 1/2"** and **GWB 1/4"** with the thickness modified to match.

5. Test each of the new types and click **OK**.

6. Save the family.

7. Start a new project.

8. In the *View* tab>*Create* panel, click 🖫 (Drafting View) and give it a generic name.

9. Switch back to the family file and load it into the project.

    Note: *Switch to the drafting view and in the Annotate tab>Detail panel, click* ▦ *(Detail Component) and select the new type if required.*

10. Test each of the linear family types in the drafting view, as shown in Figure 6–50.

Figure 6–50

11. Save and close the family file.

12. Close the project without saving.

End of practice

Practice 6f
Create Line-Based Families – Electrical Trunking

Practice Objectives

- Create a line-based model family.
- Test the family in a project.

In this practice, you will create a line-based model family using a profile and a sweep for trunking, as shown in Figure 6–51. You will add a control and assign a family category and then use the new family in a project.

Figure 6–51

Task 1: Create a line-based model family.

1. On the Home screen, in the *Families* area, click **New...**.

2. In the *New Family* dialog box, navigate to the practice files *MEP>RFT* folder, select **Generic Model line based.rft**, and click **Open**. The family template includes three reference planes, a reference line, and a labeled dimension, as shown in Figure 6–52.

Figure 6–52

3. Save the family as **Trunking.rfa** in the practice files *MEP>RFA* folder.

4. In the *Create* tab>*Forms* panel, click ✏️ (Sweep).

5. In the *Modify | Sweep* tab>*Sweep* panel, click ✏️ (Sketch Path).

6. Sketch the path from intersection to intersection of the reference planes and lock it. If needed, use **Align** to help you lock it in place, as shown in Figure 6–53.

Figure 6–53

7. Click ✓ (Finish Edit mode).

8. In the *Modify | Sweep* tab>*Sweep* panel, click 📐 (Load Profile).

9. In the practice files *MEP>RFA* folder, select **Trunking Profile.rfa**. If you did not complete *Practice 6c: Create 2D Families – Electrical Trunking Line Profile*, use **Trunking MEP Profile.rfa** in the practice files *MEP>RFA* folder.

10. Select **Trunking Profile** from the *Profile* drop-down list, as shown in Figure 6–54.

Figure 6–54

11. Click ✔ (Finish Edit mode).

12. Flex the **Length** dimension to verify that the sweep moves as expected, as shown in Figure 6–55.

Length = 4' - 0"   Length = 6' - 0"

Figure 6–55

13. Finish with a length of **4'-0"**.

14. In the *Create* tab>*Control* panel, click ⊹ (Control).

15. In the *Modify | Place Control* tab>*Control Type* panel, click ⊹ (Double Vertical).

16. Place the control as shown in Figure 6–56.

Figure 6–56

17. In the *Create* or *Modify* tab>*Properties* panel, click 🖳 (Family Categories and Parameters).

18. In the *Family Category and Parameters* dialog box, set the *Filter list* to **Electrical** and select **Electrical Fixtures**, as shown in Figure 6–57, then click **OK**.

Figure 6–57

19. Save the family.

Task 2: Test the family in a project.

1. In the practice files *MEP* folder, open **Fire Station-MEP.rvt.**
2. Open the Electrical>Power>Floor Plans>**1-Power** view and zoom on the training rooms.
3. Switch back to the family file and load it into the project.

   Note: If the command is not already started, in the Systems tab>Electrical panel, click
   (Electrical Fixture) *and in the Type Selector, select **Trunking**.*

4. In the *Modify | Place Devices* tab>*Placement* panel, click (Place on Work Plane).

5. Add trunking to the training rooms as shown in Figure 6–58. Use the **Flip** control if needed to verify it is on the outside of the wall.

Electrical fixtures

Electrical Fixtures : Trunking : Trunking

Figure 6–58

6. Save and close the project and family files.

End of practice

Practice 6g
Create Line-Based Families – Services Symbol Array

Practice Objectives

- Create a symbol family.
- Create a line-based family.
- Add an array to the line-based family.
- Add family types.
- Test the family in a project.

In this practice, you will create an annotation symbol using a label that will be added to a line-based detail family. You will add parameters and create an array parameter. You will then associate a parameter in the label with a parameter in the line-based family and create a series of family types, as shown in Figure 6–59. You will also test the family in a project.

Figure 6–59

Task 1: Create an annotation symbol with a label.

1. On the Home screen, in the *Families* area, click **New...**.

2. In the *New Family* dialog box, navigate to the practice files *MEP>RFT* folder, select **Generic Annotation.rft**, and click **Open**.

3. Zoom in to read the red note and then delete it. The family category of this example does not matter at this time.

4. Save the family as **Services Symbol.rfa** in the practice files *MEP>RFA* folder.

5. In the *Create* tab>*Text* panel, click A (Label).

6. Click near the intersection of the reference planes to place the label.

7. In the *Edit Label* dialog box, click (Add Parameter).

8. In the *Parameter Properties* dialog box, create a **Type** parameter with the *Name* of **Letter** and the *Data Type* set to **Text**, as shown in Figure 6–60. Click **OK**.

Figure 6–60

9. In the *Edit Label* dialog box, click (Add parameter(s) to label) and set the *Sample Value* to **A**, as shown in Figure 6–61. Click **OK**.

Figure 6–61

10. Move the label so it is at the intersection of the reference planes and resize boundary leaving some room on both size for longer text. Verify that the properties match what is shown in Figure 6–62.

Figure 6–62

11. Click in an empty area in the view and in Properties, select **Keep Text readable**.

12. Save the family.

Task 2: Create a line-based family.

1. Start a new family based on **Detail Item line based.rft** from the practice files *MEP>RFT* folder. The family template includes three reference planes, a reference line, and a labeled dimension, as shown in Figure 6–63.

Figure 6–63

2. Save the family as **Services Lines.rfa** in the *MEP>RFA* folder.

3. In the *Create* tab>*Detail* panel, click (Line).

4. In the *Modify | Place Lines* tab>*Subcategory* panel, expand the Subcategory list and select **Light Lines**.

5. In the Options Bar, toggle off **Chain**.

6. Sketch a line from the left intersection of the reference planes to the right intersection of the reference planes and lock it into place, as shown in Figure 6–64.

Figure 6–64

7. Add a reference plane offset 6" to the inside of each of the existing reference planes, then add dimensions, as shown in Figure 6–65.

Length = 4' - 0"

0' - 6"   0' - 6"

Figure 6–65

8. Select one of the 6" dimensions and in the *Modify | Dimensions* tab>*Label Dimension* panel, click 🗒 (Create Parameter). Create a type parameter for **Text Offset**. Apply the same label to the other 6" dimension, as shown in Figure 6–66.

Length = 4' - 0"

Text Offset = 0' - 6"   Text Offset = 0' - 6"

Figure 6–66

9. Save the family.

Task 3: Add an array.

---

1. Switch to the Services Symbol family and load it into the Services Lines family.

2. Place the label, which displays as **?**, on the reference planes' intersection and then align and lock it into place, as shown in Figure 6–67.

Text Offset = 0' - 6"

?

Figure 6–67

---

3. Select the symbol, then in the *Modify | Generic Annotations* tab>*Modify* panel, click 🔲 (Array).

4. In the *Modify | Array* tab>*Array* panel, verify that the **Linear** and **Group and Associate** options are selected, set the *Number* to **4**, and set *Move To* to **Last**. Select the innermost reference planes as the start point and end point, as shown in Figure 6–68.

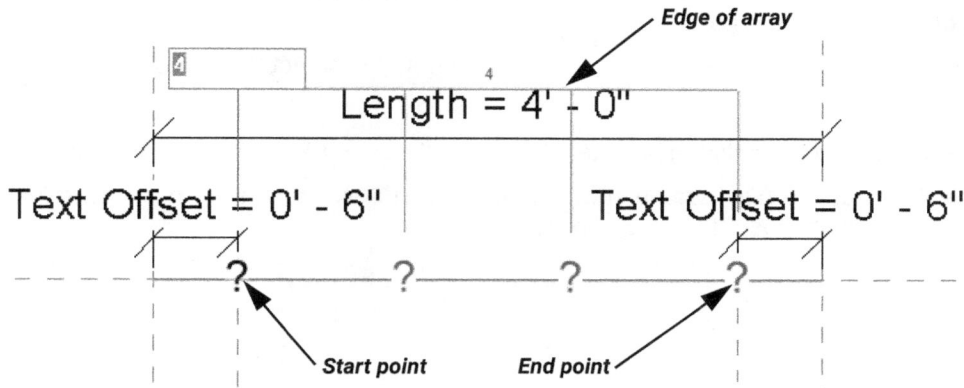

Figure 6–68

5. Align and lock the last label of the array to the text offset reference plane.

6. Click one of the **?** in the array, then select the edge of the array, as shown in Figure 6–69.

   • **Hint:** Hover over the edge of one of the arrayed elements and press <Tab> until the edge of the array (dashed lines) highlights to select the edge of the array.

7. In the *Modify | Array* tab>*Labeling* panel, click 📝 (Create Parameter) to create a label.

Figure 6–69

8. In the *Parameter Properties* dialog box, name the parameter **Number of Labels**, verify it is set to **Type**, and group it under **Other**. Click **OK**.

9. Open the *Family Types* dialog box and flex the parameters to ensure that they are working as expected by changing the *Length* value and clicking **Apply**.

10. Save the family.

Task 4: Create family types.

1. Open the *Family Types* dialog box again and at the bottom, click (New Parameter).

2. Create a new type parameter named **Service** with the *Data Type* set to **Text**. Click **OK** twice to exit out of the dialog boxes.

3. Select one of the labels. Press <Tab> to ensure that you select the symbol, not the group.

4. In Properties, click **Edit Type**.

5. In the *Type Properties* dialog box, next to *Letter*, click (Associate Family Parameter).

6. In the *Associate Family Parameter* dialog box, select **Service**, as shown in Figure 6–70. Click **OK** twice to close the dialog boxes.

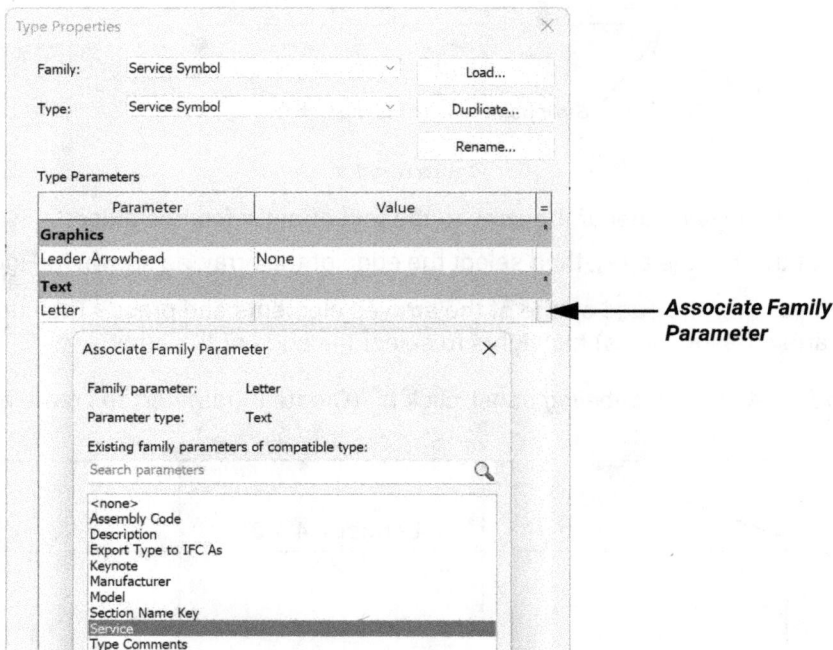

Figure 6–70

7. Open the *Family Types* dialog box again and set the value for *Service* to **A**. Click **Apply**. The letters should update as shown in Figure 6–71.

Length = 4' - 0"

Text Offset = 0' - 6"   Text Offset = 0' - 6"

A   A   A   A

Figure 6–71

8. Remain in the *Family Types* dialog box and at the top, click ◻ (New Type). Name the *Type* **Compressed Air** and click **OK**.

9. Create several other new types and change the *Service* value, as follows:

Type	Service Value
Hot Water Heating Supply	HW
Hot Water Heating Return	HWR
High Pressure Steam	HPS
Medium Pressure Steam	MPS
Low Pressure Steam	LPS

10. Save the family.

11. In the practice files *MEP* folder, open the project **Fire Station-MEP.rvt**.

12. Open the Coordination>All>Floor Plans>**Site** view.

13. In the *View* tab>*Windows* panel, click ▨ (Close Inactive).

14. Switch back to the Services Lines family and load it into the project.

15. Draw the service lines by first selecting the type from the Type Selector and then drawing in the view. If the **Detail Component** command did not start, in the *Annotate* tab>*Detail* panel, click ▦ (Detail Component). Draw several of the lines in the project, as shown in Figure 6–72.

Figure 6–72

16. Save and close the project and families.

End of practice

Practice 6h
Create Line-Based Families – Solar Panel Array

Practice Objectives

- Create a line-based model family.
- Apply an array.
- Add parameters to define the interactions of the array.
- Test the family in a project.

In this practice, you will create a line-based model family using a solar panel component. You will array the component and then set up parameters to define the number of panels set up in an array. You will test the line-based solar panel family in a project, as shown in Figure 6–73.

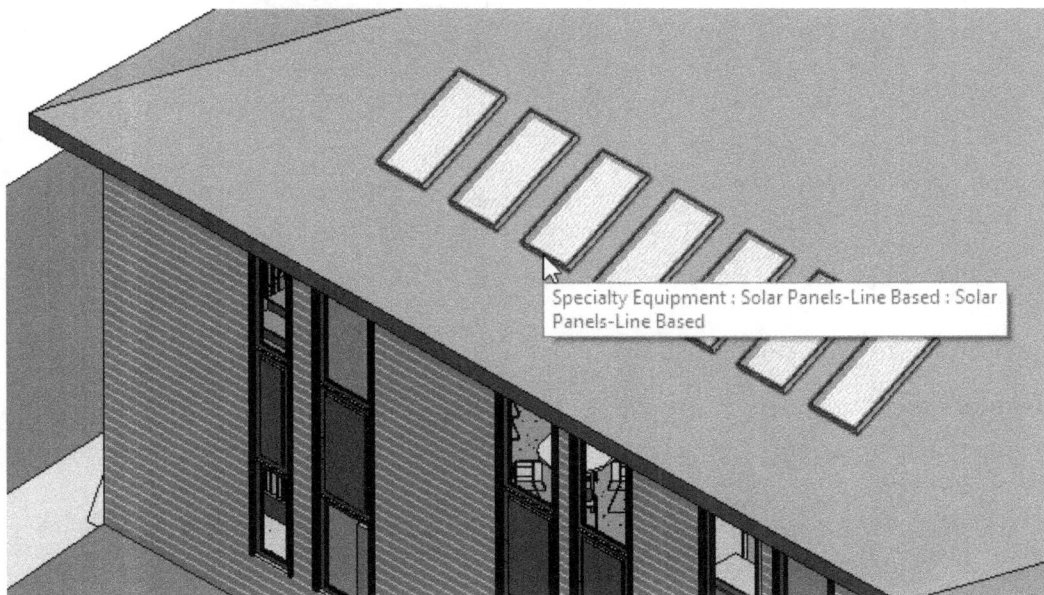

Figure 6–73

Task 1: Insert and array a component.

1. On the Home screen, in the *Families* area, click **New...**.

2. In the *New Family* dialog box, navigate to the practice files *Architectural>RFT* folder, select **Generic Model line based.rft** and click **Open**. The family template includes three reference planes, a reference line, and a labeled dimension, as shown in Figure 6−74.

Figure 6−74

3. Save the family as **Solar Panels - Line-Based.rfa** to the practice files *Architectural>RFA* folder.

4. Change the *Length* parameter to **9'-0"**.

5. In the *Create* tab>*Model* panel, click (Component).

6. An alert displays telling you that no component is loaded in the project. Click **Yes** to load one.

7. Navigate to the practice files *Architectural>RFA* folder, select **Solar Panel.rfa,** and click **Open**.

8. In the *Modify | Place Component* tab>*Placement* panel, click (Place on Work Plane).

9. Place the component and align and lock it to the reference planes, as shown in Figure 6–75.

Figure 6–75

10. Start the **Array** command and select the solar panel component, then press <Enter>. In the *Modify | Array* tab>*Array* panel, verify **Group and Associate** is selected, set the *Number* to **2**, and set *Move To* to **Last**. For the first pick, click on the solar panel, and for the second pick, click to the right to place the array as shown in Figure 6–76. The exact distance does not matter at this time.

Figure 6–76

11. Align and lock the edge of the second solar panel to the right and horizontal reference planes.

12. Save the family.

Task 2: Add parameters.

1. Click ⌖ (Modify). Select one solar panel in the array and select the edge of the array, as shown in Figure 6–77.

   - **Hint:** Hover over the edge of one of the arrayed elements and press <Tab> until the edge of the array (dashed lines) highlights. Select the edge of the array.

Figure 6–77

2. In the *Modify | Array* tab>*Labeling* panel, click ▤ (Create Parameter) to create a label.

3. In the *Parameter Properties* dialog box, in the *Parameter Data* area, type **Number of Panels** for the *Name* and select **Instance**. Group the parameter under **Constraints**, as shown in Figure 6–78. Click **OK**.

Figure 6–78

4. Open the *Family Types* dialog box. Change the *Number of Panels* to **3** and click **Apply**.

5. Test other numbers and you can see that there is an issue with more than 3 panels when the Length is set to **9'-0"**.

6. In the *Family Types* dialog box, at the bottom, click ⬜ (New Parameter).

7. In the *Parameter Properties* dialog box, create the parameter shown in Figure 6–79. Then, click **OK**.

Parameter Data

Name:

| Minimum Panel Distance | ○ Type |

Discipline:

| Common ⌄ | ⦿ Instance |

Data Type:

| Length ⌄ | ☐ Reporting Parameter |

Group parameter under:

| Constraints ⌄ | (Can be used to extract value from a geometric condition and report it in a formula or as a schedulable parameter) |

Tooltip description:

<No tooltip description. Edit this parameter to write a custom tooltip. Custom

Edit Tooltip...

Figure 6–79

8. Set the *Minimum Panel Distance* to **3'-6"**.

9. Set the formula for the *Number of Panels* to **Length / Minimum Panel Distance**, then click **Apply**.

10. Test out different lengths and distances to flex the family, such as the example shown in Figure 6-80.

Figure 6-80

11. Finish the testing by setting the *Length* to **9'-0"** and the *Minimum Panel Distance* to **3'-0"**.

12. Save the family.

Task 3: Test the family in a project.

1. In the practice files *Architectural* folder, open the **Fire Station.rvt** project.

2. Switch back to the family and load it into the project.

3. In the *Modify | Place Component* tab>*Placement* panel, click ✉ (Place on Face).

4. Select the south facing side of the roof where you want to place the solar panels and draw a string of solar panels across the roof, as shown in Figure 6–81.

Figure 6–81

5. Click ⌖ (Modify) and select the solar panels.

6. In Properties, in the *Constraints* area, change the *Minimum Panel Distance* to **3'-6"**. The number of panels changes with the new distance.

7. Save and close the project and family files.

End of practice

6.3 Creating In-Place Families

In-place families use standard family tools to create elements that are unique and specific to the project in which you create them and are not expected to be reused in any other project. These might include built-in furniture, custom door or window openings, and roofs.

In-place families should only be used if you are doing a one-time project specific modification. If you think a family might be used again, you should create a loadable component family for it.

- In-place family elements have a wide range of family categories to choose from to reflect the element type.

- If an in-place family in another project is needed, you can copy and paste it into your current project.

- If the element is a host element, such as a wall, you can add elements to it, such as doors or windows.

- Elements, such as in-place doors and windows, can be copied and moved within their host.

- Complex stairs can be created as an in-place family.

- In-place family elements can be aligned and locked to project elements so they move together.

- Ensure that reference planes are drawn in the family. If you tie an in-place family to an external reference plane and delete the reference plane, you lose the family.

- In-place families are rarely used in the MEP disciplines.

How To: Create an In-Place Family

1. In a project, in the *Architecture* tab>*Build* panel, *Structure* tab>*Model* panel, or *Systems* tab>*Model* panel, expand (Component) and click (Model In-Place).

2. In the *Family Category and Parameters* dialog box, you can filter the list to display only the disciplines needed or enter a category in the *Category name search* field, as shown in Figure 6–82.

Figure 6–82

3. Select a *Family Category* and click **OK**. In the *Name* dialog box, enter a name for the new family and click **OK**.

4. The *Family Editor* tabs display in the ribbon. Use the tools like reference planes, dimensions, labels, forms, connectors, and parameters to create the elements you want to have in the family.

5. In the *In-Place Editor* panel, click ✔ (Finish Model) to create the in-place element.

Practice 6i
Create In-Place Families – Door Opening

Practice Objectives

- Create an in-place door family and opening.
- Add trim for the in-place door family using a sweep based on a 2D profile.

In this practice, you will create a door in-place family and add an odd-shaped opening. Using a sweep, you will add a profile for door trim, as shown in Figure 6–83.

Figure 6–83

Task 1: Create an in-place door family.

1. Start a new project based on the **Imperial-Architectural Template.rte** file found in the practice files *Architectural>RTE* folder.

2. Save the project as **Sample Opening.rvt** in the practice files *Architectural* folder.

3. Verify you are in the **Floor Plan: Level 1** view, then draw a **10'-0"** high wall in the horizontal direction.

4. In the *Architecture* tab>*Build* panel, expand (Component) and click (Model In-Place).

5. In the *Family Category and Parameters* dialog box, set the *Filter list* to **Architecture** and then set the *Family Category* to **Doors**. Click **OK**.

6. Name the in-place family **Odd Shaped Opening**.

7. The Family Editor tools display in the ribbon. In the *Create* tab>*Datum* panel, click

    ⌂ (Reference Plane) and draw a reference plane along the center of the wall. Name it **Center of Wall,** as shown in Figure 6–84.

    Note: The reference plane is used to specify the work plane. It does not impact the shape of the wall.

    Center of Wall

    Figure 6–84

8. Switch to the **Elevations: South** view and zoom in on the wall.

9. In the *Create* tab>*Model* panel, click ⬜ (Opening).

    *Note: If you have more than one wall in the project, you are prompted to select a host for the opening. Click **OK** and select the wall.*

10. Draw an opening similar to that shown in Figure 6–85. The exact design does not matter; ensure that it is at least the width and height of a standard door opening. The sketch must be closed.

    Figure 6–85

11. Click ✔ (Finish Edit Mode), but do not click **Finish Model.**

Task 2: Add a sweep for the trim and sketch a profile.

1. In the *Create* tab>*Work Plane* panel, click ▦ (Set).

2. In the *Work Plane* dialog box, set the *Name* to **Reference Plane: Center of Wall** and click **OK**.

3. In the *Create* tab>*Forms* panel, click 🗂 (Sweep).

4. In the *Modify | Sweep* tab>*Sweep* panel, click ⬡ (Sketch Path).

5. Click 🖉 (Pick Lines) and select the lines around the opening. Do not close the sketch to make one continuous loop.

6. Click ✔ (Finish Edit Mode).

7. In the *Modify | Sweep* tab>*Sweep* panel, click 🗔 (Edit Profile).

8. In the *Go To View* dialog box, select **Floor Plan: Level 1** and click **Open View**.

9. Zoom in on the red dot. Draw the profile shown in Figure 6–86. The profile must be closed. You do not need to add the dimensions.

Figure 6–86

10. Click ✔ (Finish Edit Mode) twice.

11. Click ✔ (Finish Model).

12. View the new cased opening in several views.

   - Drawing the profile in the in-place family keeps the size of the trim directly connected to the selected wall and opening. If you were to change the size of the wall, the frame will not update since there are no constraints applied to the width of the frame.

13. If time permits, edit the in-place family. Go to **Floor Plan: Level 1**, select the frame, and edit the sweep, then select the sweep and click **Edit Profile**. Align and lock the profile sketch lines that are around the wall, then dimension and lock the dimensions in place, as shown in Figure 6–87. Change the wall type to see if it was successfully constrained.

   - **Hint:** You will need to dimension from the outer sketch line to the wall and lock it.

Figure 6–87

14. Save and close the project.

End of practice

Practice 6j
Create In-Place Families – Concrete Corbeling

Practice Objectives

- Create a 2D profile and use it in an in-place family to create a concrete corbel.
- Join the corbeling to the wall.

In this practice, you will draw a profile of a corbel and then use it in an in-place family to create a sweep, as shown in Figure 6–88.

Figure 6–88

Note: A Corbel is a stepped bracket, designed to support a weight. It projects from a wall and is created from a building material, such as concrete, stone, or wood.

Task 1: Create the profile.

1. Create a new family based on the **Profile-Hosted.rft** template found in the practice files *Structural>RFT* folder

2. Save the family as **Corbel.rfa** to the practice files *Structural>RFA* folder.

3. Change the scale to **3"=1'-0"** and draw the four reference planes shown in Figure 6–89.

    Note: The dimensions are for information only.

Figure 6–89

4. In the *Create* tab>*Detail* panel, click ⌐ (Line). Draw the profile shown in Figure 6–90. Lock all lines to their aligned reference planes.

    Note: The Family Editor does not display as many tabs or panels because fewer commands are required to create a 2D profile.

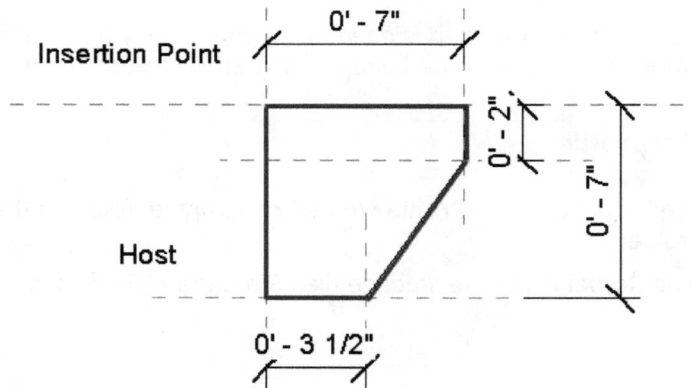

Figure 6–90

5. Save the family.

Task 2: Add a new wall sweep using the profile.

1. In the practice files *Structural* folder, open **Concrete-Structure.rvt**.
2. Open the **Structural Plans: Level 1** view.
3. In the *Structure* tab>*Model* panel, expand ▦ (Component) and click ▦ (Model In-Place).
4. In the *Family Category and Parameters* dialog box, set the *Filter list* to **Structure** only, select **Walls**, and click **OK**.
5. In the *Name* dialog box, type **Wall Corbeling** and click **OK**.
6. In the *In-Place Editor,* in the *Create* tab>*Forms* panel, click ▧ (Sweep).
7. In the *Modify | Sweep* tab>*Sweep* panel, click ⌔ (Sketch Path).
8. Use the Draw tools to sketch the lines shown in Figure 6–91 along the exterior side of the walls.

Figure 6–91

9. Click ✔ (Finish Edit Mode).
10. In the *Modify | Sweep* tab>*Sweep* panel, click ▧ (Load Profile).
11. In the *Load Family* dialog box, navigate to the **Corbel.rfa** profile created in the previous task. Select it and click **Open**.
12. In the *Sweep* panel, click ▧ (Select Profile).
13. In the *Profile* list, select **Corbel**.
14. In the Quick Access Toolbar, click ⌂ (Default 3D View).

15. Zoom in on the profile location and note that it is facing into the wall, as shown in Figure 6–92.

Figure 6–92

16. In the Options Bar, click **Flip**.

17. In Properties, edit the *Vertical Profile Offset*, or using the temporary dimension, lower the corbel (negative) **-6"** in the Y-direction, as shown in Figure 6–93.

Figure 6–93

18. Click ✔ (Finish Edit Mode).

19. With the new corbel sweep still selected, in Properties, in the *Materials and Finishes* area, next to *Material*, click **<By Category>**, then click ⬚ (Browse).

20. In the *Material Browser*, select **Concrete - Cast-in-Place Concrete** and click **OK**.

21. In the *Modify | Sweep* tab>*In-Place Editor* panel, click ✔ (Finish Model).

Task 3: Join the corbel to the wall.

1. Open the **Structural Plans: Level 1** view.

2. Draw a wall section across the wall and corbel, as shown in Figure 6–94.

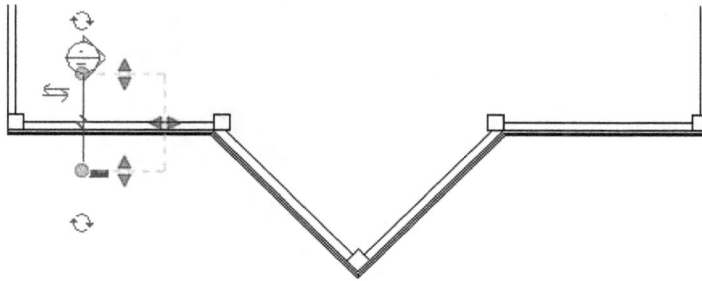

Figure 6–94

3. Open the section. You can see that the wall and corbel are still considered separate entities, as shown in Figure 6–95.

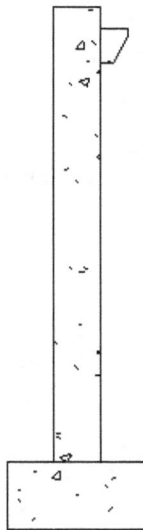

Figure 6–95

4. In the *Modify* tab>*Geometry* panel, click ⬤ (Join). Select the wall and then the corbel. It becomes part of the existing wall, as shown in Figure 6–96.

Figure 6–96

5. Save and close the project.

End of practice

6.4 Working with Shared Parameters

Shared parameters can be used across multiple projects or families and are stored in a .TXT file outside of any projects or families, which protects it from being changed. You can only reference one shared parameter file (.TXT) at a time, but it can be used across multiple elements in a model.

Creating Shared Parameters

Shared parameters can be created wherever there is an option to create a parameter (as shown in Figure 6–97), including in *Schedule Properties* (creating a field) and in the *Family Types* dialog box.

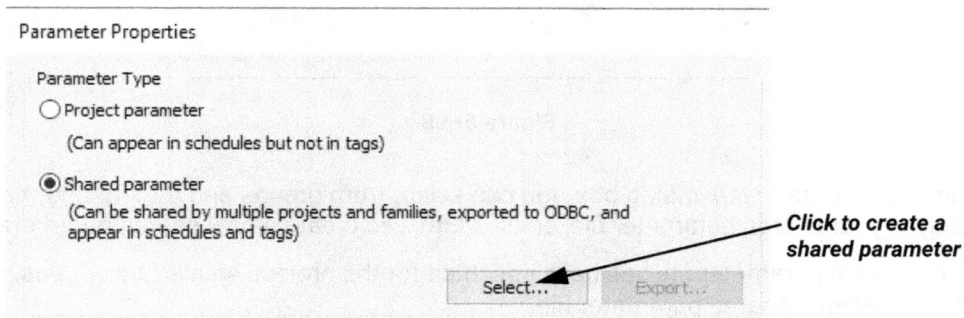

Figure 6–97

* You can also directly open the *Edit Shared Parameters* dialog box by clicking (Shared Parameters) in the *Manage* tab>*Settings* panel.

   Note: *If you are creating shared parameters in a family file, do it only for elements that constrain or flex the geometry and are used in a schedule.*

How To: Create a Shared Parameter

1. Start the process of adding a parameter in Project Parameters, schedules, or family types.

2. Set the *Parameter Type* to **Shared parameter** in the *Parameter Properties* dialog box, as shown in Figure 6–98.

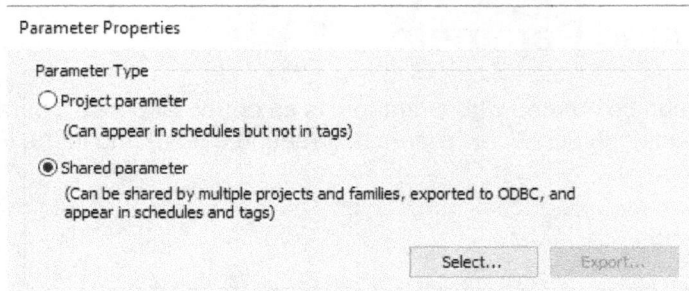

Parameter Properties

Parameter Type

○ Project parameter
  (Can appear in schedules but not in tags)

◉ Shared parameter
  (Can be shared by multiple projects and families, exported to ODBC, and appear in schedules and tags)

Select...   Export...

Figure 6–98

3. Click **Select...**.

4. In the *Shared Parameters* dialog box, you can select from groups and parameters that are already in your shared parameter file, or click **Edit...** to create a new shared parameter.

    *   If no shared parameter file has been specified for the project, an alert box opens. Click **Yes** to select a shared parameter file.

    Note: Shared parameters are stored in a text file that should be placed in a network location available to everyone. This ensures consistency between projects and team members by maintaining naming standards and limiting typical typing errors with spaces and case sensitivity.

5. In the *Edit Shared Parameters* dialog box, shown in Figure 6–99, click **Create...** to create a shared parameter file or **Browse...** to select an existing one.

Figure 6–99

6. Creating groups for related parameters makes working with numerous names much easier. In the *Groups* area, click **New** to create a new parameter group.

7. In the *New Parameter Group* dialog box, shown in Figure 6–100, type a new name and click **OK**.

    Note: Only one shared parameter file can be active in a project at a time. Therefore, create one main file with multiple groups instead of creating many files.

Figure 6–100

8. In the *Edit Shared Parameters* dialog box, in the *Parameters* area, click **New** to create a new shared parameter.

9. In the *Parameter Properties* dialog box, type a *Name* for the parameter and set the *Discipline* (**Common, Structural,** or **Electrical**) and *Data Type* using the drop-down lists. You can also add a tooltip. The dialog box is shown in Figure 6−101.

Figure 6−101

10. Click **OK**.

11. In the *Edit Shared Parameters* dialog box, once you have the parameters in place, you can:

    *   Click **Properties...**to display the contents of the Parameter Properties. You cannot modify them.
    *   Click **Move...** to switch a parameter from one parameter group to another.
    *   Click **Delete** to remove a parameter. Be careful about using this because it might impact the current project and any other projects that use the parameter.

12. When you have finished creating the shared parameters, click **OK** to close the *Edit Shared Parameters* dialog box.

13. Continue with the other steps required to add the parameter to the project, family, or schedule.

How To: Add a Shared Project Parameter to a Project

1. In the *Manage* tab>*Settings* panel, click ⬚ (Project Parameters).

2. In the *Project Parameters* dialog box, shown in Figure 6–102, click **New Parameter**.

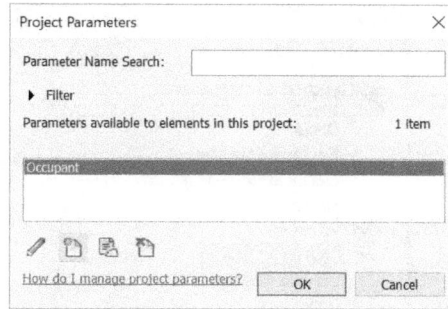

Figure 6–102

3. In the *Parameter Properties* dialog box, select **Shared parameter** and click **Select....**

4. In the *Shared Parameters* dialog box, set the *Parameter group* and select the *Parameter* that you want to add to the project, as shown in Figure 6–103 (you can only add one parameter at a time). Click **OK**.

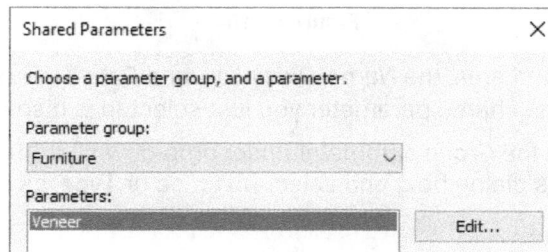

Figure 6–103

- If the parameter you want to use does not exist, click **Edit....** to create a new shared parameter.

5. In the *Parameter Properties* dialog box:

   - In the *Categories* area, select the categories to which you want the parameter to apply, as shown in Figure 6–104.

   Note: Use the Filter List to limit the number of categories available.

Figure 6–104

   - In the *Parameter Data* area, the *Name*, *Discipline*, and *Data Type* drop-down lists are grayed out, while the shared parameter you just selected is displayed.

6. Select an option from the *Group parameter under* drop-down list (this is where it displays in the *Element Properties* dialog box) and select **Instance** or **Type**, as shown in Figure 6–105.

Figure 6–105

7. Click **OK** twice to add the parameter to the project.

Practice 6k
Work with Shared Parameters in Architectural Projects

Practice Objectives

- Create shared parameters in a project.
- Create an annotation tag family and link the shared parameters into the tag.
- Add the shared parameters to a family and insert them into the project along with the associated tags.
- Create a schedule using the shared parameters including the project, tag, and family.

In this practice, you will create shared parameters through project parameters and use them in a family, tag, and schedule, as shown in Figure 6–106.

<Office Information>		
A	**B**	**C**
Employee	Extension	Department
Sarah	1236	Drafting
Shelby	1237	Drafting
McKinely	1238	Drafting
Miles	1241	Engineering
Jefferson	1240	Engineering
Vance	1239	Engineering
Dan	1234	Sales
Julie	1235	Sales
Samuel	1233	Sales

Figure 6–106

Task 1: Create shared parameters.

1. In the practice files *Architectural* folder, open **Office-Layout.rvt**.

2. In the *Manage* tab>*Settings* panel, click 📇 (Project Parameters).

3. In the *Project Parameters* dialog box, click **New Parameter**.

4. In the *Parameter Properties* dialog box, select **Shared parameter** and click **Select...**.

   - If an alert box displays asking if you want to choose a new file, click **Yes** and go to Step 6.

5. In the *Shared Parameters* dialog box, click **Edit...**.

6. In the *Edit Shared Parameters* dialog box, click **Create...**.

7. In the *Create Shared Parameter File* dialog box, navigate to the practice files *Architectural* folder and save the new file as **Office-Parameters.txt**.

8. In the *Groups* area, click **New**. Type the name **Office Information** and click **OK**. This becomes the current group, as shown in Figure 6–107.

Figure 6–107

9. In the *Parameters* area, click **New...** and create three new shared parameters using the following information. When finished, click **OK**.

Name	Discipline	Data Type
Extension	Common	Integer
Employee	Common	Text
Department	Common	Text

10. In the *Edit Shared Parameters* dialog box, click **OK**.

11. In the *Shared Parameters* dialog box, shown in Figure 6–108, select **Department** and click **OK**.

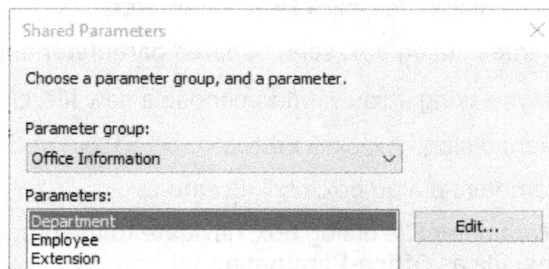

Figure 6–108

12. In the *Parameter Properties* dialog box, in the *Parameter Data* area, group the parameter under **Other** and make it an **Instance** parameter. In the *Categories* area, set the *Filter list* to **Architecture** and in the Categories list, select **Furniture** and **Furniture Systems**, as shown in Figure 6–109.

Figure 6–109

13. Click **OK**. **Department** is added to the shared parameters in the project.

14. Repeat the process for **Employee** and **Extension**.

15. Click **OK** to finish creating the project parameters.

16. Save the project.

Task 2: Create a tag with shared parameters.

1. Create a new family based on the **Generic Tag.rft** template found in the practice files Architectural>*RFT* folder.

2. Save the family as **Office-Information.rfa** to the practice files Architectural>*RFA* folder.

3. Zoom in, read the information in red, and delete the note.

4. In the *Modify* tab>*Properties* panel, click 🖳 (Family Category and Parameters).

5. In the *Family Category and Parameters* dialog box, verify the *Filter list* is set to **Architecture** and set the *Family Category* to **Furniture System Tags,** as shown in Figure 6–110. Click **OK**.

Figure 6–110

6. In the *Create* tab>*Detail* panel, click ⎰⎱ (Line). Draw a box, starting at the crossing of the two reference lines, as shown in Figure 6–111. Do not add the dimensions; they are for reference only.

Figure 6–111

7. In the *Create* tab>*Text* panel, click A▤ (Label).

8. Use the default type, **Label: 3/32"**.

9. Click inside the box you just created.

10. In the *Edit Label* dialog box, which includes a list of the multi-category parameters supplied with Revit, click 🗋 (Add Parameter).

    Note: In the Parameter Properties dialog box, you can only create shared parameters.

11. In the *Parameter Properties* dialog box, click **Select...**.

12. The shared parameters you created earlier should be available by default in the *Shared Parameters* dialog box. Select **Extension**, as shown in Figure 6–112, and click **OK**.

Figure 6–112

13. Click **OK** until you reach the *Edit Label* dialog box.

14. Select **Extension** and click ⇥ (Add parameter(s) to label). Click **OK** to insert the label into the family.

15. Click ⬉ (Modify) and select the new label. Resize the outline of the text box to fit inside the box. Move the label so that it is centered in the box, as shown in Figure 6–113.

Figure 6–113

16. Save the family and load it into the project **Office-Layout.rvt**.

Task 3: Add shared parameters to a furniture family.

1. Click ⬉ (Modify) and continue working in the **Office-Layout.rvt** project.

2. In the *Architecture* tab>*Build* panel, click 🗗 (Component).

3. In the *Modify | Place Component* tab>*Mode* panel, click ⬇ (Load Family).

4. In the practice files *Architectural>RFA* folder, open **Work-Station-Cubicle.rfa**.

5. Place workstations in the lower rooms in the left building, similar to what is shown in Figure 6–114.

Figure 6–114

6. Click � (Modify) and select the new workstation.

7. In the *Modify | Furniture Systems* tab>*Mode* panel, click ▱ (Edit Family).

8. In the *Properties* panel, click ▱ (Family Types).

9. At the bottom of the *Family Types* dialog box, click ▱ (New Parameter).

10. Select **Shared Parameter** and click **Select...**.

11. The shared parameters you created earlier are also available in this family file. Add each of the parameters from the *Office-Information* category into the family as an Instance parameter in the *Other* category.

12. In the *Family Types* dialog box, set the *Extension (default)* to **1234**, as shown in Figure 6–115. The other values can be left blank.

Figure 6–115

13. Click **OK**.

14. Save the family file and load it into the **Office-Layout.rvt** project. Overwrite the existing version and its parameter values.

15. Add several other cubicles in various offices.

Task 4: Add tags and create a schedule.

1. In the *Annotate* tab>*Tag* panel, click ⬚ (Tag by Category).

2. In Properties, uncheck the checkbox for *Leader Line*, then select the workstations and tag each of them. The default **1234** extension number should display on each tag, as shown in Figure 6–116. Adjust the tags as needed.

Figure 6–116

3. Select a workstation. In Properties, the *Extension*, *Employee*, and *Department* parameters should be available in the *Other* area, as shown in Figure 6–117.

Figure 6–117

4. Change the *Extension*, and add an *Employee* name and a *Department*.

5. Repeat with several other workstations.

6. In the *View* tab>*Create* panel, expand ▦ (Schedules) and click ▦ (Schedule/Quantities).

7. In the *New Schedule* dialog box, verify the *Filter list* is set to **Architecture**. Create a new **Furniture Systems** schedule and set the *Phase* to **Phase 1**, as shown in Figure 6–118. Click **OK**.

Figure 6–118

8. In the *Schedule Properties* dialog box, on the *Fields* tab, add the **Family and Type** parameter to the *Scheduled fields* list, then add **Extension**, **Employee**, and **Department**, as shown in Figure 6–119.

Figure 6–119

9. At this point, you can modify the other schedule properties as needed. Click **OK** when you are finished. The schedule should display the information you entered in the workstation's properties. Change the name of the schedule to **Office Information**, **Hide** the *Family and Type* column, and move the *Employee* column in front of the *Extensions* column, as shown in Figure 6–120.

\<Office Information\>		
A	B	C
Employee	Extension	Department
Sarah	1236	Drafting
Shelby	1237	Drafting
McKinely	1238	Drafting
Miles	1241	Engineering
Jefferson	1240	Engineering
Vance	1239	Engineering
Dan	1234	Sales
Julie	1235	Sales
Samuel	1233	Sales

Figure 6–120

10. Save and close the project.

11. If time permits, you can copy the Office Information tag and change the *Family Category* to **Furniture Tags**. Then you can use the new tag to tag the desks in the project. Furniture and Furniture Systems are different categories and cannot use the same tag.

End of practice

Practice 6I
Work with Shared Parameters in MEP Projects

Practice Objectives

- Create a schedule that uses shared parameters.
- Add the shared parameters to a family file and note the impact on the schedule.

In this practice, you will create a mechanical equipment schedule and add shared parameters to the project through the schedule. You will then modify and add the shared parameters in a family file and update the family in the project. The shared parameters then populate the schedule, as shown in Figure 6–121.

<Mechanical Equipment Schedule>						
A	B	C	D	E	F	G
Mark	Type	Height	Width	Depth	Gas Line Diameter	Liquid Line Diamete
1	HP060C	44 3/4"	38 7/8"	34 3/4"	1"	1/2"
2	HP060C	44 3/4"	38 7/8"	34 3/4"	1"	1/2"
3	HP060C	44 3/4"	38 7/8"	34 3/4"	1"	1/2"
4	HP060C	44 3/4"	38 7/8"	34 3/4"	1"	1/2"

Figure 6–121

Task 1: Create a schedule and add shared parameters.

1. In the practice files *MEP* folder, open **Townhouse-Complex.rvt**. Note that four heat pumps have been added to the townhouses.

2. In the *View* tab>*Create* panel, expand ⊞ (Schedules) and click 🗠 (Schedule/Quantities).

3. In the *New Schedule* dialog box, set the *Filter list* to **Mechanical**, select the *Category* of **Mechanical Equipment**, and click **OK**.

4. In the *Schedule Properties* dialog box, in the *Fields* tab, select the following fields: **Mark** and **Type**. The rest of the parameters need to be shared parameters.

5. In the center of the dialog box, click 🗋 (New Parameter).

6. In the *Parameter Properties* dialog box, select **Shared parameter** and click **Select...**.

   • If an alert box displays asking if you want to choose a new file, click **Yes** and go to Step 8.

7. In the *Shared Parameters* dialog box, click **Edit...**.

8. In the *Edit Shared Parameters* dialog box, click **Create...**.

9. In the *Create Shared Parameter File* dialog box, navigate to the practice files *MEP* folder and save the new file as **Townhouse-Parameters.txt**.

10. In the *Groups* area, click **New**. Type in the name **Heat Pump Information** and click **OK**. This becomes the current group, as shown in Figure 6-122.

Figure 6-122

11. In the *Parameters* area, click **New**. Create new shared type parameters using the following information. When finished, click **OK**.

Name	Discipline	Data Type
Height	Common	Length
Width	Common	Length
Depth	Common	Length
Gas Line Diameter	Common	Length
Liquid Line Diameter	Common	Length

12. In the *Edit Shared Parameters* dialog box, click **OK**.

13. In the *Shared Parameters* dialog box, select **Height,** as shown in Figure 6−123, and click **OK**.

Figure 6−123

14. In the *Parameter Properties* dialog box, in the *Parameter Data* area, verify that *Group parameter under* is set to **Dimensions**, as shown in Figure 6–124.

Figure 6–124

15. Click **OK**. **Height** is added to the scheduled fields.

16. Click ▯ (New Parameter) again.

17. In the *Parameter Properties* dialog box, select **Shared parameter** and click **Select...**.

18. This time you do not have to create a shared parameter file, as the files created in the previous steps are available. Select **Width** and click **OK** twice to apply the parameter to the scheduled fields.

19. Repeat the process and add the rest of the new shared parameters in the order shown in Figure 6-125.

Figure 6-125

20. Click **OK**. The Mechanical Equipment Schedule displays but only includes values for the **Mark** and **Type**, as shown in Figure 6-126. The shared parameters are not yet identified in the Heat Pump family.

<Mechanical Equipment Schedule>						
A	B	C	D	E	F	G
Mark	Type	Height	Width	Depth	Gas Line Diameter	Liquid Line Diamete
1	HP060C					
2	HP060C					
3	HP060C					
4	HP060C					

Figure 6-126

21. Save the project.

Task 2: Add shared parameters to a family.

1. Open the Mechanical>HVAC>**Floor Plans: Ground - Mech** view and select the heat pump labeled **1**.

2. In the *Modify | Mechanical Equipment* tab>*Mode* panel, click ⬚ (Edit Family). The family file opens in the Family Editor.

3. In the *Properties* panel, click ⬚ (Family Types).

4. In the *Family Types* dialog box, several of the parameters that already exist in the family display (as shown in Figure 6–127), but they are not connected as shared parameters.

Parameter	Value	Formula	Lock
Family Types			✕
Type name: HP060C			
Search parameters			
Constraints			⌃
Default Elevation	0"	=	☐
Dimensions			⌃
Width	38 7/8"	=	☐
Liquid Line Radius	1/4"	=	☐
Gas Line Radius	1/2"	=	☐
Fan Radius	16 3/8"	= Depth / 2 - 1"	☑
Height	44 3/4"	=	☐
Depth	34 3/4"	=	☑
CenterY	17 3/8"	= Depth / 2	☑
CenterX	17 3/8"	= CenterY	☑

Figure 6–127

Note: Note how the name is the same, but since the parameter is a Family Parameter, Revit does not see the previously created parameters as the same. This is what Shared Parameters do - they connect the different areas (project, families, tags, and schedules).

5. Select the **Width** parameter and in the *Parameters* area, click ✎ (Edit Parameter).

6. In the *Parameter Properties* dialog box, select **Shared Parameter** and click **Select...**.

7. The shared parameters you created earlier are also available in this family file, as shown in Figure 6–128.

Figure 6–128

8. Select **Width** and click **OK** twice. The existing parameter is now connected with the shared parameter.

9. Repeat the process with the **Height** and **Depth** parameters.

   Note: The information stored in the Heat Pump family for the Liquid Line and Gas Line are set to a radius, because it is required by the connectors. Therefore, you have to add Parameters and formulas for the diameters.

10. In the *Family Types* dialog box, click 🗋 (New Parameter).

11. In the *Parameter Properties* dialog box, select **Shared parameter** and click **Select....**

12. In the *Shared Parameters* dialog box, select **Gas Line Diameter** and click **OK**.

13. Set it as a **Type** parameter and group it with the **Dimensions** group. Click **OK**.

14. Repeat the process for **Liquid Line Diameter**.

15. Set the following for the two diameter parameters, as shown in Figure 6–129:

- *Gas Line Diameter*
  - *Value:* **1"**
  - *Formula:* **= Gas Line Radius * 2**
- *Liquid Line Diameter*
  - *Value:* **1/2"**
  - *Formula:* **= Liquid Line Radius * 2**

Parameter	Value	Formula	Lock
Constraints			
Default Elevation	0"	=	☐
Dimensions			
Depth	34 3/4"	=	☑
Gas Line Diameter	1"	=Gas Line Radius * 2	☐
Height	44 3/4"	=	☐
Liquid Line Diameter	1/2"	=Liquid Line Radius * 2	☐
Liquid Line Radius	1/2"	=	☐
Gas Line Radius	1/4"	=	☐
Fan Radius	16 3/8"	=Depth / 2 - 1"	☑
CenterY	17 3/8"	=Depth / 2	☑
CenterX	17 3/8"	=CenterY	☑
Width	38 7/8"	=	☐

Family Types — Type name: HP060C — Search parameters

Figure 6–129

16. Click **OK** to close the *Family Types* dialog box.
17. Save the family to the practice files MEP>*RFA* folder.

Task 3: Load the family and modify the schedule.

1. In the *Create* tab>*Family Editor* panel, click 📲 (Load into Project).

2. Overwrite the existing version and its parameter values.

3. Open the Mechanical Equipment Schedule. The values for the parameters are now included. Add headers for the dimensions, as shown in Figure 6–130.

<Mechanical Equipment Schedule>						
A	B	C	D	E	F	G
		Overal Dimensions			Pipe Dimensions	
Mark	Type	Height	Width	Depth	Gas Line Diameter	Liquid Line Diameter
1	HP060C	3' - 8 3/4"	3' - 2 7/8"	2' - 10 3/4"	0" - 1"	0" - 0 1/2"
2	HP060C	3' - 8 3/4"	3' - 2 7/8"	2' - 10 3/4"	0" - 1"	0" - 0 1/2"
3	HP060C	3' - 8 3/4"	3' - 2 7/8"	2' - 10 3/4"	0" - 1"	0" - 0 1/2"
4	HP060C	3' - 8 3/4"	3' - 2 7/8"	2' - 10 3/4"	0" - 1"	0" - 0 1/2"

Figure 6–130

4. Typically the values for these parameters should only be in inches. To fix this, in Properties next to **Formatting** parameter, click **Edit...**.

5. The *Schedule Properties* dialog box opens with the *Formatting* tab selected.

6. In the *Fields* area, select **Height** and click **Field Format...**.

7. Uncheck **Use project settings**, then change the *Units* to **Fractional inches** and the *Unit Symbol* to ". Click **OK**.

8. Repeat this for the rest of the length based parameters so that they display in inches and not in feet and inches.

9. Click **OK** to close the dialog box. The schedule updates as shown in Figure 6–131.

<Mechanical Equipment Schedule>						
A	B	C	D	E	F	G
		Overall Dimensions			Pipe Dimensions	
Mark	Type	Height	Width	Depth	Gas Line Diameter	Liquid Line Diameter
1	HP060C	44 3/4"	38 7/8"	34 3/4"	1"	1/2"
2	HP060C	44 3/4"	38 7/8"	34 3/4"	1"	1/2"
3	HP060C	44 3/4"	38 7/8"	34 3/4"	1"	1/2"
4	HP060C	44 3/4"	38 7/8"	34 3/4"	1"	1/2"

Figure 6–131

10. Save and close the project.

End of practice

Practice 6m
Work with Shared Parameters in Structural Projects

Practice Objectives

- Create shared parameters in a project.
- Use the shared parameters in a family, associated tag, and schedule.

In this practice, you will create shared parameters through project parameters and use them in a family, tag, and schedule, as shown in Figure 6–132. The context here is a public plaza with columns, some free-standing and some supporting canopies and roofs. Each column will have custom brackets for banners, flags, etc.

		<Structural Column Schedule>		
A	B	C	D	E
Column Location Mark	Mark	Bracket Type	Bracket Offset from Base	Bracket Finish
A-1	1	Banner	12' - 0"	Metal
A-2	2	Banner	12' - 0"	Metal
A-3	3	Banner	12' - 0"	Metal
A-4	4	Banner	12' - 0"	Metal
A-5	5	Banner	12' - 0"	Metal
A-6	6	Banner	12' - 0"	Metal
A-7	7	Banner	12' - 0"	Metal

Figure 6–132

Task 1: Create shared parameters.

1. In the practice files *Structural* folder, open **Events-Plaza.rvt**.
2. In the *Manage* tab>*Project Settings* panel, click (Project Parameters).
3. In the *Project Parameters* dialog box, click **New Parameter**.
4. In the *Parameter Properties* dialog box, select **Shared parameter** and click **Select...**.
   - If an alert box displays asking if you want to choose a new file, click **Yes** and go to Step 6.
5. In the *Shared Parameters* dialog box, click **Edit...**.

6. In the *Edit Shared Parameters* dialog box, click **Create...**.

7. Save the new file as **Plaza-Parameters.txt** in the practice files *Structural* folder.

8. Create a new parameter group. In the *Groups* area, click **New...**. Type the name **Columns** and click **OK**. This becomes the current group, as shown in Figure 6–133.

Figure 6–133

9. In the *Parameters* area, click **New...** and create three new shared parameters using the following information. When finished, click **OK**.

Name	Discipline	Data Type
Bracket Type	Common	Text
Bracket Offset from Base	Common	Length
Bracket Finish	Common	Material

10. In the *Edit Shared Parameters* dialog box, click **OK**.

11. In the *Shared Parameters* dialog box, select **Bracket Type,** as shown in Figure 6–134, and click **OK**.

Figure 6–134

12. In the *Parameter Properties* dialog box, in the *Parameter Data* area, group the parameter under **Other** and make it an **Instance** parameter. In the *Categories* area, filter the list based on **Structure** and select **Structural Columns,** as shown in Figure 6–135.

Figure 6–135

13. Click **OK**. **Bracket Type** is added to the shared parameters in the project.

14. Repeat the process with the **Bracket Offset from Base** and **Bracket Finish** parameters.

15. Click **OK** to finish creating the project parameters.

16. Save the project.

Task 2: Create a tag with shared parameters.

1. Start a new family based on the **Generic Tag.rft** template found in the practice files *Structural>RFT* folder.

2. Zoom in, read the information in red, and delete the note.

3. In the *Properties* panel, click 🖳 (Family Category and Parameters).

4. In the *Family Category and Parameters* dialog box, verify the *Filter list* is set to **Structure** and set the *Family Category* to **Structural Column Tags**, as shown in Figure 6–136. Click **OK**.

Figure 6–136

5. In the *Create* tab>*Detail* panel, click 🔲 (Line). Draw a box, starting at the crossing of the two reference lines, as shown in Figure 6–137. Do not add the dimensions. They are for reference only.

Figure 6–137

6. In the *Create* tab>*Text* panel, click 🖍 (Label).

7. Use the default type, **Label: 3/32"**.

8. In the *Modify | Place Label* tab>*Format* panel, set *Justification* to ☰ (Align Text Center) and ☰ (Align Text Top).

9. Click inside the box you just created.

10. In the *Edit Label* dialog box, which includes a list of the multi-category parameters supplied with Revit, click 🗋 (Add Parameter) at the bottom of the dialog box.

   Note: In this dialog box, you can only create shared parameters.

11. In the *Parameter Properties* dialog box, click **Select...**.

12. In the *Shared Parameters* dialog box, the shared parameters you created earlier should be available by default. Select **Bracket Type**, as shown in Figure 6–138. Then, click **OK**.

Figure 6–138

13. Click **OK** until you reach the *Edit Label* dialog box.

14. Select **Bracket Type** and click ⤓ (Add parameter(s) to label).

15. Repeat with the **Bracket Offset from Base** and **Bracket Finish** parameters. In the *Break* column, select the option for the first two parameters, as shown in Figure 6–139. This forces each parameter to be on a separate line.

Figure 6–139

16. Click **OK** to insert the label into the family.

17. Click ▷ (Modify) and select the new label. Resize the outline of the text box so that it fits inside the box, and move the label so that it is top-centered in the box, as shown in Figure 6–140.

Figure 6–140

18. Save the new family with the name **Column-Bracket-Tag.rfa** to the *Structural>RFA* folder.

19. Load the family into the project **Events-Plaza.rvt**.

20. The **Tag** command is automatically started. In Properties, check the checkbox next to *Leader Line*. Tag one of the columns.

21. The tag is empty as shown in Figure 6–141, because no values have been added to the parameters.

Figure 6–141

22. Save the project.

Task 3: Add tags and modify information.

1. In the *Annotate* tab>*Tag* panel, click 🏷 (Tag All).

2. In the *Tag All Not Tagged* dialog box, select **All objects in current view**, select the *Category* **Structural Column Tags** with the *Loaded Tags* set to **Column-Bracket-Tag.** Select **Leader** and click **OK**.

   - All of the columns are tagged. The tags are blank but display question marks when selected, as shown in Figure 6–142. This is because the corresponding information has not been entered into the properties.

Figure 6–142

3. Select a column.

4. In Properties, scroll down to the *Other* area. The **Bracket Finish**, **Bracket Offset from Base**, and **Bracket Type** parameters are available but have no information stored in them yet, as shown in Figure 6–143.

Figure 6–143

5. Right-click on the column and select **Select All Instances>Visible in View**.

   - In this case, you will set the default values for all columns once. Individual columns can be changed later.

6. In Properties, set the *Bracket Finish* to **Metal**, *Bracket Offset from Base* to **12'-0"**, and *Bracket Type* to **Banner**.

7. Select two or three individual columns, and in Properties change the *Bracket Type* to **Sculptural** and the *Bracket Offset from Base* to **15'-0"**. The tags update only for those columns, as shown in Figure 6–144.

Figure 6–144

8. Save the project.

Task 4: Create a structural column schedule.

1. In the *View* tab>*Create* panel, expand ▦ (Schedules) and click ▦ (Schedule/Quantities). Create a new building component schedule for structural columns.

2. In the *Schedule Properties* dialog box, in the *Fields* tab, add the **Column Location Mark** parameter and then add **Mark**, **Bracket Type**, **Bracket Offset from Base**, and **Bracket Finish**, as shown in Figure 6–145.

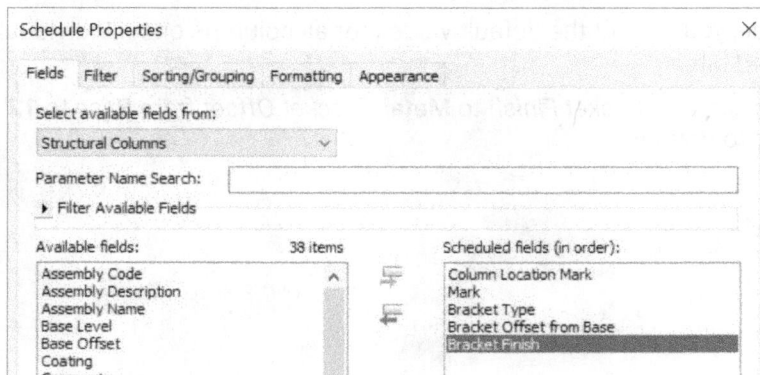

Figure 6–145

3. Sort by the *Column Location Mark* and click **OK**. The schedule should display the information you entered in the column's properties, as shown in Figure 6–146.

<Structural Column Schedule>				
A	**B**	**C**	**D**	**E**
Column Location Mark	Mark	Bracket Type	Bracket Offset from Base	Bracket Finish
A-1	1	Banner	12' - 0"	Metal
A-2	2	Banner	12' - 0"	Metal
A-3	3	Banner	12' - 0"	Metal
A-4	4	Banner	12' - 0"	Metal
A-5	5	Banner	12' - 0"	Metal
A-6	6	Banner	12' - 0"	Metal
A-7	7	Banner	12' - 0"	Metal

Figure 6–146

4. Save and close the project.

End of practice

Chapter Review Questions

1. An in-place family is created whenever you need a custom family that is:

    a. not available in your library.

    b. built using profiles.

    c. unique and specific to the project.

    d. requiring shared parameters.

2. Which of the following are examples of elements created from a profile? (Select all that apply.)

    a. Wall reveals

    b. Desk families

    c. In-place sweeps

    d. Curtain wall mullions

3. Line-based families enable you to draw repeating elements in a line by selecting two points. These families can be made up of 2D detail elements or an array of 3D elements.

    a. True

    b. False

4. Where are shared parameters (access shown in Figure 6–147) stored?

Parameter Properties

Parameter Type

○ Project parameter

   (Can appear in schedules but not in tags)

◉ Shared parameter

   (Can be shared by multiple projects and families, exported to ODBC, and appear in schedules and tags)

Select...   Export...

Figure 6–147

a. In a text file.

b. In the current project.

c. In a shared project.

d. In the family file.

Command Summary

Button	Command	Location
	Annotation Symbol	• **File** tab, expand New
	Model In-Place	• **Ribbon:** *Architecture* tab>*Build* panel, expand Component • **Ribbon:** *Structure* tab>*Model* panel, expand Component • **Ribbon:** *Systems* tab>*Model* panel, expand Component
	Project Parameters	• **Ribbon:** *Manage* tab>*Project Settings* panel
	Shared Parameters	• **Ribbon:** *Manage* tab>*Project Settings* panel

Creating Architectural-Specific Families

Creating architectural families in Revit involves three distinct workflows: loadable component families, in-place modeling, and system families. Most common elements, like doors and windows, are built as loadable component families to ensure they are reusable and parametrically flexible across multiple projects. However, for unique site-specific conditions, such as angled cornices or custom coping, it is often more efficient to use in-place families or custom 2D profiles modeled directly within the project context. Finally, complex elements like railings function as assemblies; these are managed as system families that integrate various sub-components, including rails, balusters, posts, and panels, into a single cohesive unit.

Learning Objectives

- Create custom door and window families from existing families and templates.
- Use in-place families to create angled cornices, fascias, and copings.
- Create railing types, including the rails, balusters, posts, and panels.

7.1 Creating Custom Doors and Windows

You can create custom doors and windows by copying and modifying an existing family, enabling you to use all of the existing detailed elements and parameters. For example, in Figure 7–1 the full panel door family on the left can be transformed into the square panel on the right.

Figure 7–1

When you use a template, only the most basic elements are included. For example, in the Window with Trim template (shown in Figure 7–2), only the opening for the window, basic trim, and parameters are included. Everything else must be added.

Figure 7–2

Practice 7a
Create Custom Doors

Practice Objectives

- Create custom families based on an existing family.
- Add and modify parameters.
- Modify reference planes and dimensions.
- Set formulas for parameters.

In this practice, you will create a new door family based on an existing door family, shown on the left in Figure 7–3. For the first family, you will add a material parameter and modify an existing extrusion to use the new glass material, as shown in the middle in Figure 7–3. You will then create a copy of the family and modify the dimension and parameters and add a formula to create square panels, as shown in the right in Figure 7–3.

| Original Door | Glass Panel Door | Square Glass Panel Door |

Figure 7–3

Task 1: Create door types and specify new material.

1. In the practice files *Architectural>RFA* folder, open **Door-Interior-Single-5_Panel_Vert-Wood.rfa**.

2. Save the file in the practice files *Architectural>RFA* folder with the name **Door-Interior-Single-5_ Panel_Vert-Wood_Glass.rfa**.

3. In the *Family Types* dialog box, create a new **Type** parameter named **Interior Panel Material** with *Data Type* set to **Material** and *Group parameter under* set to **Materials and Finishes.**

4. Assign the *Value* to **Glass,** as shown in Figure 7–4. Click **OK.**

Parameter	Value	Formula	Lock	^
Construction			☆	
Function	Interior	=		
Wall Closure	By host	=		
Construction Type		=		
Swing Angle (default)	90.00°	=	☐	
Materials and Finishes			☆	
Interior Panel Material	Glass	=		
Panel Material	Cherry	=		
Frame Material	Cherry	=		
Trim Material	Cherry	=		
Door Handle Material	Aluminum	=		

Figure 7–4

5. Select the Panel Extrusion, as shown in Figure 7–5. (Press <Tab> to select the interior extrusion.)

Figure 7–5

6. In Properties, in the *Material and Finishes* area, click ▤ (Associate Family Parameter) beside *Material*, as shown in Figure 7–6.

Panel (1)	⌄	🔡 Edit Type
Constraints		�<
Extrusion End	-1 53/256"	
Extrusion Start	-1 171/256"	
Work Plane	Reference Plane : Cent...	
Graphics		☆
Visible	☑	
Visibility/Graphics Ov...	Edit...	
Materials and Finishes		☆
Material	Cherry	▤
Identity Data		☆
Subcategory	Panel	
Solid/Void	Solid	

Associate Family Parameter

Figure 7–6

7. In the *Associate Family Parameter* dialog box, select **Interior Panel Material** and click **OK**. The interior panels update to glass, as shown in Figure 7–7.

Figure 7–7

8. Create three family types. Modify the *Width* and *Height* values to match the name. You will use the new types to flex the parameters as you continue working.

   - **32" x 80"**
   - **36" x 80"**
   - **36" x 84"**

9. Save the family.

Task 2: Modify the glass panel in a separate door family.

1. Save the family as **Door-Interior-Single-5_Panel_Vert-Wood_Glass-Square.rfa**. (This enables you to have different door styles based on one original.)

2. Open the **Elevations: Exterior** view.

3. Verify the *Scale* is set to **1 1/2"=1'-0"**. This will make the dimensions easier to modify.

4. Delete the Stiles dimension on the left, as shown in Figure 7−8.

Figure 7−8

5. Add a new dimension labeled **Interior Panel Width** (Type Parameter) in the **Dimensions** group parameter, as shown in Figure 7–9.

Figure 7–9

6. Open the *Family Types* dialog box.

7. Set the *Type name* to **32" x 80"** and click **Apply**.

8. Add the following *Formula* to the **Interior Panel Width** parameter, as shown in Figure 7–10:
= **(Height - (Bottom Rail + Top Rail + (Intermediate Rail * 4))) / 5**.

Parameter	Value	Formula	L ^
Dimensions			
Interior Panel Width	9 163/256"	= (Height - (Bottom Rail + Top Rail + (Intermediate Rail * 4))) / 5	☑
Width	32"	=	☑
Height	80"	=	☑
Rough Width	34"	= Width + 2"	☑
Rough Height	81"	= Height + 1"	☑
Thickness	1 3/8"	=	☑
Stiles	4 3/4"	=	☑
Top Rail	4 11/16"	=	☑
Intermediate Rail	4 1/2"	=	☑
Bottom Rail	9 1/8"	=	☑

Figure 7–10

- Ensure that you type in all the parameter names exactly and watch the parentheses. The *Value* should solve as **9 163/256"** and it will show as grayed out.

- This formula was developed because a reporting parameter based on the height of the interior panel cannot be used in this case.

9. Click **Apply**. The entire panel set changes to a square shape, as shown in Figure 7–11. Click **OK**.

Stiles = 4 3/4"

Interior Panel Width = 9 5/8"

Figure 7–11

10. Open the 3D Views>**Preview** view.

11. Use the family types you created earlier to flex the family.

12. Save the family.

13. Create a new project and add a wall into the project.

14. Load the two doors you created into the project and test them in the wall.

15. Save and close the families. You do not need to save the project.

End of practice

Practice 7b
Create Custom Windows

Practice Objectives

- Create a custom family based on a template.
- Add trim and glass to the window.

In this practice, you will create a new window family based on a family template. You will modify the existing opening, trim it, and add materials and glass to the window, as shown in Figure 7–12.

Figure 7–12

Task 1: Create a custom window family.

1. Create a new family based on the **Window with Trim.rft** template found in the practice files *Architectural>RFT* folder.

2. Save the family to the practice files *Architectural>RFA* folder as **Arched Window with Trim.rfa**.

3. Open the **Elevations: Exterior** view.

4. Edit the sketch of the **Opening Cut** element (use <Tab> to select the Opening Cut shown on the left in Figure 7–13). Draw an arc, then lock the tangency locks, as shown on the right in Figure 7–13. Delete the extra horizontal sketch line.

Figure 7–13

5. Click ✔ (Finish Edit Mode).

6. Add a dimension to the arc and label it **Arch Radius** (a **Type** parameter in the *Dimensions* group), as shown in Figure 7–14.

Figure 7–14

7. Edit the **Trim: Extrusion** element and modify the sketch so that it matches the new arc opening, as shown in Figure 7–15.

Figure 7–15

8. Click ✔ (Finish Edit Mode).

9. Open the *Family Types* dialog box and modify the **Arch Radius** parameter to use the formula **Width/2**. Flex the model by trying different widths.

10. Set the final *Width* to **3'-0"** and click **OK.**

11. Save the family.

12. Start a new project using the Architectural template and add a wall to the project.

13. Switch back to the window family and load it into the project to test it.

14. Open a 3D view and set the *Visual Style* to 🖻 (Shaded). The window does not have glass or materials, as shown in Figure 7–16.

Figure 7–16

15. Save the project as **Window Test.rvt**.

Task 2: Add a material to the window trim.

1. Switch back to the family file **Exterior** view.

2. Set the *Visual Style* to ▦ (Shaded).

3. Select the **Trim Projection : Extrusion**.

4. In Properties, next to the **Materials** parameter, select **<By Category>**. Click ⸱⸱⸱ (Browse) at the end of the row.

5. In the *Material Browser*, under *AEC Materials>Wood*, select **Cherry** and click ⬆ (Adds material to document.), as shown in Figure 7–17.

Figure 7–17

6. Select the new material. On the *Graphics* tab, in the *Shading* area, select **Use Render Appearance**, as shown in Figure 7–18.

Figure 7–18

- By default, this material only displays when the *Visual Style* is set to **Realistic**. By using the **Render Appearance**, the color displays when the *Visual Style* is set to **Shaded** or **Consistent Colors**.

7. Click **OK** to close the *Material Browser* and apply the material.

8. Save the family file.

Task 3: Add glass to the window.

1. In the family file, open the **Floor Plans: Ref. Level** view.

2. Draw a reference plane **1"** from the exterior face of the window and lock it in place by dimensioning from the exterior reference plane to the one you just created, as shown in Figure 7–19. Name the reference plane **Glass**.

Figure 7–19

3. Open the **Elevations: Exterior** view.

4. In the *Create* tab>*Work Plane* panel, click ▦ (Set).

5. In the *Work Plane* dialog box, select the new reference plane **Glass** and click **OK**.

6. In the *Create* tab>*Form* panel, click ▣ (Extrusion).

7. Sketch and lock the outline of the glass inside the window.

8. In Properties, in the *Constraints* area, set the *Extrusion End* to **1/2"**.

9. In the *Materials and Finishes* area, click ⋯ (Browse) beside *Material*.

10. In the *Material Browser*, open the *AEC Materials* library and select the *Glass* category. Select **Glass, Clear Glazing** and click ⬆ (Add material to document), as shown in Figure 7–20.

Figure 7–20

11. In the *Project Materials* list, select the **Glass, Clear Glazing** material and in the *Graphics* tab, select **Use Render Appearance**.

12. Click **OK**.

13. Click ✔ (Finish Edit Mode). The glass material displays.

14. Save the family file.

15. Click 🗔 (Load into Project) and select **Overwrite the existing version and its parameter values**. The new glass and trim material display in the project.

16. Close the family and project.

End of practice

7.2 Creating Angled Cornices and Copings

You can create a custom cornice that follows different angles at the top of a wall by creating an in-place family instead of adding it manually or editing the wall's assembly. You can only add wall sweeps vertically or horizontally whether using the **Wall Sweep** command or by editing the assembly of a wall. For example, to add a cornice to the top of a wall following an angled profile (as shown in Figure 7–21), you would need to use a workaround, such as an in-place sweep family using a solid sweep. A solid sweep can also be used to create a coping on the top of a short wall running beside steps.

Attempting to place a wall sweep   In-place solid sweep family

Figure 7–21

Creating Fascias

You can add fascia elements to your project by adding details to your roof edges using a profile type and the **Roof: Fascia** command. Fascias can be constructed of one element or multiple elements. Another way to create fascias along an angle element is to use a model line, as shown in Figure 7–22. Typically, a fascia is applied to a roof edge but it can also be applied to a model line placed anywhere in a project.

Figure 7–22

How To: Create a Fascia Type

Note: The process is similar for creating new gutter types.

1. Open a view that displays the model line or roof edge you want to apply the fascia to.
2. Load the profile for the fascia.
    *   Fascia profile options are available in the Revit Library's *Profiles>Roofs* folder.
3. In the *Architecture* tab>*Build* panel, expand (Roof) and click (Roof: Fascia).
4. In Properties, click (Edit Type).
5. In the *Type Properties* dialog box, click **Duplicate**.
6. In the *Name* dialog box, type a name and click **OK**.
7. In the *Type Properties* dialog box, select the appropriate profile, as shown in Figure 7–23.

Figure 7–23

8. Click **OK** and the new fascia type is ready to be used.

9. In the view, hover the cursor over the roof edge. When it highlights (as shown in Figure 7–24), click to select it. The fascia profile is applied.

Applied fascia

Figure 7–24

How To: Add a Fascia Using Model Lines

1. Open the view that you want to add a fascia in. Verify the height of the fascia profile first so that you know where to put the model lines.

2. In the *Architecture* tab>*Work Plane* panel, click (Set) and select the appropriate work plane. This will need to be set if you are in an elevation or section view.

3. In the *Architecture* tab>*Model* panel, click (Model Line).

   • If you did not set the work plane and are in a view that requires it to be set, the *Work Plane* dialog box displays. Select the appropriate option in the *Specify a new Work Plane* area and click **OK**.

4. Draw the model lines on the face of the element where you want to add a fascia.

5. In the *Architecture* tab>*Build* panel, expand (Roof) and click (Roof: Fascia).

6. Select the model lines.

Creating an In-Place Sweep Family

You can create an in-place sweep family when your design needs unique geometry that a loadable family or fascia tool cannot achieve. Creating an in-place sweep allows you to have control over difficult corner transitions or when the geometry needs to follow a non-standard path that loadable families cannot follow. You can control the sweep's display by assigning it to a subcategory. You can then toggle its visibility or modify the line weights and materials of the sweep in the *Visibility/Graphic Overrides* dialog box independently from the main host component.

How To: Create an In-Place Sweep Family

1. In the *Architecture* tab>*Build* panel, expand 🔲 (Component) and click 🔲 (Model In-Place).

2. In the *Family Category and Parameters* dialog box, select a family category, such as **Casework**, **Mechanical Equipment**, or **Walls**, and click **OK**.

3. In the *Name* dialog box, enter a name for the family and click **OK**. You are placed in the Family Editor with the corresponding tabs available in the ribbon.

4. In the *Create* tab>*Forms* panel, click 🔲 (Sweep).

5. In the *Modify | Sweep* tab>*Sweep* panel, click 🔲 (Sketch Path).

   - If the *Work Plane* dialog box displays, select **Pick a plane** and click **OK**. Select the face of the wall that you want to add the sweep to.

6. Using one of the *Draw* tools, sketch a path for the sweep, as shown in Figure 7–25.

Figure 7–25

7. Click ✔ (Finish Edit Mode).

8. In the *Sweep* panel, expand the *Profile* drop-down list and select a profile.

   - If the profile needed is not loaded, click 🔲 (Load Profile) to load the profile.

9. If you want to draw a profile, verify *Profile* is set to **<By Sketch>** and click 🔲 (Edit Profile).

10. If you are not in a view that Revit can draw a profile in, the *Go To View* dialog box displays. Select a view and click **Open View**.

11. Zoom in and draw the profile, like the wall cap shown in Figure 7–26.

Figure 7–26

12. Click ✔ (Finish Edit Mode) twice.

13. Select the sweep family and in Properties, set the *Subcategory*. Setting a subcategory helps to control the family within the specified category in the *Visibility/Graphic Overrides* dialog box. Note that you are able to create a subcategory while in edit mode.

14. Click ✔ (Finish Edit Mode).

15. Switch to a 3D view to see the in-place family.

💡 Hint: Create an Object Style Subcategory

When creating an in-place sweep family, you might want the family member to be modified in the *Visibility/Graphic Overrides* dialog box separately from the main component. For example, if you are creating a cornice or coping for a wall and want to be able to toggle it off separately from the wall, you can create an object style subcategory.

1. In the *Manage* tab>*Settings* panel, click 🔲 (Object Styles).

2. In the *Object Styles* dialog box, on the *Model Objects* tab, click **New** in the *Modify Subcategories* area.

3. In the *New Subcategory* dialog box, type a *Name* and select a category from the *Subcategory of* drop-down list, as shown in Figure 7–27.

Figure 7–27

4. Click **OK**.

5. The object style is now available in the *Visibility/Graphic Overrides* dialog box, as shown in Figure 7–28. Edit the *Line Weight*, *Line Color*, *Line Pattern*, or *Material* as needed.

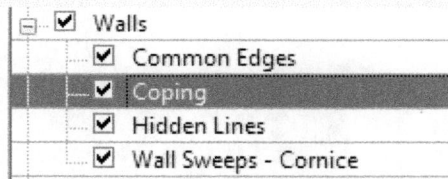

Figure 7–28

6. In the in-place family, select the object you want to add to the new subcategory. In Properties, in the *Identity Data* area, select a *Subcategory* from the list (as shown in Figure 7–29) and click **OK**.

Figure 7–29

Practice 7c
Create Angled Cornices and Copings

Practice Objectives

- Create a coping using an in-place family.
- Use model lines and roof fascia to add a profile to a sloped wall.

In this practice, you will create a coping using an in-place family with a solid sweep. You will then add a profile to a sloped wall using the **Roof: Fascia** command and a model line, as shown in Figure 7–30.

Figure 7–30

Task 1: Create a coping using an in-place family.

1. In the practice files *Architectural* folder, open **Plaza.rvt**. This is the beginning of a site design consisting of two slabs with retaining walls connected by a stair.

2. Open the **Floor Plans: Site** view.

3. Open the **Sections: East-West Site Section** view and zoom in on the lower wall that has stairs. This is where you are going to add a stone coping to the top of the wall.

4. In the *Architecture* tab>*Build* panel, expand (Component) and click (Model In-Place).

5. In the *Family Category and Parameters* dialog box, select **Walls** and click **OK**.

6. Name the family **Coping** and click **OK**.

   Note: You are placed in the Family Editor with the corresponding tabs available in the ribbon.

7. In the *Create* tab>*Forms* panel, click (Sweep).

8. In the *Modify | Sweep* tab>*Sweep* panel, click ⟋ (Sketch Path).

9. In the *Work Plane* dialog box, select **Pick a plane** and click **OK**. Select the face of the concrete retaining wall.

10. Draw the path, as shown in Figure 7–31.

Figure 7–31

11. Click ✔ (Finish Edit Mode).

12. In the *Sweep* panel, click ⟓ (Edit Profile).

13. In the *Go To View* dialog box, select **Section: Wall Section** and click **Open View**.

14. Zoom in and draw the profile, as shown in Figure 7–32.

Figure 7–32

15. Finish the profile, sweep, and model.

16. Switch to a 3D view to see the coping in place.

Task 2: Use model lines and roof fascia to add a profile to a sloped wall.

1. Open the **Sections: East-West Site Section** view and zoom in to the sloped retaining wall.

2. In the *Insert* tab>*Load from Library* panel, click ⬇ (Load Family). Navigate to the practice files *Architectural>RFA* folder and load **Wall-Profile.rfa**.

3. In the *Architecture* tab>*Model* panel, click ⁀ (Model Line).

4. In the *Work Plane* dialog box, select **Pick a Plane** and click **OK**, then select the face of the concrete retaining wall, as shown in Figure 7–33. Note that this dialog box will only display if you are in a section, ceiling plan, or elevation view.

    Note: If you use Pick Lines or draw from right to left, the fascia faces the wrong direction when it is applied.

Figure 7–33

5. In the Options Bar, set the *Offset* to **7"**. Draw a model line from right to left, down from the top of the retaining wall, as shown in Figure 7–34 (the image has been simplified for clarity).

Figure 7–34

6. In the *Architecture* tab>*Build* panel, expand ▦ (Roof) and click ▽ (Roof: Fascia).

7. In Properties, click **Edit Type**.

8. In the *Type Properties* dialog box, create a new fascia type named **Wall Sweep** using the profile you loaded earlier, and set the *Material* to **Masonry - Stone**, as shown in Figure 7–35. Click **OK**.

Parameter	Value	=
Construction		»
Profile	Wall-Profile : Wall-Profile	
Materials and Finishes		»
Material	Masonry - Stone	...

Type Parameters

Figure 7–35

9. Select the model line to place the wall sweep.

10. Open the **Site** view, then click the flip arrows to flip the profile.

11. Open the **3D views: Full View** view, as shown in Figure 7–36, to view the fascia.

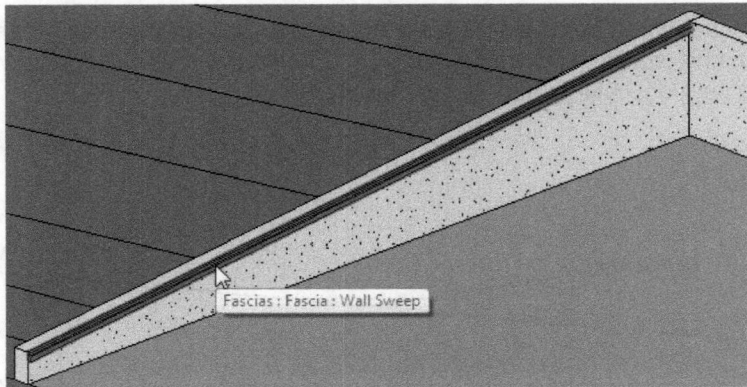

Figure 7–36

12. Save and close the project.

End of practice

7.3 Creating Custom Railings

Creating a railing is more complex than creating a standard component family, as railings consist of several preset families for the rails, balusters, posts, and panels, as shown in Figure 7–37. Once you have the collection of families ready, you can create a Railing type.

Note: When you are creating a family, see if you can modify an existing one to suit your needs. This is much faster than creating a new family from scratch and helps you learn how to construct the specific family.

Figure 7–37

- It helps to create all of the components for a Railing type (e.g., rails, handrails, top rails, posts, balusters, and panels) before creating the type.

- There are also Railing Supports (for handrails) and Railing Termination families that can be added to railings types.

Creating Rail Profiles

Top rails, handrails, and rails within a railing structure are all based on a rail profile. The rail profile is made of 2D elements that are swept along the railing lines, as shown in Figure 7–38.

Figure 7–38

- Existing profiles for rails are found in the Revit Library's *Profiles>Railings* folder.

- The **Profile-Rail.rft** template is specifically created for railings. The template indicates where to start drawing the outline, as shown in Figure 7–39.

Rail Centerline

Rail Top

Figure 7–39

- Rail profiles must be closed shapes.

- Once you have created a rail profile, you can apply it to a Top Rail or Handrail system family type.

Creating Baluster, Post, and Panel Families

Balusters and posts are created from solid elements made with extrusions and revolves. Having the correct reference planes is important for flexibility. Standard balusters also require void elements to cut the angle on stair railings.

There are three baluster templates for standard balusters, posts, and panels. The example in Figure 7–40 shows a custom baluster modified from an existing baluster family supplied with Revit.

Original baluster　　　　　*Modified baluster*

Figure 7–40

The templates for these families include reference planes for the slope angles, as shown for a baluster panel in Figure 7–41. For stair railings, you can lock the solid elements to these angles so that they respond to the slope of the stair.

Baluster Panel Elevation

Figure 7–41

- Component families are found in the *Railings* folder, with subfolders for *Balusters*, *Supports*, and *Terminations*.

- To create elements from scratch, use the following family templates:

  - **Baluster.rft**
  - **Baluster-Panel.rft**
  - **Baluster-Post.rft**
  - **Railing Support.rft**
  - **Railing Termination.rft**

💡 Hint: Adding Custom Posts

Posts are the point at which railings join. In many cases, this is the area in which railings need to change pitch and extend into adjacent railings, creating an integral, non-interrupted system. When designing a post, it is important to have a good grasp of creating custom families and to want to experiment. An example is shown in Figure 7–42.

Figure 7–42

- If you create a post as a post family, you cannot insert it as an independent component in the model. However, if you create a post as a generic model, you cannot use it in the *Baluster* dialog box and add it to a rail system. For this reason, it is recommended that you create the post family as an actual post, and then save a copy as a generic model. This gives you the option of using the post in any situation.

Creating Railing Types

Railings are a system family. To create a railing type, select an existing railing, duplicate it, and modify the parameters in the *Type Properties* dialog box. At the bottom of the dialog box, click **<<Preview** to display the railing, as shown in Figure 7–43.

Figure 7-43

- When editing a type, any changes that you make to one type impacts all instances of the railing type, as shown on the left in Figure 7-44. Make duplicate copies of the top rail and railing type before making changes so that you can have one without extensions, as shown on the right.

Figure 7-44

How To: Set the Rail Structure (Non-Continuous)

1. While editing a railing type, in the *Type Properties* dialog box, next to the **Rail Structure (Non-Continuous)** parameter, click **Edit...**.

2. In the *Edit Rails (Non-Continuous)* dialog box, click **Insert** to add a new rail to the list. You can have a single rail or multiple rails in a railing type, as shown in Figure 7–45.

   - If there are no other horizontal members, this dialog box remains empty.

Edit Rails (Non-Continuous)   ✕

Family: Railing
Type: Handrail - Pipe
Rails

	Name	Height	Offset	Profile	Material
1	Rail 1	2' 6"	0' 0"	Circular Handrail : 1"	<By Category>
2	Rail 2	2' 0"	0' 0"	Circular Handrail : 1"	<By Category>
3	Rail 3	1' 6"	0' 0"	Circular Handrail : 1"	<By Category>
4	Rail 4	1' 0"	0' 0"	Circular Handrail : 1"	<By Category>
5	Rail 5	0' 6"	0' 0"	Circular Handrail : 1"	<By Category>

Figure 7–45

3. Fill out the information about the rails as required:

Name	The name of the individual railing component. Select the name to modify it.
Height	The height for each rail from the base height.
Offset	The distance from the rail sketch line.
Profile	Select a profile in the drop-down list. You need to have the profile loaded before you can use it. (This is just a profile family, not a rail type as is required when you specify the top rails and handrails.)
Material	Specify a material for the rail. This is the only place where you can apply the material for rails.

4. Click **Up** and **Down** to move the rail to the correct location in the group.

5. Click **OK** to finish the command.

How To: Edit the Baluster Placement

1. While editing a railing type, in the *Type Properties* dialog box, next to the **Baluster Placement** parameter, click **Edit....** The *Edit Baluster Placement* dialog box has two main areas: *Main pattern* and *Posts*, as shown in Figure 7–46.

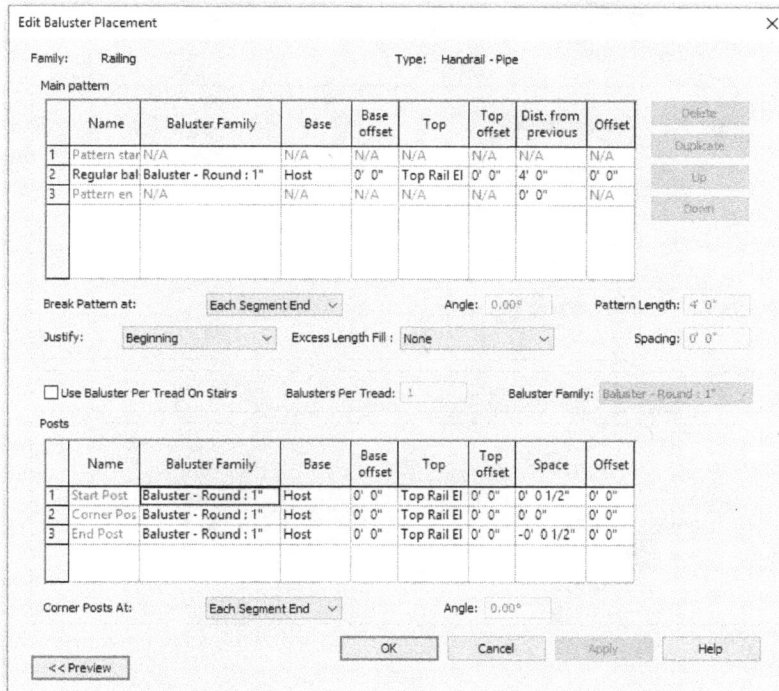

Figure 7–46

2. In the *Main pattern* area, add the baluster family and its sizes, such as the distance from the previous baluster. You can also add panels in this area.

3. If you are using a baluster on stairs and want a specific number per tread, select **Use Baluster Per Tread On Stairs** and specify the number per tread.

4. In the *Posts* area, specify the profiles for the *Start*, *Corner*, and *End* posts, and then specify their dimensions and locations.

How To: Set the Top Rail and Handrail

1. While editing a railing type, in the *Type Properties* dialog box, set up the information for *Top Rail, Handrail 1*, and *Handrail 2*, as shown in Figure 7–47.

   Note: The Top Rail is either the top of a guardrail (specify the handrail separately) or the top of the handrail (no separate handrail type needed).

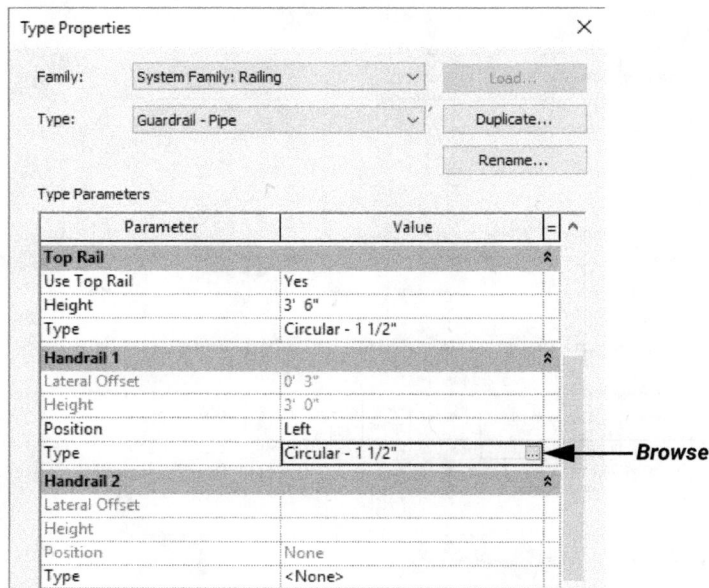

Figure 7–47

2. To select a *Type*, click ⬚ (Browse), as shown above in Figure 7–47. The *Type Properties* dialog box displays (as shown in Figure 7–48), where you can duplicate and modify type properties (including Extensions and Terminations).

Figure 7–48

- In the *Extension (Beginning/Bottom)* area, set the *Extension Style*. The properties are **None**, **Wall**, **Floor**, and **Post**, as shown in Figure 7–49.

Wall   *Floor*   *Post*

Figure 7–49

- A *Termination* can be added if required. The default rectangular termination works best with the Floor Extension style, but you can also create custom ones.

- For handrail types, you can also specify *Supports*, as shown in Figure 7–50. These are typically used if you are creating a wall-based railing type.

Supports		⌃
Family	Support - Metal - Circular	
Layout	Align With Posts	
Spacing	None	
Justification	Fixed Distance	
Number	Align With Posts	
	Fixed Number	
Identity Data	Maximum Spacing	
Keynote	Minimum Spacing	

Figure 7–50

3. If you are creating a guardrail, you also need to specify the *Type* and *Position* of the handrail. The handrail can be set to **Left**, **Right**, or **Left and Right** of the main railing as shown in Figure 7–51. The **Lateral Offset** and **Height** are read-only parameters.

Handrail 1		⌃
Lateral Offset	0' 3"	
Height	3' 0"	
Position	Left	
Type	None	
Handrail 2	Left	
Lateral Offset	Right	
Height	Left and Right	
Position	None	
Type	None	

Figure 7–51

- If you do not want to include a separate handrail in the railing type, set the *Type* to **None.**

> **💡 Hint: Additional Cleanup Options**
>
> When railings are not cleaning up as expected, ensure that the Stair Properties are correct. For example, *Rail Connections* can be set to **Trim** (as shown in Figure 7–52) or **Weld**. The **Weld** option forces a miter joint, rather than a butt joint.

Type Parameters

Parameter	Value	=
Construction		⌃
Railing Height	0' 0"	
Rail Structure (Non-Continuous)	Edit...	
Baluster Placement	Edit...	
Baluster Offset	0' 0"	
Use Landing Height Adjustment	☐	
Landing Height Adjustment	0' 0"	
Angled Joins	Add Vertical/Horizontal Segments	
Tangent Joins	Extend Rails to Meet	
Rail Connections	Trim	

Figure 7–52

When a straight rail joins an arc rail, Revit tends to distort the geometry. To fix this, select the segment of a rail in the railing's Sketch mode and modify the *Height Correction* in the Options Bar, as shown in Figure 7–53.

| Modify | Sketch Path | Slope: By Host ⌄ | Height Correction: By Type ⌄ 0' 0" |

Figure 7–53

Practice 7d
Create Custom Railings

Practice Objectives

- Duplicate and modify existing baluster and baluster panel families.
- Create a custom railing type using the baluster and baluster panel families.

In this practice, you will make copies of existing baluster and baluster panel families and modify them slightly. You will also create new Top Rail and Handrail types. You will then use the various families and types to create a new Railing type, as shown in Figure 7–54.

Figure 7–54

Task 1: Set the material of a baluster family.

1. In the practice files *Architectural* folder, open **Modern-Hotel-Railings-BIM.rvt**.
2. Open the **3D Views: Hall Balcony** view. This is the railing style you are going to use to create a new railing style.
3. Switch to the **Floor Plans: Floor 2** view.
4. In the *File* tab, expand 📂 (Open) and click 🗔 (Family).
5. In the practice files *Architectural>RFA* folder, open **Baluster-Round.rfa**.
6. Save the file as **Baluster-Round-Wood.rfa** in your practice files *Architectural>RFA* folder.
7. In the Baluster family file, in the *Manage* tab>*Settings* panel, click ⚙ (Materials). A short list of materials is available in the family and no wood materials are available.

8. In the *Material Browser*, expand *AEC Materials* and select **Wood**. In the selection set next to **Birch**, select ⬆️ (Adds material to document), as shown in Figure 7–55.

Figure 7–55

9. In the *Project Materials* area, select the **Birch** material and in the *Graphics* tab, select **Use Render Appearance**, as shown in Figure 7–56.

Figure 7–56

10. Click **OK**.

11. In the *Create* tab>*Properties* panel, click ▦ (Family Types).

12. In the *Family Types* dialog box, change the current type to **2"**.

13. Beside the *Type name*, click 🗋 (New Type) and name the new type **2" - Birch**.

14. Set the *Baluster Material* to **Birch**, as shown in Figure 7–57.

> *Note: The material for balusters cannot be set in the railing style, only in the family.*

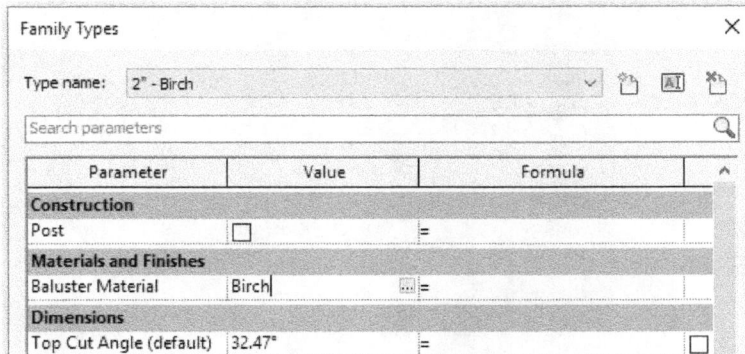

Figure 7–57

15. Click **OK**.

16. In the View Control Bar, set the *Visual Style* to ⬚ (Consistent Colors) and then to ⬚ (Realistic) to display the new wood shade.

17. Save the baluster family.

18. In the *Create* tab>*Family Editor* panel, click ⬚ (Load into Project and Close).

19. If the Modern Hotel project is the only one you have open, the family automatically loads and switches to the project file. If you have others open, select the Modern Hotel project from the list and click **OK**.

- If needed, overwrite the existing version and its parameter values.

Task 2: Modify a baluster panel family.

1. In the practice files *Architectural>RFA* folder, open the family file **Baluster Panel - Glass w Brackets.rfa**.

2. Save it as **Baluster Panel - Glass with Open Brackets.rfa** in your practice files *Architectural>RFA* folder.

3. Open the **Elevations: Left** view.

4. Zoom in on one of the brackets and select it.

5. In the *Modify | Extrusion* tab>*Mode* panel, click ⬚ (Edit Extrusion).

6. Sketch a **3/4"** radius circle inside the bracket, as shown in Figure 7–58. This creates a hole in the extrusion.

> *Note: To snap to the center of the arc, type the shortcut **SC** for Snap to Center.*

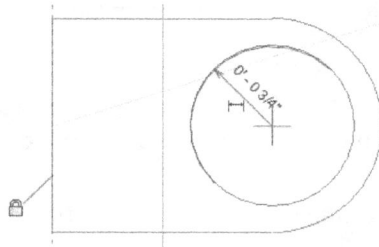

Figure 7–58

7. Click ✔ (Finish Edit Mode).

8. Repeat the process with the other three brackets.

9. Open the **3D Views: View 1** view and set the *Visual Style* to 🔲 (Consistent Colors). The panel displays with the opening in the brackets, as shown in Figure 7–59.

Figure 7–59

10. In the *Modify* tab>*Properties* panel, click 🔲 (Family Types).

11. Create a new family type named **36" w 1" Gap**.

12. In the *Family Types* dialog box, change the *Width* to **3'-0"**.

13. Click **Apply**. The panel updates, as shown in Figure 7–60. Click **OK**.

Figure 7–60

14. Save the baluster panel and load it into the Modern Hotel project.

Task 3: Create top rail and handrail types.

1. In the Modern Hotel project, in the Project Browser, expand **Families>Railings>Top Rail Type** node.

2. Right-click on **Circular - 1 1/2"** and select **Type Properties**.

3. In the *Type Properties* dialog box, duplicate the type, and name it **Circular - 1 1/2" - Birch**.

4. Change the *Material* to **Birch** and set the *Extension Style (Beginning/Bottom)* and *Extension Style (End/Top)* to **Wall**, as shown in Figure 7−61.

Figure 7−61

5. Click **OK**.

6. Repeat the process to create a new Birch Handrail type.

7. Save the project.

Task 4: Create custom railing types.

1. In the Modern Hotel project, open the **3D Views: Hall Balcony** view.

2. Select the railing.

3. In Properties, click 🔲 (Edit Type).

4. In the *Type Properties* dialog box, click **Duplicate** and name the new railing type **Hotel Balcony Guardrail - Glass Panel**.

5. Next to the **Rail Structure (Non-Continuous)** parameter, click **Edit...**.

6. In the *Edit Rails* dialog box, delete all of the Rails and click **OK**.

7. Click **OK**. The new railing displays with wooden guardrail and handrail and existing posts, as shown in Figure 7–62.

Figure 7–62

8. Select the railing and edit the Railing type again.

9. Next to the **Baluster Placement** parameter, click **Edit...**.

10. In the *Main pattern* area, next to *Regular Baluster* (in the *Baluster Family* column), change the type to **Baluster-Round-Wood: 2" - Birch**, as shown in Figure 7–63.

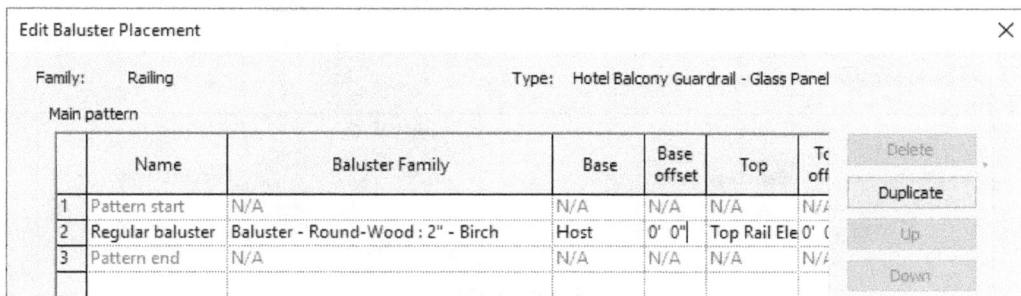

Figure 7–63

11. Click **Duplicate**.

12. In row *2*, change the *Name* to **Panel** and the *Baluster Family* to **Baluster Panel-Glass with Open Brackets: 36" w 1" Gap**.

13. Click **OK** twice and view the railings. The panel displays, but it is not in the correct location in relation to the posts, as shown in Figure 7–64.

Figure 7–64

Note: Distances between balusters is measured from center to center.

14. Edit the type again and open the *Edit Baluster Placement* dialog box. In the *Dist. from Previous* column, you can see that the settings are now **4'-0"** for both the baluster and the panel. Therefore, the baluster and panel placement is spread out.

15. Set the *Dist. from Previous* to **1'-7 1/8"** for both the baluster and panel.

16. Set *Justify* to **Beginning** and *Excess Length Fill* to **None**, as shown in Figure 7–65.

Main pattern

	Name	Baluster Family	Base	Base offset	Top	Top offset	Dist. from previous	Offset	
1	Pattern sta	N/A	N/A	N/A	N/A	N/A	N/A	N/A	Delete
2	Panel	Baluster Panel - Gla	Host	0' 0"	Top Rai	0' 0"	1' 7 1/8"	0' 0"	Duplicate
3	Regular ba	Baluster - Round -	Host	0' 0"	Top Rai	0' 0"	1' 7 1/8"	0' 0"	Up
4	Pattern en	N/A	N/A	N/A	N/A	N/A	0' 0"	N/A	Down

Break Pattern at: Each Segment End ▼   Angle: 0.000°   Pattern Length: 3' 2 1/4"

Justify: Beginning ▼   Excess Length Fill : None ▼   Spacing: 0' 0"

Figure 7–65

17. While still in the *Edit Baluster Placement* dialog box, in the *Posts* area, change the *Baluster Family* for all of the posts to **Baluster - Round - Wood: 2" - Birch** and click **OK**.

18. In the *Type Properties* dialog box, change both the *Top Rail Type* and *Handrail 1 Type* to **Circular - 1 1/2" - Birch**, as shown in Figure 7–66.

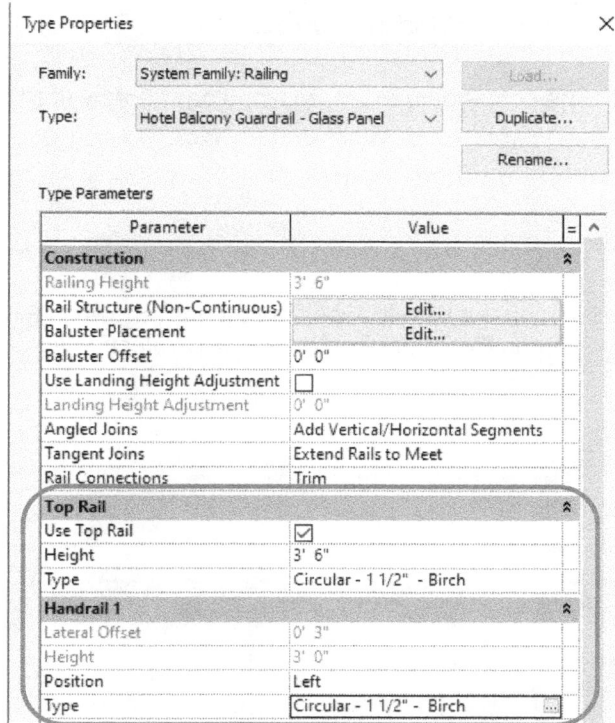

Figure 7-66

19. Close the dialog boxes and view the new Railing type. This time, the baluster to panel fit is better, as shown in Figure 7-67.

Figure 7-67

20. Save and close the project.

End of practice

Chapter Review Questions

1. It is easier and less time-consuming to create a custom door by starting with an existing door.

    a. True

    b. False

2. Based on the information in the *Family Types* dialog box (shown in Figure 7–68), if you changed the *Trim Projection Ext* value, would the *Trim Projection Int* also update?

Parameter	Value	Formula	Lock
Dimensions			
Height	4' 0"	=	☑
Default Sill Height	3' 0"	=	☑
Trim Projection - Ext.	0' 0 1/2"	=	☑
Trim Projection - Int.	0' 0 3/4"	=	☑
Trim Width - Exterior	0' 3 1/2"	=	☑
Trim Width - Interior	0' 3 1/2"	=	☑
Width	3' 0"	=	☑
Window Inset	0' 0 3/4"	=	☑
Rough Width		=	☑
Rough Height		=	☑

Figure 7–68

    a. Yes

    b. No

3. Which of the following must be in place before you can add a fascia to an angled wall? (Select all that apply.)

    a. A profile

    b. A fascia type

    c. A wall sweep

    d. A model line

4. Which of the following parts of a railing type (shown in Figure 7–69) is created by a profile?

Figure 7–69

    a. Rail

    b. Post

    c. Baluster

    d. Baluster panel

5. What is the main difference between a Baluster family and a Post family?

    a. A baluster is created using a profile and a post is created using solid forms.

    b. A baluster has top and bottom angles programmed into the family, while a post does not have any angles.

    c. Balusters can be placed on stair treads, but posts can only be placed on landings.

    d. Balusters are typically placed 4" apart, and posts are placed 3'-0" apart.

Command Summary

Button	Command	Location
	Roof: Fascia	• **Ribbon:** *Architecture* tab>*Build* panel
	Object Styles	• **Ribbon:** *Manage* tab>*Settings* panel
	Model Line	• **Ribbon:** *Architecture* tab>*Model* panel

Creating MEP-Specific Families

MEP-specific families in Revit are system-based families used to model mechanical, electrical, and plumbing systems within a project. These families include elements such as plumbing fixtures, lighting fixtures, electrical and data devices, and pipe fittings, all of which are designed to interact with MEP systems through connectors and defined parameters.

Learning Objectives

- Upgrade an architectural plumbing fixture with MEP connectors.
- Create a custom lighting fixture.
- Create a data device family that includes a tag in the family.
- Create a pipe fitting flange.

Practice 8a
Upgrade an Architectural Plumbing Fixture to MEP

Practice Objective

*   Upgrade an existing architectural toilet fixture with pipe sizes and connectors for use in a MEP project.

In this practice, you will upgrade an existing architectural toilet fixture to be used in an MEP project. You will create parameters for pipe sizes. You will also add connectors for cold water and Sanitary systems, as shown in Figure 8–1.

Figure 8–1

Task 1: Create parameters for pipe sizes.

1. In the practice files *MEP>RFA* folder, open **Toilet-Commercial-Wall-3D.rfa**.

2. Save the family as **Toilet-Commercial-Wall-3D-MEP.rfa** in the practice files *MEP>RFA* folder.

3. In the *Family Types* dialog box, add the following type parameters:

Name	Discipline	Data Type	Group
Sanitary Radius	Piping	Pipe Size	Dimensions
Cold Water Radius	Piping	Pipe Size	Dimensions

---

4. Set *Sanitary Radius* to **2"** and *Cold Water Radius* to **1/2"**. Lock the parameters.

   Note: The related diameter parameters need to be Shared because they are often used in plumbing fixture schedules.

5. Add a new parameter, but this time select the **Shared Parameter** type and click **Select...**.

6. If an alert box displays asking if you want to choose a new file, click **Yes**. If the alert box does not display, in the *Shared Parameters* dialog box, click **Edit...**.

7. In the *Edit Shared Parameters* dialog box, click **Browse...** and navigate to the **MEP.txt** parameter file found in the practice files *MEP* folder.

8. Add a new group called **Piping** and two new parameters for the following:

Name	Discipline	Data Type
Sanitary Diameter	Piping	Pipe Size
Cold Water Diameter	Piping	Pipe Size

9. In the *Edit Shared Parameters* dialog box, click **OK**.

10. In the *Shared Parameters* dialog box, select one of the new parameters and click **OK**. Make sure *Group parameter under* is set to **Dimensions** and click **OK**.

11. In the *Family Types* dialog box, click ⬚ (New Parameter).

12. In the *Parameter Properties* dialog box, select **Shared Parameter** and click **Select**.

13. In the *Shared Parameters* dialog box, select the other new parameter and click **OK** twice.

14. Set the values and create formulas for *Sanitary Diameter* and *Cold Water Diameter* based on the corresponding radius parameters, as shown in Figure 8-2.

Parameter	Value	Formula	Lock
Dimensions			⌃
Cold Water Diameter	1"	= Cold Water Radius * 2	☑
Cold Water Radius	1/2"	=	☑
Mounting Height	1' 3"	=	☑
Sanitary Diameter	4"	= Sanitary Radius * 2	☑
Sanitary Radius	2"	=	☑

Figure 8-2

15. Click **OK**.

16. Save the family.

Task 2: Add connectors.

1. Rotate the view so that the back of the toilet displays. (If the wall displays, hide it temporarily or set the *Visual Style* to **Wireframe** while you are adding connectors.)

2. In the *Create* tab>*Connectors* panel, click 🖾 (Pipe Connector).

3. In the Options Bar, select **Domestic Cold Water**.

4. Hover the cursor over the face of the pipe opening, as shown in Figure 8–3, and click to place the connector.

Figure 8–3

5. Click ⌖ (Modify) and select the connector.

6. In *Properties*, set the following values for parameters:

    *   *Flow Configuration*: **Fixture Units**

    *   *Flow Direction:* **In**

    *   Uncheck the **Allow Slope Adjustments** option

    *   *Fixture Units:* **2.5**

7. In the *Dimensions* area, click ⬚ (Associate Parameter) next to *Diameter*.

8. In the *Associate Family Parameter* dialog box, select **Cold Water Diameter**, as shown in Figure 8–4, then click **OK**.

Figure 8–4

9. The connector resizes to fit the correct pipe size.

10. Add a pipe connector for a sanitary system to the back of the fixture, as shown in Figure 8–5.

Figure 8–5

11. Select the connector and set the following properties:

   • *Diameter:* **4"**
   • *Flow Configuration:* **Fixture Units**
   • *Flow Direction:* **Out**
   • Select **Allow Slope Adjustments**
   • *System Classification:* **Sanitary**
   • *Fixture Units:* **4**

   Note: The connector will host to the center of the rectangular face.

12. From the practice files *MEP* folder, open the **Sample.rvt** file. Open a Plumbing Floor Plan view and load the family to test it.

13. Save and close the family, but do not save the project file.

End of practice

Practice 8b
Upgrade an Architectural Lighting Fixture to MEP

Practice Objectives

- Modify the light source.
- Apply a power connector.
- Create family types with different materials for the pendant and glass shade.

In this practice, you will modify a lighting fixture family with a specific light source and connector, as shown in Figure 8–6. You will also create family types using different materials.

Figure 8–6

Task 1: Set up a new light fixture family.

1. In the practice files *MEP>RFA* folder, open the family **Pendant-Light-Fixture.rfa**.

2. Open the **Elevations: Front** view. It includes reference planes for the ceiling and light source, a ceiling element, the fixture elements, and the level, as shown in Figure 8–7.

Light source reference plane

Ceiling element

Ceiling reference plane

Light source

Level

Figure 8–7

3. Select the light source. In the *Modify | Light Source* tab>*Lighting* panel, click 🔔 (Light Source Definition).

4. In the *Light Source Definition* dialog box, change the Light distribution to 🔺 (Photometric Web), as shown in Figure 8–8, then click **OK**.

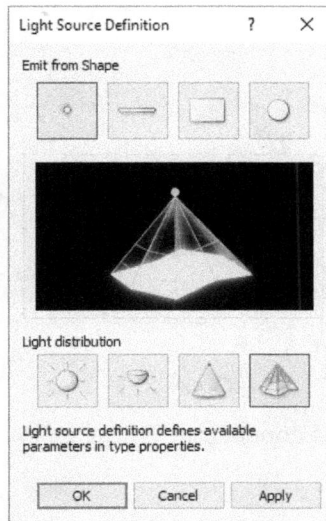

Figure 8–8

5. Open the *Family Types* dialog box and set the following values for the parameters:

    *   *Lamp:* **CF42TRT**
    *   *Apparent Power:* **44.21 VA**
    *   *Light Loss Factor>Total Light Loss Factor:* **0.85**
    *   *Initial Intensity:* **Luminous Flux, 3200**
    *   *Photometric Web File:* Click ⌞⋯⌟ and select **spot_ideal.ies** from the practice files *MEP>IES* folder
    *   *Tilt Angle:* **90**

6. Save the family.

Task 2: Add a connector.

1. Open the default 3D view and, if needed, set the *Visual Style* to **Wireframe**. Rotate and zoom in to the top of the pendant lighting fixture.

2. In the *Create* tab>*Connectors* panel, click ⫶ (Electrical Connector).

3. In the Options Bar, select **Power - Balanced**.

4. Attach the connector to the face of the pendant at the point where the pendant touches the ceiling, as shown in Figure 8–9 (it will look like only half of the pendant's face is selected, but the connector will be placed on the entire face).

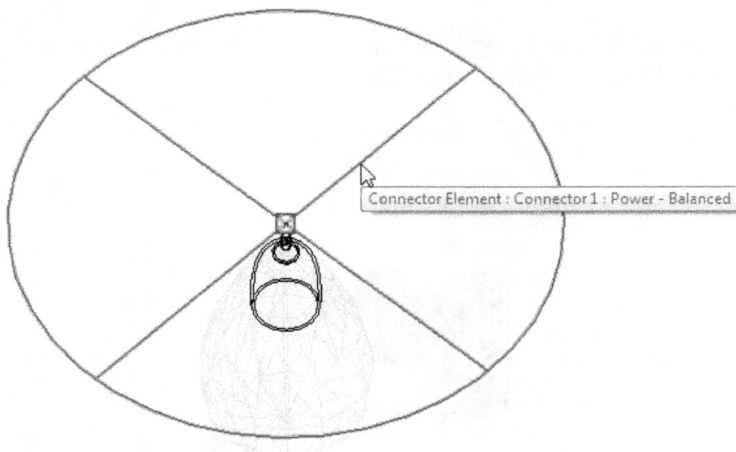

Figure 8–9

5. Click ⫸ (Modify) and select the connector.

6. In *Properties*, specify the values for the following parameters:

    •   *System Type:* **Power - Balanced** (verify)

    •   *Load Classification:* Click ⌑ and select **Lighting**

    •   *Voltage:* **277**

    •   *Power Factor:* **0.95**

7. While still in *Properties*, beside the *Apparent Power* parameter, click ⌑ (Associate Family Parameter).

8. In the *Associate Family Parameter* dialog box, select **Apparent Power**. Click **OK**.

9. Save the family.

Task 3: Create family types.

1. In the *Create* tab>*Properties* panel, click ⌑ (Family Types).

2. In the *Family Types* dialog box, beside the *Type name*, click ⌑ (New Type).

3. In the *Name* dialog box, type **Brushed Nickel and Clear Glass** and click **OK**, then click **Apply**.

4. Create another new type called **Brass and Green Glass**.

5. In the *Materials and Finishes* area, verify or set the following values for the parameters, as shown in Figure 8–10:

    •   *Pendent Material:* **Metal - Brass**

    •   *Glass Material:* **Glass - Green**

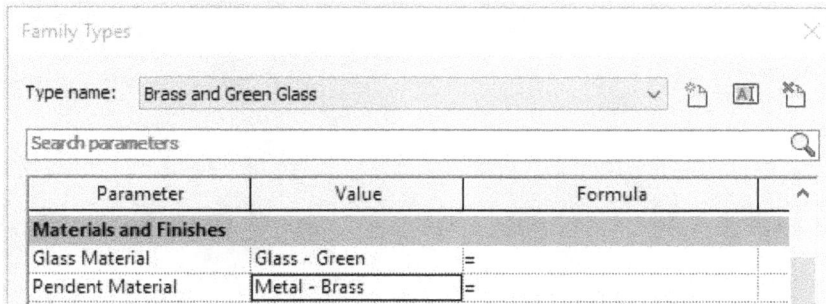

Figure 8–10

6. Click **OK**.

7. If time permits, create several other family types that use different colors of glass and different pendant materials.

8. From the practice files *MEP* folder, open **Sample.rvt**. Open an Electrical Lighting Ceiling Plan view and load the family to test it.

9. Open the Electrical>Power>3D Views>**3D Elec** view. Select the lighting fixture and use the Type Selector to change it to a different type.

    Note: To turn on the light source, open the Visibility/Graphic Overrides dialog box, expand **Lighting Fixtures***, and turn on* **Light Source***.*

10. Save and close the family, but do not save the project file.

End of practice

Practice 8c
Create a Data Device with Annotation Parameters

Practice Objective

- Create a data device with both solid elements and annotation elements.

In this practice, you will create a data device using reference planes, extrusions, and connectors. You will then add an annotation symbol to the family with its related parameters, as shown in Figure 8–11. You will also test the family in a project.

Figure 8–11

Task 1: Set up reference planes.

1. Create a new family based on the **Data Device Hosted.rft** template found in the practice files *MEP>RFT* folder.

2. Save the family to the practice files *MEP>RFA* folder as **Data Receptacle Type C.rfa**.

3. In the *Manage* tab>*Settings* panel, click ⬛ (Project Units) or type **UN**.

4. In the *Project Units* dialog box, set the *Length* units to **Fractional Inches**. Click **OK** twice to close the dialog boxes.

5. In the **Floor Plans: Ref. Level** view, set the *View Scale* to **6"=1'-0"**.

6. Zoom in closer to the intersection of the reference planes.

7. Create and dimension the reference planes, as shown in Figure 8–12. You do not need to label these dimensions as all of the data receptacles are the same size.

Figure 8–12

8. Save the family.

Task 2: Create the model extrusions.

1. Create the two extrusions shown in Figure 8–13. In *Properties*, set the *Extrusion End* for each of the extrusions as follows:

    *   Extrusion 1 = (negative) **-2 1/8"**
    *   Extrusion 2 = **3/16"**

Figure 8–13

2. Open a 3D view and set the *Visual Style* to **Wireframe**. The finished view displays as shown in Figure 8–14.

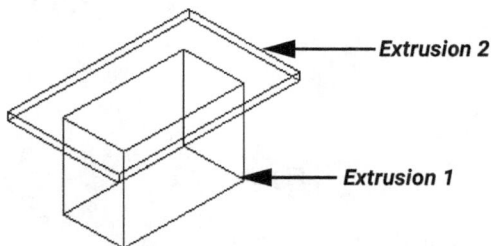

Figure 8–14

3. In the *Create* tab>*Connectors* panel, click ⚡ (Electrical Connector).

4. In the Options Bar, select **Data**.

5. Select the face of the top extrusion.

6. Click ⌖ (Modify) and select both extrusions.

7. In the *Modify | Extrusion* tab>*Mode* panel, click ⬚ (Visibility Settings).

8. In the *Family Element Visibility Settings* dialog box, uncheck **Coarse** and **Medium**. Click **OK**.

   - This causes the 3D elements to display only at the Fine detail level where it is often used to coordinate the placement of items by their real dimensions.

9. Return to the **Ref. Level** view and close the 3D view.

10. Save the family.

Task 3: Create an annotation symbol.

1. Create a new family based on the **Generic Annotation.rft** template found in the practice files *MEP>RFT* folder.

2. Save the family to the practice files *MEP>RFA* folder as **Data Device Annotation.rfa**.

3. Read and delete the red note.

4. In the *Create* tab>*Detail* panel, click ↖ (Line) and using the *Draw* tools, sketch the shape shown in Figure 8–15.

   Note: Do not add the dimension; they are for information only.

Figure 8–15

5. In the *Create* tab>*Text* panel, click ᴬ▤ (Label).

6. Click inside the new symbol sketch.

7. In the *Edit Label* dialog box, there are no parameters listed. Click 🗋 (Add Parameter).

8. Create an instance parameter named **Tag**, set *Data Type* as **Text**, and set *Group parameter under* as **Identity Data**. Click **OK**.

   Note: Ensure that this is an instance parameter.

9. Back in the *Edit Label* dialog box, add the parameter to the label and set the *Sample Value* to **A1**, as shown in Figure 8–16, then click **OK**.

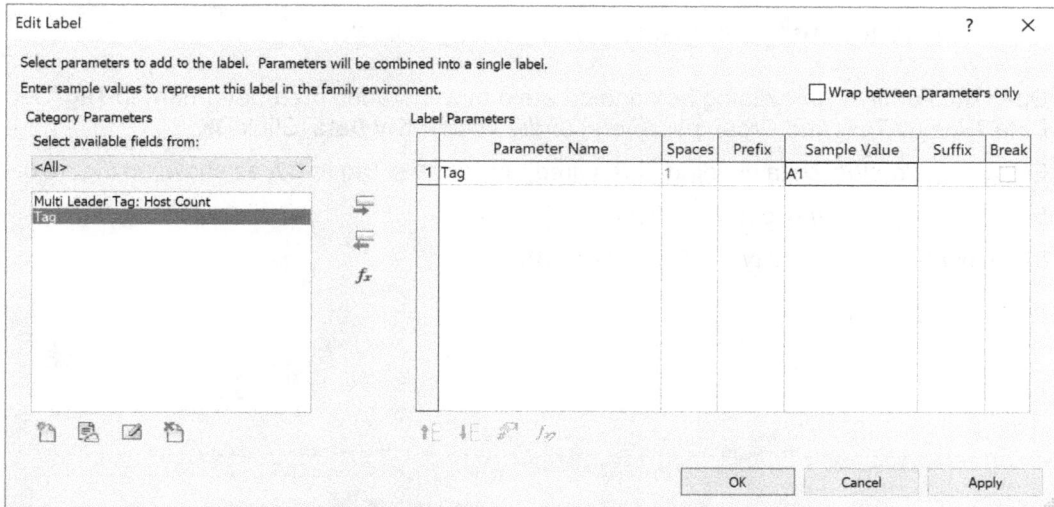

Figure 8–16

10. Select the new label and, in *Properties*, click [Edit Type icon] (Edit Type). In the *Type Properties* dialog box, set the *Background* to **Transparent** and click **OK**.

11. Relocate the label to fit inside the symbol sketch.

12. With nothing selected, in *Properties*, select **Rotate with component** and **Keep text readable.**

13. Save the annotation family and load it into the data receptacle family.

14. Place the data device annotation family at the center of the elements, as shown in Figure 8–17.

Figure 8–17

Task 4: Create instance parameters and family types.

1. Open the *Family Types* dialog box and create a new instance parameter named **Tag**. Set *Data Type* as **Text** and *Group parameter under* as **Identity Data**. Click **OK**.

2. Expand the *Identity Data* heading (if required) and set the *Tag* to **C7**, as shown in Figure 8–18.

3. Beside the *Type name*, click 📋 (New Type).

4. In the *Name* dialog box, type **C7** and click **OK**.

Parameter	Value	Formula	Lock
Constraints			
Default Elevation	48	=	☑
IFC Parameters			
Type IFC Predefined Type		=	
Export Type to IFC As		=	
Identity Data			
Tag (default)	C7	=	
Type Image		=	

Figure 8–18

5. Select the Data Device Annotation element.

6. In *Properties*, under the *Identity Data* heading, beside the **Tag** parameter, click ▯ (Associate Family Parameter).

7. In the *Associate Family Parameter* dialog box, select **Tag** and click **OK**. The parameters are associated together and the tag displays as **C7**, as shown in Figure 8–19.

Figure 8–19

8. Select the tag. In the *Modify | Generic Annotations* tab>*Visibility* panel, click ⬚ (Visibility Settings).

9. In the *Family Element Visibility Settings* dialog box, in the *Detail Levels* area, uncheck **Fine** and click **OK**.

   Note: Tags are used more in views set to the Coarse or Medium detail level.

10. If time permits, in the *Family Types* dialog box, create additional family types for C1, C2, C3, C4, C5, and C6. Under the *Identity Data* section, change the value of the *Tag (default)* parameter for each of these as you create the family type. Click **Apply** to accept the changes and click **OK** when finished.

11. Save the family.

Task 5: Test the family.

1. From the practice files *MEP* folder, open **Sample.rvt** and load the family to test it.

2. Open the **Floor Plans: 1- Power** view and set the *Detail Level* to **Coarse**.

3. Switch to **Data Receptacle Type C.rfa** and load it into the project.

4. In the *Modify | Place Component* tab>*Placement* panel, click ⬚ (Place on Vertical Face) and place the device on the wall.

5. Change the *Detail Level* to **Fine**. The 3D elements display, but not the tag.

6. Open the Electrical>Power>3D Views>**3D Elec** view and change the *Detail Level* to **Fine**. Rotate the model as needed to see the device.

7. Save and close the family, but do not save the project file.

End of practice

Practice 8d
Create a Pipe Fitting Flange (Advanced)

Practice Objectives

- Create reference planes, dimensions, and labels.
- Draw single-line representations for Coarse and Medium detail levels.
- Create solids for the Fine detail level.
- Create and apply family types.

In this practice, you will create a family file based on a template and add parameters, some of which include formulas. You will then add reference planes, dimensions, and labels and create family types to help you flex the framework. You will then create the flange components: a single-line representation for **Coarse** and **Medium** detail levels, and an extrusion and blend solid elements for **Fine** detail level, as shown in Figure 8–20. Finally, you will test the flanges in a project and draw pipe between them.

Figure 8–20

Task 1: Open a family template.

1. Create a new family based on the **Plumbing Fixture.rft** template found in the practice files *MEP>RFT* folder.

2. Save the family to the practice files *MEP>RFA* folder as **Pipe Fitting Flange.rfa**.

3. In the *Create* tab>*Properties* panel, click 🔲 (Family Category and Parameters).

4. In the *Family Category and Parameters* dialog box, set the *Filter list* to **Piping** and in the *Family Category* area, select **Pipe Fittings**.

5. In the *Family Parameters* area, verify and set the following options:

    *   Clear the **Work Plane-Based** option.
    *   Select **Always Vertical**.
    *   For the *Part Type*, select **Transition**.
    *   Clear the **Shared** option.

6. Click **OK**.

7. Type **UN** to open the *Project Units* dialog box. In the *Format* column, click the value next to *Length*.

8. In the *Format* dialog box, set the *Units* to **Fractional inches** and set the *Rounding* to **To the nearest 1/16"**. Click **OK**.

9. In the *Project Units* dialog box, set the *Discipline* to **Piping**. In the *Format* column, click the value next to *Pipe Size*. In the *Format* dialog box, set the *Rounding* to **To the nearest 1/16"** and set the *Unit symbol* to **"**.

10. Click **OK** twice.

11. Set the view *Scale* to **1"=1'-0"**.

12. Save the family.

Task 2: Create parameters.

1. In the *Create* tab>*Properties* panel, click (Family Types).

2. In the *Family Types* dialog box, click (New Parameter).

3. In the *Parameter Properties* dialog box, in the *Parameter Type* area, select **Family Parameter** (if it is not already selected) and specify the following:

    *   *Name:* **NomRad**
    *   *Discipline:* **Piping**
    *   *Data Type:* **Pipe Size**
    *   *Group Parameter Under:* **Dimensions**
    *   Select **Type**

4. Click **OK**.

5. Repeat the steps, creating instance parameters named **NomDia, FlgRad, FlgDia, PipeOD, PipeOR, RFD, RFR, RFT, FT, LTH, HT,** and **HubRad**. Define the parameters as follows:

    *   *Parameter Type:* **Family Parameter**
    *   *Discipline:* **Piping**
    *   *Data Type:* **Pipe Size**
    *   *Group Parameter Under:* **Dimensions**
    *   Select **Instance**

6. In the *Family Types* dialog box, specify the following values:

   - *FT:* **3/4"**
   - *FlgDia:* **9"**
   - *LTH:* **5"**
   - *NomRad:* **2"**
   - *PipeOD:* **4 1/2"**
   - *RFD:* **7"**
   - *RFT:* **1/16"**

   Note: *By default, the parameters are listed in alphabetical order.*

7. In the *Family Types* dialog box, enter the following formulas for the parameters (there should be no spaces in the formulas you enter):

   - *FlgRad:* **FlgDia/2**
   - *HT:* **LTH-(FT+RFT)**
   - *HubRad:* **PipeOR*1.5**
   - *NomDia:* **NomRad*2**
   - *PipeOR:* **PipeOD/2**
   - *RFD:* **FlgDia-2"**
   - *RFR:* **RFD/2**

The final information displays as shown in Figure 8–21.

Parameter	Value	Formula	Lock
Dimensions			☆
FT (default)	3/4"	=	☐
FlgDia (default)	9"	=	☐
FlgRad (default)	4 1/2"	= FlgDia / 2	☐
HT (default)	4 3/16"	= LTH - (FT + RFT)	☐
HubRad (default)	3 3/8"	= PipeOR * 1.5	☐
LTH (default)	5"	=	☐
NomDia (default)	4"	= NomRad * 2	☐
NomRad	2"	=	☐
OffsetHeight (default)		=	
OffsetWidth (default)		=	
PipeOD (default)	4 1/2"	=	☐
PipeOR (default)	2 1/4"	= PipeOD / 2	☐
RFD (default)	7"	= FlgDia - 2"	☐
RFR (default)	3 1/2"	= RFD / 2	☐
RFT (default)	1/16"	=	☐

Figure 8–21

8. Click **OK**.

9. Save the family.

Task 3: Create plan view reference planes.

1. Place three vertical reference planes **2"** apart, with one to the left of the **Center (Left/Right)** reference plane, and two on the right, as shown in Figure 8-22.

2. Name the new reference planes, as shown in Figure 8-22, with the *Is Reference* parameter set to **Not a Reference**.

Figure 8-22

3. Dimension the reference planes, as shown in Figure 8-23.

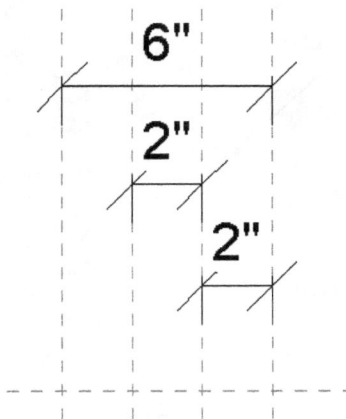

Figure 8-23

4. Apply the labels shown in Figure 8-24 to the dimensions.

$$LTH = 5"$$

$$FT = 3/4"$$

$$RFT = 1/16"$$

Figure 8-24

5. Add horizontal reference planes, dimensions, and labels on either side of the **Center (Front/ Back)** reference plane, as shown in Figure 8-25.

Figure 8-25

6. Save the family.

Task 4: Create family types so that you can test the framework.

1. In the *Properties* panel, click ⊞ (Family Types).

2. In the *Family Types* dialog box, beside the *Type name*, click ⬚ (New Type).

3. In the *Name* dialog box, type **4"** and click **OK**. Note that the existing values are applied to this type by default.

4. Click ⬚ (New Type) again. In the *Name* dialog box, type **6"** and click **OK**.

5. In the *Dimensions* area, change the parameter values as follows:

   - *FT:* **15/16"**
   - *FlgDia:* **11"**
   - *LTH:* **3 1/2"**
   - *NomRad:* **3"**
   - *PipeOD:* **6 5/8"**

6. Move the *Family Types* dialog box so that the reference planes display. Click **Apply**. The reference plane locations change according to the new parameter values, as shown in Figure 8–26.

Figure 8–26

7. In the *Type Name* drop-down list, select **4"**.

8. Click **Apply**. Note that the reference planes return to their original sizes.

9. Click **OK** to close the dialog box.

10. Save the family.

Task 5: Create plan view graphics.

1. Type **VV** to open the *Visibility/Graphic Overrides* dialog box. At the bottom of the *Model Categories* tab, click **Object Styles...**.

2. In the *Object Styles* dialog box, click **Select All**. Change the *Projection* to **5**, as shown in Figure 8–27.

Object Styles   ✕

Model Objects   Annotation Objects   Imported Objects

Category	Line Weight		Line Color	Line Pattern	Material
	Projection	Cut			
⊟ Pipe Fittings	5		■ Black	Solid	
Center line	5		■ Black	Solid	

Figure 8–27

3. Click **OK** twice to close the dialog boxes.

4. In the *Create* tab>*Model* panel, click ⌐ (Model Line). Uncheck **Chain** from the Options Bar.

5. Draw the lines shown in Figure 8–28. In the *Modify | Place Lines* tab>*Subcategory* panel, verify the *Subcategory* is set to **Pipe Fittings**. If you do not see the thickness, toggle

   ⧗ (Thin Lines). Use align and lock the lines to the reference planes.

RFT = 1/16"

Gasket reference plane

PipeOD = 4 1/2"

EQEQ

EQ EQ

FlgDia = 9"

Figure 8–28

6. Open the *Family Types* dialog box. Change the *Type name* to **6"** and click **Apply** to verify that the lines flex correctly.

7. Reset the *Type name* to **4"** and click **OK** to close the dialog box.

8. Select the three lines.

9. In the *Modify | Lines* tab>*Visibility* panel, click ⬚ (Visibility Settings).

10. In the *Family Element Visibility Settings* dialog box, in the *Detail Levels* area, clear the **Fine** option. Leave all of the others selected, as shown in Figure 8-29.

   • This enables the selected elements to be visible only at the **Coarse** and **Medium** detail levels.

Figure 8-29

11. Click **OK**.

12. In the View Control Bar, expand ⬚ (Preview Visibility Off) and select ⬚ (Preview Visibility On). Test the *Detail Levels*. When you select **Fine**, the line elements should disappear. End on **Medium**.

13. Toggle off the preview visibility.

14. Save the family.

Task 6: Create the raised face and flange extrusions.

1. In the Project Browser, open the **Elevations: Left** view.

2. Select the three model lines and temporarily hide the elements.

3. In the *Create* tab>*Forms* panel, click ▮ (Extrusion).

4. In the *Modify | Create Extrusion* tab>*Work Plane* panel, click ▮ (Set).

5. In the *Work Plane* dialog box, in the *Name* drop-down list, select **Reference Plane: Flange Thickness** and click **OK.**

6. Draw a circle at the intersection of the **Ref. Level** and **Center (Front/Back)** reference planes. Dimension the radius and label it using the **RFR** parameter, as shown in Figure 8–30.

Figure 8–30

7. Click ⬚ (Modify).
8. In *Properties*, in the *Extrusion End*, click the **Associate Family Parameter** button.
9. In the *Associate Family Parameter* dialog box, select **RFT**, as shown in Figure 8–31, then click **OK**.

Figure 8–31

10. Click ✔ (Finish Edit Mode).

11. Click ▋ (Extrusion).

12. Set the work plane to **Reference Plane: Center (Left/Right)**.

13. Draw a larger circle at the same intersection.

14. Make the temporary dimension permanent and label it as **FlgRad**. The new radius displays as shown in Figure 8–32.

Figure 8–32

15. Click ⌖ (Modify).

16. In *Properties*, in the *Extrusion End*, click the **Associate Family Parameter** button. In the *Associate Family Parameter* dialog box, select **FT** and click **OK**.

17. Click ✔ (Finish Edit Mode).

18. Open the **3D views: View 1** view. The two circular extrusions and the model lines should display. Shade and rotate the element, as shown in Figure 8–33. Flex it using the family types.

Figure 8–33

19. Save the family.

Task 7: Create the pipe connection blend.

1. Return to the **Elevations: Left** view.

2. In the *Create* tab>*Forms* panel, click 🔵 (Blend).

3. Draw a circle at the same intersection. Dimension and label it **HubRad**.

4. In the *Modify | Create Blend Base Boundary* tab>*Mode* panel, click 🔷 (Edit Top).

5. Draw a smaller circle at the same intersection as the other element. Dimension and label it **PipeOR**.

6. In *Properties*, set the *Second End* to (negative) **-4 3/16"**.

7. Click ✔ (Finish Edit Mode).

8. Open the **Elevations: Front** view. Align and lock the small end of the blend to the Weld reference plane, as shown in Figure 8–34.

Figure 8–34

9. Open the **3D Views: View 1** view and flex the types to ensure that everything is working, as shown for two possible flexes in Figure 8-35.

Figure 8-35

10. Select the model lines and temporarily hide them.

11. Save the family.

Task 8: Add connectors.

1. Continue working in the **3D Views: View 1** view. Rotate the view as shown in Figure 8-36.

2. In the *Create* tab>*Connectors* panel, click 🔲 (Pipe Connector).

3. In the *Modify | Place Pipe Connector* tab>*Placement* panel, verify that 🔲 (Face) is selected.

4. In the Options Bar, in the *System type* drop-down list, select **Hydronic Supply**.

5. In *Properties*, set the *Round Connector Dimension* parameter to **Use Radius**.

6. Hover over the small face of the blend, then press <Tab> to highlight the face and click to add the connector.

7. The arrow of the connector should be pointing outward from the geometry, as shown in Figure 8–36. If the arrow is pointing inward, click the **Flip** control.

Figure 8–36

-   The connector arrow does not indicate the direction of flow. It simply shows which side the pipe will connect from. If the arrow is pointing inward, the pipe created from the flange will run through it instead of away from it.

8. Spin the view so that the raised face is visible and apply another connector to that face, as shown in Figure 8–37.

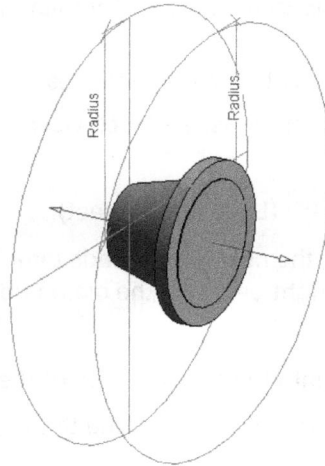

Figure 8–37

9. Click ⍟ (Modify) and select one of the connectors. In the *Modify | Connector Element* tab> *Connector Links* panel, click ⌀ (Link Connectors) and select the other connector to link the two together.

10. Select both connectors.

11. In *Properties*, for *Radius,* associate it with the **NomRad** parameter and click **OK**.

12. The connectors are resized as shown in Figure 8–38.

Figure 8–38

13. Save the family.

Task 9: Test the flange in a project.

1. Start a new project using the **Imperial-Systems Template.rte** file found in the practice files *MEP>RTE* folder.

2. Save the project as **Flange Test.rvt** to the practice files *MEP* folder.

3. Open the Mechanical>HVAC>Floor Plans: **1 - Mech** view.

4. Switch back to the family.

5. In the *Family Editor* panel, click 🗋 (Load into Project).

   • If you have one project open, the new family loads directly into it. If you have more than one project open, select the right one(s) in the dialog box.

6. You are returned to the project.

7. Place an instance of each type into the drawing area of the project.

   • If a command is not automatically started, in the *Systems* tab>*Plumbing & Fixture* panel, click 🗋 (Pipe Fitting).

8. Zoom in to display the plan view of the flanges at a **Coarse** detail level. Ensure that **Thin Lines** is toggled off so that the line weight displays, as shown on the left in Figure 8–39.

9. With **Thin Lines** on, change the *Detail Level* to **Fine**. The flanges display in detail at full size, as shown on the right in Figure 8–39.

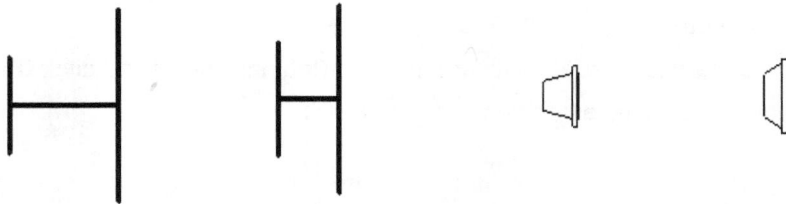

Figure 8–39

10. Ensure that the flanges are aligned with each other, and then draw pipe between them.

11. Open a 3D view.

12. Zoom in on the flanges and toggle on ⊟ (Thin Lines).

13. Change the *Detail Level* to **Fine** and type to **SD** to shade the view.

14. Spin the view to examine the flanges from all sides.

15. Save the project file.

16. Close the project and family files. Save any changes you want to keep.

End of practice

Chapter Review Questions

1. An architect has requested that you use an architectural vanity family such as the one shown in Figure 8–40, but it does not work with MEP tools. What must you do to upgrade it so that it includes MEP parameters?

Figure 8–40

a. Add pipes to the family where you want the project pipes to tie in.

b. Add connectors to the family where you want the project pipes to tie in.

c. Import an existing sink designed to work with MEP systems into the family.

d. Use one of your own families even if it does not match the architect's request.

2. Which of the following Light Source Definition distribution options enables you to specify an IES file?

a. (Spherical)

b. (Hemispherical)

c. (Spot)

d. (Photometric Web)

3. If you want to include an annotation element, such as a label that references a parameter in a family, you can only do so by creating a separate annotation tag.

   a. True

   b. False

4. How do you have a family display different elements when you change the *Detail Level* from *Coarse* to **Fine**?

   a. In the project file, select the family and in *Properties* change the detail level.

   b. In the family file, select the elements and modify the *Visibility Settings*.

   c. In the family file, in the *View Properties*, set the detail level.

   d. In the project file, set the *Visibility Settings* for the view.

5. In the *Family Types* dialog box shown in Figure 8–41, if the *Pump Length* changed to **2'-0"**, what would the value of *Radius 2* be?

Figure 8–41

   a. 5'-0"

   b. 4'-0"

   c. 4'-11"

   d. 5'-1"

Creating Structural-Specific Families

Creating structural-specific families in Revit involves modeling components that define and support a building's structural system, using three different workflows: loadable component families, in-place modeling, and system families. Common elements, such as columns, beams, braces, and foundations, are typically created as loadable families for reuse and consistency across projects, while elements for unique or site-specific conditions, like stiffener plates, may be modeled using in-place families.

Learning Objectives

- Create a gusset plate with parametric properties.

- Create an in-place column stiffener family.

- Create a floor-based family with a void that cuts out a depression in a floor when inserted in a project.

- Create a built-up column family made of steel plates.

- Create a tapered concrete column family.

- Create a truss family.

- Create a precast hollow core slab family that uses an imported CAD file for the profile.

- Create a tapered moment frame family that includes two columns with a connecting beam.

Practice 9a
Parametric Gusset Plate

Practice Objectives

- Create reference planes, dimensions, and parameters.
- Create solid geometry for the plates.
- Modify visibility settings and create family types.

In this practice, you will create a family file based on a template and create reference planes. You will then create gussets as a mass, create material parameters, and apply family types. Finally, you will toggle off the visibility of the gusset plate from the coarse detail to all views, as shown in Figure 9–1.

Figure 9–1

Task 1: Start a new family using a template and add reference planes.

1. Create a new family based on the **Structural Stiffener.rft** template found in the practice files *Structural>RFT* folder.
2. Save the family to the practice files *Structural>RFA* folder as **Parametric Gusset Plate.rfa**.
3. Open the *Project Units* dialog box. Change the *Length Format* to **Fractional inches**. This makes the dimensions easier to read.
4. Open the **Elevations: Left** view.
5. Create and dimension the new reference planes, as shown in Figure 9–2.
   - Ensure that the diagonal reference plane being added crosses the intersection of the **Center (Front/Back)** and **Ref. Level** reference planes.

Figure 9–2

6. Label one of the dimensions with a new type parameter named **Width**.

7. Select the other two dimensions and apply the same parameter to them.

8. Flex the parameter to test the stability of the framework.

9. Set the *Width* to **8**".

10. Save the family.

Task 2: Create front view reference planes.

1. Switch to the **Elevations: Front** view and create two reference planes, **1/4"** on either side of the **Center (Left/Right)** reference plane and add dimensions. Label the overall dimension as **Thickness**, as shown in Figure 9–3.

   Note: Modify the scale so that the dimensions are clearly displayed.

Figure 9–3

2. Flex the parameter to test the stability of the framework.

3. Set the *Thickness* to **1/2"**.

4. Save the family.

Task 3: Create family geometry.

1. Switch to **Elevations: Left** view.

2. In the *Create* tab>*Forms* panel, click ▊ (Extrusion). In the *Extrusion* panel, set the *Depth* to **1/2"**.

3. Draw individual lines across the outside intersections of the reference planes, and lock all five lines to the reference planes, as shown in Figure 9–4.

   *Note: Use the **Align** command to help lock the lines to the reference plane.*

Figure 9–4

4. Click ✔ (Finish Edit Mode).

5. Switch to the **Elevations: Front** view. Align the left and right sides of the extrusion with the reference planes you created earlier and lock them.

6. Switch to a 3D view and shade the model.

7. In the *Create* tab>*Properties* panel, click ⊞ (Family Types) to flex the model to ensure that everything is working together. The model displays as shown in Figure 9-5.

Figure 9-5

8. Save the family.

Task 4: Add material parameters.

1. Open the *Family Types* dialog box.

2. At the bottom of the dialog box, click 🗋 (New Parameter).

3. Create an instance parameter named **Material** and set the *Data Type* to **Material**. The group automatically updates to **Materials and Finishes**, as shown in Figure 9-6. Click **OK**.

   *Note: Setting the parameter as an **Instance** makes it easier to modify it in the project file.*

Figure 9-6

4. In the 3D view, select the plate.

5. In *Properties*, in the *Materials and Finishes* area, click ⊡ (Associate Family Parameter) next to *Material*.

6. In the *Associate Family Parameter* dialog box, select **Material**, as shown in Figure 9–7, then click **OK**.

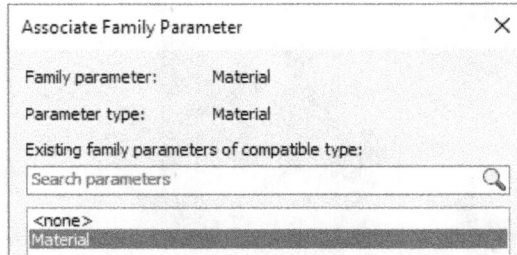

Figure 9–7

7. In *Properties*, the **Material** parameter is now marked with the = sign, as shown in Figure 9–8. Therefore, when the family is loaded into a project, you can control its material using Properties.

Figure 9–8

Task 5: Change the visibility settings in a family.

1. Select the extrusion.

2. In the *Modify | Extrusion* tab>*Mode* panel, click 📷 (Visibility Settings).

3. In the *Family Element Visibility Settings* dialog box, clear the **Coarse** option, as shown in Figure 9–9, so that the gusset plate does not display at a **Coarse** detail level.

Figure 9–9

4. Click **OK**.

5. In the *View Control* panel, select ▨ (Preview Visibility On).

6. Change the *Detail Level* to **Coarse**, **Medium**, and **Fine**. The outline of the Gusset Plate remains in the **Medium** and **Fine** detail levels but disappears in the **Coarse** detail level.

7. Toggle off the preview visibility.

8. Save the family.

Task 6: Create family types.

1. Open the *Family Types* dialog box.

2. Create three family types. Set the *Name* and the *Width* parameter of each as follows:
   - **8"**
   - **10"**
   - **12"**

3. Use the new types to flex the gusset plate family.

4. Save the family.

5. Start a new project using the **Imperial-Structural Template.rte** file from the practice files *Structural>RTE* folder. Open a 3D view and set the *Detail Level* to **Medium**.

6. Insert one of each Plate type into the project.

7. Shade the view using the shortcut **SD**.

8. Select one of the Plates. In *Properties*, apply a material to it. Repeat with the others using different materials.

9. Save and close the family and project files.

End of practice

Practice 9b
In-Place Column Stiffeners

Practice Objective

- Create an in-place family in a detail view.

In this practice, you will create a stiffener plate to strengthen a column's flange, as shown in Figure 9–10.

Figure 9–10

1. In the practice files *Structural* folder, open **Column-Stiffeners.rvt**. The file opens in the **Structural Plans: Level 2** view.

2. In the Project Browser, open **Detail Views: Detail 0**. It displays a column supporting a beam and concrete on metal deck slab, as shown in Figure 9–11.

Figure 9–11

3. The column requires stiffeners to strengthen its flanges. In the *Structure* tab>*Model* panel, expand ⬛ (Component) and click ⬛ (Model In-Place).

4. In the *Family Category and Parameters* dialog box, set the *Filter list* to **Structure** and select **Structural Stiffeners**, as shown in Figure 9–12. Click **OK**.

Figure 9–12

5. Enter a name for the stiffener plate, as shown in Figure 9–13.

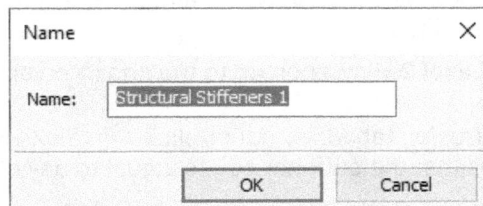

Figure 9–13

6. You are now in the In-Place Editor. In the **Detail 0** view, draw two horizontal reference planes and name them, as shown in Figure 9–14. These reference planes assist in locating the stiffener plates.

7. Align and lock the reference planes to the related beam, as shown in Figure 9–14, so they move with the depth of the beam.

Figure 9–14

8. In the *Create* tab>*Forms* panel, click (Extrusion).

9. In the *Work Plane* dialog box, select **Reference Plane: Top of Beam** in the drop-down list and click **OK**.

10. In the *Go To View* dialog box, select **Structural Plan: Level 2**. Click **Open View**. This view is used to draw the stiffener plate.

11. In the **Structural Plans: Level 2** view, zoom in to the grid intersection **1A**.

12. In the *Modify | Create Extrusion* tab>*Draw* panel, click (Pick Lines). In the Options Bar, select **Lock**. This ensures that the stiffener edges adjust to any changes to the column size.

13. Select and trim the perimeter of the inside face of the column, as shown in Figure 9–15.

    Note: You might need to zoom in very close to display the faint background image.

Figure 9–15

14. Click **Modify**.

15. Select the radius inside corners (arcs) and lock the tangency locks. This maintains the tangency of the arcs to the horizontal and vertical lines when the column size changes, as shown in Figure 9–16.

Figure 9–16

16. Click **Modify**.

17. In *Properties*, set the *Extrusion End* value to (negative) **-1**", as shown in Figure 9–17.

Figure 9–17

18. Click ✔ (Finish Edit Mode).

19. Switch to the **Detail 0** view. Note that the stiffener plate is located under the **Top of Beam** reference planes.

20. Select the stiffener plate and click 🔘 (Copy). In the *Copy* panel, unselect **Constrain**. Select the starting point as the bottom of the stiffener plate and copy it halfway down between the two reference planes.

21. Select the copied stiffener plate and click **Edit In-Place**.

22. Select the stiffener plate. In the *Modify | Extrusion* tab>*Work Plane* panel, click **Edit Work Plane**.

23. In the *Work Plane* dialog box, select **Reference Plane: Bottom of Beam** and click **OK**. The plate moves into a new position.

24. The stiffener plate thickness must be adjusted upward. Select the new stiffener plate and change the *Extrusion End* to **1**". Align and lock the left and right sides to the column.

25. In the *In-Place Editor* panel, click ✔ (Finish Model).

26. Open the **Default 3D View**. Align and lock the front face of both stiffener plates to the front face of the column, as shown in Figure 9–18.

Figure 9–18

27. In the **Level 2** view, select the column and from *Properties*, change it to a different size to verify that the stiffener plates follow.

28. In the **Detail 0** view, select the beam and from *Properties*, change to different sizes to test that the stiffener plate moves with the different sizes.

   • If needed, in the Detail 0 view, select the Structural Stiffener you created and re-align the bottom extrusion to the **Bottom of Beam** reference plane, as shown in Figure 9–19.

Figure 9–19

29. Save and close the project.

End of practice

Practice 9c
In-Place Slab Depression

Practice Objectives

- Create a floor-based family by setting up the parametric framework.
- Create a void form for a depression in the floor.
- Apply the family in a project.

The slab depression family is an important host-based family that you need to modify for your projects. In this practice, you will create a slab depression using a template file and apply it in a project, as shown in Figure 9–20.

Figure 9–20

Task 1: Create a family and add reference planes, insertion points, and dimensions.

1. Create a new family based on the **Generic Model floor based.rft** template found in the practice files *Structural>RFT* folder.

2. Save the family to the practice files *Structural>RFA* folder as **Slab Depression Component.rfa**.

3. In the *Create* tab>*Properties* panel, click ⊞ (Family Categories and Parameters).

4. In the *Family Category and Parameters* dialog box, select **Structural Foundations** and click **OK**.

5. In the *Create* tab>*Datum* panel, click ⊡ (Reference Plane).

6. Add the horizontal and vertical reference planes and dimensions, as shown in Figure 9–21.

Figure 9–21

*Note: Ensure that you set these parameters and the one below to **Instance** parameters. This ensures that they can be set in the project each time they are placed.*

7. Label the horizontal dimension as **Slab Depression Length** and the vertical dimension as **Slab Depression Width**. In both cases, set the parameter to **Instance**. The parameters display as shown in Figure 9–22.

Figure 9–22

8. Flex the parameters to test them.

9. Open the **Elevations: Front** view where you create the depth of the depressed slab.

10. Add another reference plane **3"** down from the reference level. Add a dimension between the reference level and the new reference plane. Label the dimension as **Slab Depression Depth** and set it as an **Instance** parameter, as shown in Figure 9–23.

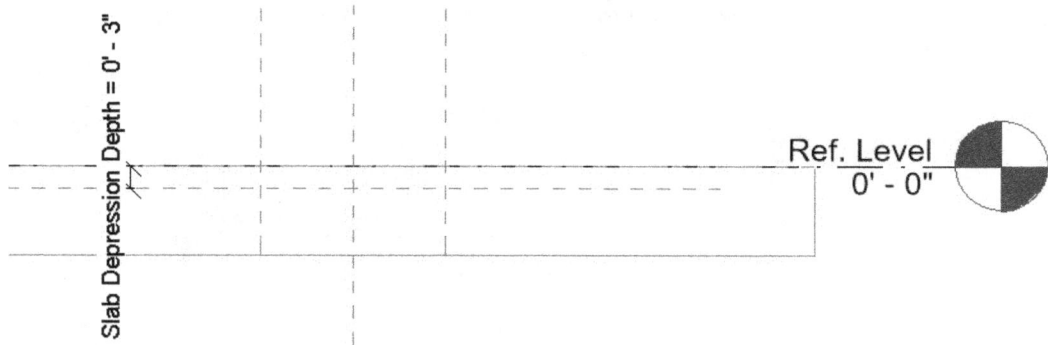

Figure 9–23

11. Flex the parameters to test them.

12. Save the family.

Task 2: Create the depressed area for the slab.

Now you will create the depressed area for the slab by creating a void form and locking it to the reference planes.

1. Switch to the **Floor Plans: Ref. Level** view.

2. In the *Create* tab>*Forms* panel, expand ⬚ (Void Forms) and click ⬚ (Void Extrusion).

3. In the *Draw* panel, click ⬚ (Rectangle).

4. Add the rectangle by clicking at the top left corner of the intersecting reference planes and then the bottom right corner. Click the lock controls to constrain the void form to the reference planes, as shown in Figure 9–24.

Figure 9–24

5. Click ✔ (Finish Edit Mode).

6. Open the **Elevations: Front** view.

7. In the *Modify* tab>*Modify* panel, click ⬚ (Align).

8. Select the lower reference plane first and then pick the bottom of the void form, as shown in Figure 9–25. Select the lock control to constrain the bottom of the void form to the reference plane.

Figure 9–25

9. Still in the **Align** command, select the reference level and pick the top of the void form. Select the lock control to constrain the top of the void form to the reference level.

10. In the *Modify* tab>*Geometry* panel, click ⬭ (Cut Geometry) and pick the void form and the slab object. (The order of the selection does not matter.)

11. Open a 3D view to see the depression in the slab object. Type **SD** to shade the view, as shown in Figure 9–26.

Figure 9–26

12. Use the *Family Types* dialog box to flex the depression.

13. Close the dialog box.

14. Save the Depressed Slab component family file. Do not close the family file.

Task 3: Test the component family file.

1. Start a new project using the **Imperial-Structural Template.rte** file and save the file in the practice files *Structural>RTE* folder as **Depressed Slab Example.rvt**.

2. Open **Structural Plan: Level 1** and click (Close Inactive Views).

3. In the *Structure* tab>*Foundation* panel, click (Structural Foundation: Slab). Create an **8"** **Foundation Slab** in the new project.

4. When the slab has been created in the project file, return to the **Slab Depression Component.rfa** family file.

5. In the *Family Editor* panel, click (Load into Project).

6. If it is not automatically started, start the (Component) command.

7. Pick a location for the slab depression. The insertion is based on the origin in the family file. The default insertion point is at the center of the recessed slab.

8. Select different views to display the depression. Cut some sections through it.

9. To change the size of slab depression, return to the **Floor Plans: Level 2** view, and select the component.

10. In *Properties*, change the values to any size, as shown in Figure 9–27.

Figure 9–27

11. Return to the 3D view and Section view to see the new shape of the depressed slab.

12. Save and close the project and family files.

End of practice

Practice 9d
Built-Up Column

Practice Objectives

- Set up the parametric framework for a column.
- Use extrusions to create the sides of the column.

Revit has an extensive structural columns library to meet many standard types and sizes in the industry. However, there is still a need for built-up (custom) made columns. In this practice, you will create a built-up column from steel plates, as shown in Figure 9–28.

Figure 9–28

- The analytical line is already incorporated into the family in the structural system family template. Therefore, it is not required to be created in the new family.

Task 1: Set up reference planes and dimensions.

1. Create a new family based on the **Structural Column.rft** template found in the practice files *Structural>RFT* folder.

2. Save the family to the practice files *Structural>RFA* folder as **Built-Up Column.rfa**.

3. In the **Structural Plans: Lower Ref. Level** view, add reference planes to the inside of the four exterior reference planes using ⌖ (Pick Lines) with an *Offset* of **2"**, as shown in Figure 9–29.

Figure 9–29

4. Delete the vertical **EQ** dimensions to prevent over-constraining and re-insert new vertical EQ dimensions at the inner reference planes, as shown in Figure 9–30.

Figure 9–30

5. Place single dimensions horizontally and vertically above the EQ dimensions, as shown in Figure 9–31.

Figure 9–31

6. Select the horizontal dimension and label it. Set the *Name* to **Primary Plate Length** and select **Instance**, as shown in Figure 9–32.

   *Note: The **Instance** option enables the value to be modified per element.*

   Figure 9–32

7. Follow the same procedures for the vertical dimension, naming it **Secondary Plate Length**.

8. Add four more dimensions and label them, as shown in Figure 9–33. Set the **Instance** parameters for these new dimensions to determine the thickness of the primary and secondary plates.

   Figure 9–33

9. Flex the sizes to ensure that they are moving together.

10. Save the family.

Task 2: Create the plates.

1. In the *Create* tab>*Forms* panel, click ▢ (Extrusion) to create the plates. Only one plate can be created at a time because each extrusion must be a closed loop.

2. Sketch the rectangle, based on the start and end points shown in Figure 9–34.

   • Lock the lines to the reference planes.

   • Leave the **Extrusion Start** and **Extrusion End** parameters as default. The column height is adjusted later by aligning with other reference planes.

Figure 9–34

3. Click ✔ (Finish Edit Mode).

4. Create another extrusion at the bottom, as shown in Figure 9–35, making sure to lock the extrusion lines. Click **Finish Edit Mode**.

Figure 9–35

5. Create the secondary plate (sketch shown in Figure 9–36) and repeat on the other side. Click **Finish Edit Mode**.

Figure 9–36

6. Flex the sizes to ensure that the extrusions move as expected.

7. Open the **Elevations: Front** view to establish the height of the column.

8. Use 📐 (Align) to align the four plates to the **Upper Ref. Level.** Select the **Upper Ref. Level** and then the top of a plate and lock it in place. Repeat this procedure until all four plates are locked to the **Upper Ref. Level** and **Lower Ref. Level**, as shown in Figure 9–37.

   Note: Ensure that the view is in Wireframe mode to see all of the plates.

Figure 9–37

9. Set the *Visual Style* of the view to **Hidden Line**. Note that the secondary plates behind the primary plates disappear.

10. Use Symbolic Lines to display the secondary plates with hidden lines. In the *Annotate* tab> *Detail* panel, click 🗇 (Symbolic Line).

11. In the *Modify | Place Symbolic Lines* tab>*Subcategory* panel Type Selector, select **Hidden Lines (projection)**.

12. In the Options Bar, verify that the **Chain** option is cleared. Draw a line from the intersection of the **Upper Ref. Level** and the inside reference planes on both sides of the column, as shown in Figure 9–38. Lock these lines to both the **Upper** and **Lower Ref. Levels** and the reference planes.

Figure 9–38

13. Temporarily hide the reference plane category so you can see the new lines, as shown in Figure 9–39.

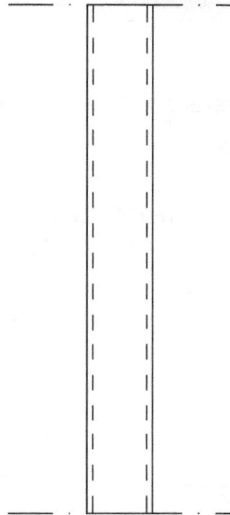

Figure 9–39

14. Flex the sizes and **Upper Ref. Level** height.

15. Reset Temporary Hide/Isolate.

16. Save the family.

17. To test the Built-Up Column, start a new project using the **Imperial-Structural Template.rte** file from the practice files *Structural>RTE* folder and load the **Built-Up Column** family into the new project, as shown in Figure 9–40. Navigate from one view to another to see the new column. Add other columns and change the size and offset from the level.

Figure 9–40

18. Save and close the family and project files.

End of practice

Practice 9e
Tapered Concrete Column

Practice Objectives

- Create reference planes and parameters as the framework of the column family.
- Create geometry using a solid blend.

In this practice, you will create a tapered concrete column using a column family template. You will create its geometry using a solid blend and add a taper parameter that can be modified, as shown in Figure 9-41.

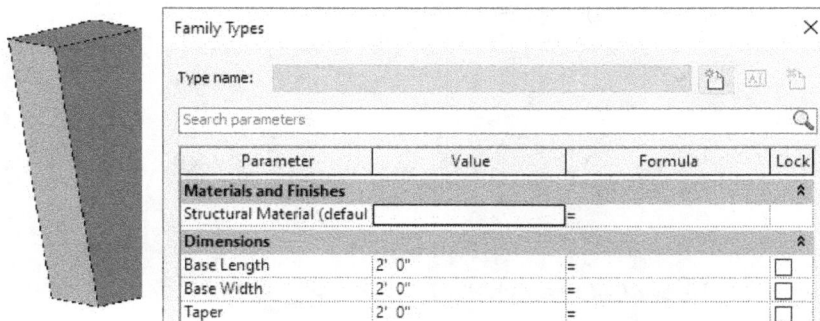

Figure 9-41

Task 1: Create reference planes and parameters.

1. Create a new family based on the **Structural Column.rft** template found in the practice files *Structural>RFT* folder.

2. Save the family to the practice files *Structural>RFA* folder as **Tapered-Concrete-Column.rfa**.

3. Add dimensions and labels for the **Base Width** and **Base Length**, as well as a reference plane named **Taper**. Create them as a **Type** parameters. Dimension and label it, as shown in Figure 9–42.

Figure 9–42

4. Flex the sizes to test the framework.
5. Save the family.

Task 2: Create geometry.

1. In the *Create* tab>*Forms* panel, click ⬙ (Blend).
2. Sketch the base of the blend and lock it, as shown in Figure 9–43.

Figure 9–43

3. Click ⬚ (Edit Top), sketch the top of the blend (the overhanging taper - it is larger than the base) and lock it, as shown in Figure 9–44.

Figure 9–44

4. In the *Mode* panel, click ✔ (Finish Edit Mode).

5. Open the **Elevations: Front** view.

6. Align and lock the blend to the **Upper Ref. Level**, as shown in Figure 9–45.

Figure 9–45

7. Open the **3D Views: View 1** view and shade it. Rotate to display the taper side of the column, as shown in Figure 9–46.

Figure 9–46

8. Use the *Family Types* dialog box to flex the column.

9. Reset the default values and close the *Family Types* dialog box.

10. Save the family.

11. If time permits, you can create family types using various dimensions and test them in a project.

12. Save and close the family files.

End of practice

Practice 9f
Truss Family

Practice Objectives

- Start a truss family and add reference planes and labels.
- Add top chord, bottom chord, and web layout lines.

In this practice, you will create a truss using a truss family template. You will add reference planes, create parameters, and add chords and webs to form the structure of the trusses, as shown in Figure 9–47. You will then test it in a project.

Figure 9–47

Task 1: Add reference planes and labels.

1. Create a new family based on the **Structural Trusses.rft** template found in the practice files *Structural>RFT* folder**.**

2. Save the family to the practice files *Structural>RFA* folder as **Custom Truss.rfa.**

3. Add the reference planes, dimensions, and labels (Instance parameters) shown in Figure 9–48.

Figure 9–48

4. Open the *Family Types* dialog box and scroll down to the *Dimensions* area. Add the formula *Top Chord Length* = **Truss Length / 3** (as shown in Figure 9–49) and click **Apply**.

    Note: If you forgot to set any of the labels as Instance parameters, you can edit it in the Family Types dialog box.

Dimensions			
End Height Left (default)	4' 0"	=	☐
End Height Right (default)	4' 0"	=	☐
Top Chord Length (default)	26' 8"	= Truss Length / 3	☑
Truss Length (default)	80' 0"	=	☑
Truss Height (default)	10' 0"	=	☑

Figure 9–49

5. Click **OK**.

Task 2: Add the top chord, bottom chord, and web layout lines.

1. In the *Create* tab>*Detail* panel, click ⬙ (Top Chord).

2. In the Options Bar, verify that the **Chain** option is cleared so that you can lock each line as it is created.

3. Starting from the left vertical reference plane, draw the top chord, locking each sketch before you draw the next, as shown in Figure 9–50.

Figure 9–50

4. In the *Modify | Top Chord* tab>*Draw* panel, click ⬙ (Bottom Chord).

5. Draw the bottom chord, across the bottom of the truss, as shown in Figure 9–51. Lock the bottom chord sketch line in place.

Figure 9–51

6. In the *Create* tab>*Detail* panel, click (Web). In the Options Bar, verify that the **Chain** option is not selected.

7. Draw vertical web lines, as shown in Figure 9–52. Dimension and set them EQ in three different sets.

Figure 9–52

*   Start at the far left reference plane and work over to the right.
*   Ensure that you dimension to the vertical reference planes where available or the truss will not flex correctly.
*   DO NOT mirror the Web lines as this might cause undesirable results or errors in the truss family.

8. Add diagonal web members to the left of the truss, from the top chord to the bottom chord. Start from the far left side working toward the center of the truss. Repeat the process from the other direction. The final outcome is shown in Figure 9–53.

Figure 9–53

- Snap to the intersections of elements. Type **SI** to force the snap points.
- DO NOT mirror the web lines, as this might cause errors when the truss is loaded into a project.

9. Flex the geometry.

10. Reset the values to the dimensions shown in Figure 9–53.

11. Save the family.

12. Load the truss into a project and test it.

- Note that the default framing sizes might be too large. In the truss family (or in the truss type in the project), set appropriate framing members for the chords and webs.

13. Save and close the project and family files.

End of practice

Practice 9g
Precast Hollow Core Slab

Practice Objectives

- Create a family using the Structural Framing - Beams and Braces template.
- Use a CAD file to modify the sketch of an extrusion.
- Assign a material to the extrusion.
- Set visibility settings for Medium and Fine detail levels along with simple geometry for the Coarse detail level.

In this practice, you will use the **Structural Framing - Beams and Braces.rft** file as the base of the hollow core slab. You will modify an existing extrusion and import a CAD drawing to assist in setting up the new profile. You will assign a material to the extrusion and establish the visibility settings for **Medium** and **Fine** detail levels. You will then draw a second extrusion with a simple rectangular profile, assign the material and set the visibility settings so that it only displays at a **Coarse** detail level as shown in Figure 9–54.

Detail Level: Coarse   *Detail Level: Medium and Fine*

Figure 9–54

Task 1: Import a CAD file into a family template to create the hollow core geometry.

1. Create a new family based on the **Structural Framing - Beams and Braces.rft** template found in the practice files *Structural>RFT* folder.

2. Save the family to the practice files *Structural>RFA* folder as **Precast-Hollow-Core-Slab.rfa**.

3. Close any other projects or family files that you might have open.

4. Open and tile the following views:
   - **Floor Plans: Ref Level**
   - **Elevations: Front**
   - **Elevations: Left**
   - **3D Views: View 1**
5. In the **Elevations: Left** view, zoom in on the geometry.
6. Select the extrusion. In the *Modify | Extrusion* tab>*Mode* panel, click (Edit Extrusion).
7. Select the outline geometry (as shown in Figure 9–55) and the reference planes that are part of the extrusion and delete them from the view.

Figure 9–55

Note: In this example, a CAD drawing is used to create the geometry of the hollow core slab.

8. In the *Insert* tab>*Import* panel, click (Import CAD).
9. In the *Import CAD Formats* dialog box, navigate to the practice files *Structural>CAD* folder. Select **Precast-Hollow-Core-Slab.dwg** and then set the following options, as shown in Figure 9–56:
   - Select **Current View Only**
   - *Colors:* **Black and White**
   - *Layers:* **All**
   - *Import units:* **Auto-Detect**
   - *Positioning:* **Auto - Center to Center**

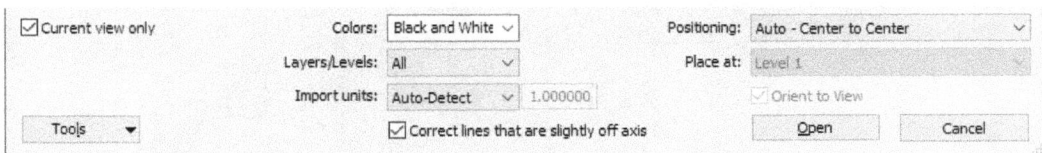

Figure 9–56

10. Click **Open**.

11. A message box opens prompting you about exploding import instances. Click **Yes** to continue. The family now includes the sketch lines from the AutoCAD drawing, as shown in Figure 9–57.

Figure 9–57

12. To select the material for the hollow core slab, in *Properties*, in the *Materials and Finishes* area, select **<By Category>**, and then click ⸛ (Browse).

13. In the *Material Browser*, select **Concrete-Precast Concrete,** as shown in Figure 9–58.

Figure 9–58

14. Click **OK** to close the dialog boxes. The material is assigned.

15. Click ✔ (Finish Edit Mode).

16. Click in empty space to release the selection.

17. In the 3D view, zoom out to display the slab. Set the *Visual Style* to ▦ (Shaded) to display the new slab with the concrete material applied, as shown in Figure 9–59.

Figure 9–59

18. Save the file.

Task 2: Establish visibility settings.

1. Select the new extrusion.

2. In the *Modify | Extrusion* tab>*Mode* panel, click 🗗 (Visibility Settings).

3. In the *Family Element Visibility Settings* dialog box, in the *Detail Levels* area, verify that **Coarse** is cleared, as shown in Figure 9–60.

Figure 9–60

4. Click **OK**.

5. In the View Control Bar, click 🖿 (Preview Visibility On).

6. Test the *Detail Levels*. In the **Coarse** detail level, the extrusion should not display.

7. Activate the **Floor Plans: Ref. Level** view. Align and lock the extrusion to the **Member Left** and **Member Right** reference planes.

8. Activate the **Elevations: Left** view.

9. In the *Create* tab>*Forms* panel, click 🗗 (Extrusion). In the *Work Plane* dialog box, select **Pick a plane** and click **OK**. Select the face of the existing extrusion.

10. Draw a rectangle around the perimeter of the hollow core slab and lock it in place.

   * Start the rectangle at the lower left corner.

   * To select the appropriate upper right corner, press <Tab> once to force the horizontal temporary dimension, as shown in Figure 9–61.

Figure 9–61

11. In *Properties*, set the *Extrusion End* to (negative) **-8'-0"** and the *Material* to **Concrete - Precast Concrete**.

12. Click ✔ (Finish Edit Mode).

13. Activate the **Floor Plans: Ref. Level** view.

14. Align and lock the new extrusion to the **Member Left** reference plane, as shown in Figure 9–62.

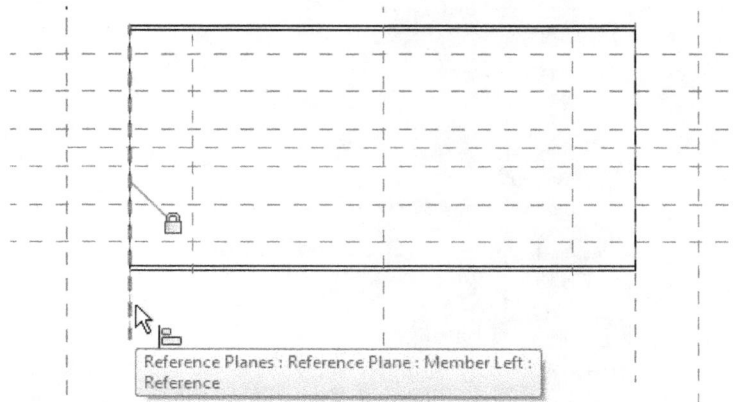

Figure 9–62

15. Align the other end to the **Member Right** reference plane.

16. Select the new simple rectangular extrusion.

17. In the *Modify | Extrusion* tab>*Mode* panel, click 🔲 (Visibility Settings).

18. In the *Family Element Visibility Settings* dialog box, in the *Detail Levels* area, clear **Medium** and **Fine**, as shown in Figure 9–63.

Figure 9–63

19. Click **OK**.

20. Release the selection and preview the different *Detail Levels*.

21. Save the file.

Task 3: Add hidden lines.

1. Activate the **Floor Plans: Ref. Level** view.

2. In the View Control Bar, set the *Visual Style* to 🔲 (Wireframe).

3. In the *Annotate* tab>*Detail* panel, click ▦ (Symbolic Line).

4. In the *Modify | Place Symbolic Lines* tab>*Subcategory* panel, set *Subcategory* to **Hidden Lines [projection]**.

5. In the *Modify | Place Symbolic Lines* tab>*Draw* panel, click ╱ (Line). In the Options Bar, clear the **Chain** option. Lock the lines as you draw them.

6. Draw hidden lines horizontally along the edges, as shown in Figure 9–64. You cannot see them as you draw because they are in the same location as the elements displayed through the wireframe view.

Figure 9–64

7. In the View Control Bar, set the *Visual Style* to ▱ (Hidden Line). The hidden lines should be displayed.

8. Select the 12 hidden lines that you just created.

9. In the *Modify | Lines* tab>*Visibility* panel, click ▱ (Visibility Settings).

10. Set the visibility of only the lines to the **Medium** and **Fine** detail levels.

11. Save the family.

12. Start a new project using the **Imperial-Structural Template.rte** file from the practice files *Structural>RTE* folder and load the family into the project.

13. Using ▱ (Beam), draw a beam using the new **Precast-Hollow-Core-Slab** family.

14. Test the visibility settings in the plan and elevation views.

15. Close but do not save the project.

16. Save and close the family.

End of practice

Practice 9h
Tapered Moment Frame

Practice Objectives

- Set up reference planes, reference lines, and parameters as the framework of the family.
- Create geometry for the columns and beams of the family.

In this practice, you will use the family template file **Structural Column.rft** as the basis of the tapered moment frame. You will create reference planes, reference lines, and parameters and then create the geometry for the columns and tapered beam using both solid sweeps and extrusions, as shown in Figure 9–65.

Figure 9–65

Task 1: Set up the reference planes and parameters.

1. Create a new family based on the **Structural Column.rft** template found in the practice files *Structural>RFT* folder.
2. Save the family to the practice files *Structural>RFA* folder as **Tapered-Moment-Frame.rfa**.

3. Add dimensions and labels for **Overall Length** and **Column Width** to the existing reference planes, as shown in Figure 9–66. Create them as **Type** parameters.

Figure 9–66

4. Open the *Family Types* dialog box

5. In the *Family Types* dialog box, change the values of *Column Width* to **1'-0"** and *Overall Length* to **26'-0"**, as shown in Figure 9–67. Click **OK**.

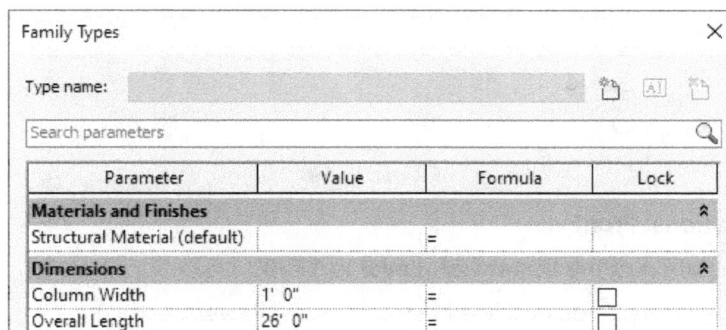

Figure 9–67

6. Zoom out and extend the horizontal reference planes beyond the new vertical reference planes, as shown in Figure 9–68.

   - Unpin the **Front/Back** reference plane to lengthen it. Click on the **Pin** icon to pin the reference plane back in place so that it will not move when you add dimensions and labels.

Figure 9–68

7. Add two new horizontal reference planes with associated dimensions and label (type parameter) to represent the **Beam Width**, as shown in Figure 9–69.

   - **Hint:** Use **Pick Lines** with an *Offset* of **2"** and place them inside the existing outer reference planes.

Figure 9–69

8. Open the **Elevations: Front** view.

9. Change the *elevation* of the **Upper Ref. Level** to **13'-0"**.

10. Extend the reference planes and levels so that they all overlap.

11. Add a reference plane on top of the **Upper Ref. Level**, as shown in Figure 9–70, and lock it into the level.

12. Add reference planes and labels (type parameters), as shown in Figure 9–70.

Figure 9–70

13. Add **Column Base** and **Column Top** reference planes and labels on the other end of the frame. (Do not use Mirror.)

14. Temporarily hide the **Upper Ref. Level,** but not the associated reference plane.

15. Draw two reference lines from the intersection of the top and outside reference planes to the center vertical reference plane, as shown in Figure 9–71. Lock the end of the reference lines to the related reference planes.

Figure 9–71

16. Reset **Temporary Hide/Isolate**.

17. Flex the framework. End with the **Upper Ref. Level** height of **13'-0"** and **Beam Middle** height of **12'-0"**.

18. Save the family file.

Task 2: Create the geometry for the tapered columns.

1. In the *Create* tab>*Forms* panel, click 🦋 (Sweep).

2. In the *Create* tab>*Work Plane* panel, click ▦ (Set).

3. In the *Work Plane* dialog box, select **Reference Plane: Center (Front/Back)**, as shown in Figure 9–72. Click **OK**.

Figure 9–72

4. In the *Modify | Sweep* tab>*Sweep* panel, click 🖉 (Sketch Path).

5. In the *Draw* panel, ╱ (Line) is selected by default. In the Options Bar, verify that the **Chain** option is selected.

6. Sketch the path for the column of the moment frame. Align the two vertical sketch lines to their parallel reference planes.

7. Align and lock the angular sketch line to the reference line, as shown in Figure 9–73.

   Note: Draw the left vertical sketch first. The profile is drawn in this plane.

Figure 9–73

8. In the *Mode* panel, click ✔ (Finish Edit Mode).

9. In the *Modify | Sweep* tab>*Sweep* panel, click ⬚ (Edit Profile).

10. When the *Go To View* dialog box opens, select **Floor Plan: Lower Ref. Level**. Click **Open View**.

11. If you have not already done so, zoom out to see the full framework and expand the Reference lines to the ends.

12. Zoom in on the profile target and draw a rectangle **3/4" x 1'-0"**. Lock it to the reference planes, as shown in Figure 9–74.

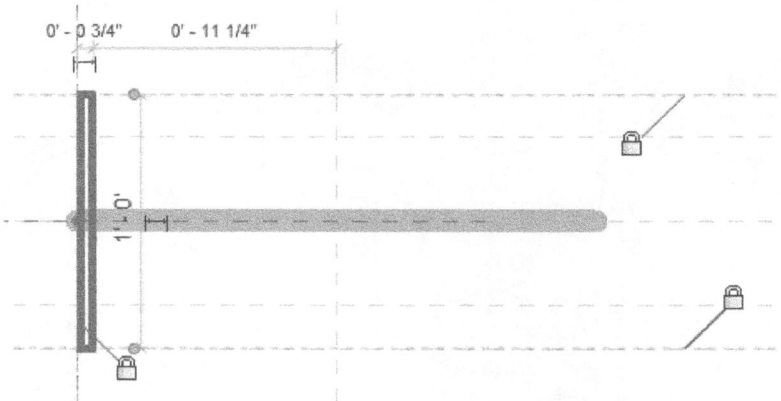

0' - 0 3/4"   0' - 11 1/4"

1' - 0"

Figure 9–74

13. Click ✔ (Finish Edit Mode) twice to finish the profile and the sweep.

14. Open the **3D Views: View 1** view. Rotate and shade it to display the column up to this point, as shown in Figure 9–75.

Figure 9–75

15. Return to the **Elevations: Front** view.

16. Click ▨ (Extrusion) and set the *Work Plane* to **Reference Plane: Center (Front/Back)**.

17. In the *Modify | Create Extrusion* tab>*Draw* panel, click ⚓ (Pick Lines). In the Options Bar, select **Lock**.

18. Zoom into the sweep that was created earlier and select all of the interior lines, as shown in Figure 9–76.

    Note: The lines are automatically locked to the selected lines because you selected the ***Lock*** *option.*

Figure 9–76

19. In *Properties*, set the values of the *Extrusion End* to **3/8"** and *Extrusion Start* to (negative) **-3/8"**, as shown in Figure 9–77.

Figure 9–77

20. Click ✔ (Finish Edit Mode).

21. Display the column profile in a shaded 3D View and return to the **Elevations: Front** view. (**Hint:** Press <Ctrl>+<Tab>.)

22. Mirror the new tapered column (both extrusion and sweep) along the center vertical reference plane, as shown in Figure 9–78. Edit the sketch and align and lock it to the front and back reference planes.

Figure 9–78

23. Edit the path sketch of the mirrored sweep and align and lock the sketch to the reference lines.

24. Flex the framework to ensure that everything is working as expected.

25. Save the family file.

Task 3: Create the geometry for the tapered beam.

1. Open the **Elevations: front** view, if not already in it.

2. Start the **Sweep** command and add a path, as shown in Figure 9–79. Use **Pick Lines** with the **Lock** option on and select the angled reference lines.

Figure 9–79

3. Click ✔ (Finish Edit Mode).

4. In the *Modify | Sweep* tab>*Sweep* panel, click 🖼 (Load Profile).

5. In the *Load Family* dialog box, navigate to the practice files *Structural>RFA* folder. Select **Tapered-Frame-Profile.rfa** and click **Open**.

6. In the *Profile:* drop-down list, select **Tapered-Frame-Profile**, as shown in Figure 9–80.

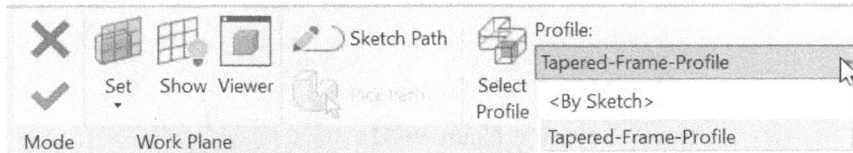

Figure 9–80

7. Click ✔ (Finish Edit Mode).

8. Display the top plate of the beam profile in a 3D view, as shown in Figure 9–81.

Figure 9–81

9. Return to the **Elevations: Front** view and create another sweep for the beam's bottom flange using the sketch for the path shown in Figure 9–82 and the same profile family. Lock the path ends to the reference planes.

    Note: You can temporarily hide existing solid elements so that you can attach the sketch to the reference planes.

Figure 9–82

10. The final 3D view should display as shown in Figure 9–83.

Figure 9–83

11. Return to the **Elevations: Front** view and add an extrusion using the interior of the previously created sweeps, as shown in Figure 9–84. Set the *Extrusion End* to **3/8"** and *Extrusion Start* to (negative) **-3/8"**. Use **Pick Lines** and in the Options Bar, select **Lock**. Select all of the interior lines of the sweep. Trim the sketch as needed. Click **Finish Edit Mode**.

Figure 9–84

12. Open the 3D view and move it to one side. Open the *Family Types* dialog box and flex the geometry of the **Tapered Moment Frame** parameters, as shown in Figure 9–85.

Figure 9–85

13. Save the family file.

14. Create a new structural project, load the family, and test it.

15. Save and close the project and family files.

End of practice

Chapter Review Questions

1. How do you change a standard dimension to a parameter-based dimension, as shown in Figure 9–86?

Figure 9–86

   a. In the Type Selector, select a parameter-based type.

   b. In *Properties*, change the *Value*.

   c. From the ribbon, create a label by clicking on **Create Parameter**.

   d. In the *Family Types* dialog box, in the *Parameters* area, click **Add**.

2. Why would you create an in-place family rather than a component family?

   a. An in-place family can be used several times in the current project only.

   b. An in-place family is used once in the current project for a specific location and size.

   c. A component family cannot be modified to fit the specific location.

   d. A component family cannot be joined to other elements in the project.

3. Which of the following Generic Model family templates would you use to create a slab depression?

   a. Generic Model wall based.rft

   b. Generic Model face based.rft

   c. Generic Model line based.rft

   d. Generic Model floor based.rft

4. In a truss family, is the highlighted element shown in Figure 9–87 a chord or a web?

Figure 9–87

a. Chord

b. Web

5. When assigning material to a solid form you can select the **Associate Family Parameter** option. The option to select the material is grayed out, as shown in Figure 9–88. Where do you assign the material?

Figure 9–88

a. In the *Family Types* dialog box, select the associated parameter and select the material.

b. In the *Manage* tab>*Settings* panel, click 🌑 (Materials) and select the material.

c. In the *Modify* tab>*Geometry* panel, click 🔲 (Paint).

d. In the *Family Category and Parameters* dialog box, specify the material in the *Family Parameters* area.

Appendix

A

Additional Management Tools

There are many tools available in Revit® that you can use when creating and using templates and projects. This appendix provides details about several additional tools and commands that are related to those covered in this guide.

Learning Objectives

- Set up units, snaps, temporary dimensions, and arrowheads.
- Create object styles for components that include line weight, color, pattern, and material.
- Create patterns used in the **Filled Region** command and for cut and surface patterns in materials.
- Create materials and material libraries that can be used in multiple projects.
- Review mechanical settings (for ducts and pipes).
- Review electrical settings (for wiring, cable trays, and conduits).
- Review structural specific settings.
- Create view list, sheet list, and note block schedules.
- Modify the keyboard shortcuts and double-click function of the mouse.
- Create new Project Browser organization layouts for views, sheets, schedules, and panel schedules.

A.1 General Settings

A variety of settings are available to help you customize the projects you create and keep everything consistent with your office's standards. Other settings can make the process of working in Autodesk Revit more productive.

Specifying Units

You will select Imperial or Metric units when you create the project template if starting with the Revit None Template; otherwise, new project templates will take on the base project template that was selected. You can also set up the Project Units with specific formats and options. For example, if you are working on a Civil project where everything is set up in feet, you specify **Decimal Feet** as the Length Format. For an international metric project, you can specify the length units as Meters, Centimeters, or Millimeters.

How To: Set Up Project Units

1. In the *Manage* tab>*Settings* panel, click ▣ (Project Units) or type **UN**.

2. In the *Project Units* dialog box, in the *Format* column, click the button next to the unit type that you want to modify, as shown on the left in Figure A–1. The related *Format* dialog box opens, as shown on the right in Figure A–1.

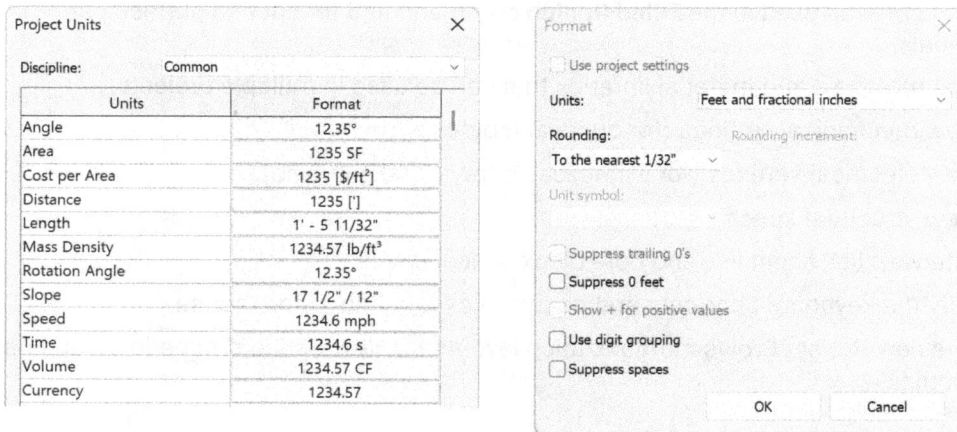

Figure A–1

3. Set the *Units*, *Rounding*, and other options as required.

4. In the *Project Units* dialog box, you can also select the *Discipline* (**Common** by default) and change the Unit format for each discipline. The other options are **Structural**, **HVAC**, **Electrical**, **Piping**, **Energy**, and **Infrastructure**. The options vary according to the discipline-specific software in use.

5. Click **OK** to close each dialog box.

Format Options

Each unit has specific formatting options. The option is grayed out if it is not applicable to that unit type.

Units	Select the type of units in the *Units* drop-down list. The list will differ depending on which format you are editing.

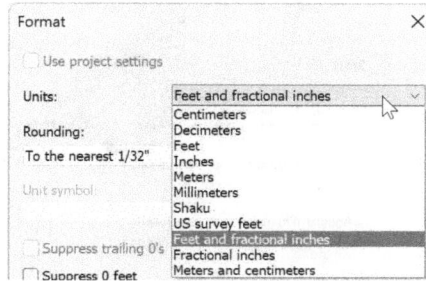

Rounding	Specify how precisely you want the dimensions to be rounded. The options depend on the *Units* you selected.
Unit Symbol	Specify which unit symbol you want to display for the selected units, such as **$** for currency or **None**.
Suppress trailing 0's	(For decimal-based units) If selected, this option removes any trailing 0s. For example, it displays 1.5 instead of 1.50 if you are using two decimal places.
Suppress 0 feet	(Imperial Units only) If selected, this option removes the 0 in front of a dimension in inches only. For example, the dimension displays as 4", rather than 0'-4".
Use digit grouping	If selected, the unit uses the Decimal symbol/digit grouping specified in the *Project Units* dialog box.

Suppress spaces	(Imperial Units only) If selected, this option removes the spaces between the feet and inches, so that a dimension reads 1'-2", rather than 1' - 2".

- The **Use project settings** and **Show + for positive values** options are grayed out when setting units for the project or template. This dialog box is used when creating dimension styles or specifying label formats when the options are available.

Snap Settings

The *Snaps* dialog box (shown in Figure A–2) enables you to set which snap points are active and set the dimension increments displayed for temporary dimensions (both linear and angular). In the *Manage* tab> *Settings* panel, click ᗰᗰ (Snaps) to open the dialog box.

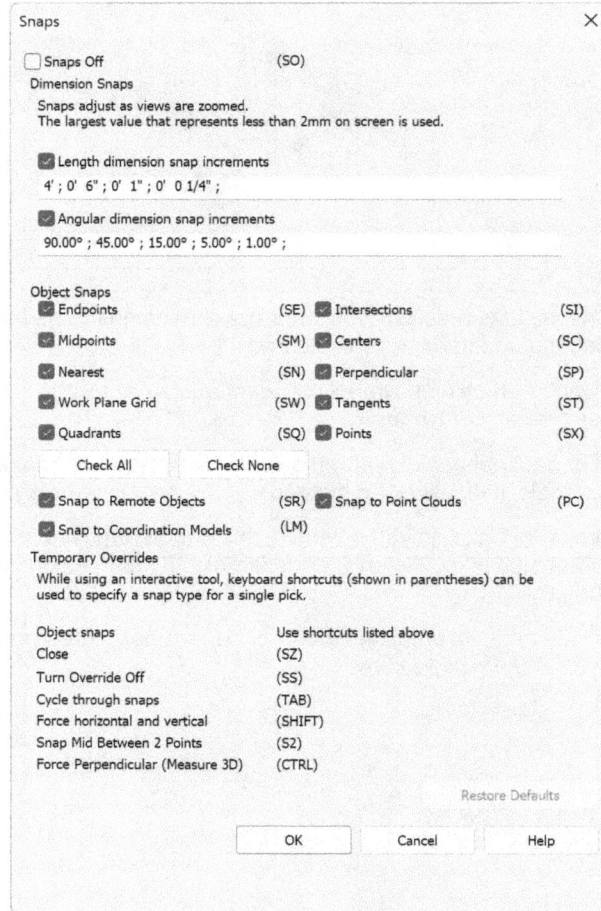

Figure A–2

Note: Keyboard shortcuts, such as the ones listed here, are part of the User Interface and apply to all projects.

- Snap overrides are listed as keyboard shortcuts in parentheses, next to the corresponding snap. When a snap override is used, the cursor finds that specified snap type in your view until something is selected.

- Snap overrides can be used while inside a command by right-clicking and selecting **Snap Overrides** and then selecting the one that you want to use from the list.

Temporary Dimension Settings

Temporary dimensions display when you draw or edit elements in a view. By default, they measure from the center lines of walls to the center lines of openings, as shown in Figure A-3.

Figure A-3

- When you move a witness line to another element or part of an element, the location is remembered in the current session of program.

You can control where temporary dimensions are placed by default. In the *Manage* tab>*Settings* panel, expand ✎ (Additional Settings) and click ⊢⊙ (Temporary Dimensions) to open the *Temporary Dimension Properties* dialog box, as shown in Figure A-4.

Figure A-4

- You can set up these properties in the project template file or modify them at any time. They do not affect existing elements in your project.

- Individual users can control the size of the temporary dimension text in the *Graphics* area of the *Options* dialog box.

Setting Up Arrowheads

A variety of arrowhead types are supplied with Revit, including open and filled arrow styles, tick marks, and dots. You can also create custom styles by duplicating an existing style and defining the parameters, such as the *Arrow Style* shown in Figure A–5. In the *Manage* tab>

Settings panel, expand 🔧 (Additional Settings) and click ⇄ (Arrowheads) to open the dialog box.

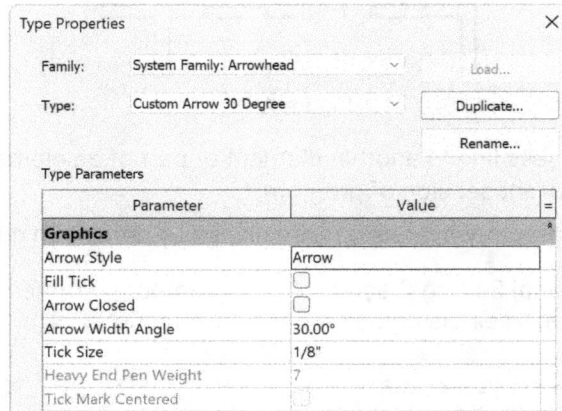

Figure A–5

- Arrowheads are used by text (with a leader), tags, and dimensions.

- The templates include loop leaders, typically used in MEP projects, that can be set as *Tick Mark* for dimensions and *Leader Arrowhead* for text, as shown in Figure A–6. You can also create an Arrow Style using Loop in the Arrowhead settings.

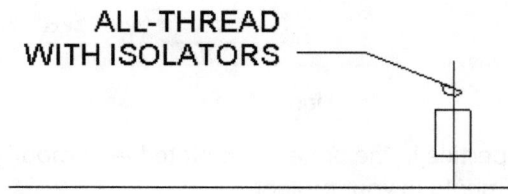

Figure A–6

A.2 Creating Object Styles

Every element in Revit contains object styles that control how its components display in various views. For example, the *Doors* element includes the *<Hidden Lines>*, *Elevation Swing*, *Frame/Mullion*, *Glass*, *Opening*, *Panel*, and *Plan Swing* as components, as shown in Figure A–7. The *Elevation Swing* is set to a light line weight, displayed in black with a dashed line pattern. It does not have any material attached to it, but the *Glass* component does.

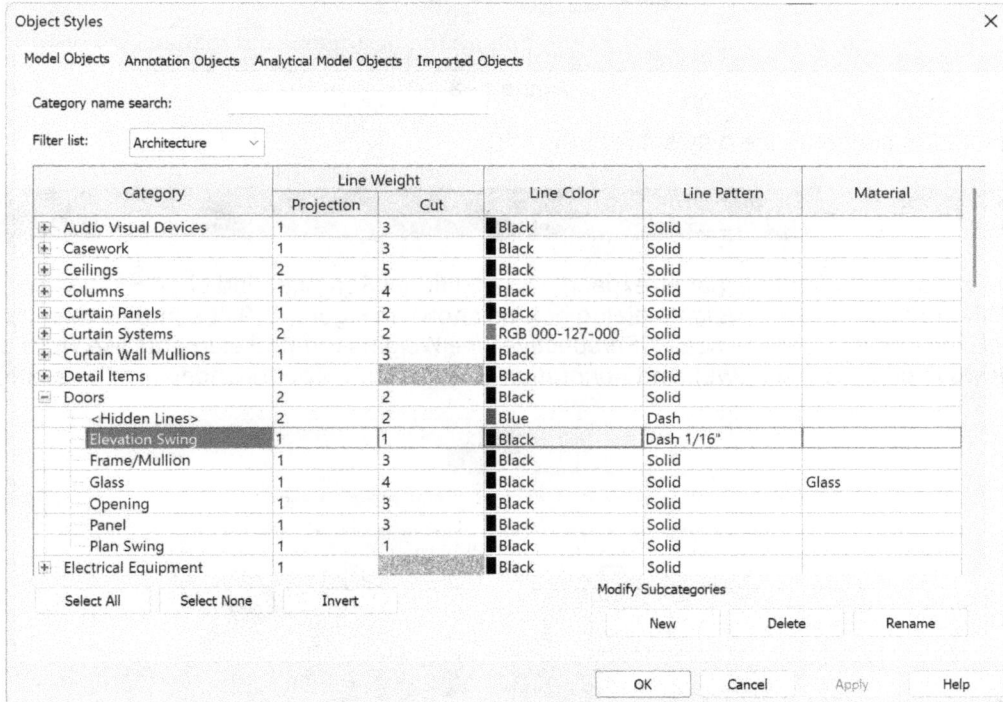

Figure A–7

- In the *Manage* tab>*Settings* panel, click ⬚ (Object Styles) to open the *Object Styles* dialog box.

- To modify an object style, select the category or subcategory to change and then select an option in the appropriate column in the drop-down list or dialog box.

- Most categories enable you to create subcategories. For example, you can create subcategories for reference planes that can be toggled off while leaving other reference planes visible in a view.

Line Weights

Line weights for model elements can be set for a **Projection** (in elevations) or **Cut** (in section and plan). For example, a wall displays a heavy line weight while the door and window cuts are lighter, as shown in Figure A–8.

Figure A–8

- Annotation elements are only set for projection.

Hint: Setting Line Weights

In the *Manage* tab>*Settings* panel, expand (Additional Settings) and click (Line Weights) to open the *Line Weights* dialog box, as shown in Figure A–9. It contains three tabs: *Model Line Weights* (vary by scale), *Perspective Line Weights* (control elements like walls and windows in perspective views), and *Annotation Line Weights* (not dependent on the scale).

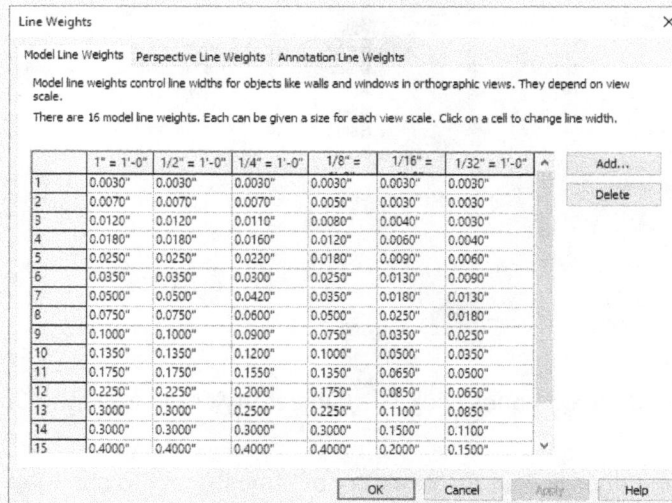

Figure A–9

You can customize the line weights in each tab and add scales as required for the model line weights.

Line Color

When you select **Line Color** in the *Object Styles* dialog box or elsewhere, the *Color* dialog box opens, as shown in Figure A–10. You can select a color from the *Basic colors* table or enter values in the *Hue, Sat, Lum, Red, Green,* and/or *Blue* fields and adjust the slider on the right side to alter the amount of black or white used to create a needed color. If you specify **No Color**, the item will assume the color of the parent category or use the color black. For example, if you set the *Line Color* for *Panel* under the *Door* category to **No Color**, it will assume the door's line color.

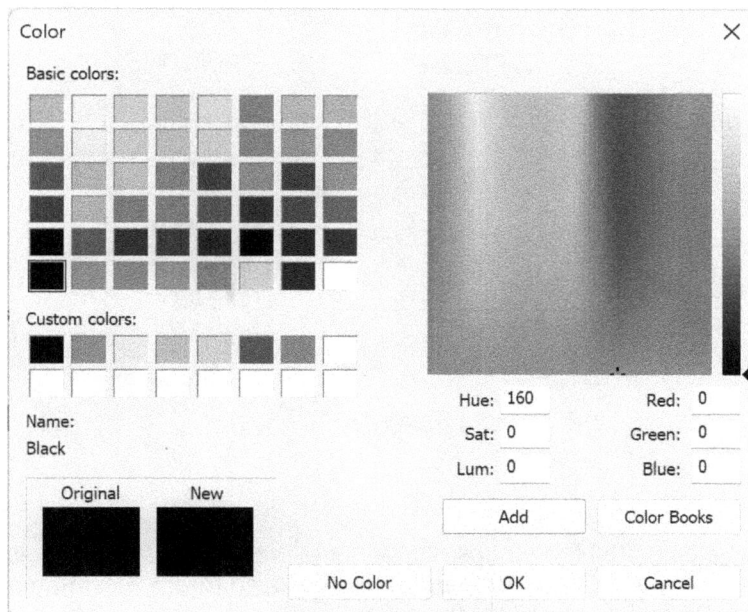

Figure A–10

Click **Color Books** to select from thousands of colors, including options from the Pantone color system, as shown in Figure A–11. Typically, most elements in Revit are black for printing purposes. When you shade and render, the elements take on the color of the assigned material. Therefore, these dialog boxes are opened when you create materials.

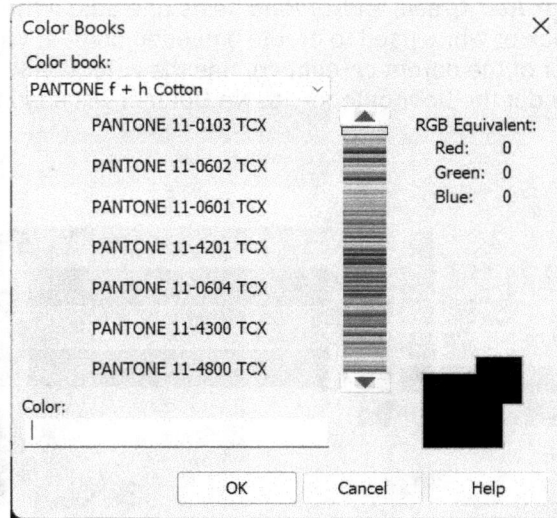

Figure A–11

Line Patterns

Line patterns can be specified for various components in the *Object Styles* dialog box. In the example shown in Figure A–12, the line pattern **Dash** is used for the elevation door swing and the line pattern **Dash dot** is used for the callout bubble.

Figure A–12

How To: Create Line Patterns

A wide variety of patterns are supplied with Revit and you can create your own with a series of dashes, spaces, and dots.

1. In the *Manage* tab>*Settings* panel, expand ✐ (Additional Settings) and click ☰ (Line Patterns) to open the *Line Patterns* dialog box.

2. In the *Line Patterns* dialog box, click **New**.

3. In the *Name* dialog box, type a name for the pattern and click **OK**.

4. In the *Line Pattern Properties* dialog box, add a list of dashes, spaces, and/or dots and specify their values, as shown in Figure A–13. *Space* is always the option after a dash or dot. You do not have to enter a value for dots.

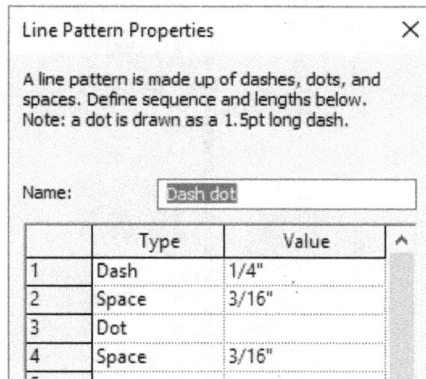

Figure A–13

Line Styles

Line styles are a specific type of object style used with the sketching tools. They are not part of the *Object Styles* dialog box, but are created in a similar way.

In the *Manage* tab>*Settings* panel, expand (Additional Settings) and click (Line Styles). In the *Line Styles* dialog box (shown in Figure A–14), specify the *Line Weight*, *Line Color*, and *Line Pattern* for each line style.

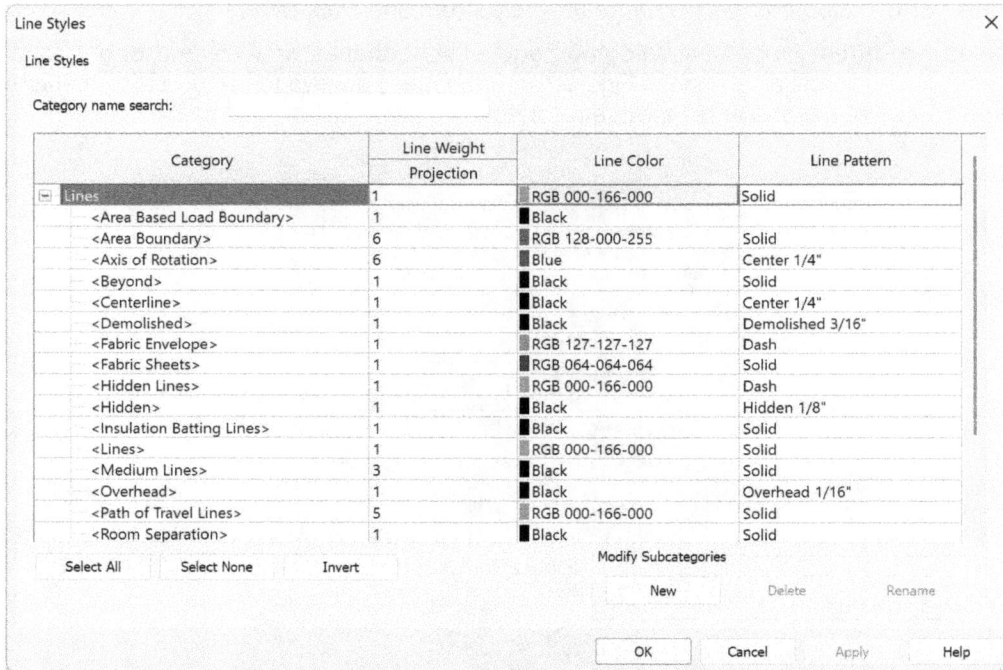

Category	Line Weight Projection	Line Color	Line Pattern
Lines	1	RGB 000-166-000	Solid
<Area Based Load Boundary>	1	Black	
<Area Boundary>	6	RGB 128-000-255	Solid
<Axis of Rotation>	6	Blue	Center 1/4"
<Beyond>	1	Black	Solid
<Centerline>	1	Black	Center 1/4"
<Demolished>	1	Black	Demolished 3/16"
<Fabric Envelope>	1	RGB 127-127-127	Dash
<Fabric Sheets>	1	RGB 064-064-064	Solid
<Hidden Lines>	1	RGB 000-166-000	Dash
<Hidden>	1	Black	Hidden 1/8"
<Insulation Batting Lines>	1	Black	Solid
<Lines>	1	RGB 000-166-000	Solid
<Medium Lines>	3	Black	Solid
<Overhead>	1	Black	Overhead 1/16"
<Path of Travel Lines>	5	RGB 000-166-000	Solid
<Room Separation>	1	Black	Solid

Figure A–14

A.3 Creating Fill Patterns

Fill patterns are used by the various **Filled Region** commands and material specifications. In the *Manage* tab>*Settings* panel, expand 🔧 (Additional Settings) and click ▦ (Fill Patterns). Select from two types: **Drafting** and **Model**.

- Fill patterns can also be created while you are working in the *Visibility/Graphic Overrides* dialog box. When you select a Fill Pattern override, the dialog box displays ⌐…⌐ (Browse), which opens the *Fill Patterns* dialog box.

Drafting patterns are symbolic. The view scale controls the size of the pattern, as shown on the left in Figure A–15. These are used in details and in plan or section cuts.

Model patterns are full scale to the actual elements they represent. They do not change if the view scale changes, as shown on the right in Figure A–15. These patterns are primarily used in elevation and plan views.

Using the buttons at the bottom of the *Fill Patterns* dialog box, you can, edit, create, delete, and duplicate fill patterns, as well as export fill patterns to a .PAT file.

Figure A–15

- In the *Type Properties* dialog box for filled regions, you can set the background to **Opaque** or **Transparent.**

How To: Create New Fill Patterns

1. In the *Manage* tab>*Settings* panel, expand 🔧 (Additional Settings) and click ▨ (Fill Patterns).

2. In the *Fill Patterns* dialog box, select the type of pattern you want to create: **Drafting** or **Model**.

3. Click 📋 (New Fill Pattern).

4. In the *New Pattern* dialog box, type a name for the pattern.

    Note: The PAT file can be created specifically for Revit, or it can be based on an AutoCAD® PAT file.

5. For a simple pattern (as shown in Figure A–16), specify the *Type* as **Basic** and select **Parallel lines** or **Crosshatch** and type values for the *Line angle* and *Line spacing*.

Figure A–16

6. For a complex pattern (as shown in Figure A–17), specify the *Type* as **Custom**. Then, click **Import...** and select a PAT file and a pattern. Set the *Import Scale* as required.

7. For drafting patterns, specify the *Orientation in Host Layers* as **Orient to View, Keep readable,** or **Align with element**.

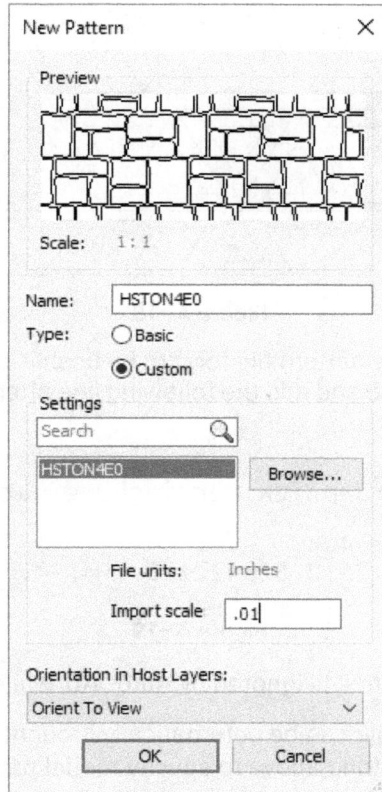

Figure A–17

8. Click **OK** to finish. The pattern can now be used to create a filled region type or used in a material.

Importing Patterns from AutoCAD

Pattern files (PAT) can be imported from the AutoCAD software, such as the Escher pattern shown in Figure A–18.

Figure A–18

One change must be made in the pattern file for it to be usable as a model type of pattern in Autodesk Revit. Open the PAT file and add the following line after the title of a custom hatch, as shown in Figure A–19.

```
*AR-HBONE, Standard brick herringbone pattern @ 45 degrees
;%TYPE=MODEL
45,         0,0,          4,4,                    12,-4
135,        2.828427125,2.828427125,  4,-4,       12,-4
```

Figure A–19

- A line with a semicolon in front it is ignored by AutoCAD, while the type is specified for Revit.

- Any pattern in the **Acad.pat** file can be automatically brought in as a drafting pattern. However, you must add the string above to specify model patterns.

A.4 Creating Materials

When you shade or render Revit models, their appearance depends on the materials that have been associated with the elements, as shown in a shaded view in Figure A–20. Materials also include information that can be used in material takeoff schedules and in energy and structural analysis. You can use materials supplied with Revit or create custom materials.

Figure A–20

- Materials can be assigned in several ways: using ⊕ (Paint) on faces, setting it in the layers of system families (such as walls and floors), and in object styles. You also assign materials when you create other component families, such as doors and furniture.

- Materials consist of 2D graphic settings for shading, surface, and cut patterns and the 3D rendering appearance, as well as physical and thermal properties. You can also include identity data, such as manufacturer, model, and keynotes.

Material Libraries

Materials are stored in libraries, which can be shared between Revit projects and AutoCAD®, Autodesk® Inventor®, Autodesk® Showcase®, and Autodesk® 3ds Max® software. Before creating custom materials, it is recommended that you create a custom library. Materials can be copied between the current project and the library.

- You can also use Transfer Project Standards to bring in all the materials from another project into the current project.

- Older versions of materials may need to be updated with appearance assets, as shown in Figure A–21. All legacy materials still work but they may not be as complex and nuanced when rendering.

Figure A–21

How To: Create a Material Library

1. In the *Manage* tab>*Settings* panel, click ⊛ (Materials).

2. At the bottom of the *Material Browser*, expand ▦ (Creates, opens and edits user-defined libraries) and select **Create New Library**, as shown in Figure A–22.

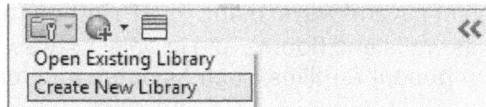

Figure A–22

3. In the *Select File* dialog box, navigate to the appropriate folder, type a *File name* and save the library. The Material Library displays in the Library list without any materials displayed.

4. Create new materials as required in the current project. Then drag and drop both new and existing materials from the project materials into the new library as shown in Figure A–23.

    Note: Libraries that come with Revit are locked. You can copy materials from them but cannot add or change materials in them.

Material Browser - Concrete Masonry Units

Figure A–23

How To: Create a Material

1. In the *Manage* tab>*Settings* panel, click ⚙ (Materials).

2. In the Material Editor, expand ◷ (Creates or duplicates a material) and select either **Create New Material** or **Duplicate Material**, as shown in Figure A–24. If you are duplicating a material, select an existing material similar to what you want to use first.

    Note: You can also right-click on an existing material in the Material Browser and select Duplicate.

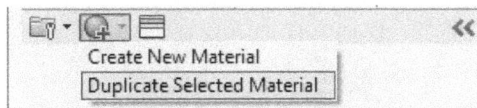

Figure A–24

3. A new material is added to the current project. Modify the name of the material or right-click on the material name in the *Material Browser* and select **Rename**.

- Duplicated materials include all of the properties of the existing material as shown for a new Aluminum material in Figure A–25.

4. Fill out the information on each of the tabs.

- Before changing the material's default information on the *Appearance*, *Physical*, or

  Thermal tabs, ensure you first duplicate the material's assets by clicking ▢ (Duplicate this asset), as shown in Figure A–25, so you do not override the default assets.

Figure A–25

5. Click **Apply** and add additional materials as required.
6. Click **OK** when you are finished.

Identity Tab

In the *Identity* tab, you set up the *Descriptive Information*, *Product Information*, and *Revit Annotation Information* for the material, as shown in Figure A–26. This information can be used in material takeoff schedules.

Figure A–26

Graphics Tab

In the *Graphics* tab (shown in Figure A–27), you set how a material displays in shaded or hidden line mode.

Figure A–27

- The *Shading* area controls how the material displays when an element is shaded. If you want the shaded view to resemble the rendered view, select **Use Render Appearance**. The color and other options are modified to match the Render Appearance selection. Alternatively, you can set up a color and transparency ratio. Only use this if the render appearance would be too dark or otherwise not suit the use.

- The *Surface Pattern* and *Cut Pattern* areas enable you to select a fill pattern and color to display on a surface or in a section cut. The surface and cut patterns can be set for *Foreground* and *Background*. Surface patterns stay true to size. Cut patterns are drafting patterns, which change size according to the view scale.

Appearance Tab

In the *Appearance* tab, you can set different aspects of a rendered material, including **Information**, the type of material (in this example Masonry is selected as shown in Figure A–28) and other parameters depending on the type of material you are working with. Note that changing the asset changes all of the information, so check if that is an option first.

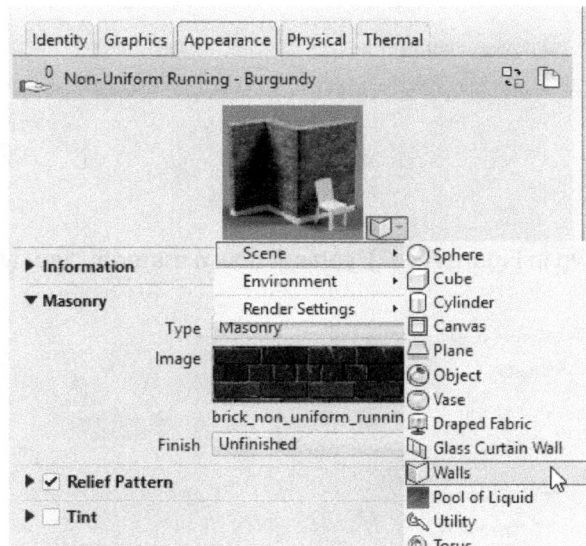

Figure A–28

- You can select how to display the preview of the material by expanding the Scene list next to the graphic, as shown in Figure A–28 above.

- You can modify the *Render Settings* of the preview to either **Draft Quality** or **Production Quality**.

- If you duplicate a material and then change asset-related information (such as the Image or Color) the original material also updates. To prevent this from happening, duplicate or change the asset before making changes.

Physical Tab

In the *Physical* tab, you can specify information about the physical properties of the material. The options vary by material type, as shown in Figure A-29.

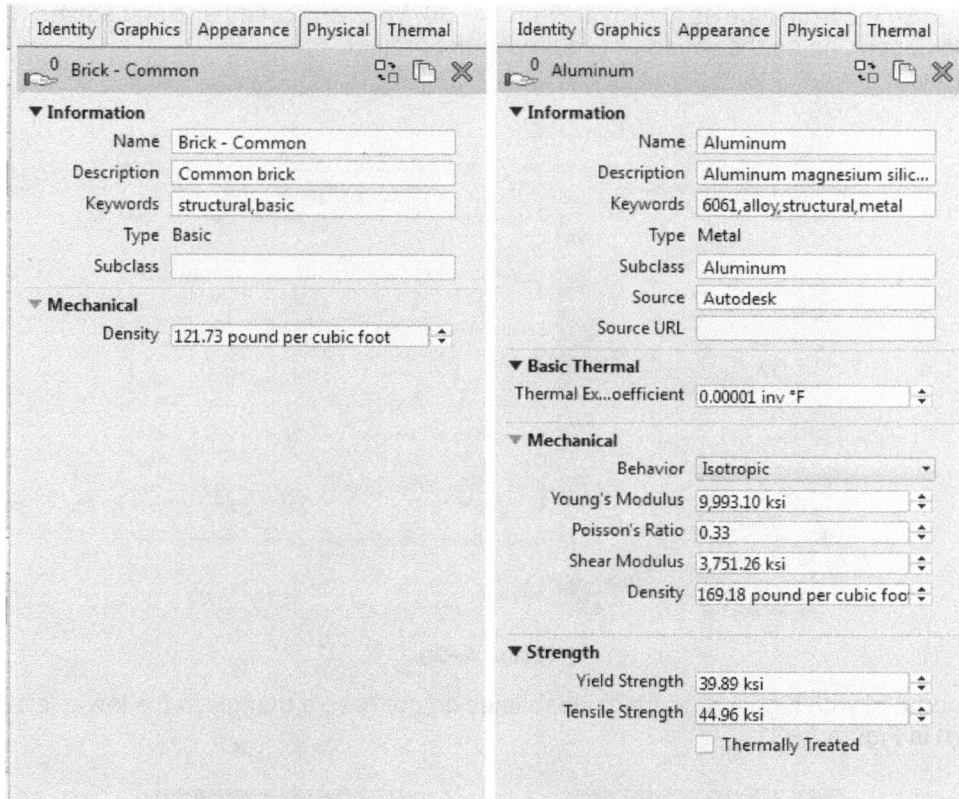

Figure A-29

- Some materials, such as **EPDM Membrane** or **Vapor Retarder**, do not have physical properties, but do have thermal properties.

- Analytical surface and Default materials do not have physical or thermal properties.

- As changing the asset changes all of the information, you should check to see if that is an option first.

Working with Assets

Physical Assets contain preset parameters for materials. These assets are available in the *Appearance*, *Physical* and *Thermal* tabs. Autodesk provides an extensive library of assets that are divided by material type as shown in Figure A–30. You can modify and add assets to materials depending on the variables required in the project.

Figure A–30

Assets updated with higher rendering capabilities do not have a triangle in the lower left corner, as shown in Figure A–31.

Original Cherry Asset   *Updated Cherry Asset*

Figure A–31

How To: Replace an Asset for a Material

1. In the *Material Browser*, select the material that you want to modify.

2. In the *Appearance*, *Physical*, or *Thermal* tab, click (Replaces this asset).

3. In the *Asset Browser* dialog box, hover the cursor over the required asset and click

    (Replaces the current asset in the editor with this asset), as shown previously in Figure A-30.

4. Close the *Asset Browser*.

*   The assets are filtered by type. Therefore, you need to modify the Appearance asset by clicking through the *Appearance* tab, etc.

*   You can create new assets by duplicating an existing one and then modifying the parameters.

A.5 Settings for Mechanical Projects

In addition to the standard settings common to all Revit projects, Revit also has specific mechanical settings that can be used in a template or a project.

In the *Manage* tab>*Settings* panel, expand 🔲 (MEP Settings) and click 🔲 (Mechanical Settings), or in the *Systems* tab>*HVAC (or Mechanical, or Plumbing & Piping*) panel title, click ⌐ (Mechanical Settings), as shown in Figure A–32. Alternatively, you can type **MS**.

Figure A–32

Mechanical Settings

Mechanical settings enable you to preset many items relating to duct and pipe sizes, conversion settings, and other key defaults, as shown in Figure A–33.

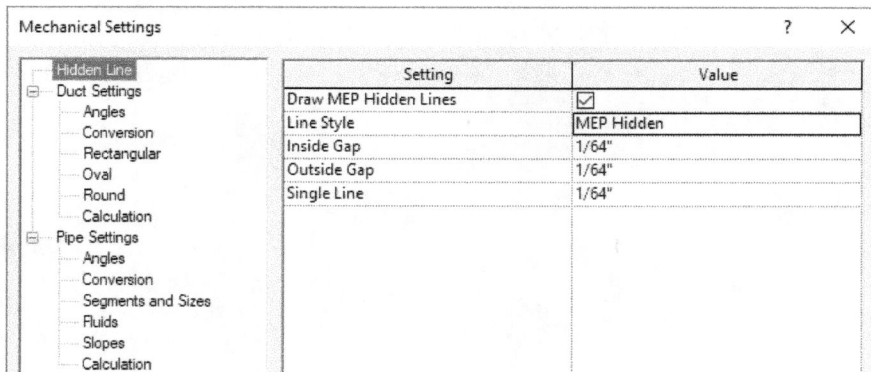

Figure A–33

Hidden Line

If the **Draw MEP Hidden Lines** option is selected, hidden lines display to indicate pipes and ducts that are below other pipes and ducts, as shown in Figure A–34.

Figure A–34

The **Line Style**, **Inside Gap**, and **Outside Gap** options enable you to specify how the hidden lines display.

Angles

In the *Angles* category you can specify the limits on the angles that can be used as ducts or pipes are being drawn, as shown in Figure A–35. This is most often used with piping.

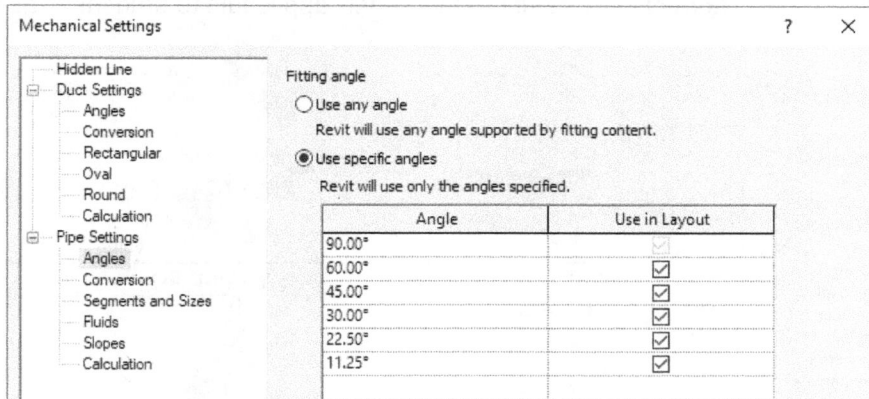

Figure A–35

- The **Duct Settings>Angles** options also include **Set an angle increment** for determining the angle values.

Duct Settings

For the **Single Line Fittings** option, the first two settings relate to how fittings display in a single line view, as shown in Figure A–36. If the **Use Annot. Scale for Single Line Fittings** option is selected, the single line fittings display at the same size on every sheet, regardless of the view scale. The **Duct Fitting Annotation Size** option enables you to specify the size at which the fittings should be displayed.

Figure A–36

The **Air Density** and **Air Viscosity** options are used when sizing the ducts. The remaining options set the separators and suffixes that are used for duct objects.

Conversion

The *Conversion* area is used to set the routing solutions for ductwork. The settings for the *Main* and *Branch* options can be set separately for each system type. You can specify the *Duct Type*, *Middle Elevation*, and *Flex Duct Type* settings (this is only applicable to branches), as shown in Figure A–37.

Figure A–37

Rectangular, Oval, and Round

The **Rectangular, Oval,** and **Round** options enable you to adjust the sizing tables. The *Size* column lists all of the sizes. You can click **New Size...** to add a size to the list and **Delete Size** to remove sizes from the list.

In addition, you can specify whether a size displays in the size lists (to be available when you place a new duct or select existing ducts) or if the size is used by the sizing routine (automatic sizing of duct branches and systems), as shown in Figure A–38.

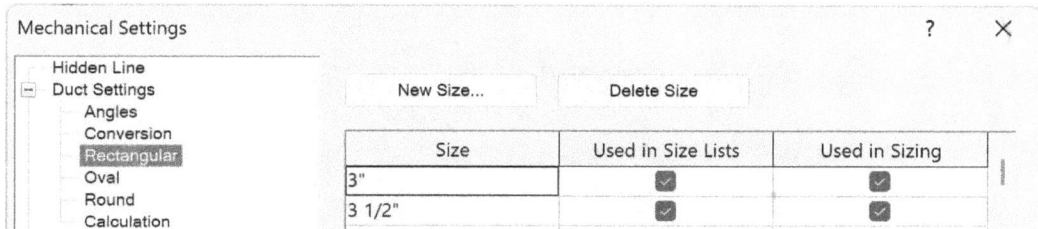

Figure A–38

- For example, if you do not want the sizing routine to use any odd numbered sizes, clear the **Used in Sizing** option for all odd-numbered sizes.

Pipe Settings

Most of the options in the *Pipe Settings* area are identical to or similar to those in the *Duct Settings* area.

Pipe Segments and Sizes

Pipe segment and size settings are more complex due to the many different materials and connections available. Each material has its own roughness, connection types, schedule/types, and sizes that correspond to each combination, as shown in Figure A–39.

Figure A–39

The actual size lists are identical in function to those for ducts, except for the inclusion of the **ID** (inside diameter) and **OD** (outside diameter) parameters.

- Click 🗋 (Create New Pipe Segment) to open the *New Segment* dialog box (as shown in Figure A–40), where you specify new Material, and/or Schedule/Type for the segment.

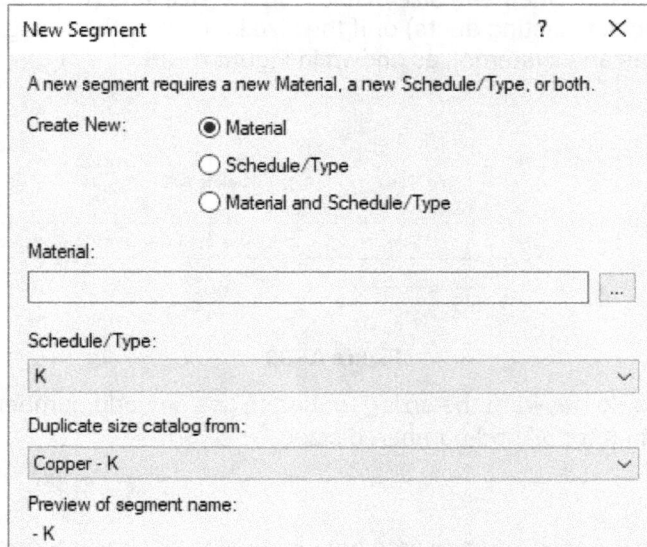

Figure A–40

- To delete a segment, click 🗋 (Delete Pipe Segment).

Fluids

The *Fluids* area enables you to specify the viscosity and density of fluids at different temperatures, as shown in Figure A–41. You can add or delete fluid types, and for each type, add or delete temperatures.

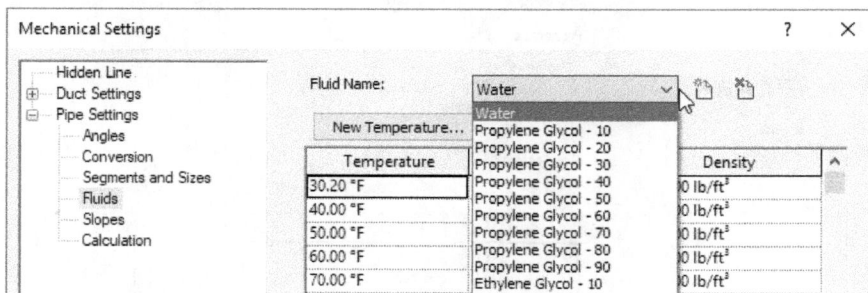

Figure A–41

Slopes

In the *Slopes* area, you can add or delete typical slopes used in a project, as shown in Figure A–42.

Figure A–42

Calculation

Both Duct and Pipe settings include methods for Pressure Drop that are specific to their needs, as shown for Pipe Settings in Figure A–43. For pipes, the calculation method for converting fixture units to flow for plumbing fixtures is also included.

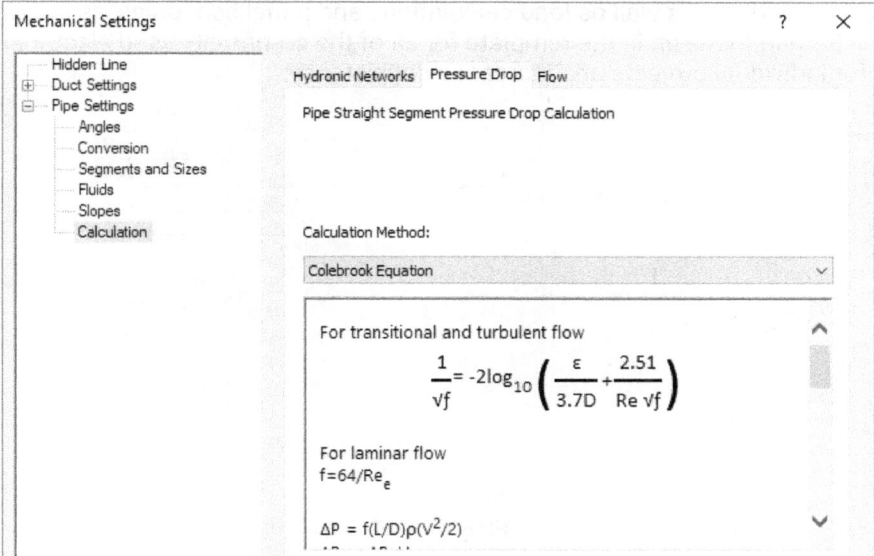

Figure A–43

A.6 Settings for Electrical Projects

In addition to the standard settings common to all Revit projects, Revit also has specific electrical settings that can be used in a template or a project.

- In the *Manage* tab>*Settings* panel, expand 🖳 (MEP Settings) and click 🖳 (Electrical Settings), or in the *Systems* tab>*Electrical* panel title, click ↘ (Electrical Settings), as shown in Figure A–44. Alternatively, you can type **ES**.

Figure A–44

In the *Electrical Settings* dialog box, you can preset many options relating to wiring, voltage, cable trays, and conduits, as well as load calculations and panel schedules, as shown in Figure A–45. Setting these up in the template for all of the commonly used electrical settings, saves time for individual projects and increases consistency.

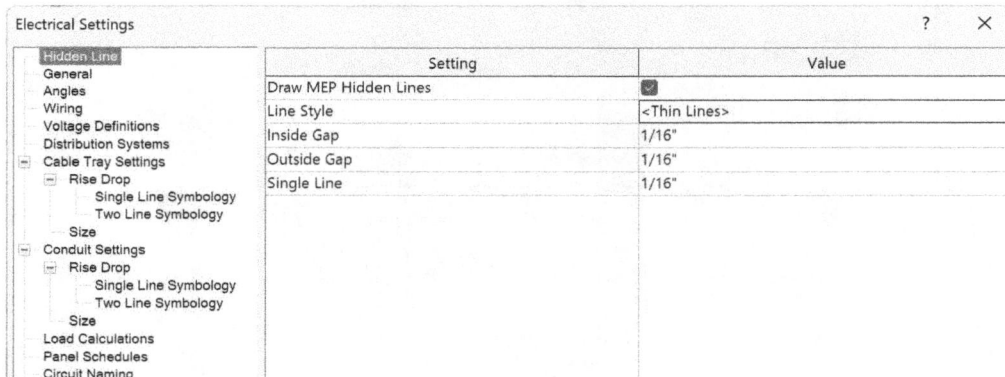

Figure A–45

General

The parameters in the *General* area affect the display of electrical information. The **Electrical Data Style** option sets how the power information displays in the **Electrical Data** parameter in the Instance Properties of the electrical component. The **Circuit Description** option sets the formatting of the circuit description.

Wiring

The *Wiring* area enables you to specify how wires and wire sizes are displayed in the view. The **Tick Mark** families need to be preloaded into the template so that they can be selected in this area, as shown in Figure A–46.

Electrical Settings

Setting	Value
Gap of Wiring Crossing	0' - 0 1/16"
Hot Wire Tick Mark	Long Wire Tick Mark
Ground Wire Tick Mark	Long Wire Tick Mark
Neutral Wire Tick Mark	Long Wire Tick Mark
Slanted Line across Tick Marks	No
Show Tick Marks	Always
Arrow for Multi-Circuits Home Run	Multiple Arrows
Home Run Arrow Style	Arrow Filled 15 Degree

Navigation tree (left panel):
- Hidden Line
- General
- Angles
- Wiring
- Voltage Definitions
- Distribution Systems
- Cable Tray Settings
  - Rise Drop
    - Single Line Symbology
    - Two Line Symbology
  - Size
- Conduit Settings
  - Rise Drop
    - Single Line Symbology

Figure A–46

Voltage Definitions

In the *Voltage Definitions* area, you can specify the minimum and maximum voltages of devices that can be added to the distribution systems of a specified voltage. For example, Revit permits devices ranging from 110V to 130V on a 120V distribution system, as shown in Figure A–47. You can also add or delete definitions.

Electrical Settings

	Name	Value	Minimum	Maximum
1	120	120.00 V	110.00 V	130.00 V
2	208	208.00 V	200.00 V	220.00 V
3	240	240.00 V	220.00 V	250.00 V
4	277	277.00 V	260.00 V	280.00 V
5	480	480.00 V	460.00 V	490.00 V

Navigation tree (left panel):
- Hidden Line
- General
- Angles
- Wiring
- Voltage Definitions
- Distribution Systems
- Cable Tray Settings
  - Rise Drop
    - Single Line Symbology
    - Two Line Symbology

Figure A–47

Distribution Systems

The *Distribution Systems* area sets the distribution systems that are available in your project, as shown in Figure A–48. You can edit the names by selecting them. The options for *Phase* are preset and affect the options that are available in the *Configuration* and *Wires* columns, determine whether *L-L Voltage* or *L-G Voltage* is available, and set the *High Leg Phase* for analytical systems with a 4-wire configuration. You can add more systems and delete existing systems if they are not assigned to devices in the current project.

	Name	Phase	Configuration	Wires	L-L Voltage	L-G Voltage	High Leg Phase
1	120/208 Wye	Three	Wye	4	208	120	None
2	120/240	Three	Delta	4	240	120	B
3	120/240 Single	Single	None	3	240	120	None
4	480/277 Wye	Three	Wye	4	480	277	None

Figure A–48

Cable Tray and Conduit Settings

Cable trays and conduit settings include rise drop symbology and sizing, as shown in Figure A–49.

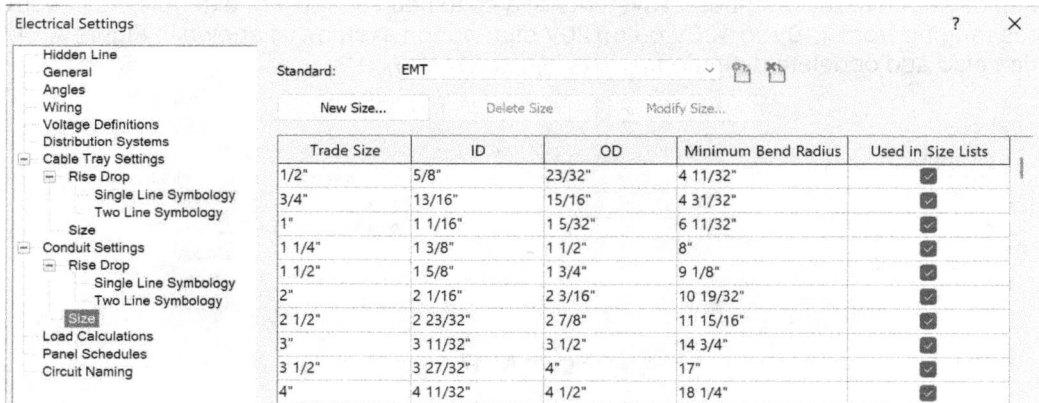

Standard: EMT

Trade Size	ID	OD	Minimum Bend Radius	Used in Size Lists
1/2"	5/8"	23/32"	4 11/32"	✓
3/4"	13/16"	15/16"	4 31/32"	✓
1"	1 1/16"	1 5/32"	6 11/32"	✓
1 1/4"	1 3/8"	1 1/2"	8"	✓
1 1/2"	1 5/8"	1 3/4"	9 1/8"	✓
2"	2 1/16"	2 3/16"	10 19/32"	✓
2 1/2"	2 23/32"	2 7/8"	11 15/16"	✓
3"	3 11/32"	3 1/2"	14 3/4"	✓
3 1/2"	3 27/32"	4"	17"	✓
4"	4 11/32"	4 1/2"	18 1/4"	✓

Figure A–49

Load Calculations and Panel Schedules

The *Load Calculations* area allows you to set the load calculations for panels, as shown in Figure A–50. Click **Load Classifications** to create or edit load classification types that can be specified for panels and electrical connectors used in a project.

* Load classifications are assigned to device connectors, and demand factors are assigned to load classifications.

* Uncheck **Run calculations for loads in spaces** to improve system response and performance.

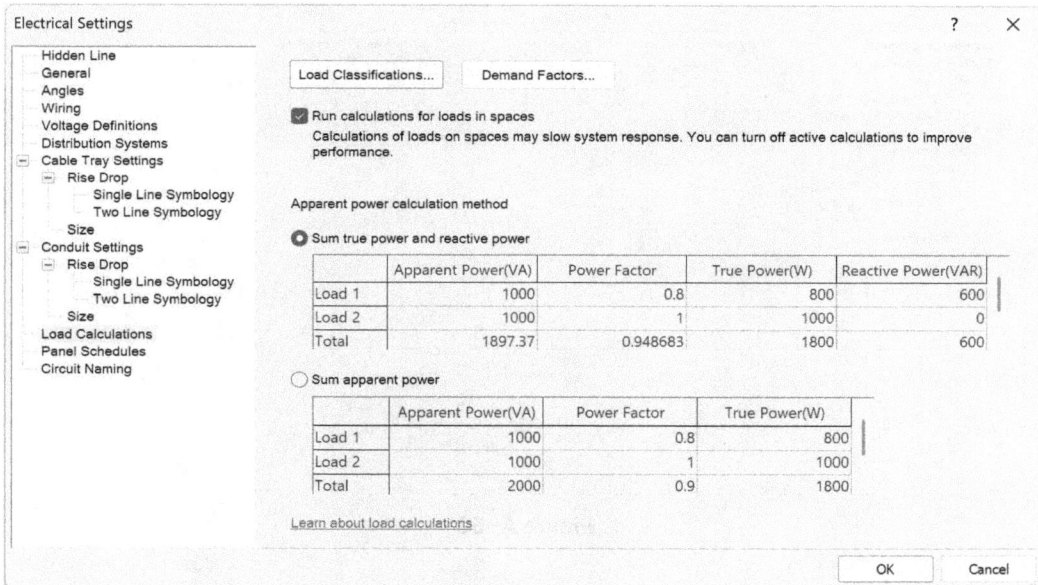

Figure A–50

The *Panel Schedules* area (shown in Figure A–51) enables you set up labels and other options for the default panel schedule.

Figure A–51

Circuit Naming

Create a custom *Circuit Naming Scheme Name* by defining one or more parameters, as well as an optional suffix, prefix, and separator. You can then specify this custom circuit scheme for an electrical equipment's *Circuit Naming* parameter in Properties. You can specify a project naming scheme by selecting one from the *By Project - Circuit Naming Scheme* drop-down list, as shown in Figure A–52.

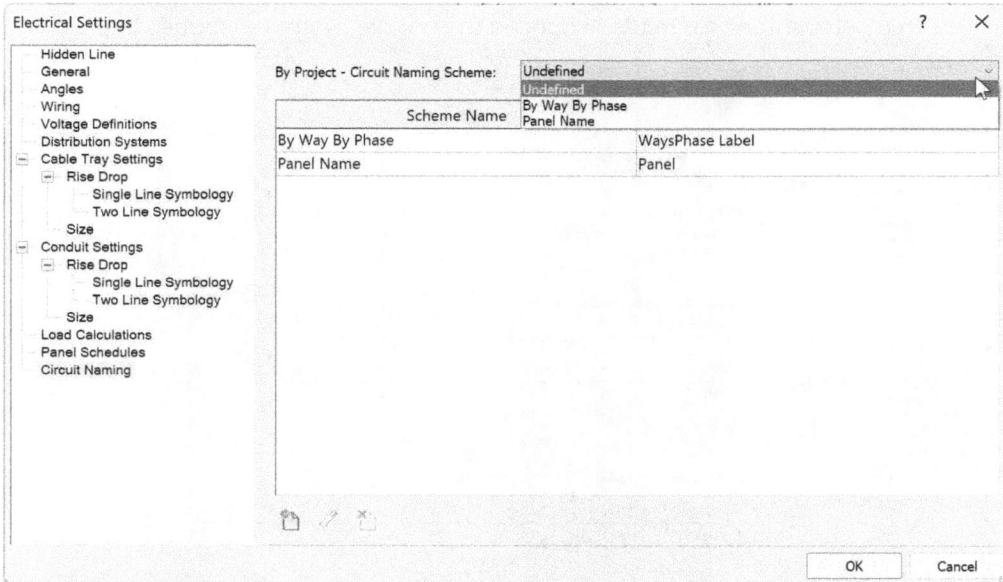

Figure A–52

A.7 Settings for Structural Projects

In addition to the standard settings common to all aspects of Revit, there are structural settings that need to be customized.

- In the *Manage* tab>*Settings* panel, expand *Structural Settings* and click 🖼️ (Structural Settings), or click the arrow in the *Structure* tab>*Structure* panel title.

Symbolic Representation Settings

You can specify the brace symbolic lines that will display in plan views to determine how braces will display above or below the level in the *Structural Settings* dialog box, as shown in Figure A–53. You can also specify symbolic cut back distance, connection types, and the annotation symbol used. You need to pre-load the structural connection annotations and symbols.

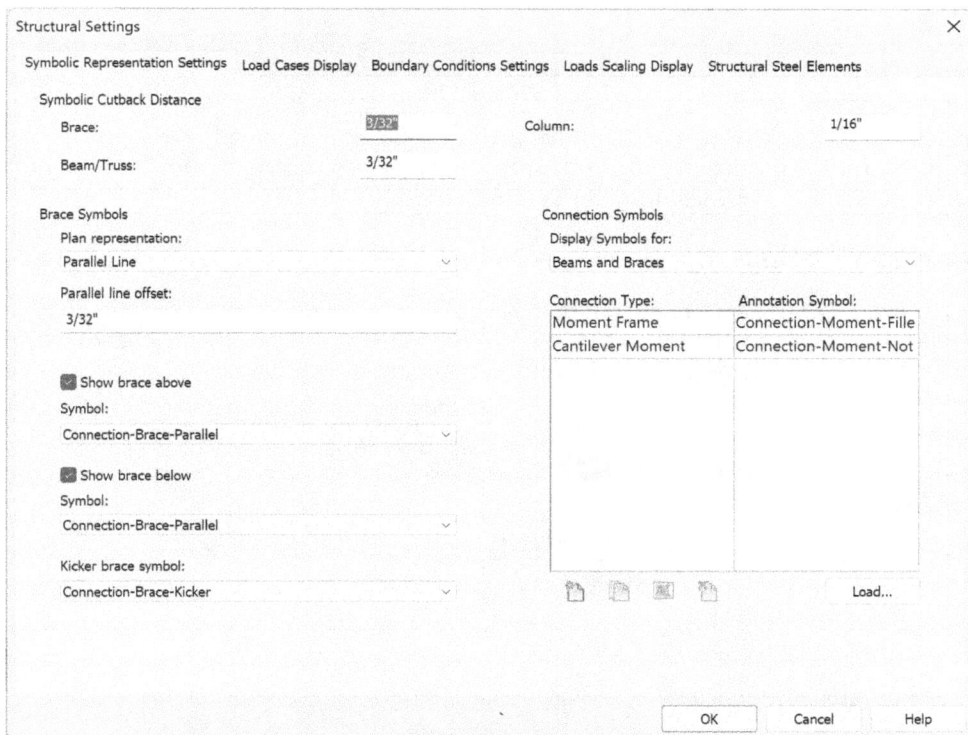

Figure A–53

The **Symbolic Cutback Distance** setting represents the distance that cuts a framing member back from a column or into another framing member. This cutback distance is symbolic and does not affect the 3D view. For example, in plan, beams do not extend into the column and there is a gap between them, as shown in Figure A–54. The same connection in 3D displays the beams back from the column, which is more consistent with a real-world situation.

Figure A–54

The *Brace Symbols* and *Connection Symbols* areas enable you to specify the kinds of symbols that are shown for the braces in plan, and for frame and shear connections. For many of these items, only one symbol is loaded into the default template.

Load Cases Display

The *Load Cases Display* tab (shown in Figure A–55) is used in correlation with the load cases and combinations to define the different types of loads used in a project. These vary by project and by region and typically require the input of a company's engineer.

Figure A–55

Boundary Condition Settings

On the *Boundary Conditions Settings* tab, you can select the family symbols used for boundary conditions, as shown in Figure A–56 (from left to right: **Fixed**, **Pinned**, **Roller**, and **User Defined**).

Figure A–56

The structural templates typically include four boundary condition families: **Fixed**, **Pinned**, **Roller**, and **Variable**. They are assigned to the corresponding boundary conditions, as shown in Figure A–57.

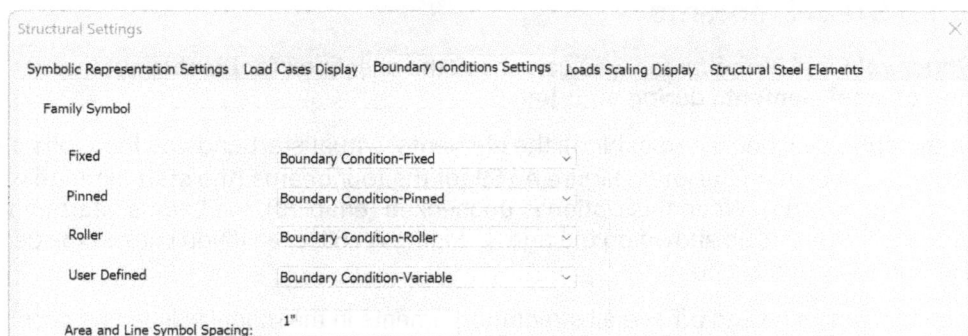

Figure A–57

- You can create new boundary condition families, load them into the template, and select them from the drop-down lists as required.

Loads Scaling Display

On the *Loads Scaling Display* tab, in the *Define Generic Load Scale* area, you can select **Use Project Settings** (as shown in Figure A–58), then set the minimum and maximum load values and arrow lengths for the entire project.

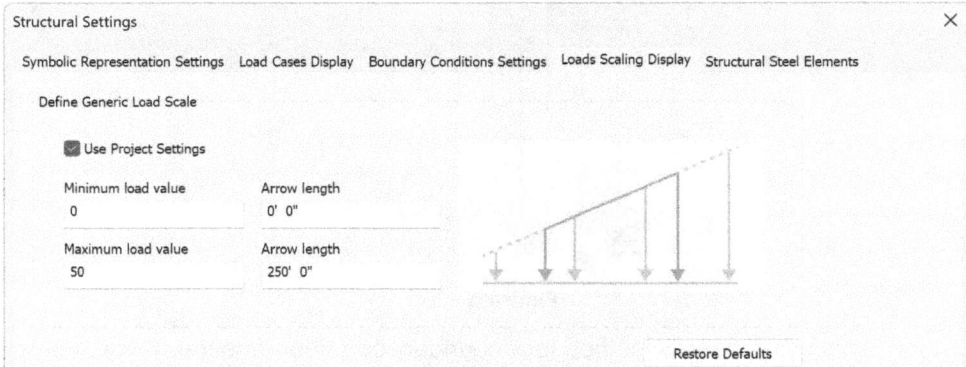

Figure A–58

Structural Steel Elements

On the *Structural Steel Elements* tab, you can check the checkbox for **Disable automatic shortening of steel elements during auto-join**.

- When the option is checked (disabled), the elements' actual start and end locations are displayed, as shown on the left in Figure A–59 for the four beams (the start location was the center of the column). When this option is unchecked (enabled), the beams' start and end locations will shorten, as shown on the right in Figure A–59, even if you clicked the center of the column as your start point.

- You can toggle this on and off and all structural elements in the model will update accordingly.

- The results from disabling the automatic shortening will only display when the *Detail Level* is **Medium** or **Fine**.

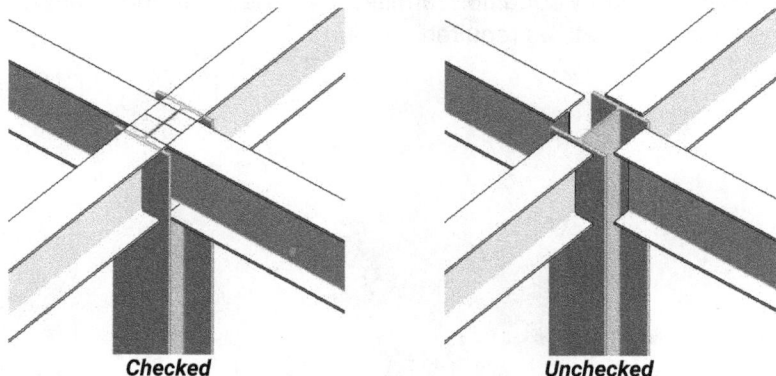

Checked *Unchecked*

Figure A–59

A.8 Additional Schedule Types

In addition to the standard schedule/quantities and material takeoff schedules, several other schedule types can be created in Revit, as shown in Figure A–60. **Sheet List** schedules keep track of all the sheets and **View List** schedules keep track of all of the views used in a project. **Note Block** schedules can be used to create a custom style of keynotes.

> *Note: More information on **Graphical Column** schedules is found in the the Autodesk Revit: Fundamentals for Structure guide.*

Figure A–60

Sheet List Schedules

A sheet list schedule (shown in Figure A–61) is used to keep track of all of the sheets in a project and any list sheets that could be added. Sheet lists are often used by architects to display all of the sheets in a building project. This includes any consultant sheets that are not in the architectural project file, as they would only be in the Sheet List schedule and not created as actual sheets.

Figure A–61

How To: Create a Sheet List Schedule

1. Open a project template file (or a project).

2. In the *View* tab>*Create* panel, expand ▦ (Schedules) and click ▱ (Sheet List).

3. In the *Sheet List Properties* dialog box, in the *Fields* tab, select the **Sheet Number** and **Sheet Name** and add them to the *Scheduled fields* list, as shown in Figure A–62.

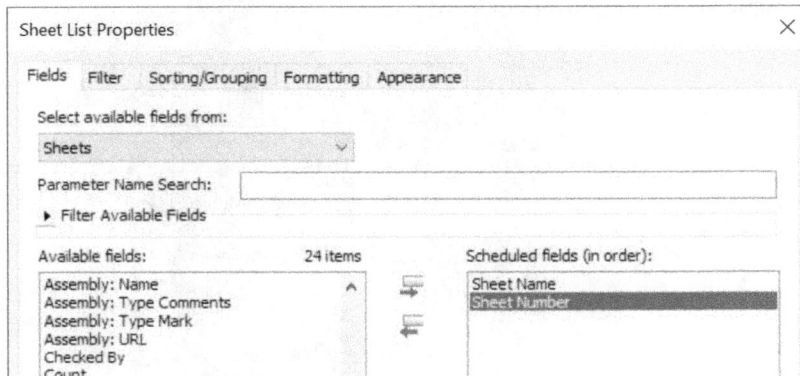

Figure A–62

4. Depending on the complexity of your sheet naming scheme, you can also modify items on the *Filter* and *Sorting/Grouping* tabs.

5. Click **OK** when you are finished.

6. You are placed in the schedule view with the two parameters displayed. Stretch out the columns as shown in Figure A–63.

    Note: If sheets are already in the project, they display here.

Figure A–63

7. In the *Modify Schedule/Quantities* tab>*Rows* panel, click ▦ (Insert Data Row).

8. A new row is added below the schedule names. If no sheets are in the project, it comes in automatically as **A101** and **Unnamed**.

9. Add as many rows as you need. If you are using a numbering scheme such as A1xx for site plans, A2xx for Floor Plans, A3xx for Detail plans, etc., then you should rename the sheet number for the first row of a set before creating more rows so that they increment automatically.

10. In their respective columns, type a *Sheet Number* and *Sheet Name*, as shown in Figure A–64. Note that this sheet does not display in the *Sheets (all)* section in the Project Browser.

Figure A–64

How To: Create a New Sheet Based on a Placeholder Sheet

1. In the *Modify Schedule/Quantities* tab>*Create* panel, click □ (New Sheet). You can also access the command on the *View* tab or right-click on *Sheets* in the Project Browser.

2. In the *New Sheet* dialog box, select the placeholder sheet you want to use, as shown in Figure A–65. To select more than one, hold <Ctrl> or <Shift> as you select.

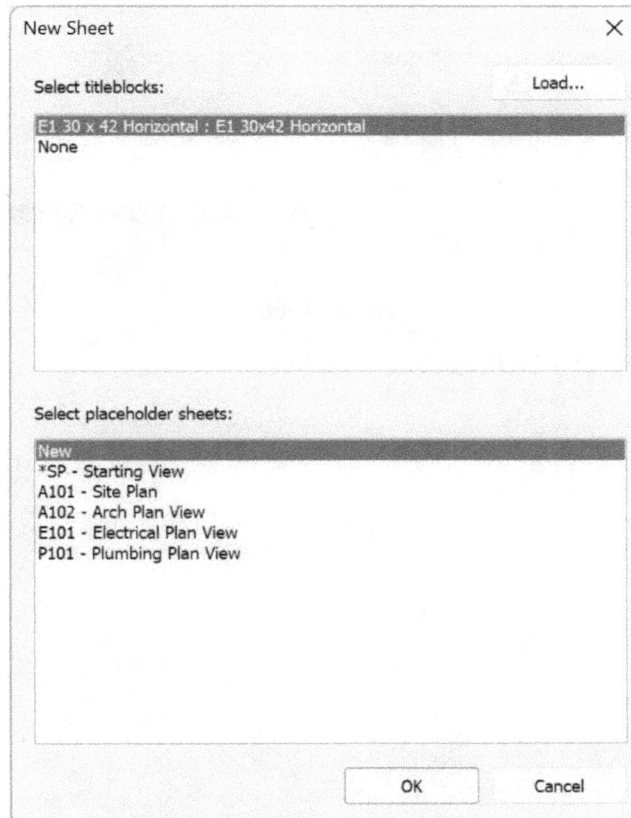

Figure A–65

3. Click **OK**. The new sheet is created in the project.

• You can import the sheet list schedule into another project, but it does not import the associated sheets. That is because they are part of the project, not the schedule view.

View List Schedules

View list schedules are similar to other schedules in their construction. The difference is that the available fields are gathered from the view, as shown in Figure A–66 . This type of schedule can be very helpful when you are creating copies of view and want to modify the phase, discipline, or other information about the view.

In the *View* tab>*Create* panel, expand ⊞ (Schedules) and click 🗎 (View List).

Figure A–66

• You can also add fields from Project Information.

Note Blocks

Note blocks enable you to create a schedule of all the generic annotation elements in the model. They are a way of creating a custom keynoting system if the internal system in Revit does not work for you. It requires you to create an annotation symbol with at least two parameter labels for a number and text (as shown in Figure A–67) and a note block schedule that uses the same options.

Figure A–67

How To: Create and Use Note Blocks

1. Create a generic annotation symbol with the required parameters.

2. Load it into the project.

3. Using the **Symbol** command, place the note block symbol in the project. You can add a leader after you have placed it, as shown in Figure A–68.

4. Select the symbol and in *Properties*, assign the number and text, as shown in Figure A–68.

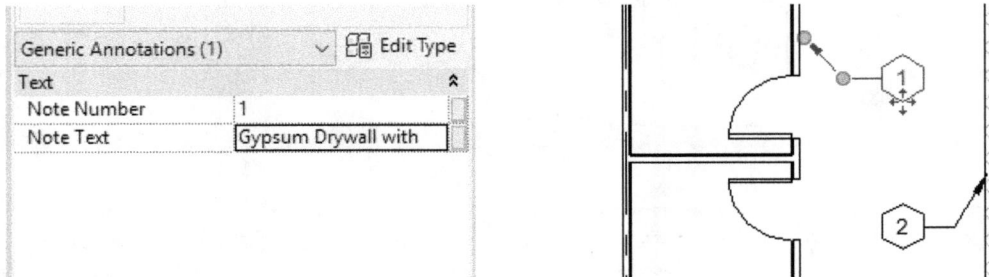

Figure A–68

5. In the *View* tab>*Create* panel, expand ⊞ (Schedules) and click ▤ (Note Block).

6. In the *New Note Block* dialog box, select the Family, as shown in Figure A–69. Then, click **OK**.

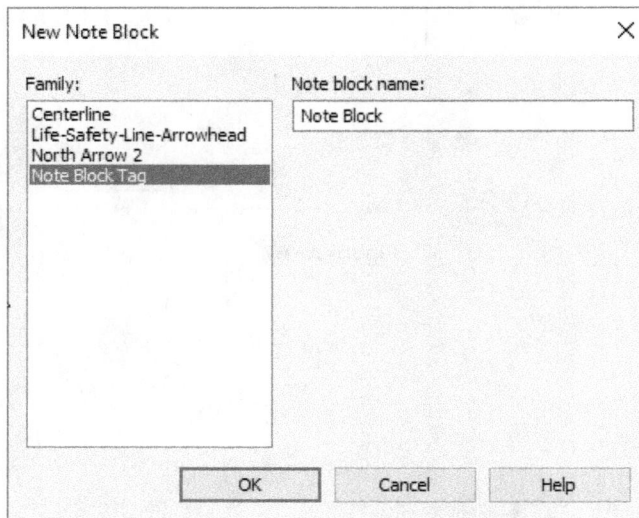

Figure A–69

7. In the *Note Block Properties* dialog box, select the required fields (as shown in Figure A–70), make any other modifications as required, and click **OK** to created the schedule.

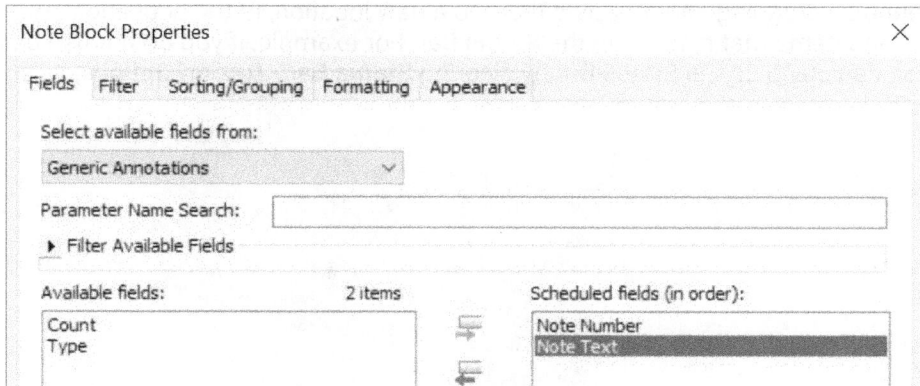

Figure A–70

8. Modify the schedule as required and place it on the sheet with the corresponding view, as shown in Figure A–71.

Figure A–71

A.9 Basic User Interface Customization

The Revit User Interface has a variety of features that can be customized. From moving ribbon panels around by dragging and dropping them to a new location, to the activation and location of palettes, and items that display on the Status Bar. For example, if you do not use design options, you can clean up the Status Bar by clearing **Status Bar - Design Options**, as shown in Figure A–72.

Figure A–72

You can also customize other parts of Revit, including which tabs display in the ribbon, customizing keyboard shortcuts, specifying how the double-click functions work and setting up the Project Browser organization.

Configuring the Ribbon

Revit is used by many different disciplines, including architecture, structure, mechanical, electrical, and plumbing. All of these tools are set up to display in the ribbon by default. Most users only need access to a specific set of tools and the interface can be customized to suit those needs.

How To: Configure the Ribbon to Suit Your Needs

1. In the *File* tab, click **Options**.
2. In the *Options* dialog box, in the left pane, select **User Interface**.

3. In the *Configure* area, in the *Tools and analyses* list (shown in Figure A–73), clear all the options that you do not want to use.

Note: You are not deleting these tools, just removing them from the current user interface.

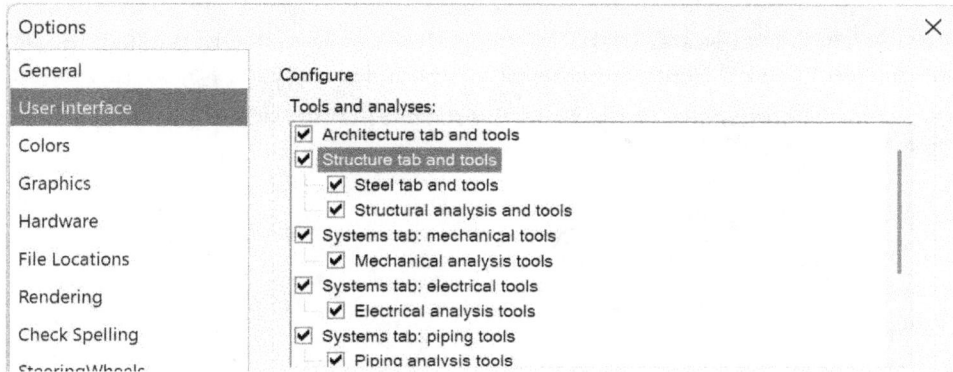

Figure A–73

Customizing Shortcuts

A helpful customization is to set up the keyboard shortcuts for frequently used commands. These are not saved by project, but on each computer. To display the shortcuts that are already available, hover the cursor over a tool, such as **Text**, to display the tooltip that displays the associated shortcut, as shown in Figure A–74.

Note: When you type keyboard shortcuts, you do not need to press <Enter> or <Spacebar>.

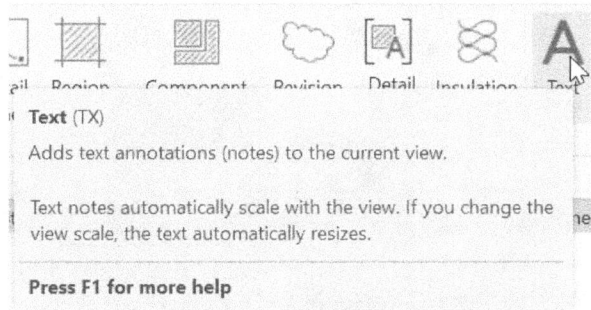

Figure A–74

How To: Customize the Keyboard Shortcuts

1. In the *View* tab>*Windows* panel, expand [icon] (User Interface) and click [icon] (Keyboard Shortcuts).

   - Alternatively, in the *File* tab, click **Options**. In the *Options* dialog box, select the *User Interface* pane. In the *Configure* area, click **Customize...** next to *Keyboard shortcuts*.

2. In the *Keyboard Shortcuts* dialog box, use **Search** or **Filter** to narrow the search, as shown in Figure A−75.

Figure A−75

3. Select the command that you want to add or modify.

4. Enter a shortcut in the box next to *Press new keys*, as shown in Figure A−76, and click **Assign**.

Figure A−76

5. Click **OK** when you have finished.

- To remove shortcuts, select the shortcut, and click **Remove**.

- You can import or export the shortcut file to be used in other stations of Revit than the one on which they were created. When you export to XML, all of the commands are exported. You can then add the required shortcuts to the XML file and import them into your program.

- You can assign a shortcut to a command even if it is already being used. For example, **LL** is used for the Level command (as shown in Figure A–77), but you can assign LL to another command. A *Duplicate Shortcut* dialog box displays, alerting you that the shortcut is currently assigned and how to cycle through the options.

Figure A–77

Customizing Double-Click Settings

When you double-click on elements, you can specify what you want this to do. For example, by default, double-clicking on a family, such as a chair, column, or plumbing fixture, opens the element in the Family Editor. In most cases that is not something you want to do, editing the type would be better. You can change this in the *Customize Double-click Settings* dialog box, as shown in Figure A–78.

Figure A–78

How To: Customize Double-Click Settings

1.   In the *File* tab, click **Options**.

2.   In the *Options* dialog box, in the *User Interface* pane, in the *Configure* area, next to *Double-click Options:* click **Customize...**.

3.   Select the method that you want to use for each of the element types.

Project Browser Organization

When starting a project using the supplied Revit templates, the Project Browser has a default organization, which is to show all view types. When working with complex projects, it can help to organize the views, sheets, schedules, and panel schedules so that it is most useful to the methods used in your firm. It is easy to switch between different organizations, and you can create custom ones to suit your work, as shown in Figure A−79.

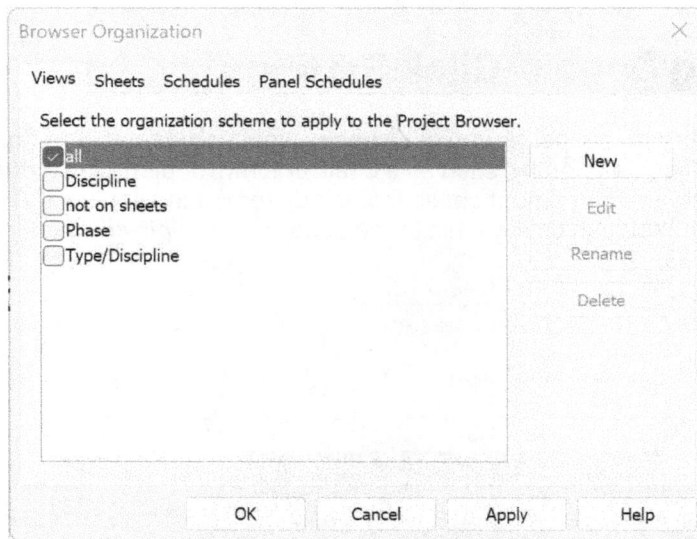

Figure A−79

If the default organization schemes do not suit your needs, you can modify and duplicate a view type to create a new type that allows you to group views together for ease of access.

How To: Change the Project Browser's Organization Scheme

1.   Select the **Views (all)** node at the top of the in the Project Browser.

2. In the Type Selector, select the organization type that you want to use, as shown in Figure A–80.

   Note: The name of the current organization type will display in parentheses next to Views in the Project Browser.

Figure A–80

- You can also switch the organization for **Sheets**, **Schedules**, and **Panel Schedules** by selecting the respective node and changing the type in the Type Selector.

3. The Project Browser updates to sort the views by the selected scheme (e.g., for the **Type/Discpline** scheme, it will sort by view type and then by discipline). Figure A–81 shows the difference between the **all** and **Type/Discipline** browser organization types.

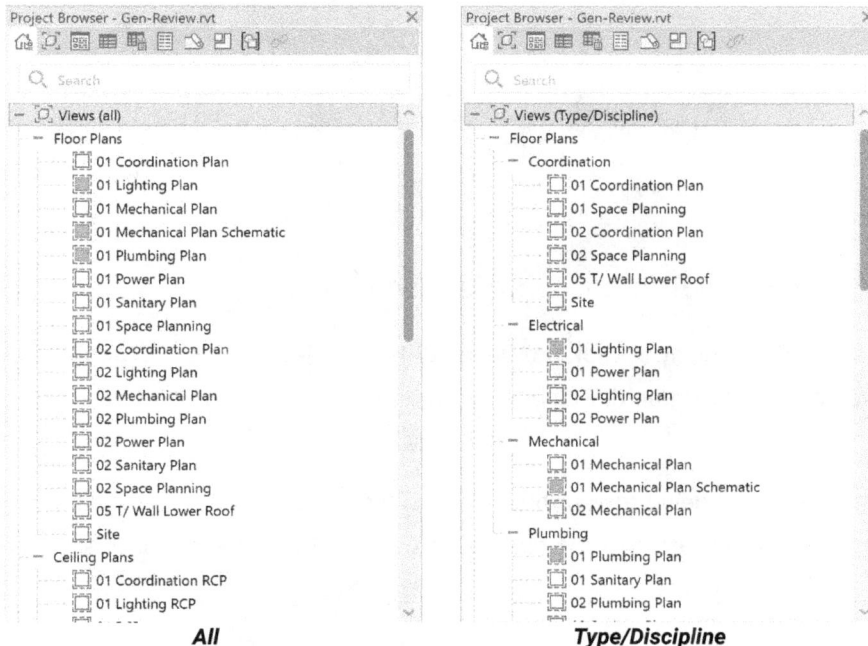

All   *Type/Discipline*

Figure A–81

- Alternatively, in the Project Browser, right click on **Views (all)** and select **Browser Organization...** (as shown in Figure A–82), or in the *View* tab>*Windows* panel, expand ⊟ (User Interface) and click ⊡ (Browser Organization).

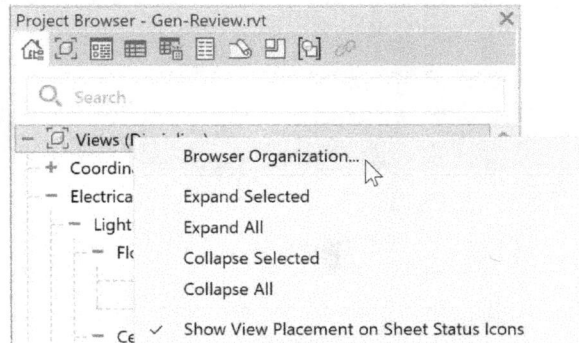

Figure A–82

In the *Browser Organization* dialog box, select a different scheme (e.g., **Type/Discipline**), as shown in Figure A–83, and click **OK**.

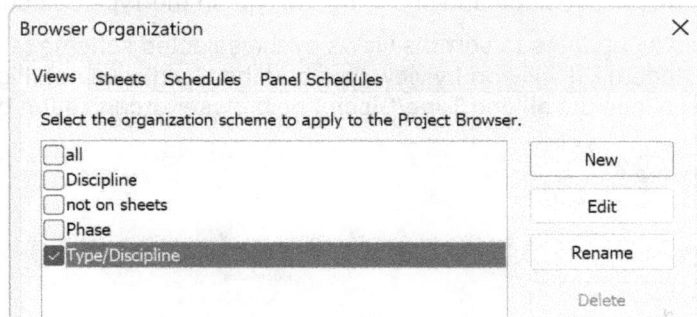

Figure A–83

How To: Create a New Browser Organization Type

1. In the Project Browser, right-click on **Views (all)** and select **Browser Organization...**.
2. In the *Browser Organization* dialog box, select the tab for the section of the browser you want to create a organization type for (*Views, Sheets, Schedules*, or *Panel Schedules)* and click **New**.
3. Enter a name for the new browser organization type and click **OK**.
4. In the *Browser Organization Properties* dialog box, on the *Filtering* tab, specify the filtering rules, as required.

5. On the *Grouping and Sorting* tab, assign the various groups as required. The example shown in Figure A–84 is by discipline, which is an organization type that is used most often in MEP templates.

Figure A–84

6. Click **OK**.

7. In the *Browser Organization* dialog box, you can continue to create new organization types. Click **Apply** between sets if you are creating multiple organizations, and click **OK** when you have finished.

How To: Create New View Types to Group Similar Views

1. In the Project Browser, select a view of the type you want to create a group for.

2. In *Properties*, verify that it says the correct view type (e.g., **Floor Plan**) in the Type Selector and click **Edit Type**.

3. In the *Type Properties* dialog box, click **Duplicate...**.

4. In the *Name* dialog box, type a name for the group (e.g., **Level 1**), as shown in Figure A–85, and click **OK**.

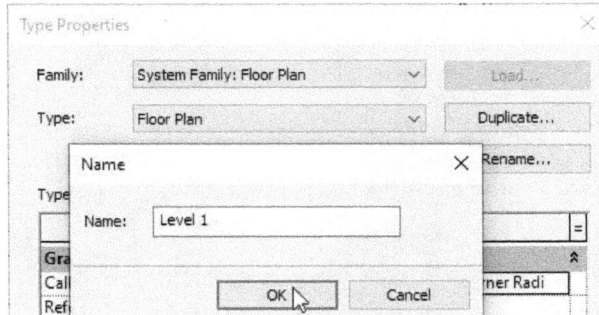

Figure A–85

5. Click **OK** in the *Type Properties* dialog box.

6. In the Project Browser, the new group will display as its own node, as shown in Figure A–86.

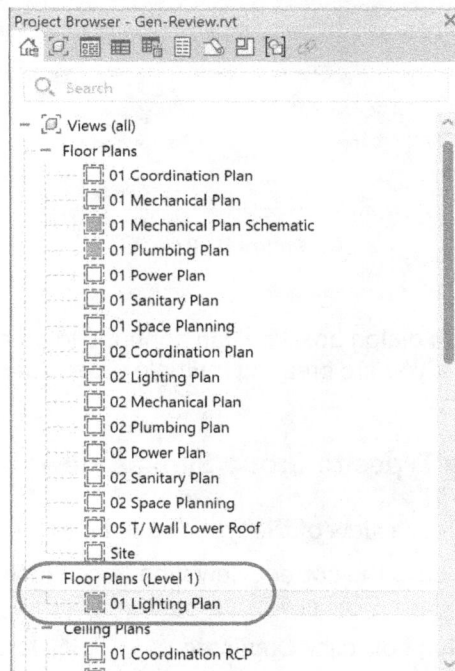

Figure A–86

7. You can select other views of the same type and set their view type to this new group. For example, select another floor plan view in the Project Browser, then in the Type Selector, select the group (e.g., **Level 1**), as shown in Figure A–87.

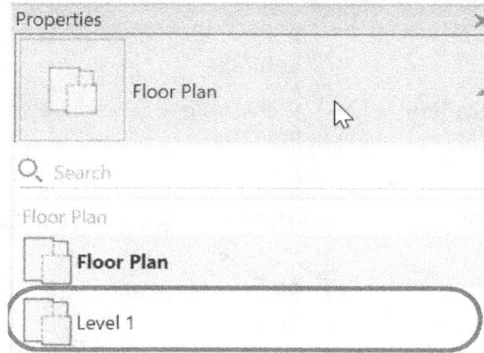

Figure A–87

- The view is moved into the **Floor Plans (Level 1)** group.

Command Summary

Button	Command	Location
	Arrowheads	• **Ribbon**: *Manage* tab>*Settings* panel, expand Additional Settings
	Browser Organization	• **Ribbon**: *View* tab>*Windows* panel, expand User Interface • *File* tab: Options>*User Interface* tab
	Electrical Settings	• **Ribbon**: *Manage* tab>*Settings* panel, expand MEP Settings
	Fill Patterns	• **Ribbon**: *Manage* tab>*Settings* panel, expand Additional Settings
	Keyboard Shortcuts	• **Ribbon**: *View* tab>*Windows* panel, expand User Interface • *File* tab: Options>*User Interface* tab
	Line Patterns	• *Ribbon*: *Manage* tab>*Settings* panel, expand Additional Settings
	Line Styles	• **Ribbon**: *Manage* tab>*Settings* panel, expand Additional Settings
	Line Weights	• **Ribbon**: *Manage* tab>*Settings* panel, expand Additional Settings
	Materials	• **Ribbon**: *Manage* tab>*Settings* panel
	Mechanical Settings	• **Ribbon**: *Manage* tab>*Settings* panel, expand MEP Settings
	Note Block	• **Ribbon**: *View* tab>*Create* panel, expand Schedules
	Object Styles	• **Ribbon**: *Manage* tab>*Settings* panel
Options	**Options**	• Ribbon: *File* tab
	Project Units	• **Ribbon**: *Manage* tab>*Settings* panel • **Shortcut**: UN
	Sheet List	• **Ribbon**: *View* tab>*Create* panel, expand Schedules
	Snaps	• **Ribbon**: *Manage* tab>*Settings* panel, expand Schedules

Button	Command	Location
	Structural Settings	• **Autodesk Revit Structure** • **Ribbon:** *Manage* tab>*Settings* panel
	Temporary Dimensions	• **Ribbon:** *Manage* tab>*Settings* panel, expand Additional Settings
	User Interface	• **Ribbon:** *View* tab>*Windows* panel
	View List	• **Ribbon:** *View* tab>*Create* panel

Index

* 9 7 8 1 9 6 7 6 2 5 5 0 5 *